THE MIND AND HEART OF LOVE

by the same author

*

THE NATURE OF BELIEF

THOMAS AQUINAS

MIRAGE AND TRUTH

CHRISTIAN MORALS

PAIN AND THE PROVIDENCE OF GOD

DEATH AND LIFE

THE MIND AND HEART
OF LOVE

LION AND UNICORN
A STUDY IN
EROS AND AGAPE

by

M. C. D'ARCY, S.J.
M.A. (OXON)
MASTER OF CAMPION HALL
OXFORD

FABER AND FABER LIMITED
24 Russell Square
London

First published in Mcmxlv
by Faber and Faber Limited
24 Russell Square London W.C.1
Second impression June Mcmxlvi
Third impression November Mcmxlvi
Printed in Great Britain
at the Bowering Press Plymouth

SERVUS DOMINAE
ET
ANCILLAE DOMINI

The lion and the unicorn were fighting for the crown;
The lion beat the unicorn all round the town.

But my horn shall be exalted like that of the unicorns. (*Psalm* 91.)

The face of a young lion towards the palm tree.
(*Ezechiel* 41.)

And he built his sanctuary as of unicorns, in the land which he founded for ever. (*Psalm* 77.)

My inheritance is become to me as a young lion in the wood. (*Jeremias* 12.)

Nepthali, a hart let loose, and giving words of beauty. (*Genesis* 49, 21.)

He played with lions as with lambs.
(*Ecclesiasticus* 47, 3.)

The wounded Hart
Looms on the hill
In the air of thy flight and is refreshed.
(*St. John of the Cross.*)

Hunters can catch the unicorn only by placing a young virgin in his haunts. No sooner does he see the damsel, than he runs towards her, and lies down at her feet, and so suffers himself to be captured by the hunters. The unicorn represents Jesus Christ, who took on him our nature in the virgin's womb, was betrayed to the Jews, and delivered into the hands of Pontius Pilate. (*Thirteenth-century legend.*)

The lion and the unicorn were fighting for the
    crown;
The lion beat the unicorn all round the town.

But my horn shall be exalted like that of the
    unicorn. (*Psalm* 92.)

The face of a young lion toward the palm tree.
    (*Ezekiel* 41.)

And he built his sanctuary as of unicorns, in the
    land which he founded for ever. (*Psalm* 78.)

My inheritance is become to me as a young lion in
    the wood. (*Jeremias* 12.)

Nephtali, a hart let loose, and giving words of
    beauty. (*Genesis* 49, 21.)

    He played with lions as with lambs.
       (*Ecclesiasticus* 47, 3.)

      The wounded Hart
      Looms on the hill
In the air of thy height and is refreshed.
    (*St. John of the Cross.*)

Hunters can catch the unicorn only by placing a
young virgin in his haunts. No sooner does he see
the damsel, than he runs toward her, and lies down
at her feet, and so suffers himself to be captured by
the hunters. The unicorn represents Jesus Christ,
who took on him our nature in the virgin's womb,
was betrayed to the Jews, and delivered into the
hands of Pontius Pilate. (*Thirteenth-century legend.*)

PREFACE

One of the wisest teachers of philosophy I ever knew, John Cook Wilson, used to cut short the speculations of his pupils on the nature of knowledge by drily remarking: 'You must already know what knowing is, for otherwise you would not be seeking to know what it is; and besides you cannot get outside it in order to criticise it.' We do not, perhaps, need love in order to study the nature of love, but we must from experience know so well what love is that it may seem idle to ask questions about it. That does not stop people, however, from asking questions, and the more questions are asked the more difficult does it become to find a thread to lead us out of the maze the questions reveal. Every lover will tell us that his love is unique; he will listen with impatience to explanations and repeat the old cry: Da amantem et sentit quod dico; only another lover, with love like mine, can understand. But as a special quality in all loving need not interfere with there also being something common, I will by-pass this difficulty. It is hard enough to find something common in the variety of descriptions which have been given of it in memoirs, stories, lyrics, and epics. Love appears in all literature, not as a passing episode, but as the marrow of it. But with what a bewildering variety of incident and type! We have to take into consideration not only maternal love but the love of the child for its parents, not only the awakening desires of adolescence but the binding affection of a David and Jonathan. Dante's emotions on seeing Beatrice are not the same as the love of Romeo for Juliet or of Tristram for Isolde or Othello for Desdemona. Penelope and Cordelia are both constant, but their love is not alike.

The ancients, taking friendship as the natural expression of affection, made a triple division of love. They based this division on the presence or absence of the motive of self-interest. The lowest form was, therefore, selfish; above this came the love which is pure enjoyment, and highest of all was the love of another for his or her own sake. On the same basis they made, also, the still more straightforward distinction of the loves of concupiscence and benevolence. These divisions have lasted down the ages, but they have to some extent been ousted by distinctions drawn from psychological and psychoanalytical theories of the impulses and the sentiments. Christianity has made a special contribution by its doctrine of charity, the new and startling doctrine, that is to say, of God's manner of loving man and man's graced response to that love. No account of the nature of love can afford to leave this out, because it has had a transforming effect on civilization and added a new dimension to our conception of love. The power and novelty of Christian 'charity' are best illustrated in the two well-known passages from St. Paul, the one from the letter to the Romans, where St. Paul asks: 'Who shall separate us from the love of Christ?'—and the second from the thirteenth chapter of First Corinthians: 'If I speak with the tongues of men and of angels, and have not charity, I am become as sounding brass, or a tinkling cymbal. . . .' Of the transforming effect I hope to give plenty of evidence in what is to follow. To mention now only two authors whose views I outline and criticise in this book, namely, Denis de Rougemont and Anders Nygren, no one can fail to see what a singular and decisive importance they attribute to Christian charity, or, as they call it, Agape.

There are, therefore, many kinds of love, so many, in fact, that any attempt to link them together may seem to be doomed to failure. Let me explain, therefore, how it is I have come to write this book. Like everybody else, I suppose, I took for granted when I was young that in love was to be found all that was most excellent, and as I had the good fortune to be brought up in the belief that a God, who was infinitely loving, existed, I had, as I still believe, the easiest and happiest way of approaching the subject. But soon problems began to multiply, fascinating problems which will occupy thinkers, as well as lovers, to the end of time, and of some of these problems the chapters to follow will treat. But one of the failings of the human mind is to jump to conclusions too quickly, and to make a pattern with insufficient data. Love does not change its face, but it has many expressions, and a lack of experience and too happy a lot led me to interpret it without some of its lines and without its shadows. Discovery depends so much on our having a trained eye and a mature vision, on our being enlightened by our own experience to notice what is there before us. Pieces of evidence and decisive clues are missed through lack of attention, or because the hunt, so to speak, is not up in our own souls. I knew, for instance, when young the stories of Eros and Psyche, of Dante and Beatrice and Tristram and Isolde; they had a secret which stirred more than the imagination, and they were clearly symbols and pointers as much as they were stories; but their bearing on the problems which exercised me was hidden for a long time. What is true of stories holds equally with pregnant sayings. No one can read without a stir of the heart such sayings as: 'Our heart is uneasy until it shall rest in Thee'; 'I sought what I might love, in love with loving, and safety I hated, and a way without snares'; 'Tu ne me chercherais pas, si tu ne me possedais'; or even: 'for each man kills the thing he loves'. But having read them and been stirred, we can pass on quite blind to their possible interconnection. But when the hunt is up and the quarry is in sight, the most unsuspected pieces of evidence leap to the eye. Aristotle, for example, when he is writing on physics or metaphysics, is as dry and remote as a mathematician, and yet, as the idea I now hold about love grew in my mind and spread out, of all unlikely places the chapters of Aristotle on the coming to be and passing away of organic life took on a new colour. They had become no longer remote, but relevant. In the development of the ideas in this book the passages from Aristotle are, then, a landmark. Of books read there are nearly always a few which stand out as landmarks; or rather, when one is in process of producing an idea of one's own, they deserve to be called midwives. So great an effect, indeed, do such books have, that it is difficult at times to be sure what is one's own and what is borrowed from them. What they say has been so assimilated that it seems to be personal and original.

Among such books I will mention those which have most influenced me to agreement or disagreement. The earliest in time is Pierre Rousselot's *Problème de l'Amour au Moyen Age*. Rousselot claimed to have discovered a divergence of view about the nature of love among the Scholastics who preceded St. Thomas Aquinas. His discovery has been declared to be a mare's nest by Gilson and other unfriendly critics. It is not my intention to defend Rousselot. But even granted that he was wrong in his main contention, he nevertheless presented a problem which is in no sense imaginary. He did show that it is possible to have a conflict of loves, and that, in fact, there are two tendencies which are not easily reconciled. The first is serene and poised; the second ecstatic and poignant. The first explains adequately why it is so natural to love oneself and seek one's own happiness and perfection. But as it is so naturally self-centred, it does not explain so easily how a man can love another, even God, more than himself. The second kind of love, with its emphasis on self-sacrifice, did explain the love of one's neighbour and of God and the contempt of self; but it in its turn seemed inadequate to justify self-perfection as an end.

Now, as so often happens, reflection on this problem was excited by another book which seemed to dovetail into that of Rousselot. Anders Nygren had written three volumes on *Eros and Agape*, and he, too, held that there were two kinds of love, the one egocentric and the other theocentric. His thesis ran counter to that of Rousselot in that he wished to sweep away all vestiges of Greek and Scholastic thought on love from the Christian idea of Agape. He maintained that self-centred love had crept into Christian thinking, been baptized by St. Augustine and as a result had contaminated medieval thought. Criticism of both these authors brought me near to a personal view, which I thought could avoid the weaknesses of both these authors and be far more embracing. It would fit the dance of the atoms and the to-and-fro movement in the inanimate world; it would give meaning to much that was obscure in the relations of animal love and in the evidence from human pathological cases. In the discussion of this view with others I was told that what I said about self-sacrifice and death would find corroboration in what Freud had written on the death-instinct. As, however, I was anxious to keep my thought my own on this delicate matter and could truthfully say that my memory of Freud's view was too dim for it to influence me, I did not look up what he had written until I had completed my own thought.

Much more germane to my theme was a book, written by a friend of mine, Hunter Guthrie, and called *Introduction au Problème de l'Histoire de la Philosophie*, which good fortune, again, put into my hands just at the right time. The title of this book is too general to give a proper idea of its contents. What Hunter Guthrie sets out to do is to overhaul the meaning of a human person as a thinking and willing being. To do this he employs what is known as the phenomenological method. That is to say, he tries to go behind the variety of human experience, determined in part as it is by heredity and education, and detect the faint pulsations of our common humanity as expressed in will and thought. This he calls examining 'the thinker in his purely *a priori* condition'. Like others who use this phenomenological method he brings into play the terms, existence and essence. (Those who have read Kierkegaard, even if they are not well acquainted with metaphysics, will remember the importance that writer attached to the term 'existence'.) Now those who study philosophy have to learn much about this distinction between essence and existence, but it was not till I had read Hunter Guthrie's book that I saw the full significance of these distinctions in relation to the different sorts of love. So once again a chance reading of a book enabled me to string together what had hitherto been unconnected in my mind.

Lastly and quite recently I came across *Passion and Society*, a translation by Montgomery Belgion of *L'Amour et l'Occident* by Denis de Rougemont. I knew of the wayward conception of love entertained by the troubadours in the early Middle Ages through reading the important work of Mr. C. S. Lewis, *The Allegory of Love*; but it was not till I began reading *Passion and Society*, which dealt with the same subject, that I caught the connection between this romantic love and what I had discovered in psychology and metaphysics. And so it has come about that various authors, writing on very disparate subjects, Rousselot on a spiritual and moral problem, Nygren on religion, Aristotle on the nature of change, Hunter Guthrie on metaphysics, and Denis de Rougemont on Provençal poetry and troubadour love, shuffled the thoughts in my mind and helped to form them into a pattern.

In the following pages I will move through these authors and their views to the conclusions which I wish to establish. Love is such a vast subject offering so many temptations to delay over new and beguiling turns and twists of it that a writer would never reach an end if he did not make up his mind to concentrate on one aspect of it. In connecting up one great historical manifestation with a great philosophical tradition and by contrasting what some have called the Greek approach by Eros with the Christian approach by Agape, I hope to make a pattern which may convince and serve, if examined, to connect together traits which I have not time to mention. If the word love be used not too loosely I believe that some all-embracing conceptions can be adopted, though when the branches have to be examined in detail, each will need a volume of explanation. Think for a moment of all the strange varieties of love we come across in human conduct, and what a limitless expanse any anthology of love opens up to us.[1] I have been glancing at favourite lines of verse: 'Odi et amo', 'As Lines so Loves oblique may well Themselves in every Angle greet: But ours so truly parallel, Though infinite can never meet', 'Out upon it I have loved three whole days together. And am like to love three more, if it prove fair weather', 'A well tamed Heart, For whose more noble smart Love may be long choosing a dart'. These and countless other passages need a long commentary. The reader, as it is, will find quite enough commentary in what is to follow and as much philosophy as he will be able to stomach.

For fear, however, lest in the method which I intend to follow, the thread of the argument be lost, I will put down here a summary, which must, alas, be as deceptive as it may appear simple. To some the simplicity may suggest that I have in mind some kind of hybrid or counterfeit philosophy which uses metaphors and poetic expressions when hard and rigorous analysis is required. Truly there is a way of speaking and writing on deep subjects which can appeal to undisciplined minds but to those who want truth is only exasperating. It gains its effect by ambiguous words and by the use of emotional instead of logical associations. I can only defend myself at the moment by saying that I am fully aware of the danger, and if in this summary I appear to suggest, for instance, that the changes in the physical world can be described in terms of desire

---

[1] What Lord Wavell, in his Anthology (*Other Men's Flowers*) has called, 'love young and simple . . . love romantic . . .; love practical . . .; love uxorious . . .; love gay and willing . . .; love oriental . . .; love explanatory, as of the poet who was unfaithful to Cynara in his fashion; love valedictory . . .; love submissive . . .; curtain-lecture love . . .; love misdirected and betrayed . . .; love in the twilight . . .; and many others.'

and love, or that all desire, as it occurs in the lower orders of living beings, is equivalent in any way to what we know as human love, I beg the reader to wait on what is to come for a proper explanation.

The simplest statement of the law which governs what is highest and lowest in the Universe can be called that of 'Give and Take'. In the most elementary changes in the physical world there is gain and loss, the taking on of something and the passing on of what once was and no longer is. Aristotle describes such change in terms of matter and form, where there is always something determinable which is made determined and something which actively determines, and gives it form. Something seems to slide away into nothingness itself while being at the same time a provider of what is to come, and something enters into possession. This principle is seen more clearly in the continuation of life. There is always a duality, of which one aspect is negative as compared with the other: one gives and the other takes. The giving is a surrender and implies a certain passivity, perhaps even unto death and extinction. The desire which is felt by the two parties in this momentary or prolonged union accords with the role played. There is the whoop of triumph, the exultant mastery in the act of possession and on the other side there is a joy in self-surrender even to absorption and total extinction in the being of the other. It may be that this latter desire or emotion is due to a primary urge for the species and its continuation, and since there is in the lower forms of life no true individuality in either participant, there is nothing to prevent the owner of the instinct from rushing in joy to its death. The important point to notice is the universal fact of duality. What we meet in the animal world and in human beings has its analogies in art and literature and science. Science deals with the positive and negative energy and inertia; art with major and minor chords, the rise and fall of the accent and the limiting and controlling power on matter of the form, which Coventry Patmore called 'creation's crowning good, wall of infinitude'. So ubiquitous, indeed, is this phenomenon of duality that it has found expression even in philosophy, in all those systems which go by the name of 'dialectic'.

The universality of this 'dialectic' must not, however, be exaggerated. On closer examination important differences between what are superficially alike usually reveal themselves, and it is all important to emphasize the unique status of man. In so far as he is kin to the animals we can boldly point to analogies between them, but human love has something which animal love never has. The difference can be best expressed in saying that the higher actions of man have an intrinsic value and that man has a personal dignity. This dignity implies a radical difference between human love and any lower form of love. It forbids alike the brutal possessiveness which marks the positive, male surge of animal passion and the total self-yielding of feminine ecstasy. In creatures which are swayed by animal passion the male instinct is to dominate and take, the female to yield and give. They are unhindered by any moral considerations, by mutual respect. It is sufficient that they should get what they want and that the species should be continued. In taking, therefore, and giving they fulfil their nature—and it does not matter whether the lion or the lioness, the actual male or female of the species, lord it so long as the two distinct and complementary loves are present in one way or another. Both are needed and together they suffice, the feminine as the love which surrenders for the sake of the other or the continuation of the species, and the male as the love which seeks its own and possesses, whether it be rampant or, as we shall see later, cognitive.

Now, whereas in nature these instincts go their own way, careless often of individual life, on the human level each self must grow in the taking and giving and each is a sacred life which must be respected. A new cycle begins; the two loves are present and are sublimated if the lower passion is lifted up, as it should be, to the ends of spirit. Every human person has these two loves within him, with one usually predominant, but the sacrificial impulse has a new direction. The contrast between animal and human love is admirably described in the lines of Donne:

> *All other things to their destruction draw,*
> *Only our love hath no decay;*
> *This no to-morrow hath nor yesterday,*
> *Running it never runs from us away,*
> *But truly keeps his first, last, everlasting day.*

But within the soul is more than a human love and that is why I say that the sacrificial love has a new direction. In the equality which should exist in true human love it has not its full outlet; there is more to it than a mere equality, for it is now the expression of the secret mark of human beings, namely their creatureliness, the frail-as-gossamer hold on our nature, which we call existence or persistence in being. We are hangers on, courtiers of the Absolute; we can be unmade as quickly as we are made, and in that dependence is felt dimly the ultimate love of the rivulet for its source. That is why in the mystics' terminology the soul is enraptured and its life is stolen away, and it is in the dark night that the total denuding of self is accomplished. But whereas the primitive impulse was to loss of self, 'for I was flax and he was flames of fire', in that region where the self meets the Lord of life, there is communion and not death; 'My very ashes in their urn, shall, like a hallowed Lamp, for ever burn'. Finally, this law of the two in one, of giving and taking, is to be found in its primordial and perfect expression in God Himself, where in the mutual love of the Trinity all is given without loss, and all is taken without change, save that a new Person is revealed in this wondrous intercommunion Who is Love itself.

The method I have used may be compared to a fugue, where by fugue is meant the more or less exact reproduction by several voices of the statement of a leading part. If love be composed of two leitmotifs in the way I suggest, the evidence for this hypothesis must be sought in more than one sphere of human activity, and even further afield in the behaviour of other creatures. Each new piece of evidence will repeat the main theme in its own way and make it emerge more clearly, and that is why I have not scrupled to appeal to poets and modern psychologists as well as to philosophers and theologians. The different voices coming in one after another will, I hope, leave the reader at the end with the conviction that the main theme is true. The method involves many repetitions, and if the reader finds these boring I beg him to skip them—on one condition, however, that he is sure that he has grasped the tenor of the argument. I have tried to keep the argument light by avoiding, so far as possible, technical terms. Those who have been trained in a certain school of scholarship may complain that what I have written does not belong to any known genre of scholarly work. I cannot see that this matters so long as the truth is made manifest. The 'wissenschaftliche' distinctions can become a burden instead of a gain, for the Sabbath was made for man and not man for the Sabbath. Towards the end of the book, however, I have been forced, in order to give a solid foundation to my view, to have recourse to metaphysics. The reader untrained in the abstractions of philosophy may find this hard going, but as I hope that he will have already grasped the general argument of the book by the time he reaches these chapters, the omission of them will not be so serious as in other types of books written on a different method. The advantage of a cumulative argument is that some items in it can be neglected without total loss, however much the artistic unity of the whole may suffer.

While writing this book I got my friend, Patrick Pollen, to do a coloured drawing for me, which seemed to contain in it almost everything I wanted to say. My hope was to have it for a frontispiece, but unfortunately that has not proved possible. I mention the drawing because it will explain, what otherwise might seem mysterious, the many references to the Lion and the Unicorn. My original title for this book was the Lion and the Unicorn, and the drawing showed these two heraldic beasts supporting, as in the royal arms, a shield shaped like a heart. The Lion symbolizes that noble and ignoble love which is leonine and lordly and asserts itself in pride and self-respect and honour. In other words it stands for self-centred love. The Unicorn, on the other hand, is suited for the Anima. In most of the legends the Unicorn is a fierce beast, but Christianity has made it gentle and likened it to the fawn which pants for the waters of life and is ready for self-sacrifice. With this clue I hope that the symbols of the Lion and the Unicorn will be clear.

Of the many books which have been written on human and divine love, I refer to only a few. The omission of names must not be taken to imply that I think slightingly of their treatment of the subject. It is true that I have not used what they have written, but the reason is that I deemed it wiser to decline their help rather than risk being distracted from my own line of thought.

M. C. D'Arcy

CONTENTS

PREFACE   *page* 9

INTRODUCTION   21

I. COURTLY AND PASSIONATE LOVE   27

    APPENDIX ONE   41

    APPENDIX TWO—GNOSTICISM   47

II. EROS AND CHRISTIAN THEOLOGY   54

    APPENDIX ONE   73

    APPENDIX TWO—CARITAS   76

III. THE PROBLEM OF SELF-CENTRED LOVE   84

    APPENDIX—ON PURE OR UNSELFISH LOVE   101

IV. FRIENDSHIP   104

V. REASON AND WILL   124

VI. LOVE AND THE SELF   156

    APPENDIX—LOVE AND SELF—INDIVIDUAL

    AND PERSON   169

VII. ANIMUS AND ANIMA   174

VIII. RECAPITULATION   194

IX. LOVE AND SYMPATHY   206

X. SACRIFICE   236

XI. PHILOSOPHICAL BACKGROUND   248

XII. PHILOSOPHICAL BACKGROUND—*cont.*   274

XIII. PERSONALITY   292

    APPENDIX—THE VIEW OF ST. THOMAS

    AQUINAS ON THE RELATION OF LOVE

    AND INTELLECT   304

XIV. HUMAN AND DIVINE   308

INDEX   331

19

CONTENTS

		page 9
PREFACE		
INTRODUCTION		11
I. COURTLY AND PASSIONATE LOVE		27
APPENDIX ONE		44
APPENDIX TWO — GNOSTICISM		47
II. EROS AND CHRISTIAN THEOLOGY		64
APPENDIX ONE		77
APPENDIX TWO — CARITAS		80
III. THE PROBLEM OF SELF-CENTRED LOVE		85
APPENDIX: A NOTE ON ENGLISH LOVE		101
IV. FRIENDSHIP		108
V. REASON AND WILL		124
VI. LOVE AND THE SELF		150
APPENDIX: SEX AND THE INDIVIDUAL PERSON		160
VII. ANIMUS AND ANIMA		174
VIII. RECAPITULATION		193
IX. LOVE AND SYMPATHY		200
X. MIRROR		230
XI. PHILOSOPHICAL BACKGROUND		248
XII. PHILOSOPHICAL BACKGROUND — II		274
XIII. PERSONALITY		302
APPENDIX: THE VIEW OF ST. THOMAS AQUINAS ON THE RELATION OF LOVE AND INTELLECT		304
XIV. HUMAN AND DIVINE		308
INDEX		331

INTRODUCTION

And there the lion's ruddy eyes shall flow tears of gold—W. BLAKE.

> For softly neared the ne'er accredited
> White creature, like a hind the unmerited
> Loss of her fawn lamenting with sad eyes.
> —The Unicorn by R. M. RILKE.
> Translated by J. B. LEISHMANN.

In a famous passage St. Paul told his converts that he could show them a 'more excellent way', the way of charity. So much has this word 'charity' suffered in the course of time that it is almost unsafe now to use it. Certainly the meaning which St. Paul gave to it is so overgrown with other senses that an equivalent should be found. The difficulty is to find that equivalent. Love is a better English word, but love covers a multitude of sins and virtues. A word which is still strange, but has not yet been spoilt is Agape, and within recent years it has come into fashion, especially in connection with or in contrast to another Greek word, Eros. Eros is more familiar, and as a result has become less definite. It can represent the god of love, as in the story of Eros and Psyche, or the love, which, in the chorus of Sophocles, swoops into life and makes men mad; it can be the spiritual and philosophic love which Plato describes, or sexual excitement—as in our word 'erotic'. Coventry Patmore uses it for saintly contemplation, de Rougemont for dark passion. Agape, however, is still reserved for the specifically Christian form of love, and is nearly equivalent to St. Paul's 'charity'.

In the course of this book the proper meaning of Agape or charity will, I hope, become clear. The Christian theological meaning of love is precise, and this meaning has overflowed on to the more general meaning of love and enriched it. We may with justice say that as the dominant note of barbarism is will and that of culture, especially the culture influenced by Greek ideas, is reason or intellect, so that of Christendom is love. At times when the struggle for existence is fierce and it is a question of sauve qui peut, the will to live and to master one's environment is naked and unashamed. Once nature has been tamed and men have found it better to live together in a society, reason has more scope and is more highly valued. It is reason, after all, which distinguishes man from the beasts and raises the civilized man above the barbarian. Reason, moreover, seems to give man a defence against fate. By its aid he can exercise control over what formerly he feared, over nature, and even to some

21

extent over the powers which were thought to rule nature and man. By reason a man discovers his own nature, the sources of comfort in the mind and in the heart. With the new self-reliance following on this discovery he can steel himself against adversity and make his own happiness.

But all this time the position of love is ambiguous. A barbarian has too little self knowledge to withstand the gusts of his passions, and so his loves are a mixture of the savage and the fearful. He is sufficiently human to balk at unrestrained lust, and in fear he surrounds himself with customs and taboos. Fate and the Almighty Power are hostile and quick to punish him. Hence with his darkened intelligence he cannot read love into the decrees of fate; his love sinks and tends to be subhuman. The civilized man at first seeks the answer for everything in his new-found power of reason. He hopes to dissipate his fears and to build a city which is safe from every kind of foe. But love does not easily fit into such plans, and moreover the plans do not work out. Nature is not so easily conquered; his fellow human beings do not behave so rationally; hysteria lies close behind reason and the passions defy it; and the presence of an unknown fate or Almighty Power looms behind everything. At this juncture, while reason still leads the way and is exalted, the best take refuge in a philosophical religion. The mind has touched the Absolute, and in the riches of beauty and truth and goodness, which abide there, the wise man hopes to find happiness. The highest life consists in the possession of these treasures.

This spiritual quest can be named love, and is called the 'love of wisdom'. It has, however, very little relation with human love, and it is reserved for an élite. Human love is still a pariah; the love of husband and wife is accepted, but not honoured, and other less worthy friendships are sung by the poets. There is still no sign from heaven, no exemplar in the spiritual world, no sanction, to give love an exalted, still less the supreme position in human life. By accident, however, or by an historical necessity, something did happen, which had an incalculable effect on the future of Western civilization. The mystery religions of the East encountered the philosophy of Greece, and out of this encounter came a new religious philosophy or philosophic religion. In mingling they gave to each other what each lacked. The Greek wisdom had no contacts with earth; its happiness was in reason and thought and the fruits of these. The mystery religion, on the other hand, was the child of passion and it lived on passion. The madness which love excites was changed from a brutal passion into an ecstasy, a divine frenzy. The god seized the worshipper and possessed him or her with irresistible might. The Greek had been taught to avoid extremes, but now a new inspiration seized him.

O glad, glad on the mountains
To swoon in the race outworn,
When the holy fawn-skin clings
And all else sweeps away,
To the joy of the quick red fountains,
The blood of the hill-goat torn,
The glory of wild-beast ravenings
Where the hill-top catches the day,
To the Phrygian, Lydian mountains
'Tis Bromios leads the way.

(EURIPIDES, *Bacchae* 135)

This wild and savage religion of ecstasy met the Greek philosophy; dark passion met intellectual love. The effect looks surprising. Instead of a clash there was fusion. The savage and physical delight shifted to a spiritual one; the love of truth changed into a desire of fusion with the god or goddess. The contact of the world's most civilized man with this ecstatic passion seemed to release a pent-up desire in him and introduced a new note into his poetry and love of what was around him.

And all the mountains felt
And worshipped with them; and the wild things knelt,
And ramped and gloried, and the wilderness
Was filled with moving voices and dim stress.

(EURIPIDES, *Bacchae* 723)

This new change is usually connected by scholars with the name of Orpheus and Orphism, but as it spread and took on new features and new elements of philosophy it became a tendency more than a definite form of religious thought, and can be summed up in the name, Gnosticism.

The effect of all this on the understanding and esteem of love was profound. Eros had gained in dignity; it was now fully human instead of being a form of lust, and even the reasonable philosopher could talk of fusion with the divine. But something was still wanting, the absence of which time and again proved fatal to expectations. Primitive and savage man was conscious of opposition all round him, and he feared the gods. His love therefore had no friendly tutelage from on high; it was unbridled by reason and without spiritual direction. Civilized man could rely on his interior strength; he could love himself at the cost of nature and the unknown God. He himself, the one being of whom he was sure, could love beauty and goodness in the sense that he could desire to make them his own. As to the gods, if they indeed existed, the less he tried to compete with them the better. 'Know thyself' was sufficient. 'Desire not, thou soul of mine, life of the immortals, but drink thy fill of what thou hast and what thou canst.' (Pindar, *Pythian*, iii, 59.) This is the love of a man who has no real friends and is uncertain of the reception he would get were he to meet the gods. But his mind has opened for him a new world of spirit; he can explore there and fill his soul with its riches and comfort. Clearly this is a one-sided attitude; it is partly a self-defence mechanism, a shield of protection against the menace of the world around and of fate, and it is partly acquisitive and possessive. A human being cannot live alone in a world of his own desires and shaping, and so love has a habit of turning the tables on him and putting him at the feet of another. Human beings are like children who at one moment are exhibitionists and at the next are hiding behind their mother's skirts; the Lord Angelo whose 'blood is very snow-broth', who blunts the natural edge of his appetites 'with profits of the mind, study and fast', surrenders everything, even virtue, to Isabella.

This is what happened to selfish Eros. It changed its face if not its name, and became captive instead of captor. The Greek pride was shaken by the encounter with the mystic passion of the East. Those who had learnt wisdom and self-control at the Academy listened to a music which took them out of themselves; they talked of a home in the spiritual world to which they belonged and sought for fusion with the One.[1] The reign of love, it might be hoped, would now succeed to that of Will and Reason. It is true that a new era was about to begin, an era of love, but it was to be the Christian love of Agape and not of Eros. The union of East and West, of reason with passionate desire, of possessive with dispossessive love, was too imperfect to be fertile. The future was to see an oscillation between one or other form of Eros, the cult of the dark passion or the worship of self, the belief in reason or the flight from it to other resources, an egocentric humanism or a mystic salvation from self by union with the Absolute. The lion and the unicorn went fighting round the town. There was never any permanent, true peace between them, never any tranquil love filling the human landscape and disposing of all things sweetly. Agape alone had the power to end the conflict and pitch a Jacob's ladder between heaven and Charing Cross. The perfection of love, as we shall argue, is to be found in personal friendship, whether between a man and a woman, between man and man or between man

---

[1] Nietzsche summed up the change in his comparison of the worship of Apollo with the cult of Dionysus. As Miss J. E. Harrison writes in her *Prolegomena to the Study of the Greek Religion*, paraphrasing Nietzsche: 'Apollo, careful to remain his splendid self, projects an image, a dream, and calls it *god*. It is illusion—Schein—, its watchword is limitation—Maass, Know thyself, Nothing too much. Dionysus breaks all bonds; his motto is the limitless—Uebermaass—, Excess, Ecstasy', pp. 446–7.

and God. When God revealed himself as love, the last fear was removed from man's heart. Neither God nor nature nor other human beings were enemies and a menace. They could all be looked at with interest and love, and in the case of persons love could be mutual. Even Eros, if it knows its own nature, can go with Agape. In the next two chapters we shall study two illuminating, if inadequate attempts to make a covenant between them.

CHAPTER ONE

COURTLY AND PASSIONATE LOVE

I have two luxuries to brood over in my walks, your loveliness and the
hour of my death. O that I could take possession of them both in the
same moment.—KEATS to Fanny Brawne.

These terms, classic and romantic, stand for more than difference of style.
The classic sees man as master and the romantic as victim of his environment.—ALEX COMFORT.

> *Whereupon she (the Soul) enveloped in the figure of a fawn*
> *Struggles with Death; suffering a probationary penance.*
> *At one time, invested with royalty, she beholds the light;*
> *At another, cast down into misery, she weeps.*
>
> . . . . . .
>
> *She seeketh to escape from the bitter chaos,*
> *But knoweth not how to pass through.*
> *For this cause send me, O Father!*
> *I will go down holding the Souls,*
> *I will pass through all the Aeons;*
> *I will reveal all the mysteries;*
> *I will manifest the forms of the gods;*
> *And the secrets of the holy way.*
> *I will teach, giving unto them the name of Gnosis.*
>
> —Hymn quoted by HIPPOLYTUS

Once upon a time the education of children used to begin with
the Bible, the fairy tales of Grimm and Hans Andersen and the
Arthurian legend, and so deep was their influence that the ideals
of truth and romance seemed to be identical. The image of the search
for truth was the quest of the Holy Grail, Galahad was the perfect knight,
true or tragic love lay in the stories of Elaine and Iseult and stood before
the eyes in the pictures of the Divina Beatrix and the Blessed Damosel.
Now that taste has changed, it is difficult for a younger generation to
realize how closely woven into thought and imagination was the romantic
ideal of love. Novels, and painting and poetry, all fed the imagination
on romance. Most of the Victorian poets tried their hand at the Arthurian
legend, and copies of Pre-Raphaelite paintings were everywhere. Even
the most puritanical and strict of parents and governesses could see no
harm in such stories as the tale of Tristram and Isolde and Lancelot and
Guinevere; they were as Christian as *Pilgrim's Progress* and the deeds

27

of a St. Louis and Joan of Arc. Romance gave a dream-like quality to warlike and amatory acts and seemed to bestow on them even a heavenly grace.

Times, however, have changed, and romance has vanished, and few now read the *Idylls of the King* and look at the pictures of Rossetti and Burne-Jones with the same rapture. The limitations of the Victorians have been exposed, and the somewhat acid comments of critics have penetrated the mind. Freed from their prepossessions many began to wonder how the themes of Tristram and Isolde and Lancelot and Guinevere could have been thought of as highly moral or even Christian; they seemed to be more fitly described, in the words of one commentator, as 'an epic of adultery'. A few years ago Mr. C. S. Lewis published his work on *The Allegory of Love*, and this to many appeared definitive. It made clear, beyond contention, the singular difference between the romantic or courtly and troubadour love and that of the Christian ideal. To those who had been brought up in Victorian days the truth came as a shock; they had had, as I have said, their imaginations so soaked in images of romance that they had subconsciously identified Christian and romantic love. Now they had to learn that while Christianity extolled marriage and constant fidelity, the troubadours gave not a thought to marriage, but sang of a fair lady and of love outside the marriage bond.

This was disconcerting enough to the simple, but worse was to come. In 1939 a book, entitled *L'Amour et l'Occident*, by M. de Rougemont, was published in France, and it has been translated into English by Montgomery Belgion with the title, *Passion and Society*. In this book de Rougemont dares what Lewis refrained from doing: he tries to explain why the love of the romantics is so different from that of Christian love; —and here the surprise comes—the reason given is that romantic love springs from an unholy and forbidden source, the strange, wild Eros, the necromancing and unbaptized witch, who is an implacable foe of Christianity and ever seeks to cast her spells over the true lover. There are two loves, so de Rougemont holds, which fight for man's soul, Eros and Agape, and each has its own definite characteristics which enable us to recognize it. Agape is there for all to see in the Christian teaching; Eros, on the other hand, in a Christian world has to conceal itself and goes disguised under symbols.

Now the most representative example of Eros is, so de Rougemont argues, to be found in the story of Tristram and Isolde, as it was developed by the troubadours and the courtly poets. We are accustomed to think of the story as a typical human story, simple in its construction and tragic. This is a delusion, and the quickest way to correct this superficial impression is to grasp the extraordinary inconsistencies in the original story. Tristram is depicted as the sworn knight of King Mark; as such, he has, by all the laws of chivalry, duties towards the king, his feudal lord, which he must on his honour fulfil. The writer of the story makes him at times act heroically so as to keep his pledge; and yet on other occasions, with the obvious collusion and agreement of the author, Tristram forswears himself and makes a cuckold of his master. If we ask an explanation of this mystery the author has it ready. We are told that Tristram is a victim of his destiny and that he is acting on the summons of passionate love. This passionate love is his fate, and at the same time it is his own true love. To get this right the author at one moment suggests that Tristram's actions are due to a love potion, which he cannot resist, and at another that it is Tristram's own passion which is driving him on. The treatment of the mutual love of Tristram and Isolde is equally ambiguous. We are left uncertain whether that love is physical or entirely spiritual. The plain meaning of the story is that the lovers sinned together, but according to one of the earliest versions Tristram never has physical contact with Isolde. When King Mark comes upon the lovers he sees a drawn sword lying between them, that is, the accepted symbol of their continence. Not only are they not lovers, they do not even care for each other when they are together, and Tristram hands Isolde back to Mark. But as soon as she is absent from him the passion begins all over again. The point of this will be lost to a modern reader, but by the devotee of a certain cult which flourished at the time the point would be immediately taken. A Gnostic and follower of the Catharist heresy would see in these ambiguities the staging of his creed. Tristram and Isolde are both smitten with Eros, the dark passion, and it belongs to the nature of this passion that its victim should be in love, not with any physical loved object, but with love itself; the dark passion draws the lover away from all that is earthly and living to seek death. There is death in the love potion, and it is the symbol of what must be if Eros, La Belle Dame sans Merci, beckons. Such passion can never be slaked until it is consummated in the dark night of death. The love, which Tristram and Isolde feel, as they gaze into one another's eyes, is for sorrow and unhappiness; it is a wound which cannot be healed:

> *Old tune so full of sadness*
> *That singst thy sad complaint.*
> *Through evening breezes came that strain,*
> *As once my father's death I learned in childhood;*
> *Through morning twilight, sadder sounding,*
> *As to me my mother's fate was told.*
> *He who begot me died, she dying gave me birth.*

The olden ditty's mournful plaint, E'en so to them its numbers came,
That strain that asked, that asks me still,
What fate for me was chosen,
When there my mother bore me,
What fate for me?
The olden ditty once more tells me:
'Tis yearning and dying. . . . Yearning now calls for death's repose.

These words, then, and the movement of the story, with its mysterious and symbolical incidents, de Rougemont interprets in terms of Eros. 'The love of love has concealed a far more awful passion, a desire altogether unavowable, something that could only be "betrayed" by means of symbols, such as that of the drawn sword and that of perilous chastity. Unawares and in spite of themselves, the lovers have never had but one desire—the desire for death. Unawares, and passionately deceiving themselves, they have been seeking all the time simply to be redeemed and avenged for "what they have suffered"—the passion unloosed by the love potion. In the innermost recesses of their hearts they have been obeying the fatal dictates of a wish for death; they have been in the throes of the *active passion of Night*.' Since this passion is more a force than an awareness it must be clothed in symbol, and the material for handling such symbols was present in the twelfth century in magic and the rhetoric of chivalry. Hence the writers of these romances can be found adopting symbols which reappear again and again, and the brooding beauty of these symbols with the dark hints contained in them heightened the passion of the romantic poetry.

By their very success these romantic writers must, so de Rougemont claims, have appealed to something in the breast of European man. 'The tremendous success of the Tristram romance shows', he says, 'whether we like it or not, that we have a secret preference for what is unhappy.' This lies behind the silly sentimentalism of the romantic movement in Germany and the decadence at the end of the nineteenth century as well as the torments and ecstasies of the seventeenth-century poets. 'Suffering and understanding are deeply connected: death and self-awareness are in league; and European romanticism may be compared to a man for whom sufferings, and especially the sufferings of love, are a privileged mode of understanding.' Or as a greater one wrote: 'All lovers young, all lovers must consign to thee, and come to dust.'

After having thus analysed the meaning of the love theme in Tristram and Isolde, de Rougemont gives us the historical setting and his explanation in terms of Eros and Agape. To some perhaps his interpretation may have up to now sounded far-fetched, but what he has to say of the back-

30

ground of thought in the period during which the ideal of courtly love developed brings us back to reality. The poetry of courtly love took its rise at a certain point of time and in definite localities. It has certain definite and very remarkable features, so remarkable indeed as almost to baffle historians. For what has to be explained is that at a time when the West of Europe was settling down to accept a Christian ethos and culture, when the writ of feudal law ran everywhere and the sacrament of marriage was universally accepted, there nevertheless sprang up an ideal sung of in poetry which ran counter to feudal custom and celebrated a love outside the marriage bond. This new ideal influenced all writers. As Charles Albert Cingria wrote: 'The whole of the Occitanian, Petrarchian, and Dantesque lyric has but a single theme—love; and not happy, crowned, and satisfied love (the sight of which yields nothing), but on the contrary love perpetually unsatisfied and but two characters; a poet reiterating his plaint eight hundred, nine hundred, a thousand times; and a fair lady who ever says "No".' The ordinary woman in this feudal age was much more a chattel than an ideal, and yet side by side with her came the dream of a woman at the very vision or thought of whom the heart of man is wounded beyond curing.

Many solutions of this problem have been suggested; that of de Rougemont is as follows: From its earliest years Christianity had had a persistent enemy, and this enemy, which had been crushed for a time, gained a new energy at the beginning of the Middle Ages. The generic name of this enemy is Gnosticism or Manichaeanism. In the first centuries of Christianity it had syncretized many of the beliefs of the prevalent cults, especially those from the East. As time went on it gathered into itself some of the endemic beliefs and superstitions of the Celts, who, as all know, had a remarkable influence on the early civilization of Europe. As the Celts spread they brought with them their belief in a kind of immortality which is always shrouded and made forlorn by its close association with death. In his work on *Les Celtes*, H. Hubert writes that they had 'certainly elaborated a metaphysic of death. They had meditated on death a great deal. It had grown into a familiar companion, whose disturbing nature, however, they deliberately disguised.' In their prevalent myths it is a woman who figures most prominently, a woman who stirs up the belief in immortality and can be called even the symbol of eternal desire, but she is also the dark lady, one whose dwelling is in darkness and whose charm is fatal. Spiritually conceived she is that vanishing vision which calls man out of the world, but in a less spiritual age she may represent what is unholy and be to her followers the eternal courtesan. To the Tristrams, however, she is that Eros whose song of love is heard in the night, which is more illuminating than the transient gleams of day when the soul of man is imprisoned among earthly forms. In the Celtic pantheon there are gods both of darkness and light, and in this conception they join thought with those Indo-European religions whose mythologies tell of a conflict between the principles of light and darkness, Ormuz and Ahriman. In this latter mythology the rival powers are seen most clearly, but they figure in almost all, and there are common motifs which gradually lead to a confusion or syncretization of many of the gods and goddesses. Even in the philosophical aspirations of the time there is something similar. As Dill wrote: 'The mystic who dreamt of an ecstasy of divine communion, in which the limits of sense and personality might be left behind in a vague rapture of imaginative emotion, found in the spectacle of her (Isis) inner shrine, a strange power far surpassing the most transporting effects of Eleusis.' In all is present a sense of the uncleanness of this world and an escape through purification, through a kind of death into the darkness where union with the Magna Mater could be found. The Greek genius mated with the wild dark ecstasy of the Eastern religions and produced a view of life which in time came to resemble a despairing version of the Christian faith. I say 'despairing' because it thought too despairingly of life in this world and sought an escape from it; it sought escape in a kind of death, which by a subtle perversion could all too easily be loved for its own dark self; and it despised man and recked so little of his personal worth that it would willingly dissolve him in the divine essence. In the Greek literature there is also, as Walter Pater pointed out long ago, the 'worship of sorrow'. Nietzsche has made familiar to us the distinction of the Dionysiac and Apolline element. The Apolline is sunny and human and reasonable, the Dionysiac is passionate and otherworldly, and it can be very cruel and very sad. But the dark side of the Greek wishfulness is seen best of all in the story of Persephone, the legend of the woman who is taken to the dark regions and wedded to the god of the dark. When then we talk of the Graeco-Roman culture it is important to remember this dark side in the legends and in the philosophy, as we may expect to find it reappearing in some form or other in the early Christian civilization which owed so much to the Graeco-Roman influence.

De Rougemont, then, suggests that in Manichaeanism the unwanted voices of the ancient religions and philosophies are raised again and speak the old theme, though with perhaps new emphases. They wanted not the communion of the Christian ideal but an essential, if mystical, union with God; they also, to use the expression of Plotinus, hated to be human; the body is carnal, the subject of a lower principle, and the soul must avoid contact with it and all that is human, and its only joy can consist in the very denial of the world and of itself; its unhappiness is the token of its deliverance. On the other hand the Church applied the doctrine of the Incarnation and Redemption, which was a scandal and folly to the Manichaeans, to man's acts, sacramentalizing the chief of them and viewing even the world as a quasi sacrament, and love of 'neighbour' as love of God himself. It is not surprising if the deeply-imbedded pagan myths began again to be heard in the land and to be propagated in a disguised form by those who rebelled against the Christian yoke, once the Church was able to enforce its discipline. Therefore, as de Rougemont concludes: 'The cultivation of passionate love began in Europe as a reaction to Christianity (and in particular to its doctrine of marriage) by people whose spirit, whether naturally or by inheritance, was still pagan.'

Now we know that Manichaeanism lived on, that it broke out in Spain in the heresy which is called Priscillianism, and that at the beginning of the Middle Ages the Church was engaged in rooting out as most dangerous certain tendencies which were then making themselves felt. The name by which they went was Catharism, and there is a striking family resemblance between its doctrines and those of Manichaeanism and the whole of the Gnostic philosophy. These doctrines de Rougemont summarizes as follows: 'God is love. But the world is evil. Therefore God cannot be the author of the world, or its darkness, or of the sin by which we are hemmed in. . . . Man is a fallen angel, imprisoned in matter, and on that account subject to the laws of the body—in particular the most oppressive of these, the law of procreation. But the Son of God came to show the way back to the Light. The Christ was not incarnated; he but put on the appearance of a man. . . .' Three other points are worth mentioning, first, that the place of the Third Person of the Blessed Trinity is taken by the Mother of God, the feminine source of love; second, that those who are perfect should avoid touching their wives if they are married, and thirdly, there are two classes, the perfect and the mere believers, the latter of whom alone are permitted to marry and have traffic with this world's concerns. This heresy has been called the Church of Love, and it has its secret signs and symbols which appear in the troubadour poetry.

As will be noticed, the doctrine is highly spiritual, but as so often happens, an over-emphasis on the spiritual brings a recoil to its opposite, and there can be no doubt that this religion which rejected the Incarnation as too materialistic became at times an excuse for sensualism and the licence of dark desire. Many of the troubadours extolled the purer forms of Catharsis, and dwelt on the dolorous joy of unsatified longing and on the virtue of chastity. The Lady of their dreams kept her inviolable state and was more an ideal or dream vision than a woman of flesh and blood. But they scoffed at the marriage bond and the ordinary laws of feudalism. They sang of a passion which can never be requited in this world, of death as preferable to any human reward and of the duty of separation from the beloved. As song and music moved north they encountered the Celtic fervour with its brooding on death and greyer passion. No wonder, then, that actual sin is committed, that Tristram is the paramour of Isolde, even though it be destiny in the form of a love potion which drives him to disloyalty, that Lancelot is debarred from finding the Holy Grail by his sin, and that it is left for the true Catharist, the pure of heart, like Perceval and Galahad, to have the vision. The combination of the southern courtly and religious love with the northern Celtic melancholy and love of sensual delight is thus the final phase in a development which ends with the Tristram myth, and the acceptance of all that it imports into European civilization. As de Rougemont writes: 'A Celtic background of religious legends—which, as it happens, were at a very remote period common to both the Iberian South and its langue d'oc; customs of feudal chivalry; semblances of Christian orthodoxy; a sometimes very compliant sensuality; and, finally, the individual fancy of each of the poets—there, when all is said and done, are the materials thanks to which the doctrine of Love underwent its transmutations. In this way was the Tristram myth born', and in this guise did the passionate form of love conquer.

We can now gather up some of the arguments which de Rougemont has been developing and show his conclusions in the light of Eros and Agape. We are accustomed to think of Christianity as imposing itself on a world prepared for it by the Greek philosophy and love of reason and by the universal social and legal system of Rome. But we now know that a religion with a supposedly otherworldly aspiration and a wilder kind of love stirred the Near East and Mediterranean society before the coming of Christ, and for a long time struggled on as the rival to Christianity. Even after Christianity won the day it did not die; but it had to be an alien. Its philosophy of life was therefore disguised and it continued to be disguised under poetic symbol and myth even when a period came which was favourable to its resurrection. These symbols are seen in the poetry of the troubadours and later in the poetry of the Arthurian legends and perhaps above all in the story of Tristram and Isolde. It is irrelevant to ask whether the troubadours were fully conscious of the heresy they were preaching. No one can answer that question. What can be said, however, is that the symbols were of much greater importance than we now are inclined to think. We have lost the sense of symbols as we have tended to look to the lowest factors of explanation instead of the higher ones as the key to problems. We now explain mysticism in terms of medicine and pathology; the ancients explained the sensible by religion and by the highest philosophy of which they could think. To the medieval mind passionate love is determined and justified by a theory of the soul and its final destiny. Once however this passionate love had been accepted and taken for granted by European man he began to use it, without thought of its origins and implications, as a common and natural emotion. He vulgarized it and exploited it in novels and plays, and thereby committed himself more and more to a tolerance of sin and lawlessness and to the extenuation of all passion in the name of romance and experience. De Rougemont notes with irony how little aware our modern novelists and apologists of passion are of the origins and true character of the love they describe and exalt. They do not know that they have changed Montsalvat into a Venusberg.

The second half of *Passion and Society* gives a persuasive account of the process whereby the religion of the Tristram myth worked itself out in literature and conduct, of 'the gradual profanation of the myth, its conversion into rhetoric, and in turn the dissolving of the rhetoric together with the thorough popularization of its content'. At intervals after the first divine rapture faded and failed there would come a new surge of liberation, but as the years passed and the content of hope diminished the cry of liberation became more and more shrill and melancholy, and literature had to turn in upon itself and feed from its own interior until it was left with an empty heart, a weariness with passion and sexual experience and given over to virulence and hate or an unregenerate mysticism. Eros may be still magniloquent or plaintive, but 'the tropes of passionate discourse and the hues of its rhetoric can never become more than the glow of a resurgent twilight and the promise of a phantom bliss'.

The story of this decline does not bear directly on the theme of Eros, and, therefore, I must confine myself to stressing one point in that story. According to de Rougemont passionate love took its place in Western culture in the legend of Tristram and Isolde. What was a stranger and alien became imperceptibly part of the European tradition and was even taken for a positive contribution to Christianity. It is as when the mistress of one of the royal Stuarts was given a title and admitted into society so that in time her descendants were accepted on equal terms by all. Or we may describe the change by comparing it to the domestication of a wild animal, when the wolf has become so doglike as to lie down in amity with the lamb. What de Rougemont calls Eros, the passionate desire of the Catharist, became the current coin of the educated, of mystics and saints as well as the poets and later story-tellers. All know how influenced St. Francis of Assisi was by the ideal of courtly love and the songs of the troubadours, and what a part romantic love plays in the mystical poetry of a Jacapone da Todi. Part of our trouble in interpreting Dante is the uncertainty of the figure of Beatrice. There are those who would see in her nothing but the symbol of grace or wisdom or supernatural love, while others believe that Dante's words must be taken literally as telling of his lifelong love for the child, the daughter of Folco Portinari. We do not know how far great poets like Dante were aware of the ambiguousness of their symbolic language; still less do we know whether St. Francis had any suspicion of the use made of courtly love by heretics. It seems most unlikely that he could have had any such suspicion. This throws some doubt on the thesis of de Rougemont unless we compare the liking of St. Francis and the early Franciscans for the troubadours to the use which the first Jesuits made of the classical humanism of the Renaissance despite its pagan and Neo-Platonic inspiration. The example of the Franciscans was soon followed by others, and in many a Christian mystic orthodox thought is expressed in the ambiguous language of the Catharists. No doubt the Neo-Platonic tradition is also partly responsible for this, as the writings of Denis the Areopagite were thought to be those of a disciple of St. Paul. When we come to St. Teresa of Avila we move in the atmosphere of courts and chivalry, as they made their last stronghold in Spain, but the centuries had taken the sting out of the passionate words. Nevertheless it would be easy to make out from the numerous expressions of love used by St. Teresa an argument that her experience belonged to the passionate love of Eros, as defined by de Rougemont. All the courtly words are there in her writings and she favours language about the dark night, the unhappiness of absence and the death which love demands. By themselves such phrases might make us pause, and they have led many a modern critic into error; but we have to take into account counterbalancing phrases and what we know independently of St. Teresa's life. The main body of her doctrine is so firmly imbedded in the finest tradition of Christian mysticism and sanity that we can be sure that here, if anywhere, the most supernatural and orthodox love is being experienced and written down.

The lesson to be learnt from the discovery of such language in St. Teresa is rather this, that in the seventeenth century the origin of passionate love had been forgotten and that a kind of rhetoric of Eros had become so widespread as to affect the very terms, though not the content, of holiness. The effect of this on secular love literature was bound to be unwholesome, and we may wonder whether it did not also change the mood though not the substance of the orthodox tradition. Pierre Rousselot, in an essay on the Middle Ages (*The Life of the Church*, p. 190), noted a change over from the thirteenth century spirituality of the 'pleasure of the heart in the Holy Cross' and 'grievous joy' to one 'in which meditation on the Passion always has something more painful and harsh about it'. He quotes, too, the evidence of Male in his *L'Art religieux de la Fin du Moyen Age* that the intellectual piety of the thirteenth century is in marked contrast with the emotionalism prevailing in the fifteenth. It may be possible to attribute this change in part to the influence of the death motif and the passion for suffering love, and we might trace further connections in the centuries which succeeded. Such an influence could not change the substance of Christian spirituality, but it might give it a tinge of colouring as when men turn their eyes more frequently to the Crucifixion with less thought of the Resurrection which followed. Devotion and art within the Church usually reflect to some degree the movements which are going on outside it, and if within the last century in secular experience we have seen the dereliction of a passion which feeds on itself and an infinity which has no content we may detect within Christian spirituality a habit which likes to explore the psychology of the spiritual life and the stages of mysticism.

I have given the setting of de Rougemont's doctrine of Eros because he himself chose to give the historical background and the dramatic history of it, and without these the meaning he attaches to it and Agape might be misunderstood. It must be noted, however, that even if his history be inaccurate and his interpretation of the Tristram myth exaggerated, his analysis of Eros and Agape may still be right. What then does he mean by these two loves? Plato, he tells us, spoke of Eros as a kind of frenzy or enthusiasm which reaches its culmination in the union with what is divine. 'Eros is complete Desire, luminous Aspiration, the primitive religious soaring carried to its loftiest pitch, to the extreme exigency of purity which is also the extreme exigency of unity.' It expresses an urge beyond that of sexual love, beyond even all that can satisfy man in ordinary life. It has a note of infinity, so that mortal joys only increase the wound of love. The soul lives by a perpetual renunciation of the finite because the finite fails to give it what it wants, and it cannot rest until it passes beyond desire, never to return, and embraces and is lost in the All. This passion finds the language of day and night most appropriate to its movement, and that is why 'from India to the shores of the Atlantic, though in the most varied forms, there is expressed a same mystery of Day and Night, and a same mystery of the *fatal* struggle going on between them inside men'. Almost as universal as the image of Day and Night is that of the Woman. 'Eros has taken the guise of Woman, and symbolizes both the outer world and the nostalgia which makes us despise earthly joys. But the symbol is ambiguous, since it tends to mingle sexual attraction with *eternal* desire.' That is why Tristram sings of night and is led to his doom by a woman whom he should not touch. 'Iseult is no more, Tristram no more, and no name can any longer part us'. As Novalis wrote: 'Our vows were not exchanged for this world.' Other passages from Novalis bear the mark of this romantic ideal of love.[1] 'When pain is being shunned, that is a sign that one no longer wants to love. Whoever loves must everlastingly remain aware of the surrounding void, and keep the wound open.' 'A union formed even unto death is a marriage bestowing on each a companion for Night. It is in death that love is sweetest. Death appears to one still alive as a nuptial night, the heart of sweet mysteries.' 'May thy spiritual fire devour my body; may I be closely united with thee in an ethereal embrace, and then may our nuptial night endure for ever and ever.'

To such lovers there can be no contentment in the marriage bond. It belongs to that world which is evil; it can serve only physical pleasure and should therefore be despised. Eros draws away from such things and like Narcissus gazes into the water to see its own sad love. All that is human has dissolved and ceased to be, even itself at the end. This last phase is most noticeable in the East, where the soul is invited to fly from all multiplicity and unite itself with the One. Whatever interpretations be put upon some of the doctrines in the East, there can be no doubt that taken together they seem to agree in minimizing the part of the individual person; the stress is on union with the All or the One, and they must have been understood by the multitudes as teaching a fusion or absorption. With this view, as de Rougemont points out, Rudolf Otto in his *West-Ostliche Mystik* agrees. He distinguishes Eastern and Western mysticism in terms of Eros and Agape and maintains that such Eastern writers as Sankara condemn the world for its flux and variety and place perfection in complete fusion and unity. Neo-Platonism belongs to the Eastern type and therefore such a Christian writer as Eckhart 'differs completely from Plotinus, though he is always represented as his pupil. Plotinus also is the publisher of a mystical love, but his love is throughout not Christian agapé, but the Greek eros, which is enjoyment, and enjoyment of a sensual and supersensual beauty arising from an aesthetic experience almost unknown to Eckhart. In its finest sublimation it still bears within it something of the eros of Plato's *Symposium*: that great Daemon, which is purified into a divine passion out of the ardor of procreation, yet even then retains a sublimated element of the original passion.'

Such then is Eros as understood by de Rougemont. Agape, on the other hand, is Christian love, and differs totally from Eros. It is essentially Christian and, so to speak, created by the generosity of God in the Incarnation. The Incarnation does what seems impossible to the human

---

[1] De Rougemont quotes Novalis as a typical example of the 'romantic', and therefore anti-Christian, lover. But it must be remembered that Novalis wrote the *Hymns to the Night* after the death of his bride, and that his longing for death is in order to be united with his bride and Christ.

imagination, it reconciles and brings together the infinite and the finite. Eros rushes to the funeral pyre of all that is finite; it destroys and is the sarcophagus of poor human flesh and spirit. Night and Day, being incompatible, and men being deemed creatures of Night, men can only achieve salvation by ceasing to be, by being 'lost' in the bosom of the divine. But in the doctrine of Christianity this process is inverted and death is swallowed up in victory. Death is only a condition and in the death of the self the new life begins here and now and irradiates all creation. The temporal is not just a shadow, not a ladder to be kicked away; the overflowing life of communion with God begins here and now in the present, as the Word of God was made flesh and dwelt amongst us. The dignity of what is human is thereby established, and as the poet Jammes said, 'toujours le suivit le printemps'. 'Love now still begins beyond death, but from that beyond it returns to life. And in being thus converted love brings forth our *neighbour*. . . '. To love according to this new way is a positive act and an act of transformation. Eros had pursued infinite becoming. Christian love is obedience in the present. For to love God is to *obey* God, Who has commanded us to love one another. . . . The symbol of Love is no longer the infinite *passion* of a soul in quest of light, but the *marriage* of Christ and the Church.' That is why the Christian mystic reaches perfection in a kind of marriage and seems to show such quiet activity when he is most at rest and also to be free from all the ecstasy and passion which marked the preceding stages. This, too, is the reason why the struggle between Eros and Agape manifested itself on the crucial question of marriage. The disciples of Eros despised marriage and sought their ideal outside it. The Church saw how deadly to its teaching this form of love was and fought it ruthlessly at the beginning of the Middle Ages, as at all times. Eros does not really wish that there should be two in love; one of them must cease to be, and this feeling is so strong as to seem irresistible and to be the working of destiny. But Agape accepts the other and thus guards and foments mutual love, heightening that love by that promise of fidelity which boldly challenges evil and fate:

> *If I be false or swerve a hair from truth*
> *When time is old and hath forgot itself,*
> *When waterdrops have worn the stones of Troy,*
> *And blind oblivion swallow'd cities up;*

then says the true lover, 'I have forgotten love and what it means.' Moreover, married love wants the good of the beloved, and when it acts on behalf of that good it is creating in its own presence the neighbour. And it is by this roundabout way through the other that the self rises into being a person—beyond its own happiness. Thus as persons a married couple are a mutual creation, and to become persons is the double achievement of 'active love'.[1]

De Rougemont concludes by emphasizing the more general results of failing to distinguish between passion and true love, Eros and Agape. The failure causes the general breakdown of our European civilization; and, in particular, it is the breakdown of marriage which indicates in short the general collapse. 'There are other indications, and in the most various spheres—the cult of multiplicity, the poetry of escape, the way nationalist passions encroach upon culture—whatever tends to wreck the person.' The old barbarism is upon us openly in the passion for war which is a form of the romantic yearning for death or in the craving for unrestricted experience. Europe is possibly going to succumb to the fate it has thus prepared for itself. But obviously it is not Christianity—as so many writers allege—that will be responsible for the disaster. The catastrophic spirit in Europe is not Christian. On the contrary it is Manichaean. That is what those who identify Christianity with Europe commonly overlook. Everything European is not Christian. If therefore Europe were to succumb to its evil genius, it would be through having cultivated for too long the para-Christian or anti-Christian religion of passion.

I have already said that it is not necessary to agree with all the argument in *Passion and Society* to learn much from it on the nature of Eros and Agape, or rather on sharply contrasting modes of loving. I intend to take up later the distinction which de Rougemont makes, as it is now time to pass on to another interpretation of Eros. But before doing so I must make it clear that provocative and stimulating as is this account of de Rougemont's, it would be unwise to accept it as it stands. The reasons in short are two. The first is that he does not explain how the passion of Eros can be transformed into Agape: and yet some such transformation must take place if the 'passionate' language of many Christian mystics belongs to Agape and not to Eros. Many of the mystics use the language of night and death. St. Teresa of Avila has a special liking for the images of courtly love, and it is difficult to justify them if these images always betoken the presence of Eros. But a much more important difficulty is this, that de Rougemont allows for no kind of love in between the pagan passion of Eros and the Christian and supernatural love of charity. It would seem as if the world outside Christian love had to live by one desire alone, the desire to be free from this clogging world, to deny it and by death pass into fusion with the All. Now it may be argued

---

[1] I beg the reader to notice this passage as it bears on a problem which will be discussed in a later chapter.

that this form of love is very common in ancient times and has returned upon us with the decadence of Christian culture. Plato in Orphic mood may have yielded to it, and Neo-Platonism with its contacts from the East may have fallen a victim to it. But the general Greek conception of love is of a far less wild type; it is Apolline and not Dionysiac, and in the most systematic of Greek thinkers love is described in terms which do not suit the passion of Eros as de Rougemont describes it. There must in fact have been a quiet ordered love in all civilizations; one which lacked the specific and supernatural character of Christian Agape and yet preserved a balance and discipline. No civilization could live on the wild frenzy which alone is mentioned and contrasted with the Christian ideal by de Rougemont. Let us therefore see whether the next interpreter of Eros has anything to say of this.

APPENDIX 1—TO FIRST CHAPTER

The legend of Tristram and Isolde belongs to the genre of myth and it would be tempting to examine myths of various races to find out whether the same view of love can be discovered also in them. The work, however, has been done over and over again by anthropologists, psychologists and critics of religion. The number of stories, too, is almost infinite, and perhaps for that very reason it has been almost too easy for a critic with a prejudice or theory to find evidence for what he wants. As might be expected, the theme of love recurs again and again, and there are numerous references to a passionate love which makes a man beside himself and brings death in its train. The dark goddess also keeps appearing in the legend. For instance, in the early English mythology it was believed that at death man made a journey to an abyss where dwelt a black goddess. In the more spiritualized versions of many religions it appears that the end of all desire is a fusion with the godhead, but as this thought was above the comprehension of the multitudes a debased cartoon of it was presented for worship, and this at times worsened into an excuse for cruelty and victimization. This underworld of human passion is found too frequently in the myths and in practice for it to be an accident, and it must come into any full and proper explanation of love. Aberrations can be very revealing. De Rougemont, however, insists that Tristram has an unearthly love and abhors fleshly pleasures; and it is significant that many myths express the same longing for an ascetical purity. 'Only they whose heart is wholly sinless in despite of all . . . 'tis these alone have law to pluck its flowers to give to the goddess' (Euripides, *Hippolytus*). It is not surprising to find this oscillation between high aspiration and vulgar passion, between extreme asceticism and outbursts of sexuality. The presence of the true God is too inevitable to escape recognition, but the reaction of man is soon coloured by all his feelings and experiences. The sky and earth and the nether regions are soon peopled with the images of man's virtues and vices, and he confuses the most striking phenomena of the universe with the true nature of God. That is why the gods and goddesses multiply and why the great processes of nature, decay and death and spring and ripening are associated with the sun and moon and day and night and so easily become the pageantry of worship. As, however, the early myths evolve and are changed so as to express symbolically the overt and covert desires of the human heart, they begin to show a curious similarity and to express in one way or another what has been called the Gnostic way of life, the way which the Manichaean and the Catharist adopted. The invisible world tantalizes man and makes him dissatisfied with the fugitive passions of this life. Death becomes an obsession, and the desire for escape like a wavering needle turns now to the sunlight and now to that darkness in which the mystery of love may be woven and the soul be lost in the night of fusion and nothingness.

Some instances will help to bring out the common desire, the development of the myth and gradual syncretization. In pre-Buddhist Brahmanism the stress lies on the infirmity of human desire and self. 'He by whom man knoweth, how should He know Himself? There only where duality exists, can Consciousness exist. . . . After death, there is no more self-consciousness.' And much later when the system of Buddhism was fully formed, the contempt for all human categories of thought and human or egoistic desires remained. When asked about the survival of personality after death, the Buddha answered: 'What do I explain to you? Necessary knowledge: that is, that existence is painful; that existence is produced and renewed from life to life by desire; that man may be delivered from existence; but only by deliverance from desire.' In the religion of ancient Syria we have an excellent example of the changes a god or goddess may undergo. Ashtart, the Astarte of the Greeks, was the Ishtar of the Babylonians according to the most probable interpretation. Ishtar represented fertile nature and was regarded now as a goddess of impurity and now as a goddess of the dark passions, and as time went on she was associated with the moon-goddess and accompanies Tammuz at his slaying into the dark regions. Ishtar and Astart can be regarded as almost identical and certainly as having the same history, and it is a history which comes at the end to resemble those of the great goddesses Isis and Persephone. We can, for instance, compare the following remarkable hymn to Ishtar with what I shall quote later from the hymn to Persephone:

I pray unto thee, Lady of ladies, Goddess of goddesses!
O Ishtar, queen of all peoples, directress of mankind!

O lady, majestic is thy rank, over all the gods is it exalted. . . .
Where thou lookest in pity, the dead man lives again, the sick is healed;
The afflicted is saved from his affliction when he beholdeth thy face!
I, thy servant sorrowful, sighing, and in distress, cry to thee.
Look upon me, O my lady, and accept my supplication,
Truly pity me and hearken unto my prayer!
Cry unto me, 'It is enough', and let thy spirit be appeased!
How long shall my body lament, which is full of restlessness and confusion?
How long shall my heart be afflicted, which is full of sorrow and sighing?

During the period when the Mediterranean and the Roman Empire were intoxicated with the Indo-European religions the myth exhibits more fully the nature of human and finite desire for the infinite. In Egypt the story of Osiris and Isis started in Heliopolis, when Osiris represented the fertilizing waters of the Nile and Isis the fruit-bearing soil. But as time passed on the cult of these two grew and took into the myth many other ideas; the coarser elements in the symbolism and many of the uglier practices were dropped. When Plutarch wrote, the myth symbolized the passion for union with the godhead, a union which meant fusion and not communion. Isis reigns now in the Hidden Place and all souls pass to her in a second death and after much purification are finally merged with the pure god, becoming themselves Osiris. What the precise relations could be between Osiris, who is the sum of all perfection and Isis, who says of herself: 'I am all that hath been, and is, and is to be', it is not our concern to ask. But in Plutarch and Apuleius the language of worship of the goddess recalls what de Rougemont wrote as characteristic of 'passionate love'. The initiates to her mysteries make vigil by night, and it is during the night that they are given a token of her benign presence, when a panel in the wall was drawn back and a sight was given of the shades accompanying a faintly luminous figure. 'I trod on the very threshold of death, whereunto I had journeyed . . . gods of heaven and hell I approached and stood before them and adored them face to face.' Consider, again, the words Isis addresses to one who has invoked her help: 'And utterly remember this—this keep thou deeply hidden in thy heart, that all the remaining course of thy life is pledged to me, down to the very limit of thy last breath—for it is but just that to her, by whose beneficence thou art returning to man's life, thou shouldst repay all that thou shalt henceforth be. For life thou shalt be happy, nay, glorious, beneath my patronage; and when thou shalt have measured to an end thy allotted span, and gone to the lower world, there in the hollow heart of earth shalt thou have vision of me shining across the gloom, Queen even in the inner realm of Hades, and at last, in the heavenly fields, thou shalt be ever at my side, and I will be gracious to thee, and me shalt thou adore.'

It is, perhaps, in the Greek story of Persephone that all the symbols come together, and that the dark enchantment, the joy and the despair of passionate love are best depicted. The story is a favourite one. Pindar writes an Ode on it and Euripides a chorus: Ovid relates it twice and is followed by Statius and Claudian. The earliest version is to be found in the Homeric hymns, and of this I will give the version of Walter Pater in his *Greek Studies*.

'I begin the song of Demeter, the song of Demeter and her daughter, whom Aidoneus carried away by the consent of Zeus, as she played, apart from her mother, with the deep-bosomed daughters of the Ocean, gathering flowers in a meadow of soft grass—roses and the crocus and fair violets and flags and hyacinths, and, above all, the strange flower of the narcissus, which the earth, favouring the desire of Aidoneus, brought forth for the first time, to snare the footsteps of the flower-like girl. A hundred heads of blossom grew up from the roots of it, and the sky and the earth and the salt wave of the sea were glad at the scent thereof. She stretched forth her hands to take the flower; thereupon the earth opened, and the king of the great nation of the dead sprang out with his immortal horses. He seized the unwilling girl, and bore her away weeping on his golden chariot. She uttered a shrill cry, calling upon her father Zeus; but neither man nor god heard her voice, nor even the nymphs of the meadow where she played; except Hecate only, the daughter of Perseus, sitting as ever in her cave, half veiled with a shining veil, thinking delicate thoughts; she, and the sun also, heard her.

'So long as she could still see the earth and the sky and the sea with the great waves moving, and the beams of the sun, and still thought to see again her mother, and the race of the everlasting gods, so long hope soothed her in the midst of her grief. The peaks of the hills and the depth of the sea echoed her cry. And the mother heard it. A sharp pain seized her at the heart; she plucked the veil from her hair, and cast down the blue hood from her shoulders, and fled forth like a bird, seeking Persephone over dry land and sea. But neither man nor god would tell her the truth; nor did any bird come to her as a sure messenger.

'Nine days she wandered up and down upon the earth, having blazing torches in her hands; and in her great sorrow she refused to taste of ambrosia or of the cup of the sweet nectar, nor washed her face. But when the tenth morning came, Hecate met her having a light in her hand. But Hecate had heard the voice only, and had seen no one, and could

not tell Demeter who had borne the girl away. And Demeter said not
a word, but fled away swiftly with her, having the blazing torches in
her hands, till they came to the sun, the watchman both of gods and
men; and the goddess questioned him and the sun told her the whole
story.'

The poem then tells how Demeter in her grief hid from the gods and
dwelt among men and veiled her beauty, and looking like an old woman
she came to the house of Celeus, the king of Eleusis. She sat down at
a well and met there the daughters of Celeus and was by them invited
into the house of their father. She stayed with them and nursed Demo-
phoon, the child of Metaneira, the queen. But one day the queen looked
in upon what Demeter was doing to her child and found her holding it
in the red strength of the fire like a brand; 'for her heart yearned towards
it, and she would fain have given it immortal youth'. The mother shrieked
out, and the goddess in anger cast the child down, and putting off the
mask of age and changing her form passed out from the house. But the
mother and the daughters, overcome by fear, besought her to return
and made their father build a fair temple for the goddess. Demeter therefore returned, though she remained apart weeping for her lost Persephone.

'And in her anger she sent upon the earth a year of grievous famine.
The dry seed remained hidden in the soil; in vain the oxen drew the
ploughshare through the furrows; much white seed-corn fell fruitless on
the earth, and the whole human race had like to have perished, and the
gods had no more service of men, unless Zeus had interfered. First he
sent Isis, and afterwards all the gods, one by one, to turn Demeter from
her anger; but none was able to persuade her; she heard their words with
a hard countenance, and vowed by no means to return to Olympus, nor
to yield the fruit of the earth, until her eyes had seen her lost daughter
again. Then last of all Zeus sent Hermes into the kingdom of the dead
to persuade Aidoneus to suffer his bride to return to the light of day.
And Hermes found the king at home in his palace, sitting on a couch
beside the shrinking Persephone, consumed within herself by desire
for her mother. A doubtful smile passed over the face of Aidoneus; yet
he obeyed the message and bade Persephone return; yet praying her a
little to have gentle thoughts of him nor judge him too harshly, who was
an immortal god. And Persephone arose quickly in great joy; only ere
she departed, he caused her to eat a morsel of sweet pomegranate, design-
ing secretly thereby, that she should not always remain upon earth, but
might some time return to him. And Aidoneus yoked the horses to his
chariot; and Persephone ascended into it; and Hermes took the reins in
his hands and drove out through the infernal halls; and the horses ran
willingly; and they two quickly passed over the ways of that long journey.

neither the waters of the sea, nor of the rivers, nor of the deep ravines of the hills, nor the cliffs of the shore, resisting them; till at last Hermes placed Persephone before the door of the temple where her mother was; who, seeing her, ran out quickly to meet her, like a Maenad coming down from a mountain side, dusky with woods.

'So they spent all that day together in intimate communion, having many things to hear and tell. Then Zeus sent to them Rhea, his venerable mother, the oldest of divine persons, to bring them back reconciled to the company of the gods; and he ordained that Persephone should remain two parts of the year with her mother, and one-third part only with her husband in the kingdom of the dead. So Demeter suffered the earth to yield its fruits once more, and the land was suddenly laden with leaves and flowers and waving corn. Also she visited Triptolemus and the other princes of Eleusis, and instructed them in the performance of the sacred rites—those mysteries of which no tongue may speak. Only blessed is he whose eyes have seen them; his lot after death is not as the lot of other men.'

In this moving legend are seen as it were prefigured the more philosophic and religious symbols of the Eleusinian mysteries and also the fate of Eros down the centuries. In the great days of Athens the crowds went out to Eleusis to worship the dark goddess, who had found here a dwelling-place after much wandering in Syrian places and by the Nile. By her side was the god of ecstasy, Dionysus, who had become, now that the bacchants were hushed, the shepherd of the dead. Here, too, was the shrine of Aidoneus, the god of the dead, in a cavern near the great temple. It was he who had set the flower, narcissus, to catch the attention of the maiden in the flowery meadows, the symbol of the love which feeds on itself. The goddess of fertility of the rich spring of this life was now wedded to the spirit of the dead, and Demeter must wander in pain and ever in search for true love. This cannot be found in mortal homes; the child of Metaneira must be placed in the fire like a brand if it is to be made invulnerable. But now the mysteries show how immortality is to be won and passion can be satisfied. 'Fair indeed is the secret from the Blessed Ones, that for mortals Death is not alone no evil, but a good.' (Epitaph of the Hierophant Glaukos, second century A.D.) In the Eleusinian mysteries the initiates go down into the dark and come to a cypress tree and at a second fountain in that strange region they drink forgetfulness. But after that first drink they are beset by a nightmare vision of evil things and turn in fright to the guardians of the first fountain and are bidden to taste of the cold water which flows from the pool of Memory. It is only then that they are worthy to catch a glimpse of the goddess herself and to carry away an assurance that their fate is eternally entwined with hers. Thus fortified they partake of the sacred mysteries and finally see the mother wedded to the greatest of the gods by whom in time she shall have child, the Strong One, who is no other than each initiate, now wholly united with the godhead.

Passionate love then seeks the infinite and despises the forms of earthly communion; it withdraws and by vigils and fastings and abstention from sensual thoughts it feeds on its own image like Narcissus, and can find pleasure only in the anguish of its absence from the beloved. At length in the dark night its finite longings are rewarded by death and by absorption into the infinite.

APPENDIX TWO—GNOSTICISM

In his argument de Rougemont traces the romantic love of Tristram and the philosophy which lies behind it to Gnosticism. He tells us that 'as early as the third century there spread over the geographical and historical area that is bounded by India on the one hand and by Britain on the other, a religion that syncretized all the myths of Night and Day, a religion which had been elaborated first in Persia and then by the Gnostic and Orphic sects. This religion actually spread underground, and it is known as Manichaeanism'. It took various forms and lay behind various heresies, but there is a family likeness in these heresies. Amongst the common doctrines de Rougemont picks out that of the descent and imprisonment of the soul in matter. This is the Night and the soul is either half in love with it, because it is the dwelling of Venus, or it escapes from the darkness into the Light to be reunited with the divine element from which it has descended. De Rougemont points out, also, that 'the structure of the Manichaean faith was "in essence lyrical". In other words, the nature of this faith made it unamenable to rational impersonal and objective exposition.' He adds that this lyrical expression always goes with the intense feeling that death is 'the *ultimate* good, whereby the sin of birth is redeemed and human souls return into the One of luminous indistinction'.

That Gnosticism was a serious and even dreaded rival of Christianity is proved by the attention which almost all the best-known early Christian writers paid to it. There is abundance of evidence, therefore, about it, though the hostile attitude of the early Christians prevents us from being at all times sure of the exact nature of its teaching. St. Paul seems to have had it in mind when he warned his readers 'to beware lest any man cheat you by philosophy and vain deceit; according to the tradition of men, according to the elements of the world, and not according to Christ; for in him dwelleth all the fulness of the Godhead corporeally'. These last words on the 'pleroma' of Christ contradict a favourite view of the Gnostics. Again, Timothy is warned that there are deceivers who are for ever 'learning, and never attaining to the knowledge of the truth'. Timothy is called upon to keep that which is committed to his trust, 'avoiding the novelties of words and oppositions of knowledge falsely so called'. The Cerinthus, whom St. John had in mind in the Fourth Gospel, was a contemporary of Saturninus, who was certainly a Gnostic, and must have known Gnostic teaching both at Antioch and Alexandria. The danger which the early faith had to face lay in the attempt to spiritualize its doctrines, to deny either the truth of the corporeal existence of the Word made Flesh or His godhead. In the name of a higher truth the Christian teaching was in danger of being volatilized away into something more universal and 'spiritual'. St. Ignatius of Antioch had this in mind when he wrote that these counterfeit teachers 'abstain from the Eucharist and prayer because they do not confess that the Eucharist is the flesh of our Saviour, Jesus Christ, who has suffered for our sins, whom the Father, in his goodness, has raised from the dead'.

To judge from what we know of Simon the Magician, Basilides, Saturninus, the Pistis Sophia and other writers and writings and from the comments on them by the Christian writers, Gnosticism seems to have been one of those unfortunate forms of thought for which human beings have a chronic appetite. That is to say, it was a syncretistic philosophy and religion; it made an apparent lofty unity out of the various systems known, and by picking out what it liked and eviscerating the doctrine of its true meaning within the original system, it pretended to be the highest and most spiritual of religions and the key to all others. This tendency or habit is a chronic malady of human nature, and it is as prevalent to-day as it was at the beginning of the Christian era. It displays itself in a love for an unattached mysticism, for fantastic theogonies; it strips a philosophy of its native structure and borrows the language of its highest flights, and it loves to make a superficial harmony of the thought of East and West; it is sure to despise the body and what is most human, but usually it has to permit some of the least savoury expressions of carnal desire; it is esoteric and appeals to a strange craving in human nature for hidden symbols and double meanings. I do not know whether the inventors of these secret societies, these Mystae, followers of the Kabbala, Alchemists and Templars and Assassins and Carbonari, are as guilty as those who cannot look at any sign without suspecting dark designs or read any manuscript without seeing in it the mark of some hidden cult. So tempted are we ourselves to read more into evidence than appears that it is difficult to separate out what is genuinely gnostic from what are imagined to be its tenets. But the traits I have already mentioned seem to be fairly constant.

Gnosticism seems, then, to represent one of the strongest movements of this kind of esoteric and syncretistic inventiveness. The Christians attributed its origins to Persia and Samaria and the universalistic philosophies of Alexandria and the Near East. Some modern scholars profess to see in it the influence of more remote Eastern ideas, and certainly the mystical religions of the East in their association with Greek thought helped to formulate the general character of the later gnostic manner of thinking. How easy and tempting it is to trace influences and connect up symbols can be seen in the following passages from C. W. King's *Gnostics and their Remains* (published in 1887): 'That the Gnostics borrowed many of these symbols directly from Buddhism, adding them to their old stock of Egyptian devices, is apparent upon the inspection of any large collection of Abraxas gems. The lingering influence of this importation continually peeps out where least to be expected. In the finest known MS. of the Apocalypse, the work of a French illuminator about the middle of the thirteenth century (in the library of Trinity College, Cambridge), the most elaborate of all its decorations is the heading to chapter XIV, filling half a page. It represents "The Lamb standing upon Mount Zion", surrounded by the saints; above, is the Godhead, typified by an immense golden Quatrefoil, encompassed by the Four Beasts, which bear the names of the Evangelists; at each side and below are the Four-and-twenty Elders, arranged in groups of six, eight, and ten. Within the Quatrefoil is seen an empty throne covered with a cloth crossed by diagonal blue lines; in each diagonal so formed is painted in red a circle containing a point. This *geometrical* expression of the idea of the Deity, so opposed to the characteristic anthropomorphism of regular Gothic art, may perhaps have been inspired by the Manicheist spirit that still actuated the southern French.' The greatest value in this surmise lies perhaps in the reference to the continuing influence of Gnosticism in southern France. More topical is the same writer's engaging argument for Eastern influence on Gnostic symbols in the following passage: "Worshippers of Saeti, the Female Principle, make their sacred vase with a right angle bisected by a line; and similarly the worshippers of Isis used so to mark the vessel necessary at her rites. But the Vichnaivas have for the same object a symbol of wondrous vitality and diffusion; for it is seen equally on Greek coins and vases, on the Newton Stone, Aberdeen, in ecclesiastical sculpture, where it takes the name "Tetragrammaton", being ignorantly supposed the compounds of the letter Γ four times repeated, and its sound and power confounded with those of the sacred "Tetragrammaton", or the Hebrew quadrilateral name Jehovah. This mark is properly the symbol of Sitala, the seventh incarnation, entitled "Trithalesor", a title exactly translated by the alchemaical Trismegistus; its name is the Swastika, an emblem of Resignation; so that the figure may have passed into Byzantine art with some recommendation from a knowledge of its real meaning. In Gothic nomenclature this mark becomes the equally renowned "Fylfot", as to whose etymology the following conjecture may be hazarded. The Swastika signified at first the arms crossed over the breast, the regular Indian gesture of submission, and also the legs similarly folded as the statues of Buddha are usually represented. The symbol is evidently nothing more than the rough outline of the arms and legs thus disposed. May not therefore the Gothic name Fylfot, applied to the same hieroglyph, bear through some remote tradition a reference to its real meaning, and imply the sense of Fold-foot? In the same way the old Greeks appear to have recognized its true sense, when they changed its simple form into the three conjoined legs that so aptly allude to the name Trinacria. In all probability the great popularity of the symbol, wheresoever the Indo-Germanic race penetrated, was due to the same feeling that renders it still so respected in the land of its origin, its power as a talisman to protect all places where the figure is painted up. The exclamation "Swastika" the Hindoos still employ as a mode of assent, synonymous with "Amen", "So be it". As the symbol of Resignation the Mark forms the distinctive badge of an ascetic.'[1]

There is no reason to deny the influence on Gnosticism of ideas even from the Far East. Ideas percolate and find their way reshaped to all quarters of the world. Gnosticism is more than a local cult; it is more like a false shekinah which accompanies man in his march through time. Native cults give it a habitation and a local character. From the Persians it takes on the nature of a war between a pure principle and an evil one; in the mystic religions it exhibits the fight between darkness and light; the Hebrew version gives a twist to the theology of the Old Testament; when in contact with Greek thought it turns into Orphism, and at the meeting-place of Alexandria it becomes so spiritual and universal that it forces St. John to write the Prologue of the Fourth Gospel, and emphasize the splendour of the visible and bodily and the unique glory of the only-begotten Son of God. But whereas with other religions it has successfully set itself up as the inner and higher form of that religion, as the secret of the Bacchants, the mystics and the 'elect', when confronted with Christianity it met with a rebuff. The Church refused to make any

---

[1] This passage is relevant to what I have to say in later chapters of the two forms of love, but I have thought it wiser not to employ the symbol of the swastika for what I try to define as the passive and submissive form of love!

terms with it and denounced any version of it which introduced Christian teaching and symbols, and in so doing it manifested its own inspired genius.

The significance of the struggle between Christianity and Gnosticism has not been sufficiently realized—possibly because some of the shapes which the latter took were childish or obviously inferior. In fact, however, Gnosticism at its best represents the ever-recurring thought of humanity outside the startling good news from on high of the Christian revelation. It is a type or model or pattern which human thought always takes when left to itself, and by reference to and comparison with this type it is possible to detect whether a philosophy is of Christian or pagan origin. Gnostic philosophy is always a cult of 'essence' (a term whose meaning will be explained in a later chapter), and its ideal always swings between a self-centred ideal and one of complete abandonment or surrender to fate or a higher power. Most critics can see that a purely naturalistic out-look, an Epicurean cult, for instance, is anti-Christian, but not so many grasp the truth that a too spiritual ideal which despises the body and this earth is also anti-Christian. It is the Gnostic who considers the soul as imprisoned in the body, who reckons all that is visible and finite to be illusion, who makes himself a ladder out of this world and longs to be able to kick the ladder away. Human love in the Gnostic system is either consumed away in pride or else it is self-destructive; it never finds a happy marriage, and the intellect left without true guidance from love spins a web of truth out of its own entrails. This is what I have called the philo-sophy of essence. It means that man cannot realize, when in this state, that he is *vis-à-vis* a living real God. He proceeds, therefore, to make of God an intellectual ideal or a mysterious being who is beyond reality and in some sense the one and the all. Everything that he sees, and especially his own mind, becomes an emanation of the divine, a process or becoming. In the period just before and after the coming of Christ the fashionable idea was that of 'emanation'. Since then there have been other fashions, and it may seem as if the present one is that of evolution as an explanation of the universe. But emanation and evolution and pro-cesses and becomings and doctrines of the One and the All, of the divine being in some sense one with man and man with the divine, theories of the geometrical spirit, of supermen and reincarnations, of the unreality of time or infinite progress, beliefs in 'a Godhead, Ground, Brahman, Clear Light of the Void, which is the unmanifested principle of all manifestations', as Aldous Huxley tells us, these and an infinite number more are only the Gnostic efforts to do better than Christianity by falling back upon 'essence' and hiding away from the word of a living, creative and loving God.

The importance and the influence of the Gnostic habit of mind deserve attention, and that is why I have made so much of de Rougemont's theory of love in the Middle Ages. Love when it slips its Christian moorings floats out to sea and is blown upon by Gnostic winds. But this is not the same as to say that courtly and romantic love owe their origin entirely to a Gnostic Eros, as de Rougemont suggests. He is here evidently making a case, and not all will be disposed to agree with him. C. S. Lewis, for instance, in his magisterial work, *The Allegory of Love*, after insisting on the novelty of romantic love and suggesting various causes for its rise, says that 'some part of the mystery remains inviolate'. He is rightly sceptical of any facile explanation of these very human changes in history. 'It is certain', he tells us, 'that the efforts of scholars have so far failed to find an origin for the content of Provençal love poetry. Celtic, Byzantine, and even Arabic influence have been suspected; but it has not been made clear that these, if granted, could account for the results we see. A more promising theory attempts to trace the whole thing to Ovid; but this view . . . finds itself faced with the fatal difficulty that the evidence points to a much stronger Ovidian influence in the north of France than in the south. Something can be extracted from a study of the social conditions in which the new poetry arose, but not so much as we might hope.' Another argument which might be raised against de Rougemont is that it is strange, if the Church was so much on the *qui vive* against Gnostic influences, that it did not detect the heretical symbolism of the romantic poetry and attack with more vigour its philosophy of life. De Rougemont would answer, no doubt, that the language could look simple and innocent and yet contain an esoteric meaning. But this answer only shows the infirmity in all the quests for inner meanings, secret emblems and symbols, alchemist or Rosicrucian signs, masons' marks and evidence from the Pyramids. If the words or emblems can have a simple as well as a deeper meaning there is no surety that the user of them had any awareness of the double meaning. We have to have a host of converging signs before we can have any confidence that the writer or artist is using his material as a secret code. Now what we do know is that the Gnostic movement continued side by side with Christianity, occasionally displaying itself in some heresy, but for the most part underground. We know, too, that one of the centres of this movement was Spain, that the Priscillian heresy flourished there, and that it spread to southern France. King, in his *The Gnostics and their Remains*, says boldly that Provence was 'a fruitful source of these interesting memorials of the widespread theosophy. Gnosticism from the beginning took root and flourished in southern Gaul, as the elaborate treatise of Irenaeus attacking it, as no newly-invented thing, very clearly demonstrates'. Later the Paulicians, another Gnostic sect, infected Sicily when they came in the armies of Alexius Comnenus and spread to the south of France. The Albigensians also were suspected of holding Manichaean views, and there can be no doubt of their having influenced the peoples of Provence. Lastly, the Crusades, which were recruited so largely from France, increased the traffic of ideas between the East and the West and may have influenced ideas as they certainly influenced art. For those who think that this evidence is strong when joined with the curious resemblance between the Gnostic and Troubadour views of love, the argument may seem more than suggestive. For the thesis of this book, however, it need not be more than suggestive. At any rate, as St. Thomas remarked in the middle of a royal dinner, 'That settles the Manichees', and the Gnostics.

CHAPTER TWO

EROS AND CHRISTIAN THEOLOGY

J'attends Dieu avec gourmandise.—RIMBAUD.

Love is a desire of the whole being to be united to something or some being felt necessary to its completeness, by the most perfect means that nature permits and reason dictates.—S. T. COLERIDGE.

Oh Lord, Thou knowest that I have lately purchased an estate in fee simple in Essex. I beseech Thee to preserve the two counties of Middlesex and Essex from fire and earthquakes; and as I have also a mortgage at Hertfordshire, I beg of Thee also to have an eye of compassion on that county, and for the rest of the counties, Thou may deal with them as Thou art pleased. Oh Lord, enable the bank to answer all their bills and make all my debtors good men, give a prosperous voyage and safe return to the Mermaid sloop, because I have not insured it, and because Thou has said, 'The days of the wicked are but short', I trust in Thee that Thou wilt not forget Thy promise, as I have an estate in reversion, which will be mine on the death of the profligate young man, Sir J. L . . . . g.

Keep my friends from sinking, preserve me from thieves and housebreakers, and make all my servants so honest and faithful that they may always attend to my interest and never cheat me out of my property night or day.—JOHN WARD, once M.P. for Weymouth.

Some years ago the Swedish theologian, Anders Nygren, wrote a work in three volumes, entitled *Agape and Eros*. His main contention was as follows: The Christian revelation of love is unique. Love or Agape as revealed in the Gospels is a totally different kind of love from that known and accepted by the pagan world, and in particular by the Greeks. He, therefore, calls by the name of Eros all the forms of love which existed in the Hellenistic world which early Christianity encountered and gives the name, Agape, to the specifically new form of love which was introduced by Christianity. When Saint Paul and the first Christians went out into the pagan world they found it impregnated with the idea of Eros, and so the meeting of Eros and Agape was 'Christianity's hour of destiny'. Agape reversed all the values of antiquity, but if it wavered and made terms with Eros, then the future conception of love would become ambiguous and Christianity would for ever suffer, unless someone could prove able to bring back the original meaning of

Agape. If Nygren's view be right the result was, in fact, a compromise, and what Nygren holds to be the very central revelation of Christ was clouded over for centuries and confused with its opposite. In pagan antiquity, for instance, ethics was concerned primarily with happiness; the problem of the good was the problem of the highest good—what satisfied the needs and desires of the individual. Again as concerns the relation in religion of man with God the answer in pagan thought is egocentric. In Christianity, on the other hand, the Good is not happiness but God, and the answer to the religious question is not egocentric but theocentric.

Nygren devotes many pages to an attempt to make clear what precisely is the meaning of Christian Agape. The word actually occurs only twice in the Synoptic gospels, but that is because a special word had not been invented to distinguish the love described there from what might be confused with it. There is a new kind of love unmistakably described, and just because it is so new Nygren terms it Agape to separate it from all other forms of love. He relies on Saint Paul, who through contact with the pagan Eros was forced to make its meaning clear and use special words to describe it. The love he preached was to the Jews a stumbling block and to the Gentiles mere folly. The Jews believed in a living God, a God of righteousness and mercy, but they thought of God's justice as adjusted in some way to man's deserts and His mercy as tempered to man's plight. They were therefore shocked when Christ told them that he had come to call not the righteous but sinners to repentance. Such a declaration went far beyond the limits of the Covenant and the Law which had served them as a measuring rod of God's mercies. Christ sweeps away all such limits; he declares that God's love has no limits and is independent entirely of the merits of its recipient. 'Your heavenly Father maketh his sun to shine on the evil and the good.' God is free, and God is sovereign. His love does not need to find desert; it is not called into being by anything which man can afford or boast. The degrees of human worth are as nothing in their finiteness to God; they do not count at all. God has the initiative and in man's relation with God it is God who gives all. Nygren sums up the meaning of Agape in the Gospel under four heads. It is spontaneous and uncaused; that is to say, we can offer no explanations of it on natural grounds. It is indifferent to human merit. Human values have no place when God loves. God does not love the good on account of their goodness; the sinner equally with the righteous can be struck with the dart of God's love. Thirdly it is creative, in that what was without value, a minus number relative to God's positive reality, acquires value by the fact that it becomes the object of Agape. 'The idea of the infinite value of the human soul is not a basic Christian idea at all'; such a view belongs rather to the philosophy of Eros. When, for example, God says to the sinner, 'Thy sins are forgiven thee', this forgiveness creates the goodness and does not presuppose it in any way. Lastly Agape opens the way to fellowship with God. Man of himself, no matter whether he be legally justified or full of merit or uplifted by Eros to even a Plotinian ecstasy, has no way of attaining to this fellowship. It is a pure gift to man.

If this account appear more bewildering than enlightening, that effect is not due to any obscurity or complication in Nygren's idea of Agape. The idea is in reality extremely simple, and the apparent obscurity is due to his pressing rigidly one truth about God to, as he thinks, its logical conclusion. To some this conclusion may seem so unconventional and paradoxical as to be unreasonable. The clue, I think, is to take one truth about God without any qualification and apply it. In this case the truth is that God is sovereignly good and cannot act except out of his own free disposition, that man cannot therefore determine in any way God's actions, and, indeed, that man's own actions as finite depend upon the infinite power of God's initiative and constant causality. If we work this out in terms of love (omitting the fact that man's relative self-dependence and freewill are themselves a creation of love), we shall see that as applied to God's revelation of his love in the Gospels, all depends upon God and nothing depends upon man. With this fixed thought in his mind Nygren finds in the stories of the Parables, the Prodigal Son, the Vine-yard, the Sower, the Lost Sheep and the Unmerciful Servant, evidence for his theory of Agape. They all bring out the initiative of God in loving man. The same doctrine is wrung from the texts which give the two great commandments. Of the first of these Nygren writes: 'These words imply absolute ownership. Man's love to God can be neither *amor concupiscentiae* nor *amor amicitiae*—to use the scholastic terms—for both these have their starting point in man himself. Were it the former, the love of desire, then God, even though he be man's highest good, would in the last resort be the means to the satisfaction of man's own desires and needs. But neither is there any room for the love of friendship in a theocentric scheme, for it would imply that the human and the Divine love meet on equal terms; and this is not the case. It is excluded by the sovereignty of the Divine love.' The Second commandment is also un-caused; it proceeds from Agape. 'If ye love them that love you, what thanks have ye?' In these two commandments, therefore, is Agape comprised, and there is no third commandment, such as 'love thyself'. The intrusion of this last into Christianity and its theology is due to Eros and not Agape, and its presence is an infallible mark of Eros.

In the Pauline epistles and in the Fourth Gospel the theology of Agape is said to find fullest expression. We are so familiar with the great passages of St. Paul on charity that I can be spared quoting them. They insist on the uselessness of human action without grace, the gratuitousness of God's love and the height and depth of it. So little of self-love is there in St. Paul that he declares that he is willing to be anathema from Christ for the sake of his brethren. (*Note.*—In the Middle Ages the scholastic theologians were taxed to reconcile this recklessness of love with their doctrine of beatitude.) This love for his brethren is an outstanding trait of the Epistles, and St. Augustine noticed with surprise that when, though the Epistles are written by one on fire with love for God and Christ, when St. Paul used the word 'caritas' he nearly always means by it love for his neighbour and very seldom, if ever, love for God. This Nygren explains far less persuasively than usual by the suggestion that man's love for God hardly deserves the name of Agape, as it is not spontaneous and cannot be creative. A better word for it would be faith, because faith is receptive and our love has been received from the Holy Ghost through the diffusion of his spirit.

St. Paul's delineation of Agape was helped by his contacts with Eros. Eros must have been familiar to him because he was well aware of the dangerous rivalry of Gnosticism. In the first letter to the Corinthians, chapter 13, 'we have the first conflict between the idea of Agape and the Hellenistic spirit which here takes the form of Gnosis. But Gnosis is only another name for the idea of Eros; and it is this that gives the great Agape hymn its special interest from our present point of view . . . Paul recognizes and gives forcible expression to the opposition between the Christian and the Greek ideas of Love, between Agape and Eros-Gnosis. Eros is the soul's desire and longing to attain the blessed vision of the supersensible world in all its beauty; and Gnosis is nothing else than this 'vision of God'. With all this Paul definitely parts company in this chapter. With delicacy and sureness of touch he unveils the fundamental difference of structure between these loves which superficially are so alike. Gnosis is egocentric, Agape theocentric. The opposition is absolute; that which is true of the one is not true of the other. Agape is not puffed up; Gnosis puffeth up, but Agape edifieth.'

In the Johannine Gospel Nygren finds the final formulation of the idea of Agape. In short, it is that God is Agape, and just because God is Love it follows that 'herein is love, not that we loved God, but that He loved us'; 'we love because He first loved us'; and lastly, 'beloved, if God so loved us, we ought also to love one another'. Here is not only the statement of Agape, but the metaphysic of it in the identification of love with the very nature of God, making it sovereign and uncaused by any object outside God. There is the eternal love, the self-imparting of the Father to the Son and of the Son to the disciples and of the disciples to the brethren, and therefore we are bound to say that all Agape in man is but the overflow of the Divine Agape.[1] This is the supreme statement of Christian love, and it is found in the Johannine writings. But Nygren is too honest a writer to omit what also is to be found in these same writings, namely, a view which does not seem to accord with his interpretation. So intractable is this evidence that another interpreter might well have begun to suspect that the view just stated on the nature of Agape must be wrong or at least one-sided. Nygren takes a different stand. He admits the discrepancies and owns that even in the Johannine gospel the *motif* of the Eros-love, so alien to true Christianity, has already made its appearance. The evidence for this weakening in what is called the essential doctrine of Christianity is as follows: First, God's love must be spontaneous and uncaused, and yet St. John introduces a 'because' into this love: 'The Father Himself loveth you, because ye have loved me and have believed.' Again, since it is the overflow of the divine love in man which makes men love one another with Agape, there should be no love for particular men because of anything in them which others have not got. And yet the Agape by which all men shall know Jesus' disciples is the love that they have to one another as Christians; it is not a love directed to those outside. In other words, Agape which should be universal becomes particularistic, and what is by nature uncaused seems to have particular motives. Thirdly, as Agape is an overflow of the Divine Agape, there cannot possibly be a distinction between a true and a false Agape. What then of a text such as 'Love not the world, neither the things that are in the world. If any man love the world, the love of the Father is not in him'? Here is the very distinction between a true and false love. It seems to be implied that the same kind of love can be directed towards God or the world. Now the love of the world is here certainly Eros in Nygren's sense, because the desire is a selfish or ego-centric one. There can be no escaping the conclusion, then, that St. John must have been thinking of the love of God in terms of Eros, or rather that Eros had begun to infiltrate into the idea of Agape.

I have spent some time on Nygren's idea of Agape because in later chapters it will have to be examined and compared with other ideas. We can see already that it is markedly different from what de Rougemont described as Agape. But it is in his description of Eros that Nygren raises immediate problems. A quotation from that great scholar, von Wilamo-witz-Möllendorff will put us on the way: 'We must here make a brief

---

[1] The grave difficulties inherent in this view are not touched upon by Nygren, but even at this moment it may well be asked, if the Agape in man is truly the divine nature itself, how can man himself escape being divine or else in no relation with the love which he seems to exercise?

but emphatic repudiation of a misunderstanding which can no longer be regarded as merely harmless; namely, the idea that the Platonic Eros coincides with the Christian Agape to which Paul dedicates his hymn to Love (1 Cor. xiii). As the former knew nothing of Agape, so the latter knew nothing of Eros[1]; and if they could have met they would have made nothing of one another.' The Graeco-Roman world was ruled by the idea of Eros at the time when Christianity was first preached, and there was enough superficial similarity to deceive the unwary. By Eros Nygren means, as he says, the common idea of love which was so prevalent in the Eastern religions and in the mystery cults. 'In the idea of Eros religious longings and philosophical movements had found a meeting-point.' We have already seen what de Rougemont thought of these passionate desires which coalesced into a philosophic creed and religion and went by various names, of which Gnosticism and Manichaeanism are amongst the chief. We have also seen in the appendix to the last chapter what general character the love in the legends and myths possessed. The passion took man out of himself in a longing for the infinite to which he felt his true self belonged, and death, as the end of his mortal life, the adieu to his sojourn in an evil world and the final and annihilating stage of his fusion with the dark goddess who was also the All, exercised over him a dread fascination. Now Nygren also holds that Eros before the time of Plato is associated with a view of man as imprisoned in an earthly and sensual world. The divine in him longs for liberation or salvation, and in such cults as Orphism release was achieved by purification and by ecstasy. In other words, Eros is the passion which de Rougemont describes and its fitting philosophy is dualistic and Manichaean. But, if Nygren be right, once Eros is espoused by Plato and Platonism, a remarkable metamorphosis takes place. The mythos becomes a logos; what was essentially a wild and irrational passion is converted into an excessively rational religion. Whereas in de Rougemont's account the disciplined order of marriage is the symbol of the Christian ideal and lawless love is the mark of Eros, in this new account, it is, as we shall find, the Platonic and Aristotelian theology and the exercise of reason by the medieval scholastics, which are regarded as marks of the presence of Eros. Nygren's polemic is really directed against the rationalism of some of the early fathers of the Church and of medieval philosophy, and he salutes Luther, the bitter opponent of reason, as the Christian who led Christianity back to the way of Agape.

For a right estimate of the nature of both Eros and Agape it is all-important, therefore, to watch carefully Nygren's transposition of terms and compare his interpretation with that of de Rougemont. The reader

[1] This view is at variance with that held by Nygren.

should at the same time bear in mind that no sharp divisions can be made at any one moment of their history between the two loves. It is always, we must remember, a full human person who is loving, and in that love there are sure to be many different strands. Thought will be there and emotion, joy and sorrow, self-regarding and self-forgetting desires, the longing for fusion as well as for beatitude. Eros, for instance, in the account of it in the last chapter, sought the death of self, even to ultimate extinction, but at the same time it had a narcissus quality of self-love, as when Tristram cares more for his ideal of love than for Isolde when she is with him. But though this is so, it is possible to disentangle the main threads and according to the strength of their colour call them Eros or Agape, and it is with a distinction of this kind that we must always approach the problem of their conflict. Nygren recognizes that in the myths and mysteries Eros was identified with dark passion, and he endeavours to show that in Platonism mythos and logos joined hands, and on the whole logos took from then on the chief part. He does not, however, realize, I think, the revolutionary character of this theory and its boomerang effect upon his arguments.

Before Plato, as Nygren writes, the 'conception of the double nature of man, of the divine origin and quality of the soul, its liberation from the fetters of sense, and its ascent to its original divine home is the universal basis of the idea of Eros in every form in which it appears. The soul is fallen into the darkness of matter, it is naturally immortal and by means of asceticism and purification and ecstasy it can ascend to its proper abode.' Or as Windelband, in his *Platon*, puts it: 'The world-view which Plato reached by the way of philosophical analysis, as the unified result of all previously existing theories, was of such a character that the dogmas of the Dionysiac teaching about the soul could find a place within it and could even appear as its necessary conclusion.' That is to say, we find in the Platonic system the ancient distinctions of two worlds, the one of darkness and evil and the other of light and good, the restlessness of the soul during its habitation in the world of matter and its longing to arise and go to the world to which it rightly belongs. In the system, however, the myths which Plato uses are illustrations of his philosophy and a means of suggesting what cannot be adequately described in his dialectic. The point of junction between the new philosophy and the old story is the theory of Forms or Ideas, Forms which are the pattern of the unsubstantial imitations which we meet in this life. They are 'yonder' and because the world we meet through the senses has reality only in so far as it participates in the full reality of these Forms we can ascend by the ladder of the lower simulacra to what is subsistent, Now Eros 'is man's conversion from the sensible to the super-sensible it is the upward movement of the soul; it is a real force, driving the soul upward to seek the world of the Forms.' Such an Eros is in keeping with the Orphic and Dionysiac teaching of salvation; in fact it is the old passion in a new philosophic setting.

This philosophy is given in its mythical form in the *Phaedrus*, where the soul is said to have seen the Forms in a previous existence and so impressed has she been by the sight of the True and the Beautiful and the Good that even after she has fallen and become immersed in a body, like an oyster in its shell, she still has some recollection of those Forms and is drawn towards them. The sight of beautiful things increases her longing, her eros, for the original, and she is able to take wings to rise up to the super-sensible beauty. In the *Symposium* this movement of Eros up to the super-sensible reality is described in terms of a ladder, the heavenly ladder, an image so much loved and used by later Christian writers. 'When anyone, having the right kind of love, mounts up and begins to see the beauty present in the beautiful person, he is not far from the final goal. For the right way of love, whether one goes alone or is led by another, is to begin with the beautiful things that are seen here, and ascend ever upwards, aiming at the beauty that is above, climbing, as it were, on a ladder from one beautiful body to two, and from two to all the others, and from beautiful bodies to beautiful actions, and from beautiful actions to beautiful forms of knowledge, till at last from these one reaches that knowledge which is the knowledge of nothing else than Beauty itself, and so knows at last what Beauty really is. And when one has attained thither, O Socrates, said my Mantinean friend, there if anywhere is the life that is worth living, in the beholding of Beauty itself.'

The Eros thus described by Plato is born of Want and Energy. As the child of Want he 'takes after his mother in always having want in his train; as the child of Energy he pants after the beautiful and is full of courage and audacity.' In this image Plato wants to show how Eros is empty longing and at the same time a noble aspiration; one side of it belongs to the world of shadows, the other knows that its true home is on high. In so describing Eros Plato gives the essence of that Eros which is antithetical to Agape; for it is a kind of have-not whose nature it is to be filled with the riches of heaven. Its sense of need is the motive giving a dynamic to its desire. That is why Simmel says: 'The Hellenic Eros is a Will-to-have, even when it is used in the nobler sense of the desire to have the loved person as an object for ideal instruction, ethical training and education in culture. It is for this reason that love for the Greeks is a middle state between having and not-having, and consequently must die away when its aim is attained.' 'Everyone', says Plato in the *Symposium*, 'who desires, desires that which he has not', and it follows that the gods who have nothing which they do not want do not desire, and do not reciprocate man's love for them. Love between God and man is, in the love of Eros, all on man's side and in no sense on God's side; it is a way to the Divine and definitely excludes any idea of a descent from God to man. God already has his happiness and perfection; man has neither, and therefore the object of his love is this happiness, eudai-monia. 'Tell me, Socrates, what does he desire who loves good things? That he may have them, said I. And what will he have when he has the good things? This is easier to answer, said I; he will be happy. Yes, he said, it is through getting good things that the happy become happy. And now we have no need to go on and ask why man wishes to be happy, for we have come to the final point in our inquiry.' (*Symposium*, 204 E.)

Nygren then sums up the character of the Platonic Eros by saying, first, that 'it is impossible for Plato even to conceive of a love that is spontaneous and uncaused'. Secondly, Eros is the act of the imperfect, in as much as we love what we have not and cannot love when we are without want. Thirdly, Eros is egocentric love. This is proved by the passage just quoted from the conversation of Socrates with Diotima, and it is confirmed in the *Lysis*, where it is said that there is no friendship without desire; hence the perfectly good man can never be the friend to a second perfectly good man, because each, in so far as he is perfect, is self-sufficient.

The idea of Eros is consolidated in Plato, but in order to understand its influence on the later Catholic view of love, we must make mention of some additions to it by Aristotle and the Neo-Platonists. Aristotle extended the idea so as to make it cosmic, while at the same time reducing its religious connotation. In the Aristotelian system there is constant movement in the world of matter and the change is explained by his theory of form and matter, act and potentiality. In matter there is a passive inclination, which makes it receptive of form and forms exist or come to be in an ascending scale. Now what lies behind this universal movement is a cause, but it is a final cause, a stir which is ever passing through the universe because of the presence of the Perfect Form, the divine Being. The divine Being is wrapt up in self-contemplation, but because of his presence he draws all nature by love. He is the magnet, the object which attracts, and so Aristotle can fairly be said to make Eros the driving force of all the world, and the lower is ever striving towards what is higher than itself under the stress of Eros. It works, as Scholz in his *Eros and Caritas* says, 'in the stars as a striving for likeness to God; in the Sun as a striving to be like the stars; in ever-growing, ever-decaying Nature as the desire to become like to the Sun.' For a long period after

Aristotle the philosophical implications of his thought predominated, but when the Indo-European religions swept into the Mediterranean a new blend of philosophical beliefs and religious aspirations began to dominate. This new movement found its philosophical and theological expression in Neo-Platonism. But in the centuries which had elapsed between Plato and Plotinus the 'conception of the universe undergoes a far-reaching change of structure'. In Plato's age the problem was to explain how man could reach to God and to perfection. In the Alexandrian world-scheme the problem is to discover how what is man and what is finite can have proceeded from God. One answer had been the fall of what is in origin divine, namely, the soul, into a world which was evil. The problem then was how to find a way back. But this dualistic scheme did not satisfy the Neo-Platonists. They sought for unity, and asked themselves how the world and all that is in it could have proceeded from the divine being. The system of Aristotle, with all its intermediaries between the One and the Many, suggested an answer; but it is in Plotinus that an immense procession of all from the One and back from the all to the One is to be found. There is now a way down as well as a way up, and the idea of the heavenly ladder has been completed. I need not dwell on the particulars of the Plotinian scheme. Nygren confesses that it seems at first sight to evade many of the contrasts which he has built up between Eros and Agape. He had insisted that Eros knew nothing of a descent of God; it was necessarily confined to the ascent of man to God. But in Plotinus there is certainly a descent or emanation. Again, Eros is the love of man for God and cannot be attributed to God. Yet Plotinus expressly says that 'the higher cares for the lower and adorns it' (*Enneads* IV, 8.8). I do not think that Nygren is altogether successful in dissipating this difficulty, which cannot be answered until the sharp distinction, which we shall make later, is brought in between God as existent and creative and the idea of a divine essence. This, however, does not matter at the moment. The point which Nygren wants to make is that this heavenly ladder of Eros must have looked extremely tempting to Christian writers who were engaged on a defence of the Christian belief and building up a Christian theology. If Nygren's contention be right, they swallowed the doctrine whole and did grave damage to the truly Christian idea of love. He owns that it is difficult to blame them. When the early Christians moved into the Hellenistic world they heard talk of the love of the Perfect Being among the educated. Their own Wisdom literature suggested that there might be some kinship of thought between the Hellenistic and their own, though the former must be infinitely inferior to the good tidings they had to spread; besides, they came across images and expressions which seemed harmless and adaptable.

EROS AND CHRISTIAN THEOLOGY

Despite their suspicion of the pagan cults and their own confidence in the uniqueness of their own teaching the first Christians had to take over the language in common use. Hence in time, as Christianity grew, the language of Eros tended to intermingle with that of Agape, and by the time of the Alexandrian Fathers the Christians were fast forgetting the sharp early distinctions of the two loves and becoming more and more eager to state the faith in terms of the prevalent Greek philosophy. The proof, however, so Nygren thinks, that they kept faithfully to Agape and so saved Christianity lies in the formulation of the Creeds, and above all in their insistence on the crucial examples of Agape, the Incarnation, the Redemption and the resurrection of the body. They were, besides, quick to reject the Gnostic and the other heresies which smelt of Neo-Platonism and the mystery religions. Nygren suggests as tests of the presence of Eros, first a leaning to mysticism in preference to Revelation, then the tendency to replace faith by charity, the symbolism of the heavenly ladder, the emphasis on asceticism, deification, natural immortality, ecstasy, vision, and beatitude. It is impossible, he thinks, to reconcile the two loves; they represent two utterly opposing views of life. In one, man of himself seeks out God, in the other he is so much nothing that it is God's own love which predestines him. Eros desires the good of the self, Agape is a self-giving; Eros is man's way to God, Agape is God's way to man; Eros is the noblest form of egocentric love, Agape seeketh not its own; Eros seeks to gain its life by the possession of immortal beauty, Agape lives by God's life and therefore dares to lose its own. Eros is motivated by the beauty and value in the object, Agape bestows itself on what is quite unworthy, creates the value and is sovereign.

Such then are the two loves in this account. It remains to sketch the history of their relations in the story of Christian theology. Their spasmodic intercourse was made permanent by the genius of St. Augustine, and it is his synthesis which has influenced all subsequent thinking on the subject. 'He lives', says Nygren, 'on the frontier of two separate religious worlds, those of Hellenistic Eros and primitive Christian Agape, and his significance lies chiefly in the fact that these worlds really meet in his person and form a spiritual unity.' They met and out of the union has come what has been known since as 'caritas'. (There is, alas, no English word to translate it. 'Charity' often means just almsgiving, and we have to have the context before we can be sure that it is a translation of 'caritas'.) Everything in St. Augustine's thought on this subject can be summed up in the love which is 'caritas'. By it he means primarily a love for God and not God's love towards us. This comes out in the *Confessions*. They tell of the quest of his soul for God, our everlasting

64

good, and his heart is only at rest when God is found. His soul which had been for years darkened by matter and sense and puffed up by a disordered love of self, at length saw in the teaching of the Neo-Platonists the far-off light which, when it drew near, was transformed into the Word made Flesh which enlightens every man. But just because Neo-Platonism took him by the hand and led him to the incarnate truth, its influence was never completely shaken off. The echoes of it can frequently be heard in the *Confessions*, even in the most intimately Christian passages. 'I was amazed that I already loved Thee and not a phantasm instead of Thee. Yet I did not persist to enjoy my God, but now I was drawn to Thee by Thy beauty, now borne away from Thee by my own weight.' In such words Nygren would say that we see the sublimated Eros of Plato, the love of the good or of beauty, the desire to enjoy it, and the distinction between the false and the true love. The happy life he calls 'joy in the truth; for this is a joying in Thee, Who art the Truth, O God, my Light, health of my countenance, my God'. Of wisdom; 'Can you believe that wisdom can be anything but the truth in which the Supreme Good is seen and possessed?' God is the food of the soul: 'For within me was a famine of that inward food, Thyself, my God.'

But this is not the whole of the story. As he grew in the love of God and came to know better and better the teaching of St. Paul and the Scriptures, the note of Agape begins to sound more and more convincingly in his writings and letters. In his dispute, for instance, with the Pelagians and their doctrine of grace he attributes all to God and puts the human will and its desires in their subordinate and proper place. But in such an outstanding Christian and thinker the two loves could not lie side by side frowning at each other. If we turn to the seventh book of the *Confessions* we shall find there an attempted reconciliation which was to affect not only his permanent thought but the thought of the generations which succeeded him. He does not give up Eros. By it all men look up to God and seek him, but such is man's weakness that all his efforts are unavailing. The bent will must be straightened and then uplifted, and for this God's descent to man and His grace are necessary. 'They [the Neo-Platonists] could see that which is, but they saw it from afar off; they would not hold the humility of Christ, in which ship they could have arrived safely at that which they were able to see from afar. There is no means of crossing to the fatherland unless thou be carried by the wood [of the Cross].'

In such a Christian statement as this Agape is obviously present, but Nygren contends that Eros is nevertheless predominant. The reason is that St. Augustine starts from an egocentric or acquisitive love, a love, that is, which is set on obtaining happiness. So confused by this time had the two forms of love become that he adopts the eudaemonism of Cicero's *Hortensius*, that conception of beatitude which held pride of dlace in the school of the Roman Empire. The governing thought of it is that all seek their happiness—'there is no-one who does not love'— and such happiness lies in the final satisfaction of our nature. We are creatures, says St. Augustine, and therefore needy, and by our very nature we seek the good which is God. If our love be evil that must be because we have misdirected it to some unfitting object. Such an object drags us down and away from our God-given destiny. The way of caritas has been lost and the way of sin and cupidity chosen. Caritas is love of God, the movement upward to the everlasting; cupidity is the love of the world, the movement down to the temporal, and by turning his love to this latter man becomes bent (curvatus). By loving God we become like to Him; by loving the world we become like to it. The only distinction given here between the two loves lies in the natures of the objects loved; they are both loved in the same kind of way, which is the way of possessiveness. It would seem to follow, also, from this distinction, that God alone should be desired, seeing that in Him only is to be found our true happiness, the *vita beata*, and at times St. Augustine, following out the logic of his thought, expressly says this. 'He suffices for thee; besides Him nothing suffices thee.' 'It is God and my soul which I long to know. Nothing else? No, nothing whatsoever.' Nygren would argue that such a statement might befit the ancient mysticism with its emphasis on individualist salvation, but falls far short of the Christian Agape and profanes the divine doctrine of love for our neighbour.

ŕ This difficulty and that already mentioned of explaining any real fundamental difference between caritas and cupiditas, love of God and love of the world, stand out in St. Augustine's account. If in all loving we are necessarily loving our end, and if the love of that end be on analysis the satisfaction of our need, then there is no sharp distinction between the two loves. Again, if God alone is to be loved, how is it possible to give an unqualified assent to the second commandment to love our neighbour? The solution to this second problem is given by St. Augustine in his much-used distinction of 'frui' and 'uti', of enjoyment and use. There is, he says, a proper and legitimate love for creatures; but it must be a relative love. Everything must be loved in proportion to the value it possesses. Creatures are made by God and sing His praises; therefore in so far as they lead us to God and are part of the divine order we can enjoy them with a love which is relative. The implications of this distinction come out fully in the saying: 'Good men use the world in order to enjoy God, whereas bad men want to use God in order to enjoy the world.' That is to say, the one absolute object of enjoyment is God, but in so far as creatures partake of God's goodness and lead us to Him we must use them and can enjoy them relatively. To put the enjoyment of a creature first, however, independently of its use as a means to God, is bad. Charity, then, is an ordered love, and cupidity is a disordered love. Does this suffice to cover all that is meant by the second commandment? Whatever may be thought of this solution, does not the solution itself rest on a fundamental likeness between the love of charity and the love of cupidity, in as much as they are both self seeking? Yes and no, answers Nygren. There are many passages where St. Augustine makes the sharpest contrasts between the love of God and the love of self. The way to the City of God is by the love of God to the contempt of self. Pride and acquisitiveness are to him the most odious of vices. There are, in fact, in his mind two forms of self-love; the first consists in seeking the true good of the self; the other consists in seeking self as the true good. Caritas, then, consists in seeking one's good in the first sense; and that seeking is unselfish because the good is sought in God and not in oneself. But our unregenerate nature prevents us from being truly unselfish, from practising perfect charity, and it is not until God came near to us in grace and power in the Incarnation that we could be drawn out of ourselves by a love which makes God truly our bliss. 'Through the Incarnation we are drawn into the magnetic field of the eternal world and may taste something of the sweetness of the heavenly life.' 'When God gives himself to us in Christ, He gives us at once the object we are to love and the caritas with which to love it. The object we are to love is Himself, but Caritas is also Himself, who by the Holy Spirit takes up His abode in our hearts. Even the fact that we love God is itself entirely a gift of God.'

Such is the system which, if Nygren's interpretation be accepted, St. Augustine constructed and handed on to the Middle Ages and to the Scholastic thinkers. In the next chapter we shall see how Rousselot discerned two diverse tendencies in the doctrine of love amongst Christian thinkers before St. Thomas Aquinas, both of which claimed St. Augustine as their source. That the synthesis of St. Augustine should lay itself open to diverse interpretations is not surprising. He handed on the genuine doctrine of Agape, but also mixed with it that of Eros, and moreover he did the mixing in such a way that future thinkers took for granted that it was part of the Christian message. They could be the more easily deceived in that they had at hand the writings of Proclus and the Pseudo-Dionysius, writings which were saturated with Neo-Platonism, but apparently in harmony with some of the traits of Augustinian mysticism. These writings had a wide circulation, especially those of the Pseudo-Dionysius, because he was erroneously thought to be the disciple of

St. Paul. And as they circulated they made familiar all the typical Eros ideas and symbols, the symbol of the ascent and descent, the Alexandrian world-scheme, the doctrines of purification and union and beatitude. So it came about that alongside with the pure flower of Agape, which could never be uprooted from the Church, there grew up the weed of Eros. A perfect example is to be found in Scotus Eriugena. As Nygren writes: 'The Middle Ages are the age of transition: behind them is the Platonic doctrine of the Two Worlds, and the idea that the soul is attracted up to the world of Ideas; there is the Aristotelian idea of the ladder, the conception of Eros as the spiritual force of gravity, and of the power of the Divine to draw all things to itself on the principle of 'kinei hôs eromenon'; there are also the astral notions of antiquity, Neo-Platonic ideas of spheres that revolve one above the other, Augustine's stages of ascent, the hierarchies of Pseudo-Dionysius and John Climacus's *Ladder of Paradise*'. Even in Dante the influence can be seen. The love in it is the caritas of St. Augustine, that synthesis of Agape and Eros with all the stage scenery of Neo-Platonism.

In keeping with his principles of division Nygren is unable to pick out any medieval philosopher who is free from the influence of Eros— certainly not St. Thomas Aquinas. He remarks, in fact, that St. Thomas was so unconscious of the rival meanings of Agape and Eros that he could not understand why Dionysius took pains to defend his use of the word, Eros, and quoted two passages from the Septuagint to justify himself. St. Thomas is assumed to be no more than the medieval representative of the Aristotelian and Neo-Platonic conception of love. I say, Neo-Platonic, because it is clear that the Pseudo-Dionysius had a considerable influence on his religious philosophy. The groundwork is however that of Aristotle. 'Love is something which appertains to desire, since the object of both is what is good' (II, 1, qn. 26, a. i). 'The end of love is beatitude. . . . Since the good is the object of desire, the perfect good will consist of that which completely satisfies the will. Hence to desire happiness is nothing else than to seek to satisfy desire. This is what everyone wants' (III, qn. 5, a. 8). God alone can satisfy human desire, therefore we must love God. St. Thomas underlines this doctrine by adding that 'assuming what is impossible that God were not man's good, then there would be no reason for man to love God' (II, 11, qn. 26, a. 13, ad. 3). Such statements seem to make love essentially egocentric, and St. Thomas was aware of this and also of the fact that Christianity proffered a higher kind of love, which is known as caritas. To determine, however, the nature of this new and sacred love he does not look further than Aristotle. What Aristotle in the *Nicomachean Ethics* writes of the love of friendship is dressed up to play the part of caritas. This love of friendship is defined as wishing another well (*velle alicui bonum*), and it is used to supplement the original description of love as the desire for happiness. To Nygren and others this seems a poor substitute for the glory of Agape, and even to human lovers, the heats of love must seem poorly described by such a cool and refrigerating name as benevolence. What is worse, this love turns out to be still a form of self-love. St. Thomas reproduces the analysis of Aristotle, according to which self-love is the basis of friendship, and the friend is regarded as a part of oneself, a second self or alter ego. Commenting on this and the passage in the Summa of St. Thomas, where the love of self is stressed (II, ii, qn. 26, a. 4), Dr. Burnaby, in his Hulsean lectures, published under the title of *Amor Dei*, can hardly contain himself: 'Because unity ranks higher than union, a man's own share in the divine good must rank higher as a motive of love than the association of another with him in that sharing. The true line of Thomas's thought points rather to union as the higher unity, to escape from the illusion of the closed individual in a widening of the boundary of the self; and we may doubt whether he would have committed himself to an argument as fallacious as it is revolting to the Christian conscience, if he had not allowed the crude individualism of Aristotle to impair his own deeper intuition of the Agape, which takes man, even as it has taken God, out of himself.'

That neither Nygren nor Dr. Burnaby is here fair to St. Thomas I hope to show, but as the medieval thinkers were deeply concerned with the nature of love, I shall reserve treatment of this to the next chapter. In the meantime it will be well to sum up what Nygren considers to be the relations of Eros and Agape. After tracing the origin of Christian Eros to the mystery religions, and to that extent agreeing in part with de Rougemont, he makes a jump when Plato comes on the scene and from then onwards he equates Eros with egocentric love. This enables him to make a superficially clear and sharp distinction between Eros and Agape, egocentric and theocentric love, which he then works to death. He does not, however, see that he has forced them both into such contrasting shapes that neither is alive. Neither of them taken in complete abstraction from the other is able to reveal the true nature of human love. Eros, for instance, is said to be egocentric, to mean the desire of good for self, to be a form of self-assertion; it is primarily human and is determined by the quality of the object and therefore can be measured by the worth of the object loved; it is, above all, a will to have and to possess. Now if in this description all that was intended could be summed up in the familiar word, 'selfish', almost all would agree that such a selfish love is opposed to another kind of love which is called altruistic, or just unselfish. Human experience confirms such a distinction. But Nygren says expressly that he means the noble kind of love which is found in the songs of lovers and in the pages of high philosophy and mysticism. He thinks that all traces of self must be removed. In demanding this he is asking the impossible. Not only is the language of love in its greatest transports a mixture of joy in the beloved's happiness and joy in possessing his or her love, but pushed to the extreme a love in which the self did not enter would be no love at all. There are expressions which are used at times, even by Christian saints, which might seem to imply that the lover would like to surrender his eternal happiness for the sake of God. But this is only an extravagance, and the Christian always knows that God is not the kind of being who destroys what He has created out of love. Quite the opposite! He is the archetype of love who always wishes well to His beloved. The consequence of uprooting what Nygren calls egocentric love would be, if only he were to follow out the logic of his thought, to extinguish human love altogether. We arrive at the same conclusion if we regard more closely the nature of man. He is like other living beings in that he must by force of his nature and the instincts which proceed from it seek his own well-being. The Aristotelian argument on this matter is so obvious that once stated the general principle must be admitted. Desires spring from my nature, from what I am, and they are concerned with the preservation of my being and the development and perfection of it. In that sense I am bound up with myself in a way in which I am not bound up with anybody else, and no-one else can share my conscience and responsibilities. My sense of wrong and of good are the expression in part at least of what is dangerous or helpful to the health of my soul. It follows that I cannot help, if my love be a true one, recognizing that love is what is best for me, is my life in its supreme and, perhaps, eternal, point of exaltation. It becomes nonsense, therefore, to rule out all reference to self. As I say, to rule out the self entirely is to make an abstraction of love which has no life.

Similarly with Agape. It has two forms, God's love and our love for our neighbour. It is theocentric; indeed, God is Agape, and there is no self-love. It is banished. In Nygren's summary Agape is a self-giving; it comes down from above; it is a free gift; it is unselfish: it freely gives and spends; it is sovereign and independent with regard to its object; hence it is spontaneous, 'uncaused', and creates value in its object. Finally, 'Agape lives by God's life . . . is primarily God's own love', and 'when it appears in man, is a love that takes its form from God's own love'. Now in this description there is no mention of any distinction between grace and nature, the supernatural and the natural, and to the medieval and modern Catholic theologian, who is criticized by Nygren, this is a grave omission. The very theologian who lays such stress on the value of a properly ordered self-love, when writing of human nature, will with reserve use, when writing of grace, a language closely resembling that of Nygren's Agape. He will hold that it only causes confusion to neglect the fundamental Christian distinction of grace and nature. He will also go on to say that the real problem is not what Nygren indicates, but the relation of grace to nature, and the conciliation of much that can be called Eros with Agape. The point made here is that grace does not destroy all that is human; it perfects it and elevates it to a new dynamic, and the real problem is to work out how both nature and the supernatural life survive in their integrity in the Christian order. Nygren cuts the knot and sunders self-love and grace, nature and the supernatural completely. This does not make a peace between the two, but only a solitude in which Agape withers.

All is not however well with Agape, even though it is given the entire rule in the Christian kingdom. Nygren would have it that the Gospels proclaim his doctrine of Agape. But is this so? He quotes the Prodigal Son to prove that Agape is spontaneous and has nothing to do with deserts. But he makes no mention of the elder son, to whom most comforting words are addressed at the end of the parable on account of his long-standing fidelity. He cites the parable of the vineyard and the equal payment of all the labourers, whether they entered at an early hour or at a late hour. But here again the fact is ignored that they did offer themselves and that all did some labour. Their lot is quite different from those who remained outside. There is no need, however, to press the argument from the Gospels. Such an extreme form of the Agape theory will not work out. God is Agape, and we should naturally expect someone to be the beneficiary of that love, and as beneficiary to respond. But if this theory is taken literally there is no one to respond. There is no need of that intercommunication which is essential to love. We are told that no Eros (in Nygren's sense) should enter in in man's return of love, that it should be all Agape. But as we have seen, God is Agape. There is nothing human or personal in the response, nor can there be on this interpretation. In the elimination of Eros man has been eliminated. Of this consequence Nygren seems to be uncomfortably aware, for he says that man's return of love must be Agape and not Eros, and then goes on to say that we can hardly speak of man's response as Agape; it should rather be called faith. Agape, that is, God's love, should be used, perhaps, exclusively of man's love of his neighbour. In line with the same reasoning he suggests in one place that the 'deep truth of predestination' fits in with this interpretation. Yes, indeed, if we take 'predestination' as meaning that God arbitrarily constrains those whom He wills to be saved without any human response or act of free will on their part. That this is what

Nygren really means seems to be clear from his remark following on his reference to predestination. 'Man is to love God, not because he finds fuller and completer satisfaction of his need in God than in any other object of desire, but because God's "uncaused" love has overpowered him and constrained him, so that he can do nothing else than love God.'

This image of 'overpowering' and 'constraining' sounds like an echo of the old Dionysiac frenzy and the constraining of Persephone by the god of the dark world. It occurs frequently in the experience of the mystery religions. The classical instance is to be found in the Sixth book of Virgil: 'But the prophetess, not yet Phoebus' willing slave, is storming with giant frenzy in her cavern, as though she hoped to unseat from her bosom the mighty god. All the more sharply he plies her mouth with his bit till its fury flags, tames her savage soul, and moulds her to his will by strong constraint.' Such a constraint is the antipodes to the Christian revelation of God. Yet if we remove this last spasm of human activity and freedom we are left with a theology which may be called Christian, but is, in fact, hardly if at all discernible from pantheism or monism. If the Agape be an act which proceeds from man and at the same time has nothing human or free in it, how can that act, which is expressly declared to be divine, be anything less. And if man is literally divine, then we are back at the monism of the ancient Gnostic cult.

This is not to deny that in the Christian teaching there is a deep mystery and that much of what Nygren says of Agape is drawn from the New Testament. There is indeed a problem which can be stated in terms of Eros and Agape, but it has been wrongly formulated by Nygren; so wrongly formulated that the way out, whether by Eros or by Agape, is barred. Neither Eros nor Agape can function in Nygren's formulation. The proper way of stating the problem is surely this: that God must act with sovereign power and freedom, and we know from the New Testament and all Christian teaching that God has freely offered to man a way of life which is His own, the way of what Nygren calls Agape. God, therefore, has the initiative and by His grace does lift man up into an order of love which is above that which Nygren delineates in terms of Eros. But God does this without constraint or defiance of what is best in human nature; He makes man a co-heir with His own Divine son without destruction of his freedom or his human personality. Grace perfects nature and does not undo it. How this can be so is precisely the mystery. No Procrustean solution will do; no Pelagian overemphasis on the natural or Eros will serve, nor again an overlordship of Agape so peremptory that it leaves no room for human values. This puzzle has its repercussions in all debates about love, whether they concern grace and nature or the love of self and the love of others, personal rights and duties and duties to the State, community or motherland. There is a desire of the self to give its all and a desire to be oneself and be perfect. The principle of give and take has to be harmonized in all phases of love. This is the problem which vexed the medieval thinkers—a problem which is the same as that confronting us in Nygren's pages, but seen from another angle, and in the next chapter we must consider it.

One very important clue is given to us by a comparison of the two insights into Eros which have been shown to us by de Rougemont and Nygren, and before passing on we should be clear as to what this clue is. De Rougemont said that Eros consisted of a dark passion which was lawless and infinitely discontented with the earthly and temporal existence of the soul. Agape, on the other hand, made the best of time and of the present and wore the bonds, of marriage, for instance, as a freeman, as belonging to a new covenant with God made man. That is to say, Eros has an element of violence; it is the knightly rider on a horse who seeks to find the Grail. But it is also and more noticeably a self-surrender, a form of espousals with the dark goddess, in the night where the soul is ravished and fused with the All. Now in Nygren Eros starts with the like passion, but changes after Plato into what is an essentially intellectual and possessive form of love. What was Dionysiac has become Apolline, the feminine and clinging the most masculine and self-assertive. Eros is constantly defined by Nygren as egocentric; it wishes to have and to hold, even God, who is to be its beatitude. It will not surrender itself to the Divine love and decrease as that love increases. It has no truck with the death of self. Here therefore in varying garments the two movements of love make themselves manifest, the active and the passive, the self-assertive and the self-sacrificing, the taking and the receiving. The two keep reappearing, but they are so interwoven that we have to use the greatest care in disentangling them, and be it noted, the more they are taken apart and viewed in abstraction the less real do they become. To have issue they have to commingle. As in marriage, their presence, as we shall now see, was taken seriously by the medieval thinkers, though their full significance was not always realized.

APPENDIX ONE

To explain the first significance of Eros Nygren quotes the myth of Zagreus. 'According to this myth, Zeus had determined to bestow on his son Zagreus or Dionysus dominion over the world; but while he was still a child, the Titans succeeded in getting him into their power, and killed and devoured him. Zeus then smote the Titans with his thunderbolts, and destroyed them; and out of the Titans' ashes he formed the race of men'. This myth was a favourite amongst the Orphists, as it served to explain the rites of the Dionysiac festival. I prefer, however, to turn to another story as it brings out a feature of the early religions, which is not so conspicuous in the myth of Zagreus or Persephone. A recurring trait in the myths is the miraculous birth of a hero who is a foe to the powers of darkness, performs many great feats, has to wander and suffer and often in the end dies by treachery. Tristram and Lancelot bear some traces of this early hero, and he appears in the figure of Siegfried. He is there in the Celtic legends of Lugh of the Long Arm and Cu Chulainn, in the Assyrian and Babylonian cosmogonies in the stories of Bel and Mardok, and in more human shape in Hercules. Many of these myths can be explained adequately enough as theological dramatizations of the movements of the sun and moon and the seasons of the year, but it is not fanciful to see in them also a projection of the despairs and hopes of man and the expression of his desires. We have seen already how in the myth of Persephone the dark passion in desire is mimed. Against death and in self assertiveness the hero takes shape in dream and in aspiration. He is at first dominating and cruel, possessed of superhuman courage and masculine strength. He attains by his valiant prowess many victories and much of what he wants. He is like the sun in his glory. But often enough, though he cannot be vanquished by force, he can be tricked by womanly guile and come to grief because of an unfair doom that is laid upon him. The night comes when no hero can work. As times passes the barbaric emphasis on brute strength is slowly exchanged for a different kind of power, the power to control and rule over passion. This is the light of reason, the most lordly characteristic in man. It is by reason that the civilized man is superior to the barbarian; it is by reason that man controls his passions and shows himself most masculine; and it is by reason that man is like to the gods and possesses himself of everything. The early fighting hero has changed now into the sun god, Apollo, the ideal of the Greek, because he represents all that is definite and balanced and controlled, all that makes man superior to the beasts, and godlike. The dark powers are however always threatening this sovereignty and the gods are jealous of man's prerogative. Man may be self-possessed and capable of measuring all things, but he has moments of collapse, the voice of Pan in the night time disturbs his serenity and 'apparent dirae facies'; there are strange and terrifying eyes and lurking shapes which are close and ever menacing. These apparitions are not merely threats to man's safety; they can appeal to something within a man and exercise a fearful fascination. That is why Sophocles declares that Eros is a madness, but perhaps a divine madness. Or it may seem in another mood that the gods themselves are cruel in their passion and like to kill what they love. That is why the fate of man is in the main so tragic.

This heroic and tragic mood finds expression in the legend of Prometheus, and to some extent dovetails in with the story of Persephone. In the play of Aeschylus Prometheus tells his own story. A quarrel had broken out between the God of Olympus and the Titans. The Titans determined to subdue the gods opposed to them, but would not agree on the method to adopt. Prometheus, a Titan himself, advised that they should use craft, the new wisdom instead of brute force; but since his advice was neglected he took the side of Zeus and brought about the defeat of the Titans, who relied on brute strength. But he received no gratitude from Zeus for his help, and when Zeus designed to destroy the race of mortal men and create a new race, Prometheus circumvented him by delivering man 'from death and deep destruction'. 'I stayed man from foreknowledge of his fate. First, I implanted in his heart blind hopes. . . . And furthermore I bestowed fire upon him.' In a later discourse Prometheus describes at great length the benefits he had conferred on mankind. In man 'born witless as a babe, I planned mind and the gift of understanding.' Men had had eyes but they could not see, and ears but they could not hear; they confounded all things as shapes figured in dreams; they knew not how to build and make to themselves homes; they had no tokens of the flowery spring nor the season of ripening fruit, 'but laboured without wit in all their works, till I revealed the obscure risings and settings of the stars of heaven. Yea, and the art of number, arch-device, I founded, and the craft of written words, the world's recorder, mother of the muse'. But on himself he only heaped misery by these benefits to man, and now he is fastened to a rock on the bleak cliff in the Caucasus. The Chorus bids him be reasonable and not to sin by excess of pride. ''Tis sweet to run life's long career by hopes attended strong and bold, feeding the heart in blithesome cheer; but thee I shudder to behold by myriad tortures racked in sore distress. For thou, of Zeus unawed, hast still, in pride and sheer self-will, mortals honoured in excess.' Prometheus remains unmoved by this implied rebuke and hurls defiance at Zeus. He can do his worst, and 'down to the bottomless blackness of Tartarus let my body be cast, in the whirling waters of Destiny: for with death I shall not be stricken.' He is resolute, though he is bound to the rock for thousands of years and his vitals are to be gnawed by an eagle. In the last lines of the play as the storm of Zeus' anger gathers around him, he calls out: 'O, thou mother revered! O heavenly sky, who does shed from thy region the common light of the world, thou seest the wrongs that I suffer.'

Into the play another sufferer, Io, is introduced. She suffers because she has refused to yield to the solicitations of Zeus. Night after night dream-visions came to her, beguiling her with winning words: 'O greatly blessed maid, wherefore so long a virgin, when 'tis thine to wed the Highest? Zeus with sharp desire of thee is smitten and longs for the embrace of Cypris.' Because she did not listen to these words, she was driven forth from her home, her wit and woman's form distorted, with horned temples, and savagely pursued by Argus, the fierce earth-born herdsman of the hundred eyes, and now she has to flee across the world, maddened by the stings of a gadfly. The chorus are dismayed by her sufferings and her fate and cry out 'Never may it fall to my lot, O fate, all things fulfilling, to be called to the bed of Zeus as the bride of the Highest; never may I by lords of the heavenly host be woo'd or won; I tremble even to look on the maiden who hates her Olympian wooer, destined to wander in pain far and wide, pursued by Hera's jealous rage.' Prometheus naturally sympathises with her sufferings and the injustice done her, and he foretells that 'from her seed at last shall spring a brave and glorious Archer, who from bondage shall deliver me'. (Translation taken from *Aeschylus* by George Thomson.)

In this legend Prometheus is a Titan, and he belongs to the strong and mighty; but he is in advance of his brethren and sees that in the arts of reason true manliness is most highly manifested. His pride and strength do not, however, avail him against fate. As in so many of the myths and legends he struggles vainly against his doom, and his lot is to be unhappy. His relation with the gods and with men is conveyed in the story of the stealing of the fire. Here is something which belongs to the gods, and it is made over to man. Man now has in his possession the spark of divinity, which is also that godlike reason which puts man on a kind of equality with the Divine. But it brings suffering to Prometheus, and only at the end will the Archer deliver him. Io is similarly afflicted, and in her case it is because she has refused to be the bride of the Highest. She is now restless and can find no resting-place or home on earth. She recalls the effect of the dark passion as described by de Rougemont, but it is not too far-fetched to see in the story of Prometheus an allegory of the egocentric Eros which Nygren described in the preceding chapter.

APPENDIX TWO—CARITAS

A reader of Nygren's work might easily pick up a wrong impression of the difference between his view of 'caritas' and that of the main body of Catholic writers. He holds that caritas or Agape is entirely gratuitous, that God gives the initiative and the increase, in fact, that without God's grace man can do nothing. He contrasts with this a view that caritas is God's response to human merit, that human desire, the rapacious and levelling intellect and self-love have all a place in caritas, and in general that man's natural virtue counts and that man works with God and is graced as he deserves. Such an interpretation of the Latin Fathers and the great Scholastic writers is gravely mistaken, and seems to ignore the fundamental disinction which they all make between the natural and the supernatural, between nature and grace. In the text I have avoided emphasizing this distinction in order not to complicate the issue. For a proper understanding of caritas it is, however, essential to begin with this distinction. Caritas is essentially a grace, and therefore supernatural, and if this be misunderstood, the whole of Catholic teaching will be misunderstood. Very shortly, the meaning of the supernatural can be stated as follows: God is infinitely perfect; man belongs to a finite order of being, an order in which matter and spirit meet. Man is highest in the animal world and lowest in the world of spirit. But because he is spiritual he has a far-off kinship with God in that with his mind he meets truth and with his love he desires goodness—and God is truth and goodness and knows and loves perfectly. This means that friendship, an exchange of love, is possible between man and God. But as man's mind is so feeble and his will so contrary to have any close friendship with God would be impossible if he had to rely on his own strength. Now God might have so helped man, as an inspiring teacher draws the best out of a pupil or a great lover evokes a new responsiveness in the beloved—that man would have loved Him to the limit of his natural capacity. What we learn from the New Testament is that God did more than this. His design was and is so to animate man with His own love that man, in and through God's love or grace, should have a kind of equality of friendship, such that he could know God as God knows Himself, and love God as God loves Himself in the Blessed Trinity. This is to give man, as it were, a new dimension, to raise him far above his natural capacity. Not even God could do this to a material thing; it would crack under the strain and cease to be itself. But a being who has a mind and a spiritual will and power to love can submit to this Divine pressure on it without destruction. The reason is that a mind, as such, has no limitation, and, as I suggest, a person in being a person is *for* himself and *to* another; that is to say, he is both a living self-contained being and a living relation. On both counts a human being can remain himself while acting above his natural capacity. He is energized by the love of God; that love is diffused in his heart by the Holy Ghost so that he can say: 'Abba, Father', and enjoy equal terms of friendship with the Son of God.

Now it is this mysterious elevation of man above himself which is described in the technical language of the supernatural and of grace. The Epistles of St. Paul abound in attempts to describe it. He calls it grace, adoption, regeneration, membership in Christ. St. John's favourite name for it is 'sonship'. Furthermore, as is obvious, man can do nothing of himself to deserve this gift, to begin this life or to live it. The early Christians were told over and over again that of themselves they could do nothing. 'So then it is not of him that willeth nor of him that runneth, but of God that showeth mercy.' And again: 'For by grace you are saved through faith, and that not of yourselves, for it is the gift of God; not of works, that no man may glory. For we are his workmanship, created in Christ Jesus in good works, which God hath prepared that we should walk in them.' These are but two examples of what is a constant refrain in the New Testament and in early Christian literature. So far from there being any hesitation about this or going back upon it, Councils laid it down as an essential of the Christian faith, and the later Scholastic theologians accepted it as a first principle.

The main and orthodox Catholic tradition, as represented by the Fathers and the great Scholastic writers, is, therefore, entirely at one with Nygren in maintaining the gratuity of God's gifts of grace and charity. Their doctrine of the 'supernatural' insures that and the concomitant doctrine that man can do nothing of himself to deserve God's Agape or exercise it. Nygren unwittingly misrepresents that view and sets up a false contrast between the pure doctrine of Agape and the diluted half-human and half-divine version of it which he thinks St. Augustine canonized and St. Thomas Aquinas developed. The point of difference between their view and that of Nygren does not lie here. They both start from the same texts, but whereas Nygren so exalts Agape that no place is left for any properly human response and co-operation, the great Scholastic thinkers held on to the principle that in all friendships two are concerned and not one. Even though man's love in the new covenant of friendship with God is supernatural, that is to say, beyond his natural capacity, he does not become an automaton; he is not forced, not taken hold of willy nilly and made to love. The whole purpose of God's action is to give and not to take away, to restore and increase the dignity of the human person. This means that man must be left his freedom, his power to accept or refuse, and his power, consequently, to merit by co-operation with Divine love. As Nygren ignores man's part he oversimplifies the problem of grace and charity. He has to leave out the second half of a sentence such as that from the Book of Revelation: 'they shall walk with me in white, because they are worthy'. The real problem, as the great Catholic thinkers saw it, was to allow for the full force of grace and Agape and also for man's participation in the new supernatural friendship. It is only when this is understood that we can appreciate the care and thought given to such problems as that of grace and freewill, man's divine sonship and his ever-continuing finite status and selfhood.

So far I have used the words 'grace' and 'charity' as if they were equivalent. Some great theologians, like Scotus and Bellarmine and Lessius, have argued for the identity, but the majority make a distinction. They hold with St. Augustine that 'grace precedes charity', that charity, which is an active habit, presupposes the 'new birth' of which St. Paul speaks. This question, interesting as it is in itself, does not concern us. What is more relevant is the proper definition of caritas and its relation with that love of God which does lie within our human capacity. One well-known definition of supernatural charity runs as follows: it is the love which refers all things to God and sets God above all things, even man himself. This is a more technical paraphrase of the command by Christ that we should love God with our whole strength and with our whole mind. St. Thomas sums up the difference between natural and supernatural love in an answer to an objection: 'God, in so far as he is the general good from whom all natural good depends, is loved with a natural love by everyone; in so far, however, as He is the good who makes all happy in supernatural bliss, he is loved with a supernatural love.' The point of this is that with our natural knowledge we can have some idea of the goodness of God; we can see that all good and lovely things are but a reflection of His goodness and that they come from Him. But in the Christian Revelation we learn a new lesson about God; we are given the power to understand that God is Our Father, that His nature is love, and that He intends to share His love with us and give us a vision of His essential loveliness. The act with which we respond to this invitation is supernatural charity.

The question here debated by the theologians about the difference between natural and supernatural charity may, as they frame it, seem a little unreal. The reason for this is that, in order to make their contrasts clear, they take a theoretical example from the natural order. The God who is loved as the 'general good from whom all natural good depends' is undoubtedly very different from the God of the New Testament. But the problem is much more difficult when we appeal to experience and try from experience to make a clear demarcation. The effect of the Christian teaching has been very widespread and is not confined to those who are confessedly of the Christian faith. Pagans, too, show a love both in word and in act which seems to pass far beyond the limits of the love as laid down, for example, by St. Thomas. Lastly there are many whose mind does not seem to run with their deeds. They prove a very high degree of love by their acts, though in word they seem not to know what they are doing. Modern psychology has proved, if proof were needed, how badly a man may mistake his own motives and shy away from truth which he has been shocked into fearing. Again, we have to allow for many uncovenanted graces from God, Who desires all to enjoy His friendship. Many a man, it may be, owing to his heredity and environment and upbringing is so fixed in a certain way of viewing God and the world that it would need an extraordinary shaking up of his personality for him to see the full truth. God may, to use the vivid words of Gerard Hopkins, prefer to work within the 'burl of being' of the individual man and change 'the cleave' of it. The one law is that the man should be moved by supernatural charity.

On this relation of the natural to the supernatural not all follow St. Thomas in his clear-cut distinction. He holds that there is a substantial difference in the two kinds of love. A man cannot love God above all things and more than himself with a real and efficacious love without grace; if he appears to do so, then it is only the semblance of the real love, a pious dream or ineffective fancy. Against St. Thomas many teach that there is no such substantial difference, that a difference in mode suffices, as a child of a family might love its parents very much, but unless its love had that special quality which belongs to family affection, it would be wanting in that mode of love which is appropriate to parents and brothers and sisters. Such delicate but vital differences in love are not easy to tabulate, nor again the relation of charity to the other virtues. Some theologians so stress the importance of charity that they seem loath to give any value to other virtues, such as courage or justice or purity, unless they explicitly fall under that of charity. They quote the great saying of St. Paul that 'if I should distribute all my goods to feed the poor, and if I should deliver my body to be burnt, and have not charity, it profiteth me nothing.' They cannot, however, mean that we must always explicitly refer what we do to the love of God, and once we admit that a virtue has an intrinsic excellence of its own and that only some kind of overruling principle of life or motive is needed, the edge of the difficulty is removed. All our actions are to some extent affected by our central love; when a man is selfish at heart even his virtues are slightly tinged by this attitude, and it is a common experience to find that a man who has changed his convictions, undergone a testing and shaking experience and survived it, without permanent harm, talks, speaks and acts as a 'different person'. The whole man is in each of our acts, and that is why love does have some say as to the dress in which we clothe our virtues and our vices. The same truth can be illustrated in a more general way in the rise and decline of a culture. New beliefs which are accepted and loved influence the style and idiom in art, literature, customs and morals, and when the belief begins to fade both the appreciation and practice of the moral virtues begins to evaporate. There is a remarkable parallel between the love of a living God and the chivalry, the 'lowliness and loyalty' of our social relations. (I am thinking of the lines in Piers Plowman: 'Love and lowliness and loyalty, these shall be Lords in the land, truth to save'.) The ideal of womanhood and marriage, for instance, is girt about with dogmas; she is the image of God, she reflects the beauty of the Virgin Mother of God, the union of marriage is like to that of the soul with Christ and the Church with its Head, her fidelity is like to that of God's suffering fidelity and covenant with man. Once these dogmas begin to lose their sway the ideal of the virgin, the wife and the mother also grow dim, the moral customs and laws of purity and marriage are changed, and love is regulated by business and convenience.

The difference caused by the absence of the supernatural is unmistakable, and can easily be seen, for example, in a comparason of two such novels as Sigrid Undset's *Kristinlavransdatter* and Galsworthy's *Forsyte Saga*. In both men and women toil and suffer, love and grow estranged, and evil seems to conquer, as the seasons come and go year after year; but in the one the sin and suffering and death take place under a living Providence, and the ravages of time are redeemed in some mystery of love; whereas in the other there is no hope. But it is in such biographies as those of Emma Goldman and Jan Valtin's *Out of the Night* that the contrast is most clearly presented. All the details described may not have happened, but the life lived and the persons are drawn from their experience. In both stories we read of superlative acts of courage and resolution, astounding endurance and self-sacrifice, but the violence and the treachery, the ruthlessness regarding others' bodies and lives, fill one with pity and horror. Here is naturalism, naked and exposed, without grace. And even the virtues in this underworld without light look like the 'splendid vices' of St. Augustine. They cannot but excite admiration, for they make one understand how marvellous is the nature of man with its pride and determination and its willingness to sacrifice everything. Why these two should remain with man to the last will, I hope, become plain when the nature of the two loves by which man is driven is sketched out in the later chapters of this book.

However difficult, therefore, it may be to put one's finger on the boundary line between natural love and the supernatural, there can be no doubt of the unhappy condition of the natural when the supernatural is withdrawn. In his essay on Christianity and the Supernatural,[1] Baron Von Hügel tries to indicate some of the positive effects of grace. He says that 'decency is carried up into devotedness and homeliness into heroism.

---

[1] In *Essays and Addresses on the Philosophy of Religion*.

. . . Simple justice and average fairness are transfigured into genial generosity and over-flowing self-devotion. Competition is replaced by co-operation, indeed even by vicarious work and suffering. And now the desire for a simple survival of the natural activities and of the natural happiness, and of a dim and discursive sense of God, is replaced by thirst for the full expansion and the final establishment of the human personality in an endless life of such self-devotion and of a vivid, intuitive vision of God, supreme Author and End of all Nature and Supernature'.

Von Hügel then mentions seven virtues: courage, purity, unlimited compassion, humility, truthfulness, self-abandonment in the hands of God and spiritual joy, and gives some very touching examples in the practice of them of a supernatural quality. I will quote one of these examples as it bears on the nature of love. 'There is an Irish Roman Catholic washerwoman with whom I had the honour of worshipping some thirty years ago in our English Midlands. She had twelve children, whom she managed to bring up most carefully, and a drunken husband, an Englishman of no religion, openly unfaithful to herself. The constant standing of many years at last brought on some grave internal complications: a most delicate operation would alone save her life. Whilst resting in hospital against the coming ordeal, with the experts thoroughly hopeful of success, a visiting surgeon came round, really the worse for drink, and insisted with trembling hands upon an examination there and then. This doomed the patient to a certain death, which duly came a week later. Yet from the first moment of the fatal change to the last instant of her consciousness (so the priest who attended her throughout declared to me after all was over) she was absorbed in seeking to respond, with all she was, to this great grace of God, this opportunity of utter self-abandonment to Him, and this although she dearly loved her children, and although she knew well that her eyes would hardly be closed before their father would marry a bad woman and give her full authority over this, their mother's darling little flock. All possible plans were made by the dying woman for each of her children, and from the first moment she spontaneously exacted from the priest a promise to prevent any prosecution of the fuddled surgeon—she never stopped to consider his offence even to forgive it; it was God, and the utter trust in Him, and in the wisdom, the love of His Will, that swallowed up all the pain, physical and mental, and all possible conflicts and perplexities.'

Lastly, Von Hügel points to certain implications, which, as he thinks, are characteristic of the Supernatural. The last of these points to the distinction between all natural appreciation of God and the full Christian faith and love. 'Qualities, such as reality, transcendance, presence, existence—these are not apprehended as floating in the air, or fancied in the mind; such qualities, or the impressions of such qualities, are, however confusedly, however unuttered even to itself by the apprehending mind, felt and loved as effects and constituents of a Reality distinct from the apprehender, and yet a Reality sufficiently like the human spirit when thus supernaturally sustained and sublimated, to be recognized by this human spirit with rapt, joyous adoration as its living source, support and end.' Other religions have, he says, something similar, but 'it remains a fact that, given the truth of Theism, Christianity brings to this truth a depth of roots, a breadth of inclusions and utilizations, and a penetrative delicacy of applications matched only very partially and sporadically elsewhere. For in Christianity its faith in God is the culmination and resolution of the other four convictions and tensions—of the belief in the natural-supernatural character of human experience as a whole; of the insight into the social-solitary quality of all religion; of the apprehension that the supernatural endowment is very unequal amongst men, and that there exists one supremely rich, uniquely intimate union with God, in one particular human mind and will; and of the experience that an element of Suffering enters into every Serenity. Thus everything beautiful, true and good, of whatever degree or kind, is indeed included within Christian Theism, but it is included therein according to certain very definite principles; the whole is thus not a guess or a jumble, a fog or a quicksand; it is a certainty as rock-firm as it is rich and elastic, a certainty groped after and confirmed by all that is virile, pure, humble, truthful, tender, self-immolating and deeply joyous in the depths of man's longings and attempts.'

The full meaning of 'caritas' cannot, however, be understood without some reference to the doctrine of 'incorporation' in Christ. As we say of a child: 'How like his father'—so an Apostle, if he were alive now would say of a Christian acting with supernatural charity: 'How he reminds me of the Lord!'

> *For Christ plays in ten thousand places,*
> *Lovely in limbs, and lovely in eyes not his*
> *To the Father through the features of men's faces.*[1]

[1] Sonnet by Gerard Hopkins.

CHAPTER THREE

THE PROBLEM OF SELF-CENTRED LOVE

But if the while I think on thee, dear friend,
All losses are restored and sorrows end.

—SHAKESPEARE.

Whilst my soul, like quiet foemen;
Travelleth towards the land of heaven;
Over the silver mountains,
Where spring the nectar fountains:
There will I kiss
The bowl of bliss,
And drink mine everlasting fill
Upon every milken hill.
My soul will be a-dry before;
But, after, it will thirst no more.

—WALTER RALEIGH.

Dust as we are, the immortal spirit grows
Like harmony in music; there is a dark
Inscrutable workmanship that reconciles
Discordant elements, makes them cling together
In one society.—WORDSWORTH.

As I suggested in the last chapter, the egocentric character of love did not pass unnoticed in the Middle Ages. Nygren would reply: how could it escape notice, seeing that Eros had by then dug itself in in Christian thought and the Schoolmen of those times took over the Greek philosophy as the medium for interpreting Christian doctrine? It might be, on the other hand, that love at all times must have a dual aspect; it must be possessive and also sacrificial. We have seen reason to doubt the adequacy of Nygren's distinctions, but nevertheless it is curious to watch his problem taken up by the Scholastic writers as a serious one, which it was not easy to answer. The form it took with them was whether a man could love God more than himself. The very question shows that the egocentric nature of love was realized, and this in turn witnesses to the influence on their minds of the Greek theory of Eros. As Nygren argued, Eros after Plato consists of a desire to have and to possess. Any living being which is in process of growth acts primarily in the interests of its own nature and the perfection of the same. Now man is on all fours with other living processes in moving to his perfection. The very word 'growth' is a synonym for movement of a certain kind, and desire is the form of that movement when the living being has reached the stage of conscious feeling and will. The correlation of desire with self-perfection is therefore complete and it assumes the dignity of a metaphysical principle which cannot be denied. Now the Schoolmen of the Middle Ages took over the Platonic and then the Aristotelian philosophies, and with it their doctrine of Eros. But they had already from the long continuity of Christian teaching a still more certain view of their relations with God. God is the end of man, and we must love God with our whole heart and with our whole strength. Indeed a number of statements could be quoted to the effect that God alone must be loved. There was no possible question about that; but there could very well be a question, which would exercise the best brains, to wit, how reconcile the necessary movement of human desire which ends in the self with the duty of loving God more than the self.

This is the form the problem of Eros and Agape took in the Middle Ages, and if we are to believe Rousselot in his *Pour L'Histoire du Problème de l'Amour au Moyen Age*, two differing lines of answer were at first developed. These he divides into the Physical or Graeco-Thomist conception and the Ecstatic conception, and he contends that the two differing lines can be most distinctly observed amongst the great writers. Naturally no hard and sharp division can be made at any one moment or even in any one writer. In a great lover, like St. Bernard, both views appear again and again. Nevertheless though they jostle each other they tend to draw more and more apart, and the reason for this is simple; they each represent a different idea of love and they rest on fundamentally conflicting philosophies. As a rule, the ecstatic view will be taken by those who belong to the Augustinian tradition of 'caritas' and are influenced by the Neo-Platonist mysticism and the mystery cults. The physical or unitive view has its roots in the more balanced Greek view, which is noticeable in the Aristotelian philosophy, with its insistence on the unity of body and soul and humanistic values. The first is nearer to the dark passion, the second to egoism. Floating on the surface of intercourse and discussion were the traditional distinctions of love, of concupiscence and benevolence or cupidity and friendship; but these were of no help in solving the deeper puzzle, since even the love of benevolence might according to one party rest on egocentric love. Bossuet, for instance, in his *Instruction sur les états d'oraison*, gives a long quotation from Hugh of St. Victor, of which the following is a sample: 'What is love but to desire (*concupiscere*) and to long to have and to possess and to enjoy? If not possessed then to long to possess, and if possessed then to long to keep . . . for what is love save the very desire to possess?' Now if any language belongs to Eros and is opposed to what Nygren calls Christian Agape, these words are, and yet Bossuet calmly tells us that it is the common doctrine of all the doctors, ancient and modern. In this Bossuet certainly exaggerates, and he himself supplies a correction in another definition of love which he gives in a sermon preached in 1663, *Pour la fête de l'Assomption*:[1] Car qu'est-ce que nous entendons par le nom d'amour, sinon une puissance souveraine, une force impérieuse qui est en nous pour nous tirer hors de nous, un je ne sais quoi qui dompte et captive nos coeurs sous la puissance d'un autre qui nous fait dépendre d'autrui et nous fait aimer notre dépendance? Et n'est-ce par une telle inclination que nous devons honorer celui à qui appartient naturellement tout empire et tout droit de souveraineté sur les coeurs? C'est pourquoi lui-même voulant nous préscrire le culte que nous lui devons, il ne nous demande qu'un amour sans bornes: 'Tu aimeras', dit il, 'le seigneur, ton Dieu, de toute ta force'; afin que nous entendions que l'amour seul est la source de l'adoration légitime que doit la créature à son Créateur et le véritable tribut par lequel elle le doit reconnoître.' Yet despite this clear assertion of the opposite kind of love he can still think that love is necessarily acquisitive and possessive.

The same apparent contradiction meets us in many writers, and for that reason we can seldom be sure whether it is through inadvertence or not that they declare themselves for one or other of the two types of love. For this reason some critics of Rousselot have rejected his supposed problem as a mare's nest. But we have seen enough in the previous chapter to deny this. It does not matter who is the advocate or witness nor what form of love he is defending; the puzzle always remains how egocentric love is compatible with the pure love of our neighbour and of God. In Hugh of St. Victor self-love is clearly in the ascendant, as the quotation from his writings already given proves; and in his earlier writings this is true even of Abelard's great opponent, St. Bernard. St. Bernard traces the development of the highest love from the lowest. The lowest form is when a man loves himself for himself. Then he may love God, but not for God's sake so much as for his own. In the next stage he loves God not only for his own sake but also for God's, and finally he loves himself only because of his love of God. 'A good law, therefore, is charity and a sweet one . . .; for truly it does not destroy the servile and mercenary forms of it, but so acts that they are implemented . . .; it gives direction to cupidity. . . . When it has reached its fulfilment by grace, the body will be loved and all bodily good things for God's sake alone. But God will be loved directly for his sake.' In

---

[1] The French is so limpid and strong that I have made an exception and refrained from translation.

such a gradation it is assumed that cupidity and Agape spring from one stem, and therefore it is possible to pass from egocentric love to theocentric love without a break.

In the later writings of St. Bernard the opposing ecstatic view comes more into prominence. The characteristics of this love are that it defies the ordinary rules of reason; the lover and the beloved stand over against each other as persons, and it is this separation which causes agony. The only thing to do is to forget oneself and all that one cherishes and lose oneself in the other. Love is a bond and a gift, and the great Franciscan school of the thirteenth century, following the sacred foolhardiness of its founder, marked down gratuity and liberality as the first perfection of love. So far from seeking a satisfaction out of such an experience they longed to be crucified and to bear the marks of a crucified love in their hands and feet and side. 'In foco l'amor mi mise', . . ., and of the divine love, 'Perche m'hai si ferito?' In Baudouin, Archbishop of Canterbury, we hear again the echo of death: 'Death separates soul and body; so too love separates' (Mors dividit carissima nomina, foederaque junctissima, dividit et dilectio. . . . Dividit mors animam et carnem, dividit et dilectio). The wound of love drives the soul to such distraction as to make it forget all reason. The saying of St. Augustine, 'Love and do what you will' (Ama et fac quod vis), was accepted and appreciated. St. Bernard tells us that 'love, in this like hate, ignores the calculation of truth', and the same note is struck by a saying such as this: 'A good conscience has no fear, but love is a flame. . . . Mighty is the power of love. . . . Always does it take for granted that it is loved by what it feels it loves. No more! All other titles of majesty forgotten, the lover, who feels the heats of love within him, has thought only of the beloved.'

In this ecstatic love, then, we are far from egocentric love. The lover has no thought of himself, except that he would willingly give his all for the other. Secondly, this love is almost a dark passion; it is a fire and a wound; it is violent and sacrificial; it cares nothing for reason, because it is a madness and a rapture, and lastly it has no ulterior purpose; it seeks no reward; love is the end and consummation. Love, therefore, of this kind is above all; it looks outside itself to another person, and it is beyond reason and nature. In the Greek idea of love the ultimate Eros, which stirs and draws all hearts, is itself indifferent and uncaring of all save itself. But the God who is loved in the Epistles of St. Paul and revealed in the Gospels is a living and loving God, who has become beside himself for love of us, and has suffered an ecstasy, so that in turn man must lose himself in ecstasy and give himself up, without once glancing back, to his Almighty Lover. As St. Augustine said: 'Love slays what we have been that we may be what we were not.'

Here then, once again, are two loves in contrast, and the question is whether they can be reconciled. They are both supported by Christian thinkers, and they both have claims to be the Christian Agape. 'Why not?' someone may say. There are, as experience shows, different levels of love, and it is quite legitimate to admit both under Christian Agape. Besides, Nygren has made into a mystery what is simple, if we consult experience and introduce a few distinctions. The fundamental movement of love may be egocentric, but so far as we experience that movement and look at our motives we find that it is anything but selfish. Or we can, if we like, remove altogether so-called selfish love out of the domain of love, as for instance one of the leading thinkers of the late Renaissance did. Suarez, who was thought in his time and by his disciples to be a second St. Thomas, divided off sharply the love which is called cupidity from charity. In his treatise on Hope and Charity he places cupidity not under Charity but Hope. 'The third opinion asserts the object of Hope to be God as the summum bonum who is lovable with the love of concupiscence as serving the interests of the lover . . . and this opinion seems to be true. And to explain it I say first that beside the love whereby God is loved by charity, there is another whereby God is loved as the perfect good of the lover and to the advantage of the lover himself, and this too is a good love. . . .' In using the word 'love' here Suarez is taking love in the common sense, though, as he says, it is not charity but a form of hope. This he makes clear as he goes on: 'It is certain that God by title of being the summum bonum and lovable for himself, is the object of charity. The reason is that it is in this that charity differs from all other kinds of affection for created good and even the affection for God himself, which belongs to concupiscence or hope; for the latter loves God as the summum bonum of the lover, whereas charity loves God for himself.' And in another place he makes his distinction equally clear: 'Although the love of benevolence does not tend to its object as being the good of the lover (for then it would be not the love of benevolence but concupiscence), there is nevertheless needed some kind of connection between the lover and the loved. For example, although I may so love my father or friend that I wish them good on their account, yet this love could not exist unless I thought of them as one with me and joined to me, as Aristotle says in the Eighth Book of the Ethics.'

This treatment of the two loves may seem to some too drastic, to others to be merely verbally important. To call egocentric love hope is but to change the name, and to make those whose love is still imperfect feel that they have been cast into outer darkness because of their lack of charity. Suarez is making a great demand on the poor lover. He wants to remove all vestiges of self, and one may wonder whether he might not be forced into an awkward corner, if this exclusion of self were taken too rigorously. So far as I can see, he would have to deny that such a splendid exclamation as that of the celebrated Père Coton deserves the name of charity because it refers to God as an object which he wants to possess: 'I thank you, O God, for what you are in yourself as the greatest good I have or can possess'. The hymn attributed to St. Francis Xavier would be more after Suarez' heart: 'I love thee, Lord, yet not because I hope for Heaven thereby; nor yet since they, who love thee not, must burn eternally. . . . Not with the hope of gaining aught: not seeking a reward; But as thyself hast loved me, O ever-loving Lord'.

This answer may be regarded as a final effort to justify ecstatic love without any reconciliation with physical or unitive love. If we are to believe Rousselot, St. Thomas long before Suarez had made an effective covenant between the two. We have already seen how Nygren interprets St. Thomas and how scandalized Burnaby is with the 'crude individualism' of the answer. Certainly St. Thomas trails his coat and makes no effort to hide his debt to the Aristotelian analysis of love and friendship. In the *Commentary on the Divine Names* he says openly that 'a thing is said to be loved, when the desire of the lover regards it as his good. The attitude or disposing of the appetite to anything so as to make it its good is called love. We love each thing in as much as it is our good'. But Rousselot claims that St. Thomas escapes the net of egocentric love, and he would say that Nygren has been misled. St. Thomas is far too much of an Aristotelian to deny that everything seeks after its own good, and that therefore man, too, does the same. But he does not stop there like Aristotle. He develops the thought until the individualistic or egoistic poison in the doctrine is all drained away. He is able to do this by his theory of unity. 'We see that (in a whole) each part by a natural tendency works for the good of the whole, even to its own risk and harm . . .; hence every creature in its own way naturally loves God more than it does itself, non-living bodies by their very nature, brute beast sensitively, but a rational creature by intellectual desire, which is called love.' (Quodl. Ia 8.) It is thus by enlarging the notion of what is meant by the word 'individual' that the change-over is effected. A piece of matter that is individual is so in the dog-in-the-manger sense that it is exclusive and private without sharing or any true intercommunication. But the higher we go in the scale of things and persons the less narrow is the meaning to be attached to the unity which a being has. A man, for instance, is more one than an animal; he has more selfhood and yet he is in closer relations with other men than an animal is with others of its species. An Angel, again, is more one than a man, because a man is only part of human nature which is shared by countless others, while an angel is by definition a complete nature in itself and therefore unique in its species. Nevertheless, an angel is more intimately in touch with other beings in the universe than a man can be. Lastly, God is perfect in His unity and yet He is present to all things and more to them than they are to themselves. Now if man is in his individuality related to others with a human nature and subordinated to some extent to the common-weal, as we all recognize, he is also by his higher self, by what may be called his personality, to distinguish it from his individuality, open to some kind of union with God, as the ultimate truth to which his mind is related, and the ultimate good which he can desire.

It is by relying on this notion of individuality and unity that St. Thomas is able to break new ground and free himself from the egocentric doctrine to which Nygren thought Aristotle and his followers were committed. 'To love God above all things and more than oneself is natural not only to an angel and man but also to every creature, according as it can love sensibly or naturally. Natural tendencies can be discerned in actions which proceed from nature and without deliberation; for thus each thing does naturally what it was born apt to do. But we see that each part by a natural inclination works to the good of the whole of which it is a part, even with risk or damage to itself; as is clear when a man puts out his hand to protect his head from a sword blow, for on the head depends the welfare of the whole body. Hence it is natural that each single part should love in its own manner the whole more than itself. Hence both on account of a natural tendency and his political virtue a good citizen exposes himself to danger of death on behalf of the common good. But it is obvious that God is the common good of the whole universe and all its parts; hence each creature in its own manner naturally loves God more than it does itself. . . .' The point of this is that the duality set up by love of self and love of God is a false one; a true love of oneself is a love of God, and a true love of God means that one cherishes oneself as part of God's purposes. Cupidity will in this account mean that one's love for oneself is exclusive, and of the part independently of the whole, whereas benevolence or altruism means that one is thinking primarily of the whole, which in this case is God, before one thinks of oneself. Putting this in another way, St. Thomas says that everything tends to its proper perfection, but as this perfection is part of a divine plan of love and itself is a likeness of God, the movement of every creature is a desire for God either unconsciously or indirectly or directly. Man follows the rule, and naturally loves God more than himself. As, however, he is a rational being, this desire is translated into consciousness and reflected there. As our mode of thinking is from perceptible objects to what is invisible, from particulars to what is general, we do not start even in consciousness with a clear knowledge of God as our ultimate end, as the love which clearly draws us. It is rather a vague feeling for the good, a kind of omnibus good, and because this is easily contrasted in our thoughts with what is obviously to the advantage of ourselves, we conceive of an opposition between what is not so immediately advantageous and what is. This leads to the distinction between egocentric and altruistic love.

But it may be said that in this theory of St. Thomas the old feud between the two loves remains and that we have only covered it with words. If, indeed, the human mind were not able to see through the apparent opposition that would indeed be true, but St. Thomas claims that by virtue of the spiritual nature of the self the opposition is overcome. We as individuals are spiritual, and a spiritual being is not enclosed in a narrow individualism. Our nature shouts out to us at every turn that we are more ourselves the more we go out in sympathy and service, and our mind is so constituted as to be at its best when it is in some sense everything. Here St. Thomas takes up and utilizes the profound doctrine of Aristotle that the intellect grows by becoming what is not itself, by, as we say, absorbing knowledge. 'An intellectual nature has more affinity with the whole than other natures; for every intellectual substance is in a sense everything, in so far that it is capable of comprehending everything in its mind.' In the species of animals which are below man the good of the individual by no means coincides with the good of the whole. They destroy in order to live, whereas the mind in knowing destroys nothing which it touches and absorbs. The animal, again, is limited in its desire by the good of the species to which it belongs; it is ready to sacrifice itself without final gain for the good of that species, as when a mother defends its cubs. But man's desires go out beyond the species and all 'the flaming ramparts of the world', and he cannot give his soul to dishonour to accomplish that universal good.

To sum up, then, this solution of St. Thomas as attributed to him by Rousselot: It rests on two principles which are closely connected. The first is that of the relation of the part to the whole. In every unity or whole the part loves itself truly when it loves itself as a part and not as a separate individual. Now God is that perfection which is distilled in the universe to which man belongs. To neglect the universe and cultivate his own garden would be the gravest of sins for a being who lives in that universe. But really it is not the universe but God to whom man owes everything in whose order he has his place and work. Everything he has and is belongs to God, and therefore he must love God more than himself and love himself truly only as belonging to God. 'Just because every creature naturally by everything that it is belongs to God, it follows that by the very movement of its nature a man or an angel must love God more than itself' (Ia, Qn. LX, a. 5.) The second principle is this, that every being is drawn by its very nature to its source and unity, and in so far as this movement can be called desire or love, it loves God more than any particular object of desire. 'Everything tends to its own good for the reason that it tends to the divine likeness and not vice versa' (III Contra Gent. c. 24). But though we are made by our very nature to tend in desire to God we can feast on ourselves and ignore our tie with the universe and God. We can be isolationists. And the reason why we can do this is that in his present condition man starts blind and has only the conception of a vague general good, which has not the same vividness as the concrete desires for what now pleases his vanity and pride. We are aware, that is, of our own particular selves and our privacy before we understand how miserable and contingent that privacy is. We feel the coin of ourselves before we recognize that it belongs to the mint of God.

In providing this solution out of the writing of St. Thomas, Rousselot has undoubtedly taken the sting out of Nygren's criticism. In the light of the systematic ordering of all creaturely desires to God and the special stress laid on the open universe of the mind of a spiritual being like man, no one can accuse St. Thomas of holding a completely egocentric doctrine. But Rousselot's view has by no means found universal acceptance. Some have accused him of misinterpreting St. Thomas, and other have found fault with the theory. In a long criticism in his *Eléments d'Ontologie* P. Pedro Descoqs tries first to improve the statement of the solution and then finds even the improvement inadequate. The distinguished Thomist scholar Etienne Gilson denies the existence of the problem. He says that the writers before St. Thomas cannot be arranged into two opposing teams. They constantly change over. Nor did St. Thomas give the final *coup de grâce* to the difficulty in developing this theory of unity and of the whole. In St. Thomas the key to the answer is to be found in his elucidation of the words of Genesis that man was made in the image of God. Now if Gilson could succeed in making good this last statement he would certainly remove one difficulty in accepting Rousselot's account as entirely satisfactory. Rousselot chooses as the nodal point of St. Thomas's explanation his theory of unity and of the whole and part. But in order to make this work a great strain has to be put upon the word 'whole'. There are different kinds of wholes, but the whole to which St. Thomas's remarks are relevant is that of the body. As St. Paul says that the hand cannot say to the head, 'I have no need of you', so in general in the organism of the body a part must act as a part of the whole organism if the organism and the part are to remain healthy. But if we apply this image of the whole and part to the relations of God and the world or the self it has no direct application. It is a metaphor with all the inconveniences of a metaphor. Even the relation between one man and another or with the State falls outside that of a part, or parts, in their relation to one another, in an organism. A citizen has certain duties to the State, but he, as a person, cannot be summed up as a member and nothing more. Man has constantly to fight against a false theory of the State which would reduce him to being a part or member of it with no personal rights and no functions outside the jurisdiction of the State. Even if we amplified the idea of the State so as to make it equal to the whole human race, we should still have to limit the rights of that State over the individual person. The image, therefore, is defective. So, too, is that which St. Thomas uses of the hand and the head. (We accept it in St. Paul because we already know that it is a metaphor and that it is impossible to put into human language the grace given to man by God. It helps to express the new unity in Christ, which gives us membership and personality under His Headship.) If we take this comparison seriously we must be careful to say that it is not the hand which sacrifices itself to protect the head, but the man who has both head and hands. This defectiveness in the comparison would be unimportant if the comparison were not the basis of the argument; but here the argument gains all its force from the comparison. We want to know how a man who is by nature bound to love himself can also love God more than himself. If it can be shown that in loving himself truly he is, in fact, loving God more than himself, then the difficulty is answered. The problem is how can this happen when appearances are against it. St. Thomas says: 'Look at an organism and you will see that there a part is nothing but a part or member of the whole, and therefore in truly loving itself it is loving not itself independently of the whole but the whole to which the part belongs utterly.' But if one objects and says, 'I am not on all fours with a part; I have an independent existence which can never be reduced to being just the part of something else'; then the answer has broken down, and the difficulty remains.

Descoqs would emend the theory as exposed by Rousselot. The love of God, he says, is, in the Thomist view, the supreme perfection of man, and therefore man tends to God. God created man out of love, and as love was the motive of men coming to be, so it is the motive which governs their return to God. Like the circulation in the blood there is a continual movement of love; what was made out of love finds its end and perfection in that love, and the degree of perfection among finite things is measured by its participation in the divine love: 'The divine goodness is the measure of existing things, for we can judge the degree of nobility in their various natures by their nearness or distance from God.' And because this seal is set upon even the lowest things, they all without exception are inspired by love. 'This good thing or the other, no matter what, is desirable just in so far forth as it is a resemblance of the primal Goodness, and everything which tends to its own perfection tends to this divine resemblance.' Now if this principle holds for all created being it is verified in particular in man, who possesses intelligence and will. By the force of his nature created out of love he tends to love God and to find his perfection in being like to God, and when he fights against himself and seeks to sacrifice himself, it is to remove all trace of that self love which would separate him from his true love and his being made like to the divine goodness. When St. Thomas speaks of unity or whole and part or participation he must be understood as trying to bring out this profound truth, that we are made out of love and belong to God in an order of love, and this order of love has its exigencies as strict as those which govern the relation of a part to the whole in an organic body.

Is this more satisfying? Yes, says Descoqs, but not even yet is it completely satisfactory. It will serve as a basis for a theory, but as it stands it is too abstract and too general. Magnificent in its general sweep it neglects what is specific to human love. All seek their good, that is true, but it still suggests that the object of desire is a thing to be possessed. Now what is peculiar to human love is that it is between persons, and the relation between persons can never be the same as that between a person and a thing. A thing can be mine in a sense which is forbidden when we think of another person; a person must give, he cannot be taken, and I must give at least as much as I receive, so far as in me lies. The Thomist analysis breaks down here, as Descoqs thinks, and he tries to prove this by a crucial example. Let us suppose, he says, that in the love of friendship my affection for another is so strong as to make him an alter ego, or that in our love of God we are rapt out of ourselves by that original Beauty of which our poor selves are such faint images. Great as this love is it is not perfect human love. Love is not perfect until it is fully disinterested, until we detach ourselves from ourselves deliberately and with the intention of forgetting ourselves in the beloved; of making of ourselves a free gift without compromise or arrière pensée, hoping thereby solely to please the beloved. 'So long as this deliberate self-sacrifice, this unqualified regard for the good of the other, without any self-interest, is absent, the last perfection of love is missing: the mother who exhausts herself in labour and suffering to save her son rejects with horror any suggestion of self-interest—even though, in fact, she finds in this self-sacrifice the purest joy it is possible to conceive.' Descoqs thinks that it is only in ecstatic love that this last perfection is to be found, and for that reason he leans to a view in which the two forms of love are merged without loss. Of this I will have much to say later; so I will content myself here by citing a passage from P. de Régnon's *Etudes sur la Trinité*, to which Descoqs refers. 'It is the distinction between natural and personal love which permits us, if I am not mistaken, to solve the famous dispute between Bossuet and Fénélon. The former of these two showed the strength of his reasoning ability, when he argued that love of self was inseparable from the notion of love; but he showed a narrow spirit in reducing to this fundamental love the disinterested love of friendship and charity. Fénélon was wrong in pretending that one could renounce altogether one's own good; but his loving mind hit on a truth, when he argued that the glory of true love consisted in its being free of all self-interest and of having its own reason and end in itself.'

Gilson, as a convinced disciple of St. Thomas, is not so ready to accept any defect in his theory. He departs, however, from Rousselot both in his account of the dispute among the early Scholastic writers and in his interpretation of St. Thomas. Rousselot, he thinks, has grossly exaggerated the division of opinion among the Christian thinkers. Almost every one of the writers, whom Rousselot quotes, can be found to have held both the unitive and the ecstatic view of love. They did not recognize the problem in the way that is supposed. 'If they suffered from any internal contradiction in this respect they were certainly not aware of the fact, and we may even ask whether, in their deepest thought, they did not always deny its legitimacy.' Nevertheless, Gilson does admit that the demand made by God that He should be loved above all things and for Himself must have struck a medieval Christian as difficult, if not impossible. He was too well aware of his own beggarly condition and of the infinite distance which separated the infinite perfection of God from his own infirmity. He had therefore to find an answer, and if Gilson be right, the answer is always fundamentally the same, whether we go to the great Cistercian writers like St. Bernard or William of St. Thierry or to St. Thomas. In St. Bernard, despite what Rousselot says, the ecstatic idea of love is present equally with the physical, and moreover in the earliest of his works, where if Rousselot's interpretation were right, it certainly should not be. The truth is that we have to understand what St. Bernard and his fellows meant by natural as opposed to ecstatic. They began with the fact that the first love of our feeble nature is to love ourselves. This is carnal love, and it is due to the condition in which we were born and in which we live. Theologically the explanation of this is the Fall of man, and cupidity is his natural lot. But though fallen, or to use the word of St. Augustine, 'bent', man still possesses high dignity and is the image of God, and for that reason is capable of eternal life (*Etiam sic aeternitatis capax*). What then must be done is for this curvature to be straightened out, for this will to be rectified, so that man obeys the true law of his nature which is the love of God. In its experience the soul will, therefore, 'feel itself both like to God and faithful to itself in as much as its aptitude for divine things subsists, but at the same time false both to God and its own true nature; and hence it is rent in twain and feeling itself still like, and seeing itself in part unlike, it conceives that horror of self which is the inner tragedy of the sinner's life'. This horror of the bent self is the *raison d'être* of the ecstatic form of love; whereas the persistence, even despite the Fall, of the substantial resemblance to God, justifies the 'physical' form of love. (It will be noticed, I hope, that Nygren's view and Gilson's differ because of their different view of the effects of the Fall. Nygren leaves nothing in man with which grace or Agape can collaborate, and so he can find no room for self-love in his concept of Christian Agape; Gilson agrees with St. Bernard and St. Thomas in holding that man is only wounded by the Fall and that therefore his high dignity remains. He naturally and rightly, therefore, loves himself.) Man has to get back to his best self and become once more a true likeness of the divine, and it is Agape which enables him to do this, to go out of himself and at the same time reach the pinnacle of human grandeur. When St. Bernard speaks of ecstatic love he never uses the word 'annihilation' without some qualification, because in his mind it is man's unlikeness to God which is being destroyed, as iron reddened in the fire seems to have become fire, though it is only purified, or as air seems filled with light but remains air. All this is beautifully stated by William of St. Thierry; 'When Thou lovest us, Thou lovest us only for Thyself, wherefore the perfect law of justice forbids us too to love anything beyond Thyself. And certainly, if but great grace be granted, he who loves God may go so far that he loves neither Thee nor himself for himself, but both Thee and himself for naught but Thee. And so he is reformed in Thine image, to which indeed Thou didst create him, Thou, who in the truth of Thy sovereign nature, and in the nature of Thy truth, canst love nothing, neither man, nor angel, nor Thyself, but for Thyself.' Gilson, therefore, with some reason, after relating this doctrine of the Cistercians, asks: 'Where then is the supposed opposition between love of God and love of self? By the aid of Agape man has had his love rectified and found the yoke of God easy; he has had the roots of the "miserable dissimilitude that divided the soul from its own true nature" uprooted. Losing that whereby it is but partially itself, it finds once more the fulness of its own being, as it was when it came from the hands of God. Where then is the supposed opposition between love of God and love of self? Man is so much more fully himself as he becomes more fully a lover of God for God's sake.'

It will be obvious from the foregoing that Gilson relies more on man as an image or resemblance of God than on the analogy of the whole and the part. He criticises Rousselot for taking the latter as central in the solution of St. Thomas. Not only is it not satisfactory in itself, but it is only incidental as an illustration which St. Thomas gives to bring out his doctrine of man. The idea which governs all the thought of St. Thomas is the Scriptural image of man as made in the likeness of the Divine. It is on this he works, and as Gilson thinks, makes with it a complete answer to the difficulty which Rousselot raised. The essence of the argument is this that as man is an image of God, in loving the image truly one loves the original, and in loving the original one loves the image in so far as it is a true likeness of the original. Gilson puts this forcibly and clearly as follows: 'For if man is an image of God, the more like God he makes himself the more he fulfils his own essence. Now God is the perfection of being, Who knows Himself integrally, and loves Himself totally. If man is fully to realize his virtualities and become integrally himself he must become this perfect image of God: a love of God for God's sake. For him whose thought moves on the plane of likeness and analogy, which is that of creation, the supposed opposition between love of self and love of God has no *raison d'être*. To say that if man of necessity loves himself he cannot love God with disinterested love, is to forget that to love God with disinterested love is man's true way of loving himself. Whatever of *amour propre* he retains, makes him so far forth different from that love of God which is God; and all love of self for the sake of self that he abandons, makes him, on the contrary, like to God. But thereby it makes himself like himself. As image, the less he resembles the less he is himself; the more he resembles the more he is himself; wherefor *to be* is, for him, to distinguish himself as little as possible, to love himself is to forget himself as much as possible. And he attains his last perfection when, remaining substantially distinct from his original, he has become no more than a subject carrying God's image.'

All the strength of this argument depends upon the analogy of image. Gilson tells us that God is the sovereign good and that all finite goods are not parts of that perfect good, but in their own intrinsic, limited perfection 'analogues of the creative Good that gave them birth'. He goes on from this to argue that the good in each creature will lie in its varying degree of resemblance to the creative Goodness. Once he has justified the use of this word 'resemblance' or image the argument moves inevitably to the conclusion drawn above. But we must ask whether behind the word 'image' lies any clear meaning which will really help to the solution of the problem of self-love as opposed to unselfish love. If the creature were literally an image of the Creator in the same sense in which a photograph or a face seen in a mirror is an image of the original, the argument would be certainly conclusive. But this is not the case. The word good is predicated analogically and not literally or equivocally of God and ourselves; this comes down to saying that though there is a slender thread of unity in meaning when we use the word 'good' of a creature, there is also a vast difference. That vast difference covers everything finite, whether we speak of a flower, a human person or an angel. All these latter differ amongst themselves and imitate the divine perfection by being what they are or what they ought to be, and they all differ vastly from that divine goodness. But if all creatures imitate the divine goodness, all in their several ways, the flower by being a flower and the angel by being an angel, we have to discover what is the proper way of being human; and so we are back at our original question, whether a human being imitates God by seeking itself and its own perfection or by going outside itself to want only God. In other words, whereas the image in the mirror or the face in the clear pool is a bare representation of the original and has no other existence of its own to complicate the problem, flowers and angels and men have their own specific way of being, their own essence, growth and singular perfection, and it is this we have to consult before we can know in what way they are supposed to imitate the divine goodness. The problem therefore still seems to be very much alive. Human beings are said to be the image of God as possessing mind and will. Why then should they not attend exclusively to the cultivation of the garden of their mind and will since they have been told that in doing so they will thereby imitate the divine perfection?

Even granted, however, that Gilson's contention is right and that by the use of the analogy of image 'physical' love and ecstatic love can be reconciled, is there not something still left over? I think that if we do not press this theory of the image it does show us the direction in which we must proceed. On a metaphysical level we can see that the exquisite work of God's hands, which is man, will be more perfect the more it responds to the divine intentions, and, as a conscious creature, is more at one in soul and mind with the divine love of it. We can compare the creature, man, to a work of art which is perfect in being both fully itself and at the same time the realization of what the artist in his love conceived it to be. The two do run together smoothly. For man to seek a perfection of his own with his eyes turned upon himself instead of upon the divine goodness and love is in the light of this metaphysical doctrine plainly wrong. He should not even seek any egotistic satisfaction and try to make profit for himself at the expense of loving God. We can translate this from metaphysics to the level of experience by saying that love is in being disinterested most perfect humanly. A lover is living at the highest pitch of his selfhood when he forgets himself to think only of the beloved. As Gilson finely says: 'Love seeks no recompense; did it do so it would at once cease to be love. But neither should it be asked to renounce joy in the possession of the thing loved; love would no longer be love if it renounced its accompanying joy. Thus all true love is at once disinterested and rewarded, or let us say rather that it could not be rewarded unless it were disinterested, because disinterestedness is its very essence.'

So fine is this panegyric of true love that the reader may well think that all has been said. But let him recall what Descoqs referred to as the last perfection of love. He said that the mother who labours and suffers to save the life of her child would be shocked if asked whether any thought of self entered into her mind. Where love is at its highest the last thread of self-interest is cut, even the joy which accompanies the self-sacrifice. Now when Gilson says that love seeks no recompense and is content with the joy inherent in giving, all trace of mercenary love has been wiped out. But it will be remembered that in the ancient divisions of love, love could be profitable, sweet or disinterested and sacrificial. The first is no longer in question, but is there not a faint memory of the second in saying that the joy in giving is enough without further recompense? And is it not possible to reach to a third and higher degree when the lover burns all his bridges and gives all that he has and is for love? It would seem that there are mysteries in the two loves of Eros and Agape still to explore, and perhaps the suggestion made by de Régnon between nature and person may help.

Before passing on, however, to the subject of friendship it will be well to summarize the progress so far made. De Rougemont argued that there were two kinds of love, Eros and Agape. These two, like the Lion and the Unicorn, were fighting each other round Europe at the beginning of the Middle Ages. He traced the two loves to two different sources. The one, Eros, was a kind of dark passion, a lawless love, the survival of a religious philosophy which has always had a certain fascination for the human mind. It rests on the belief that the earth is the abode of evil and that earthly passions are to be shunned. The soul is a fallen spark of divinity and has to be reunited with its source, and this is the reason why the soul is uneasy during its earthly exile and longs to be rid of this body of death. It courts a divine love and finds the end of its tribulation in death. This gnosis marks the highest manifestation of Eros; there are also less high manifestations, counterfeits and perversions; we see this kind of Eros in the ancient orgies and wild rites. No matter what form it takes, however, it despises the law-abiding and reasonable morality—

marriage, for example—as inculcated by Christian precept. It scorns the Heleenistic or bourgeois or Christian notion that the soul can make terms with this passing, unsubstantial world. Agape, on the other hand, according to de Rougemont, relying on the Christian belief in the incarnation of the Son of God and the redemption of man, holds that eternal life begins in this world and that time is not an unreal succession of moments which pass and perish, but a golden present which can give birth to eternal vows, permanent friendships, heroic virtue and divine love. Agape is essentially Christian, but its influence varies in different ages, and we can trace the growing influence of Eros and the paganism of our civilization in the increasing dominance of free love, romanticism and the passion for death and war.

I suggested weaknesses in this presentation of the two loves, and the criticism was confirmed by Nygren's analysis of their relation and antagonism. Nygren admitted that Eros came from the loins of the dark Indo-European religions; it hankers after the mysticisms, high or low, which they cultivate. In this he is at one with de Rougemont. But in his version a change came over Eros in the adoption of it by Plato and Neo-Platonism. It then began to express the aspiration of the soul for the infinite in order that the soul should possess the infinitely divine and inebriate itself with its life. In the working out of this ideal Eros became synonymous with egocentric love, a love which is a form of cupidity in that it searches for the perfect or for God in order to make itself blessed and everlastingly happy. This ideal is the human ideal *par excellence*, and were man left to himself, perhaps, it could not be surpassed. But, in fact, the Christian faith teaches an altogether different doctrine, one which pushes Eros back into the shadows. The true God manifests himself. He is a God of freedom and mercy, and His name is Agape. Between Him and the creature, man, there is an infinite distance, which man cannot cross. The whole of the relation between God and man depends on God, on His condescension to love whom He will and when he wills. There can be no question here of man's deserts or man seeking to love God so as to reach his own happiness. God has all the initiative; He creates the love in man, and it is with a divine Agape that man lives in God's love.

In their accounts of Eros and Agape de Rougemont and Nygren diverge from each other, and it is easy to point out defects in both. What is important is the degree of similarity, the way in which experience seems to force a distinction between two forms of love, however hard it may be to state that difference correctly. It is at this point that the analysis of Rousselot becomes important, for Rousselot continues the story of Eros and Agape, though his loves are hidden under new names, and the problem is differently stated. He confirms de Rougemont's theory that into the language of love had come in the Middle Ages a new intonation and a new emphasis. The tranquil perfection of St. Thomas's synthesis did not satisfy everyone; an alien emotion and a more extravagant passion than that which St. Thomas had domesticated continued to trouble the heart and expressed itself in many ways as the Middle Ages drew to their close. He is more sympathetic with this wild love than de Rougemont; he does not believe that it is so evil that it must necessarily be torn out and thrown away. Still less does he think that what Nygren calls egocentric love is an interloper in Christian thought and spirituality. Like Nygren, and long before Nygren wrote, he detected the presence of two conflicting loves in the tradition and theology of the Church. The conflict came to a head in the problem of how man could love God more than himself. The conflicting loves discerned by Rousselot are radically the same as the egocentric and the theocentric, which Nygren contrasts. But whereas Nygren would jettison one of them, Rousselot thinks that both are required in the Christian ideal, and he is satisfied that St. Thomas succeeded in finally reconciling their claims. He is, therefore, at one with both de Rougemont and Nygren in accepting the existence of these two tendencies and in admitting their influence in theology and literature.

APPENDIX.—ON PURE OR UNSELFISH LOVE

The question which Nygren has raised about egocentric love and its compatibility with pure, disinterested love is treated by many writers besides those mentioned in the text. An answer which commends itself to many and is supported by the writer on *Charité* in the *Dictionnaire de Théologie Catholique* distinguishes between the motive of the act of love and a necessary condition for its exercise. On this view it is impossible to separate off the love of God from what is bound up with it, namely, the good it does the lover. This being so it is absurd to try to make difficulties out of a fact which is undeniable. The two belong together, and it would be as absurd to suggest that a man is not a disinterested lover of truth because it happens that he is a better man for speaking and knowing truth. The writer in the *Dictionnaire*, M. Dublanchy, admits that it is 'a universal law that every being loves itself and seeks what is suitable for its nature'. A cat likes fish and not pebbles, a fish the water and not fire—one in each case suits, the other does not; and if an object appealed in no way to a man as good for him he could not start liking or loving it. A necessary condition, therefore, for love of any kind, even the most pure, is that it should appear as advantageous to us as human beings. 'But once this condition demanded by our nature is realized, the motive of love is truly the infinite perfection (of God) as loved for itself.' The condition does not interfere at all with the disinterestedness of our motive—and this is why, according to this author, the great Christian thinkers like St. Augustine and St. Bernard and St. Thomas keep the two together without any embarrassment. The perfect example of this is to be found in the saying of St. Bernard: 'Non enim sine praemio diligitur Deus, etsi absque praemii intuitu diligendus sit.' Equally complete is the sentiment of St. Augustine: 'Nolite aliquid a Deo quaerere, nisi Deum. Gratis amate, se solum ab illo desiderate'. For this reason he can conjoin the love of God and the happiness which follows from it without any hesitation: 'Si enim Deus est summum hominis bonum, quod negare non potestis, sequitur profecto, quoniam summum bonum appetere est bene vivere, ut nihil aliud sit bene vivere, quam toto corde, tota anima, tota mente Deum diligere'. Evidence from St. Thomas Aquinas is, also, quoted as in favour of this view. Without a doubt St. Thomas held the metaphysical principle that what we desire must in some sense be good for us. We are always, he says, moved to desire an object appetitu beatitudinis seu boni proprii; and he insists that 'dato per impossibile quod Deus non esset hominis bonum, non esset ei ratio diligendi'; and again, 'Non esset in natura alicujus quod amaret Deum, nisi ex eo quod unumquodque dependet a bono quod est Deus'. When he explicitly raises the question, whether God must be loved with the love of charity for His own sake, he replies: 'Respondeo dicendum quod ly "propter" importat habitudinem alicujus causae. Est autem quadruplex genus causae; scilicet finalis, formalis, efficiens et materialis ad quam etiam reducitur materialis dispositio quae non est causa simpliciter, sed secundum quid. Et secundum quattuor genera causarum dicitur aliquid "propter alterum" diligendum . . . Primis ergo tribus modis Deum non diligimus propter aliud, sed propter seipsum . . . Sed quarto modo potest diligi propter aliud, quia scilicet ex aliquibus aliis disponimur ad hoc quod in dilectione Dei proficiamus; puta per beneficia ab eo suscepta. . . .'

As we have seen, however, in the text St. Thomas does not leave the matter here. According to one interpretation he seeks an answer in terms of the relation of part to whole, and according to another by developing the idea of human beings as images of God. Some such further explanation is clearly necessary. The distinction between necessary condition and direct motive of love is only an interim explanation. It gives us something to think about and shows us that we need not be spreadeagled by the force of the objection, the apparent contradiction between loving God and loving ourselves at the same time. But to call one love a 'necessary condition' sounds too like a verbal escape to be wholly satisfactory. It may be suggestive, but it does not answer the question how we can love God purely because of His lovableness independently of the happiness which such a love confers upon us. The theory of the two loves does meet this difficulty.

CHAPTER FOUR

FRIENDSHIP

Some people when married gain each other. Some only lose themselves.
—G. K. CHESTERTON.

I understand now for the first time the mystery of the religion whence
was born the civilization I claim as my own: 'To bear the sin of man'.
Each man bears the sin of all men.—ANTOINE DE SAINT-EXUPÉRY.
There is no savour like that of bread shared between men.—ANTOINE
DE SAINT-EXUPÉRY.

Amor ch'a nullo amato amar perdona—DANTE.

O f the authors quoted in the last chapter, not one, with the exception of Rousselot and Gilson, believes that the answer of
St. Thomas resolves the main problems of love. Nygren under-
rates it; to him it is but the stale record of the Aristotelian philosophy;
Burnaby says that it neglects the novelty in the Christian idea of friendship, and Descoqs insists that the 'physical' and ecstatic forms of love are
really distinct and can only be united if we bring in a new relation, the
personal one, to supplement all philosophic disquisitions on love.
Certainly the background of St. Thomas is to be found in Aristotle, and
this admission looks black if, as is said, Greek philosophy is so impregnated with Eros or egocentric desire. But, in truth, Aristotle has been
underestimated. In his discussion of friendship, for instance, he reaches
up to an ideal which is strangely unlike the love of self for which he is
upbraided. In the Nicomachean Ethics he distinguishes three forms of
friendship, love based on profit, that which springs from pleasure and
that based on the permanent in us. He points out that the first dies when
the profit is gone, that the second is selfish and therefore fickle. The
young are amorous and fall in and out of love, and it makes them sickly
or mad and slaves to their desire. But the third 'is the friendship of men
who are good, and alike in virtue; for these wish well alike to each other
quâ good, and they are good in themselves. Now those who wish well
to their friends for their sake are most truly friends. . . .' Their love is
based on what is good and what is permanent. It is true, nevertheless,
that when he comes to analyse this third class more thoroughly he makes
it a form of self love. The passage is so important that I must quote it
at length. 'Friendly relations with one's neighbours, and the marks by
which friendships are defined, seem to have proceeded from a man's

relations to himself. For, first, we define a friend as one who wishes and does what is good, or seems so, for the sake of his friend, or, two, as one who wishes his friend to exist and live for his sake; which mothers do to their children, and friends do who have come into conflict. And, third, others define him as one who lives with and, fourth, has the same tastes as another, or, fifth, one who grieves and rejoices with his friend; and this too is found in mothers most of all. It is by some of these characteristics that friendship is defined.' (It will be noticed how twice he refers to a mother as an example to show what he means, and a mother's love comprises all that men mean by unselfish love.) 'Now each of these is true of the good man's relation to himself (and of all other men in so far as they think themselves good; virtue and the good man, as has been said, seem to be "the measure of every class of things")'. He then goes on to show how a man wishes for himself what is good and does so for the best part in him, his intellectual part; and above all he wishes the virtuous part of himself to live and flourish. No one would wish to possess the whole world at the expense of the best element in his own life. He thus continues with the characteristics he has mentioned, showing that they apply first of all to a man's own regard for himself, that is to say, his true self; and it would seem to follow that the best friendship is based on a noble self-love. Those who are capricious or evil cannot have this third form of love which constitutes true friendship. They are fickle and at war with themselves, and because there is nothing fine in their souls they cannot genuinely love themselves.

A little later on in the same book he returns to this question, whether a man 'should love himself most or someone else'. As usual, he accepts as a premise for his argument the common-sense view, and that, as he acknowledges, condemns those who love themselves; 'a bad man seems to do everything for his own sake, . . . while the good man acts for honour's sake, and the more so the better he is, and acts for his friend's sake, and sacrifices his own interest'. Common sense is right, but as he points out it is the evil man, who assigns to himself 'the greater share of wealth, honours and bodily pleasures', who is scorned. Such men, Aristotle maintains, do not really love themselves, for they are too depraved to seek for their true selves and love that. 'If a man were always anxious that he himself, above all things, should act justly, temperately, or in accordance with any other of the virtues, and in general were always to try to secure for himself the honourable course, no one would call such a man a lover of self or blame him'. A man exercises self-control and is praised just for honouring the rational principle within him; and 'that this is the man himself, or is more so than anything else, is plain, and also that the good man loves most this part of him. Whence it follows that he is most truly a lover of self, of another type than that which is a matter of reproach, and as different from that as living according to a rational principle is from living as passion dictates, and desiring what is noble from desiring what seems advantageous. Those then who busy themselves in an exceptional degree with noble actions all men approve and praise; and if all were to strive towards what is noble and strain every nerve to do the noblest deeds, everything would be as it should be for the common weal, and every one would secure for himself the goods that are greatest, since virtue is the greatest of goods.'

If this be a doctrine of selfishness it is a very enlightened selfishness, for it is no more and no less than an exhortation to virtue. The real catch in the doctrine is in the use of the word 'good' and its meaning when applied to the self. Those who have read him carelessly or are under the impression that he must be a hedonist or advocate of selfish love, have taken for granted that he uses words just in the same sense as we do. But there hangs over the whole of Aristotle's theory of the self a cloud of uncertainty. In other places he makes a sufficiently sharp distinction between the perishable self and a spiritual part or principle which is imperishable. But how the two are related is a matter of dispute. If we say that man is one and that he possesses a lower self and a higher self, then we have to conclude that he teaches an egocentric doctrine of a very elevated kind—so elevated, indeed, that it is doubtful whether it could not equally be called an unselfish attitude. If this were not so we should have to call Lovelace selfish for preferring honour to the charms of Lucasta. If, on the other hand, this higher principle, by which Aristotle sets so much store, be something beyond the individual man, in which that individual may share, then the love of which he speaks is not ego-centric at all. But then, why does Aristotle say that the love of self comes first? We do not know, because he does not seem to have been altogether certain himself. It is possible that without the right knowledge of God his theory was bound to be only a torso. He realized that the mind of man rose above all the claims of his lower physical and emotional nature, that it touched on what was universal and true and good in a manner to which the lower self, with its importunate and exclusively selfish desires, could not attain. Therefore he says that only a good and noble man can love himself really, and that such a love means preferring what is truly good and noble to all the solicitations of the lower self. To go so far was to justify self-love without offending common sense and common moral ideas, and that was all he set out to do in his discussion of friendship. But it may be that he had an inkling of a deeper truth, which he expressed later in the same book, in the words, we must needs, 'play the immortal so far as in us lies'. This is no selfish outburst, no outcome of a mortal passion. 'Tell me,' as a friendly interpreter paraphrases him, 'is there not a love that may spring from deeper yet, even from this, that in each of us is somewhat that is good, imperishable. . . . Truly in each man's heart, God lives. And God stirring and spreading in him, prompts him to strange actions and modes of being, unaccountable even to himself. Impulses, fears, contradictions, all unreckonable. Thus under all strife, it must be that the whole Universe of things is straining, pursuing ever, yet not what one fancies, but the One. . . . And if in friendship, it be the divine which calls to the divine and answers, solved is the riddle, whether we love our friend for his sake or for ours: or rather, for the one and truer self present in him and me. Our friend is a second self, and only the divine is thus one in many; only the utterly true and good.'[1] Here is an exaltation of Aristotle's thought, which, as the writer goes on himself to say, is only saved from pantheism by the richer doctrine of union taught by Christianity. Even as it is, the view has a curious resemblance to the Eros love of the divine, the soul of all life, the One with which the soul is to be finally fused.

Whatever the uncertainty pervading Aristotle's explanation of friendship, it is not egocentric in any mean sense of the word. It is doubtful, however, whether it can be stretched so as to accommodate within it those experiences of love which have persuaded so many that love says good-bye to all self, that it is an ecstasy and not a possession. St. Thomas so works upon the Aristotelian account that he leaves all in pure light. How account, however, for the fact that he leaves with Burnaby and others the impression that love is too impersonal and too bound up with the natural perfection of the lover to suit all its flights? Burnaby believes that St. Thomas misses a proper understanding of friendship. Friendship cannot exist between a person and a thing; it is a special relation and the love which is given and taken in it is like no other. In his Hulsean lectures, published under the title, *Amor Dei*, his main study is St. Augustine, and he is able to show that Nygren does not do full justice to the richness of that saint's doctrine of love. . . . He does allow, however, that what Nygren had distinguished as Eros and Agape do at times make uncomfortable bedfellows in St. Augustine's thought, and in his preface and concluding lectures he deals with this problem. In the preface he is quietly caustic in his comments on the determination of that school of theologians to which Archbishop Söderblom, E. Brunner, Nygren and even Karl Barth belong, to insist on 'Either—Or', instead of, for instance, von Hügel's 'Both—And', in comparing the natural and the supernatural, Greek and Christian thought, mysticism and prophetical religion and Eros and Agape. The fact that St. Augustine used Neo-Platonic ideas so much does

[1] *The Goddess of Ghosts*, by C. C. Martindale, p. 132.

not necessarily weaken his Christian contribution. It is true, Burnaby thinks, that the synthesis is incomplete, and the reason is that not sufficient use was made of a third element in love. Nygren neglects this third element completely and concentrates on the two supposed rivals, Eros and Agape, but the neglect of this third element 'constitutes a serious, perhaps a fatal defect in his whole construction. Eros and Agape are not the only words for love. The Philia in which Aristotle discovered the richest endowment of human personality is strange neither to the Old Testament nor to the New. It differs both from Eros and from Agape in being a mutual relation, a bond which links two centres of consciousness in one; and the Bible knows it not only as a human relationship, like that which binds together a David and a Jonathan. 'Behind the law of Moses stands the Covenant which makes Israel God's people and Jehovah their God; beyond the Body broken on the Cross is the love wherewith the Father loved the Son before the foundation of the world, the unity into which all the friends of the Crucified are to be made perfect: that they made may be one, even as we are one . . . that the love wherewith thou lovedst me may be in them, and I in them. There surely is the Holy of Holies of the New Testament; and Nygren, with a candour which we may admire, owns that he can make nothing of it.'

It is this combination of Philia with Caritas which creates the specific quality, for instance, of the love described by St. Bernard and even by Abelard. (Abelard, as someone has remarked, must have discovered that if his own love came from Eros and was egocentric, that of Heloise was selfless.) The Christian thinkers did not have the works of Aristotle which treated of friendship before them until the thirteenth century; but they knew well Cicero's *De Amicitia*, and in that book disinterested love is described and praised. St. Thomas, as we have seen, used as his text the Nicomachean account and fails to please either Nygren or Burnaby. Duns Scotus, who belonged to the Franciscan school, and, therefore, had a bias for the ecstatic theory of love, disagreed with St. Thomas and makes love so disinterested that it is hard to keep up with it. Even the pagan will prefer to immolate himself for what he loves and admires, and if a lesser love can demand such a sacrifice, must not the Supreme Good call out naturally from man a love which would annihilate itself if such a sacrifice were needed? In the love of God the *amor amicitiae* must necessarily regard Him as good in Himself and not as good to the human lover. The fact that we know that in loving God we taste infinite happiness is no more than accidental to the love we offer, and the proof is that we pay no attention to the sweetness or the joy of the affection and turn to active self-devotion and sacrifice. Here, as Burnaby remarks, love is so selfless as to rule out not only all Eros but even the sharing which comes in Philia.

FRIENDSHIP

(At the time of the Renaissance and Reformation, and afterwards, controversies and new philosophical theories complicated and obscured this issue of the competing claims of Eros and Agape. That both Catholic and Protestant thought was deeply affected by their view of these loves cannot be doubted. The way in which their definition of faith is formulated hinges on the refusal or acceptance of an alliance by Agape with Nygren's Greek Eros. It will be remembered how unwilling Nygren is to give the name of charity to man's loving response to God's Agape; he prefers to call it faith. So also in Catholic theology some tend to put any love of God which is self-regarding under the virtue of hope, instead of charity. Burnaby points out how Protestant thought reacted not only against the intellectual tradition in Christianity which was inherited from the Greeks, but also denied any place to mysticism in Christian spirituality. Both of these, so they suspected, indicated the presence of Eros. Furthermore—and here we have an echo of de Rougemont—they relegated mysticism to a back place because it belonged to the all-too-human Indo-European mystery religions. Christianity met the challenge of these ecstatic cults with the prophetical religion of the Old Testament which was fulfilled in the New Testament. As Dr. J. Oman insisted in his *The Natural and the Supernatural*: 'In the strict sense there is no such thing as a Christian mystic, because in so far as there is use of an historical revelation and of a Church with its cult, fellowship and active service of others, the religion is not mystical.' It is possible now to see why de Rougemont, without going to this extreme, is a little uneasy at the presence of what he calls the Eros language in the writings of so many of the great Catholic mystics, especially those of the Spanish renaissance.[1] But what of the Catholic tradition, which has always admitted the mystics and encouraged them? One answer would be to deny the supposed identity in thought and will of the Catholic and non-Christian mystic. All negroes look alike when they are seen for the first time by a white man, but time and closer acquaintance reveal infinite variation in looks. So, too, a cursory examination of the language of the mystics shows a remarkable similarity, but closer inspection bids one beware. Secondly, it is quite possible for mystics to use the same kind of language and yet to differ, and for this reason that the states they are trying to describe have no

---

[1] Those, therefore, of the Protestant religion who follow Archbishop Söderblom, Nygren, Brunner, Oman and others, have an easy task in replying to what Aldous Huxley has to say on true religion in his *Grey Eminence*. In that book Huxley argues that all true religion is a discipline in the mystical life, and that the mystical way is one and the same in all the highest forms of religion. One and all provide a technique for getting into touch with the absolute, and it is essential in all these techniques that the soul should die both to itself and to the world. Now if such mysticism is a false Eros and the counterfeit of the prophetical and revelational religion of Christianity, Aldous Huxley's impeachment of the modern Christian can be dismissed without any hearing.

language adequate to express them. Their descriptions have to be eked out by negatives and cryptic phrases, and it is easy for a set of phrases to become consecrated just because they are a serviceable coinage. This is what happened in the story of Christian mysticism. The Neo-Platonist vocabulary was taken over by the Christian writers. Moreover, what scandalizes Huxley in Catholic mysticism is precisely its differentiating mark. Huxley lays it down that the mystic must make no compromise with what is finite; he must detach himself completely from all inter-mediaries. Now he complains that Catholic mysticism, after the religious revival in France, owing greatly to the influence of de Bérulle, became Christocentric instead of theocentric; that is to say, it turned back to the humanity of Christ and by that act it committed suicide. But here, on the contrary, as both Catholic and Protestant will agree, is the crowning glory of Christian spirituality. Huxley has forgotten that Christ plays a central part in the mystical life long before the time of de Bérulle, and he has mistaken the nature of Christian mysticism. However high Eros may lift man by desire, the desire remains a finite yearning, and the closer man comes to the dark and inaccessible region of the All or the absolute the less hold can he have on his own infinitesimal being and existence. But the Christian does not begin with his own craving and rely on his own technique; he begins through an adoption into the life of Christ, and as it were, sees in and through this medium. Christ is not the object, but the way and the life; His humanity does not block our vision of God, because Christ is the Companion who first passed through the veil. We see *with* His eyes and love. This grace can be spoken of in terms of fellow-ship or communion or membership, and it continually gives life more abundantly to the graced person. He goes down in humility and rises in more and more abundant new strength, so that far from being absorbed into the divinity, he enjoys a relationship far richer than that which can be promised by any technique of fusion. St. Paul summed up this unique way of ascent at the very beginning when he wrote that, 'Ye are dead, and your life is hid with Christ in God'. And this also is the reason why we can find the first phase, the death-motif, in a mystic, whom Huxley would appropriate, like Ruysbroeck: ('We long to be a stool beneath the feet of the power of God; so shall we have an humble ear to listen to the truth and life which come from the wisdom of God and a ready hand to do His most beloved will'); and the second phase of hidden life in de Bérulle: 'Our first movement must be towards Jesus, as our fulfilment, and in this seeking for Jesus, in this adherence to Jesus, in this continual and profound dependence upon Jesus, is our life, our rest, our strength and all our power of working'.

I have said that the language and the mode of description used by

Catholics have in part been borrowed from Neo-Platonist sources. It has become the habit to take very seriously and to judge the mystics by their own psychological account of their states of soul. These states and the descriptions of them are, however, always to be measured by the rule of life, which is revealed by Christ. In a book called *The Doctrine of Spiritual Perfection* Dom. Anselm Stolz suggests that we have been too occupied with the psychology of mysticism and that it is time that we should examine it, as he would say, ontologically. By that he means not so much the basis of the experience as the design or score which the singer is expressing and interpreting. He begins by pointing out that to St. Paul the third or seventh heaven to which he had been raised was in his eyes a paradisal union with God, which can be reached now or here-after at the end of a process of purification. The process begins with baptism and is ratified in the Eucharist. Owing to sin the world has to some extent fallen under the dominion of sin and Satan, and as sin separates, man is far from God. This idea so common among the early Fathers of the Church led them to lay great stress on the Incarnation as the beginning of redemption. It was the guarantee that God was in the cosmos, liberating and harrying even Hell. In the union with Christ the self won its freedom from the old dominion—and this might show itself in rapture. The more free the self becomes the more does it approach the state of Adam in Paradise; it can see God as Adam did and have power as Adam had power over physical things and over animals. That is why in the stories of holy people so often birds and beasts, such as lions or wolves or swans, become the pets of the saints. The stages of freedom and union with God through Christ are not marked out by the inner experience as in later mystical writings, but rather in terms of paradisal power, sacramental grace and charity. If in the highest con-templation seeing by spiritual vision is emphasized, there is a like emphasis on hearing. Seeing belongs rather to eternal life after death; in this world, like Moses and the prophets and the three disciples, we hear the divine voice.

Stolz brings out the difference of treatment of an identical subject between the early and later Catholic writers in a series of contrasts. The early Church thought of God as especially the formal cause of creation, in so far as He communicates being; later writers think of creatures as primarily effects of an efficient cause. In conformity with these lines of thought the one looked on grace as restoring the essential likeness of man to God which had been lost at the Fall; the second favoured the idea of holiness, culminating in the vision of God. The difference can be seen well in the language. In modern days few talk of the robe of holiness, and when they quote the words about 'putting on' Christ they do not usually advert to the image of dress. But in the early days Christian life was not so much a growth in holiness as a putting on, an investiture, because grace was so to say a real determination, a purifying and then perfecting of the image. Dress in those days was not a mere sign of dignity; it conferred the dignity; by the reception of the habit the novice becomes not in appearance only but in reality a monk. [This idea explains the importance of old investitures and of ordination, and it was common in the pagan rites.] By these and various other examples Stolz shows the change of emphasis. But where both ancient and modern, ontological and psychological, meet is in the unanimous belief that it is through assimilation to the Christ, the perfect image of the Father, by means of the sacraments of grace and by charity, that the end of the mystical life, namely, holiness or union with God, is attained. One value, however, of the old way of stating the Christian truth is that it makes null the line of criticism followed by Aldous Huxley, and shows that mysticism can thrive not on a pagan Eros but Christian Agape.)

In St. Francis de Sales and in de Bérulle and others, however, Burnaby finds mysticism completely at one with the strictest Christian spirituality. They show, moreover, that trait of Philia which is omitted by Nygren to his great loss. In the *Traité de l'Amour de Dieu*, 'the evident aim of St. Francis is to retain the warmth and fervour of Augustine's "delighting in the Lord", while purging it of the last traces of self-reference', and this he does by a delicate use of the idea of friendship, based on a real affinity of likeness between God and the soul in grace. There is 'an incomparable correspondence between God and man, for their reciprocal perfection: not that God can receive any perfection from man, but because, as man cannot be perfected but by the divine goodness, so the divine goodness can scarcely so well exercise its perfection outside itself, as upon our humanity. The one has great want and capacity to receive good, the other great abundance and inclination to bestow it. . . . The meeting of abundance and indigence is most sweet and agreeable, and no one could scarcely have said whether the abounding good have a greater contentment in spreading and communicating itself, or the failing and needy good in receiving and drawing to itself—until our Saviour had told us that it is more blessed to give than to receive. Now where there is more blessedness there is more satisfaction; and therefore the divine goodness receives greater pleasure in giving than we in receiving.'

In passages such as these which abound in the writings of St. Francis de Sales the accent of Philia can clearly be marked, and Burnaby is right in calling attention to it. To his mind it completes the story of true love, which is bound to be ill-told if Eros and Agape are made the only characters. Fellowship or communion is the *vinculum perfectionis*; for

'God has made men apt to find their completion in communion, because such communion is a likeness of the mutual love in which and through which Three Persons are One God'. Marriage prepares us for boundless charity, for marriage is a union of love in which both give and receive and commit themselves wholly to the other. It is the Christian act and sacrament, and it protests, as de Rougemont saw, against the selfish or romantic desire of Eros. It is also a symbol of perfect Agape, the kind of Agape which is universal and all-embracing. In true love, where Philia dwells, there is no possibility of a one-way relationship. It is essentially mutual. 'Reduced to its simplest terms, the existence of love in a human being means that the eye of the spirit has opened to the sunshine of good. A man has seen that which is good, and seeing it has delighted in it. His delight is acceptable, and what is accepted is a gift; he must ask who is the giver and why should anything have been given to *him*. The only answer to that question is love. He *sees* that the gift of good can be nothing but the expression of love, and that love itself is greater than any or all of the gifts in which its activity is displayed. If greater, then more to be desired; and if he can desire above all things the gift of love, if he can truly cast out of his heart all that is contrary to love, then love will be given to him, and he will have power to return it to the giver. In such fruition of a supreme good there is supreme delight, and the delight itself is radiant, "diffusive of itself", creative.'

Is this the final answer to the problem of love? Burnaby has taken the problem away from the conflicting claims of Eros and Agape and introduced a third constituent, Friendship or Philia. Already in the writings of the medieval Christian writers the idea of friendship had been entertained, but its depths had not been sounded. They had adapted the Greek treatment of it to Christian theology, and so left it still with the taint of egocentrism. But Burnaby goes to the New Testament and his Philia is drawn primarily not from Aristotelian Ethics but from the divine discourse in the Fourth Gospel at the Last Supper. There is no finishing touch needed to that discourse; it says everything that can be said of love, if we would know the heights to which it can attain, the love of God for man and how men through God's help can and should love their neighbour. We may, if we like, differ from Burnaby at times in his analysis of it, and with some of the conclusions he draws from it, but the picture is there, and it is the final masterpiece. Therefore we cannot look further if we wish to know how to love and how God wills us to love. But though Burnaby does reproduce for us in pages of great beauty the superiority of this love and its inimitable perfection, he does leave many of the problems with which we started unanswered. What is a problem is met and *solvitur ambulando*, by showing us how the saints loved and how the love which is in the Holy Trinity is the supreme example which is copied in the love wherewith Christ loves us and we love one another. But we still lack a theory which embraces the various aspects of love and brings them into a consistent pattern; we still want to know how Eros and Agape are reconciled with one another without loss and how they can be joined up in Philia; and lastly, we must seek the reason why love between persons should form a union of friendship which differs so much from the love of things or of nature or even of the Absolute.

What then is clear is that the true relation of Eros and Agape must be understood in the light of Philia. The idea of Philia is common among ancients and moderns alike, but its significance wanes or waxes according as the meaning and value of human personality is neglected or appreciated. Christianity awakened the world to a new reverence for personality and the potential glory which it possesses. It would seem, then, quite likely that in probing this notion of personality and in looking at its fruits in a new fellowship and sense of community a deeper knowledge of love might be gained. Already de Rougemont fastened on to the ideal of marriage as typical of Christian Agape, and in commenting on Rousselot's solution to the problem of egocentric desire Descoqs and de Régnon made a distinction between human nature and personality which looked important. In recent years especially among writers of the Phenomeno-logical school of philosophy, great attention has been given to the difference between two sets of formulae. The one is called the 'I'—'It', and the other the 'I'—'Thou'. Amongst the best-known books on this subject is one entitled, *I and Thou*, by Martin Buber (translated by Ronald Gregor Smith). The point of these distinctions is obvious once the distinction is made. When I am confronted with a person I react quite differently from when I am concerned with things; I cannot know nor desire nor love a thing in the same way as I do a person, and this difference is summed up in these formulae. Now at first sight this distinction seems most promising, for here if anywhere we should expect a new and refreshing analysis of Philia and be able to track down the secrets of love But, alas! Buber, despite the many imaginative and fascinating things he has to say, tells us very little about the nature of love. Here, however, are some of the points he makes.

'It' is the world of things over against the 'I'. Now 'man travels over the surface of things and experiences them. He extracts knowledge about their constitution from them: he wins an experience from them.' ' "It" does nothing to the experience itself; that is ours and the world has no part in it, save that it allows itself to be experienced. When we say "It" we mean also other persons in so far as we treat them as things. The scientist, the doctor, the philosopher, the economist, the employer, all usually do this, and in our ordinary life our acquaintances are experienced not as persons but as things. Whenever, in fact, we use the third person we are doing this'. Buber readily admits that we must so act, and says that the 'I'—'Thou' relation must be continually passing into the impersonal, though it can be revived. 'As soon as the relation has been worked out or has been permeated with a means, the Thou becomes an object among objects—perhaps the chief, but still one of them, fixed in its size and its limits'. He takes as an example an artist at work. In the moment of artistic creation I am under the command of the form which is present in a most live way to my mind. I reproduce it, but almost in the very act I 'lead the form across—into the world of "It" '. 'The same holds true of love; what is at the present moment 'Thou' is bound to become 'He', 'a sum of qualities, a given quantity with a certain shape'.

So fatal is it to regard all life as an 'I'—'It' experience that Buber seems at moments to disparage it utterly. But this is only by comparison with the 'I'—'Thou' relation. In fact, we have to live with the help of both, and if the 'It' has its defects it also has its virtues. Without it we should have no order, no series of events, no things and events bounded by other things and events, no reliable world, having density and duration. It is good to have a world which remains as long as we wish, which remains a total stranger, whether it is experienced within or without us. 'You perceive it, take it to yourself as the "truth", and it lets itself be taken; but it does not give itself to you'. (It is worth pointing out that this is the language of Eros, in the sense that knowing means taking and possessing, and that the objects loved do not give themselves to us.) 'Only concerning it may you make yourself "understood" with others; it is ready, though attached to everyone in a different way, to be an object common to you all. But you cannot meet others in it. You cannot hold on to life without it, its reliability sustains you; but should you die in it, your grave would be nothingness.' In another comparison Buber thinks of it as the chrysalis to the butterfly. But though right in its place the 'I'—'It' experience all too easily becomes totalitarian, and we escape to it from the heights to which love calls us. We are content to have pinned the person down in his story and secured his words in the library. 'They have codified, in exactly the same way, the fulfilment or the breaking of the law. Nor are they niggards with admiration and even idolatry, amply mixed with psychology, as befits modern man. O lonely Face like a star in the night, O living Finger laid on an unheeding brow, a fainter echoing footstep!' As St. Augustine said that the Platonists saw truth but from afar off and knew not the living Face of the Incarnation, so those who turn to 'It' instead of saying 'Thou', serve society by scientific experiments, co-ordinating data, admiring specimens and surrendering the present for past history. A culture can arise only when there is a 'Thou' at the beginning of it to draw the soul out of itself and inflame it. As time goes on the culture dies down into an ember; it is content to live in the past instead of being continually creative. It surrenders to a smooth causality, to trends and the weight of the past, to karma. 'Where hitherto a heaven was established in a law, manifest to the senses, raising its light arch from which the spindle of necessity hangs, the wandering stars now rule in senseless and oppressive night. It was necessary only to give oneself to Diké, the heavenly "way", which means also our way, in order to dwell with free heart in the universal bounds of fate. But now, whatever we do, we are laden with the whole burden of the dead weight of the world, with fate that does not know spirit. The storming desire for salvation is unsatisfied after manifold attempts, till it is stilled by one who learns to escape the cycle of births, or by one who saves the souls, that have fallen to alien powers, into the freedom of the children of God.'

Such is the experience of 'It'. But 'if I face a human being as my Thou, and say the primary word I-Thou to him, he is not a thing among things, and does not consist of things.' This human being is not addressed in the third person, is not 'a nature to be experienced and described'; 'but with no neighbour, and whole in himself, he is Thou and fills the heaven. . . . All else lives in *his* light'. Buber says that the word 'experience' is wrong when used of a Thou; there is a relation, but it is one of meeting. 'The primary word I-Thou can be spoken only with the whole being. Concentration and fusion into the whole being can never take place through my agency, nor can it ever take place without me. I become through my relation to the Thou; as I become *I*, I say Thou. All real living is meeting.' One consequence of this condensed hyperbole is that no human being can be really himself in a world of things; to reach his proper selfhood he has to meet another whom he addresses as Thou. In crying out, 'Thou', he is for the first time himself, an 'I'. If this be so, true love can never be understood save as a meeting of persons in a friendship; and the result of that friendship is that each becomes perfect in bowing to the other. In other words, egocentrism exists only when we love things; it disappears when we address another as Thou. Buber says this in his own way in a passage which bears closely on the problem of Eros and Agape. 'Feelings are "entertained": love comes to pass. Feelings dwell in man; but man dwells in his love. That is no metaphor, but the actual truth. Love does not cling to the I in such a way as to have the Thou only for its "content", its object; but love is *between* I and Thou. The man who does not know this, with his very being know this, does not know love; even though he ascribes to it the feelings he lives through, experiences, enjoys and expresses. Love ranges in its effect through the whole world. In the eyes of him who takes his stand in love, and gazes out of it, men are cut free from their entanglement in bustling activity. . . . Love is responsibility of an I for a Thou. In this lies the likeness . . . of all who love, from the smallest to the greatest and from the blessedly protected man, whose life is rounded in that of a loved being, to him who is all his life nailed to a cross and who ventures to bring himself to the dreadful point—to love *all men*.'

Buber sketches how in infancy the child takes note of the world and has to find for itself the meaning of that world. The world is a *thing* which has to be conquered gradually, but all the time the child tries to establish relation with it in terms of the Thou, though, of course, it has no language nor full consciousness of what it is seeking. But 'the development of the soul in the child is inextricably bound up with that of the longing for the Thou, with the satisfaction and the disappointment of this longing, with the game of his experiments and the tragic seriousness of his perplexity.' When finally the child does meet the Thou it becomes then properly an I itself. That is to say, the presence of the Thou insures the reality and plenitude of the I. This doctrine will have nothing to do with the mysticism of absorption. In the Eros of de Rougemont and Nygren alike only one tended to remain at the end of love's story. In the East the self dies in the dark night of fusion; in Neo-Platonism the soul is an emanation of the One and returns to it, or if, as has happened in the West, the self preens itself, that idealized self alone is left in the final stage. But Buber is resolute in maintaining that the duality is never overcome. Those who 'in the passion of the engrossing Eros are so enraptured by the miracle of the embrace' that they think the duality of I and Thou has been overcome are mistaken. What they call a union which dissolves all difference is 'the dynamic of relation itself'. Persons do not absorb each other. If we think that the perfection of love is absorption we are making a twofold error. First, we have fallen back into the experience of things, of essences (to this doctrine I will return later), and, secondly, we have perverted the true idea of love and followed the false trail of Tristram. Far better to accept the Christian truth and symbol of marriage. . . . 'When a man is together with his wife the longing of the eternal hills blows round about them' . . . and also to accept the earth and one's place in it. The self which will not accept any of these things and either exploits all that is given to him or makes the grand refusal, is preparing for himself a solitude of hell or extinction.

In treating his theme Buber is more suggestive than analytical, more perceptive than philosophical, but all that he does say goes to confirm what has so far been tentatively put forward. Karl Heim, in his *God*

Transcendent, takes up the distinctions which Buber has made and develops them more thoroughly. His main concern, however, is not with the problem of love, but with our relation with God. There are, however, various points which he tries to make on the way which are relevant. Accepting the distinctions of the 'I'—'It' and the 'I'—'Thou', he remarks how mysterious and obsessing has been to all thinking mankind the nature of this invisible centre-point of our being, the Self. I am able to separate myself off from the world and my fellow beings and to be alone with myself. This power has been a source both of pride and misery, of hope and despair. The Faustian Ego is filled with pride and joy and thinks the world belongs to it. The Ego of Kant 'recognizes itself as the vehicle of unconditional law'. The Ego of Fichte is conscious of its absolute freedom and power of determination. 'Buddhism sees in the separate being of the individual Ego, in its unhappy thirst for existence, the cause of all the misery of the world; and it strives for a state in which the petty self may be extinguished in order to vanish in a greater Self'. Others seek to lose themselves in some community or whole, to be the slaves of some régime and allow their individuality to 'melt away like a soft candle under a scorching flame'. Now the first truth which must be accepted about the Ego is that the I can never become an object to itself. 'I can never set myself over against myself.' When I try to do so there is always something left over, or rather the dual character of the self remains; otherwise the experiment could not even be tried. Now if the Ego can never be a thing, then most important results follow. One of these results is that the self which I examine is not my present self which is in process of becoming. Like everything which belongs to the world of objects, of 'It', it is something which has already happened. All on the side of the object is a *caput mortuum*. In this Heim agrees with Buber, for Buber tells us that 'in so far as a man is satisfied with the things he experiences and uses, he lives in the past, and for him the moment as it comes and goes has no quality of presentness. He possesses nothing but objects, and the being of objects is that of something which *has* been'. Heim's description of this is that we see a series of photographs which have been completed. We may think that we see a butterfly emerging or a chicken appearing from an egg, but what we really see is 'on the contrary, only the instantaneous pictures, which we photograph, as it were, in continuous succession'. Now if the Ego can never be reduced to the status of an object, but stands outside Space and Time, then empirical or scientific or materialist accounts of it are bound to fail. We have freed it. But if it is really outside time, then it is a supertemporal spectator and have we not made it into a 'lonely, world-free, nature-estranged monad soul', which may have strayed or fallen into this world, as the mystery religions taught and the catharist heresy held? Such a soul would but long for a return to the One and for fusion with it. Heim rejects this conception of the self or Ego, and sets it not outside time but as that which is in process of becoming as opposed to that which is measurable and is past and done with. 'The nature of the Ego', he writes, 'implies presentness, becoming, the note of the Not-yet-decided. Therefore the Ego is altogether involved in time.' But for this to be true and sound we must distinguish between that objective succession of Time, the past as it unrolls itself before us, and real lived Time, whose key words are the 'Already Decided' and that which 'is in process of being decided'. Here is a fitting human destiny, a life which moves between the already accomplished, the unalterable and what I now have with all my will and love to do and be, which is not yet decided. This latter is the present, and opens up the possibility of meeting and addressing another Thou. Not that this lived time is cut off from the time of the 'It'. What Heim calls the 'Object-Space' is 'the same universe seen from the other side'.

In thus, successfully, as he thinks, showing how the Ego is not outside time, Heim concludes that 'the Platonic conception is superseded. I am no longer to be regarded as a denizen of supermundane spheres, fallen like a star out of heaven into the soulless world of matter, there to play for a brief while the part of a sojourner. This Platonic self-interpretation of the Ego, the ground of an aristocratic attitude to life, lives on, if in an attenuated form, even in Gogarten's "Self that can never be objective", and in Heidegger's Dasein (existence in the way in which the Ego exists) as distinguished from mere Vorhandensein (existence in the way in which the world of objects exists). But it cannot persist when once we have recognized that the non-objective Subject is not contrasted with the Object simply as something different in kind, and when we have ceased to be so afraid of speculation that we dare not draw the consequence and recognize that the two infinitudes are, in spite of their being incapable of union, nevertheless in some wholly inapprehensible fashion dimensionally united. Understanding this, I come back from Plato's aristocratic exaltation of the Ego to the sober knowledge of the Self found in the Biblical writings. Then I recognize once and for all the truth I am not the creature of a different sphere from the objective world set over against me. I am a piece of "world". I belong with the cosmos to one Whole with a universal destiny.'

By this means the distinction between the 'I' and the 'It' is overcome. As to the relations between the 'I' and the 'Thou', Heim says that they meet because they act on one another. In my becoming I come up against what is not dead but alive, and so much more than alive that the opposition is one of wills. 'Your will is for me a being-acted-upon by a will opposed to mine, and my will for you is a being-acted-upon by a will opposed to yours. I am aware of you as a will with which I must settle accounts, and you are aware of me in the same fashion.' Now this tension can only be resolved in two ways, either by one submitting to the authority of the other, or by a voluntary agreement to share in comradeship and co-opera-tion. The two then become of one heart and one mind and enjoy great happiness and freedom. If it is asked how they come to agree, the answer is by means of the Word, which is the medium of intercourse. The 'Thou' which made its immediate presence felt in the tension breaks the silence, which hides it, by a Word. But, be it observed, this Word is not the language of the past, of impersonal observations and scientific or con-ventional communication. It is only the Word when two persons meet in the present, when they are both in process of making a decision and determining the shape of the future.

Heim has much more to say about the relation of the Ego to God the Transcendent, but an analysis and discussion of it would lie outside the scope of this book. I need not even criticize the argument upon which Heim relies to establish his conclusions. His method of approach is that of the phenomenologists, and his argument is influenced by his desire to overcome what he thinks to be the two main contemporary errors about God and the self. Writing in the early thirties of this century he could not but be aware of the movement among his German fellow-countrymen to divinize the race and 'be as gods'. It is interesting that he should call this movement the rise of the 'Prometheus that is in Aryan man', the rebellion of the Titans against God and the attempt to usurp His divinity. In Heim's eyes the old medieval conceptions which were once satisfactory have gone altogether now that the knowledge of the Universe has changed. He tries to show that inevitably man has come to look upon God and man as part of the Universe or else take refuge in a false and pantheistic mysticism. There seems to be no alternative save that of materialism or idealism, and no destiny for man except to share the lot of other ephemeral things or become as God himself. Fichte provides the example of an hypertrophied ego and has proved to be the prototype of far too many. But close behind, if not beside, this egotism rides a horseman who is nihilist and ready for death. Heim thinks that these two attitudes follow naturally on the current conceptions of the world and the self, and he believes that these conceptions are wrong and that his working out of the 'I'—'It' and the 'I'—'Thou' modes of relation gives the Christian and true answer.

I do not think that the light he tries to throw on a dark place is so illuminating, but then I do not think that the place is as dark as he pretends. If we are to believe Heim the world as we know it now is so different from that of the past that former philosophies about it are bound to be out of date. The thought which has been built on the new discoveries leads to nihilism and therefore without his fresh formulation of the data we stand condemned. But I do not see that the discoveries of science require any such Copernican revolution in philosophy. What Plato said, or Augustine or Descartes, need not be ephemeral or just opportunist. Truth is not the appanage of any particular time or place. If Heim were right another revolution in science might put his answer out of court. But I am sure that he thinks it more than a provisional one—and what holds true for him holds true for past thinkers. He has lumped all past thinkers together and dumped them into the waste-paper box. If he had said that the current fashionable philosophies led to the dilemma with which, as he says, we are presented, the comment would at least be plausible. But there is no reason to suppose that a past philosophy may not have possessed enough truth and wisdom to keep the Christian conceptions of God and man alive and effective. The fact is that Heim is unduly influenced by the Kantian philosophy, and what he has to say is too dependent upon the truth of Kant's distinctions. Once the world of spirit has been cut off from that of sensible experience, both suffer at the hands of philosophers and theologians. They stand 'aloof, the scars remaining, Like cliffs which had been rent asunder, a dreary sea now flows between'. Materialism tries to make the best of one cliff and Idealism of the other, and the spirit of man flits over the intervening waters, like a soul in purgatory. On which side are its origin and destiny? And if it be with spirit and so with God, how can we be sure that there is a transcendent God with Whom we can enter into relation? The spiritual geniuses of the last hundred years have twisted and turned to find an answer, and as they have assumed the Kantian dichotomy they seldom give comfort. In their turn the phenomenologists have invented this distinction of the 'I'—'It' and the 'I'—'Thou'. But in developing the distinction they have been forced to take up some very exposed positions. Is it true that the world of 'It' is necessarily of the past and what-is-done-with? Is there not the simplest of bridges between the 'I' and the 'It'; and is the ego in the peculiar relation to time assigned to it by Heim? I do not think that any of these views are correct. It seems to me quite certain that I can, for instance, look at my present self in the mirror, that I can be aware that at this moment I am sitting on a chair and looking at a typewriter, and that I am not conscious of a past pressure of my hands when I now put them together. Nor is there this gulf between myself as object and myself as subject. There is undoubtedly a distinction between the two and what I know of myself at any moment does not envelop all that I am. But this incompleteness in my knowledge is no ground for making myself as object and as subject strangers to one another.

There is no need, however, to urge these criticisms because they do not affect the issue in mind. Whether Heim's general view be right or wrong the points he makes are valuable in unmasking Eros and providing material for a final answer to the problem of love. He, like so many others, has the impression that the two extremes we have to fear nowadays are a swollen egotism and a nihilism of defeat. The one shows itself in the absolute claims of individuals to lord it over others and to proclaim the advent of individual or racial supermen; and the second is seen in the growing subjection of man and the false mysticism which eliminates all personal survival. Over and over again these two temptations of the human spirit crop up. There must be some weakness in us, some reversion to tendencies which are not fully human, to make men in every age incline to titanic aggressiveness or to contentment in extinction. Heim reinforces the argument against such tendencies by his insistence on the personal element in human relations. We may sink our personality in things or exploit them to our own selfish ends, but we cannot do that once we address another person by calling him 'Thou'. There is at once set up a new circulation, a new sharing, which others have described by the name of friendship or Philia. And in this new relation the persons do not love their personality at the expense of each other. To say so would be to miss the very heart of the relationship and to drop back into an inferior experience, which is that of things. The suggestion is that the old terms of egocentrism are no longer suitable. A proper appreciation both of what the Ego is and what the 'Thou' is makes egocentrism impossible. The only way we can react to the presence of another is by submission to his will or by co-operative action (though here Heim seems to be thinking more of the transcendent God than of fellow men).

Heim does not let us into the secret of why persons should behave as he says they must behave. It may be that in his opinion there can be no intellectual answer. Reason is all very well for objects, for consideration of the past, for scientific analysis of things, but what is not an experience but a meeting, not a discussion but an address, cannot be put down on paper, like a philosophic report. The attitude of thinkers, like Heim and Buber, is, as I have suggested, influenced by Kant's distinction of two realms, one where human reason can work, and the other where faith must take its place. In the nineteenth century this theme has been played with a large number of variations, and what is called the 'existential' school of philosophy has found in the behaviour of the 'I' a way of salvation to God away from the dull categories of the human mind. I do not think that the way does, in fact, lead to salvation, but so much

FRIENDSHIP

careful inspection of the layers of the self, so much attention to the spiritual exigencies of the Ego, are not without profit to all of us. We can use them even though we do what they forbid us and try to find a rational explanation of our love of God and of our relation with Him and with our fellow men.

CHAPTER FIVE

REASON AND WILL

And if we demand intellect of the artist rather than ratiocination the artist may also demand it of his customers. His final word will be 'Tastes differ, but not right tastes; and moral notions, but not right moral notions'.—
ERIC GILL.

> She knapped 'em o' the coxcombs with a stick
> And cried, 'Down, wantons, down.'
> —SHAKESPEARE.

> Above all things I would be one of those
> Who drive with wild black horses thro' the night,
> Torches like hair uplifted in affright
> When the great wind of their wild hunting blows.
>
> .   .   .   .   .
>
> Houses behind us fall upon their knees,
> Alleys cringe crookedly before our train,
> Squares break in flight: we summon and we seize:
> We ride and our great horses rush like rain.
> —R. M. RILKE.

Two elements co-operate in the culture of those knights of the spirit (Plato's philosopher-kings). The perfect State contains them, as two complementary stages of education: 'philosophical logos mixed with music'. Together, they are the two supreme forces of the Greek genius.
—*Paideia*, vol. II, by WERNER JAEGER.

The views of Buber and Heim which I have just examined can be traced in part to the Kantian philosophy and the Romantic movement which followed it. That Romantic movement, as always, manifested its genius in an out-of-school joy, in playing truant from reason with its dull rules and categories. The leading absolute idealists, such as Hegel, had tried to cover the gap which Kant had made between thought and reality by elevating mind to the place of God; mind had the supreme power of positing nature and the whole objective world and bringing it back again to its source by a dialectical movement. But in this attempt they were forced to introduce other factors, such as the will and struggle. The transition, for instance, in Fichte, from the Absolute Ego to the Prussian State is straightforward. 'The whole system of our ideas', he says in the *Wissenschaftslehre*, 'depends on our impulses and our will', and this will has to struggle against the world of non-egos and over the mere individual Ego. Schelling, a more imaginative genius, is driven to place tension or discord even in Absolute Spirit, something which is not God and can be called evil-to-be-overcome within God himself. Hence in his *Philosophie der Mythologie* he tries to show how there is a constant reconciliation of opposites in the development of the religious consciousness. Such high fancies favoured the growth of romanticism and abetted the abdication of the mind in favour of the will. The dialectic of opposites, however, remains and is made use of throughout the nineteenth century by thinkers who move far away from the thought of these idealists.

The breakdown of the rationalist philosophies gave the romanticists their opportunity, and they rebelled against the pretentious sanity of reason and chose to find emancipation in some new word like 'will' or 'existence'. Schopenhauer is the herald of this movement of pessimistic romanticism. To him Wagner and Nietzsche, for instance, are beholden, and it is worth noting that with Wagner the motif of the Tristram myth returns. Indeed, there is more than a superficial likeness between this romantic movement and that which de Rougemont describes in his *Passion and Society*, and we can read his interpretation of Eros all too easily into the ideas of German romanticism. In this movement are to be found the same strange traits, the love for death, the refusal to accept life as it is, the longing for what is absent, the Manichaean struggle between the good and the bad principles, and the lure of the strange and the ecstatic. Quite early in life Schopenhauer compared his pessimism with the Eastern ideas he had studied. 'In my seventeenth year . . . I was as possessed by the sorrow of the world as was Buddha in his youth at the sight of illness, old age, pain and death.' We know that he read widely in translations from the literature of the Hindus, and even found in Plato ideas which were sympathetic with his own feelings. The rift already to be found in Fichte and Schelling is made the centre of his solution to life. Our thought tells us nothing of the nature of reality; it gives us only phenomena. But behind thought is will, and it is will which gives us the innermost essence of reality. He does not prove this; he just asserts it, and because of his own pessimistic temperament he declares that this will is a dark force or power. Just as Bernard Shaw invents a Life Force, so too with equal imaginative certainty Schopenhauer posits a will. Their creation, however, is coloured by their temperaments; the same monster is advertised by one as a gospel of joy and by the other as a sentence of death. This will is never very clearly conceived. It is an universal impulse or striving and it breaks out into contrary effects, which clash with one another and bring about the suffering and evil in the world. This will is common to beast and man, and it governs all action and all movement.

Its principle is self-preservation, and it is seen in all our pleasures and pains, our fears and our hopes and our loves and our hates. It is also blind and irrational, and it gives birth to mind which recreates the world as its idea. All human beings are this will in operation, and for that reason they seek their own self-preservation, not freely, but under the compulsion of nature. With mind, however, there arises a sore conflict because the mind tends to think of life as good and to hold out to the self gay hopes and the promise of a future peace. But this optimism is false and the tragedy of man is in this, that he can conceive of bliss and never attain it; he works under the delusion that life is good, and the grim reality is that it is blind and profitless. There is one escape, however, and that is by a kind of self-denial (a reminiscence of Hindu resignation); and in art man can find a surcease from the weary struggle by losing himself in contemplation. Religion, too, is a mode of deliverance, because religion teaches man to be ascetic and to die.

The barest summary of the Schopenhauerian philosophy will suffice, because its value does not lie in the cogency of the reasoning, but in its correspondence with certain ever-recurring moods of man and in its influence on succeeding thinkers and poets. Once the reason and the will had become divorced, romance had its holiday of dionysiac excitement, and strange shapes began to appear. Eros, in de Rougemont's definition of it, proceeds through lawlessness and egoism to self-destruction. From another point of view Santayana dismisses the disciples of irrational romanticism as heralds of barbarism. 'It was', he writes in *Poetry and Religion*, 'a capital error in Fichte and Schopenhauer to assign essential fertility to the will in the creation of ideas.' 'The passions are naturally blind, and the poverty of the imagination, when left alone, is absolute. The passions may ferment as they will, they never can breed an idea out of their own energy.' 'The alleged fertility of the will is . . . disproved by experience. . . . The passions discover, they do not create, their occasions. . . . The ripeness of the passions may thus precede the information of the mind and lead to groping in by-paths without issue; a phenomenon which appears not only in the obscure individual whose abnormalities the world ignores, but also in the starved, half-educated genius that pours the whole fire of his soul into trivial arts or grotesque superstitions. The hysterical forms of music and religion are the refuge of an idealism that has lost its way; the waste and failures of life flow largely in those channels. The carnal temptations of youth are incidents of the same maladaptation, when passions assert themselves before the conventional order of society can allow them physical satisfaction, and long before philosophy or religion can hope to transform them into fuel for its own sacrificial flames.'

There is no mistaking here the contempt of the mind soaked in the traditional wisdom of the West for the barbarism which neglects reason and order. 'Reason is necessary to the perception of high beauty. Discipline is indispensable to art. Works from which these qualities are absent must be barbaric; it can have no ideal form and must appeal to us only through the sensuousness and profusion of its materials.' He singles out as examples of this barbarism Walt Whitman and Browning, but it would have been just as easy for him to take many of the other writers of the nineteenth and twentieth centuries. The divorce of will and emotion from reason has lasted a long while, and it may be that some of the dry forms of recent painting and poetry are a protest against it. But it is worth pointing out here, as there may be no opportunity of returning to Santayana's criticism, that Santayana himself exemplifies the opposite fault to that which he condemns. He himself has chosen to live among the Platonic essences and to repose in them as myths which have no real relation to existence. In place of the reality which the will demands, he has cultivated the garden of art and poetry and found in it a substitute for that reality which he thinks too boorish for the humanistic life. This is of great interest to the argument of this book, because it tends to show that essence and existence, mind and will, Eros and Agape must not be kept separate; neither of them should be exalted at the expense of the other. We have seen that Nygren failed in this, and that the theologians of the 'existential' school were struggling with their stiff 'either-or' and failing as a result to reconcile the world of 'it' with the relation of the 'I'—'Thou'. The same sorry story can be read in the works of so many others who clung to Hegelian rationalism and its progeny, scientific rationalism and Marxism, or to the Schopenhauerian will.

'The act of willing, and effort, which is its essence, are like an insatiable thirst. Life is but a struggle for existence with the certainty of being conquered. To will without motive, for ever suffering, then to die, and so on for century after century, until the crust of this planet of ours crumbles away, this is Life.' In these words of Schopenhauer, which gave him a kind of macabre joy, we can almost see the flames consuming the Valhalla of Wagner's *Gotterdämmerung*. Nietzsche imbibed the pessimism of Schopenhauer when he was a student at Leipzig, and as art was the one resource against the futility of thought, and music the highest fulfilment of art, it is no wonder that he turned to Wagner for all that he at first desired. Wagner, moreover, had turned the ancient mythology of the North into opera, and this was in accord with Schelling's principle that man could be saved not by philosophy but in a mythology which translated the ideal into act. 'The myth is not based on a thought, as the children of an artificial education suppose: but is itself a kind of thinking, which imparts a conception of the world, but imparts it in a sequence of events, acts and sufferings.' So many of the aspirations and despairs of the nordic romantics of the nineteenth century are summed up in Nietzsche that he might almost be called their outsize totem figure. He despises the conventional morality and religion; life is to be found in the freedom of the passions. 'To attack the passions at the root is to assail the roots of life.' The old frenzy of the mystery religions is the way of salvation. 'Almost everywhere it is madness which paves the way for the new thought that breaks through the barrier of revered usage and superstition.' He is incoherent as being possessed from one moment to another by those opposites which the German idealists had proclaimed to be the dialectic of truth. He is night and morning, the lion and the unicorn, St. Michael and Satan, prophet and demon. Like a horseman of the Apocalypse he rides to death chanting the joys of unbridled life. As the advocate of madness and passion he is inspired by Eros, as de Rougemont understands it, but he is also the supreme egoist whom Nygren condemns as the enemy of Agape.

In one of his letters J. Yeats writes that 'the greater the pain, the greater the pleasure—the immortal and the mortal in everlasting embrace —a nuptial embrace—not sterile'. The misery of Nietzsche was that he lived in an age and under influences which prevented him from com- bining into any rich truth the great loves and desires of his nature. Each of the opposites in him broke loose on its own account and could give a brilliant improvisation. He is the supreme example of egoism and at the same time generous; he hates religion and comes down from Sinai with new tablets; he is all for novelty, and nevertheless he preaches the old eastern doctrine of despair, the doctrine of the everlasting return. The ego throws off all disguises when he declares that 'I follow new paths and there cometh to me a new language; like all the creators, I was tired with the ancient tongues'. But the pessimism which is inherent in the dark Eros is stirred by early memories associated with religion. 'Hell has certainly not remained merely an empty sound.' Dreadful omens appear to him; perhaps he sees a stork holding a snake in its beak, and hesitating to swallow it. Or all nature suddenly becomes pale; or bright and fiery colours appear across the surface of the earth, or the ghosts of dead relations approach him, with features showing traces of dreadful suffer- ings; or the dark walls of the room in which the man is sleeping are suddenly lighted up, and there, amidst a yellow flame, he perceives instruments of torture and a motley horde of snakes and devils. 'Christi- anity has surely turned this world of ours into a fearful habitation by raising the crucifix in all parts, and thereby proclaimed the earth to be a place "where the just man is tortured to death" . . . Let us never forget that it was Christianity which first turned the death bed into a bed or agony, and that, by the scenes which took place there and the terrifying sounds which were made possible there for the first time, it has poisoned the senses and the blood of innumerable witnesses and their children.'

The Christian faith rightly taught is the exact antitoxin for such pagan fears of death, but we have to suppose that Nietzsche must have learnt of Christianity from some polluted source. As a relief from the nightmare it is no wonder if he imagined a new world guided by Apollo to joy and exquisite form and inspired by Dionysus to dance to new music. For a while the mythology of Wagner beguiled him, but when he discovered that Wagner was not prepared to accept him as an equal and that the music of Wagner was more bewitching than exalting, he looked elsewhere. 'Wagner est un névrosé.' He wished to break away from all this, to leave the twilight of the gods and pass out into the sunshine, to that divine table, the earth, trembling with new creative dictums and die-casts of the gods.' 'I wish to pass over the wide seas like a voice or a cry of joy—even until I find the Isles of the Blessed where dwell my loved ones.' The answer of Eros lay in the self, in egoism; the 'good and healthy egoism which springs from the strong soul—from the strong soul united to a superior body, to a beautiful body triumphing and strengthening. The egoistic joy of such body, of such soul, is named Virtue.'

This new ideal was pursued in book after book. In *Menschliches, allzu Menschliches*, he detected an enemy in all idealism; he attacked the accepted view of the saint, because it encouraged faith and pity. These so-called virtues were the outcome of a diseased society, a society which in its desperate efforts to escape its own ruin invented remedies which only hastened its death—remedies drawn from the World Beyond. 'It was fatigue and weariness which created the Beyond; the fatigue, which, with one bound—and a fatal bound—wishes to reach the last things—a poor ignorant fatigue, which no longer even wishes to will.' In his next books, *The Dawn of Day* and *The Joyful Wisdom*, he develops the same theme; the Superman reaches his zenith, and is saluted in the prose poem, *Thus Spoke Zarathustra*. A more critical justification is attempted in *Beyond Good and Evil* and in the *Genealogy of Morals*. 'This "I"—this most royal being, speaks of the body, even when it dreams, and exalts itself, flying with bruised wings.' 'My "I" has taught me a new pride; I teach it to men; not to hide one's head in the sands of heavenly things, but to bear it proudly, an earthly head which creates the meaning of this earth.' But inevitably the Ego coarsens, and the results of the worship of the self, its strength and power, begin to show themselves. We know too well now the cult of naked power. Nietzsche at his best is far from advocating the excesses of the doctrine of the Superman. He was far too sensitive and imaginative to have anything but detestation for the brutality of the German at the mercy of his passion. But his imagination betrayed him. 'You will have to pardon my occasionally chanting a paean of war. Horribly clangs its silvery bow. And although it comes along like the night, war is nevertheless Apollo, the true divinity for consecrating and purifying the State.' Being far different in fact from this imaginative conception of the Superman and the Ego, the genuine Nietzsche, like all men, stirred as they are by Agape as well as by Eros, can break out into such beautiful passages as the following: 'But to live without a name and even to be slightly sneered at. . . . A physician, as it were, of the poor in spirit, helping this one and that one whose head is troubled with opinions, without the latter perceiving who has actually helped him. Without any desire to appear to be in the right in the presence of his patient or to carry off a victory. . . . To be like an obscure and unknown inn which turns no one away who is in need, but which is afterwards forgotten and laughed at. To be without any advantages over others—neither possessing better food nor purer air nor a more cheerful mind—but always to be giving away, returning, communicating and becoming poorer. To know how to be humble in order to be accessible to many people and humiliating to none. To take a great deal of injustice on his shoulders, and creep through the cracks and crannies of all kinds of errors, in order that we may reach some obscure souls on their secret paths. Ever in possession of some kind of love and some kind of egoism and self-enjoyment. In possession of power, and at the same time hidden and resigned. Constantly basking in the sunshine and sweetness of grace, and yet knowing that quite near to us stands the ladder leading to the sublime. That would be life. That would indeed be a reason for a long life.'

The very virtues which Nietzsche affected to despise make their reappearance here, modesty and humility, self-restraint and pity. He writes as if he were giving his answer to the problem of egocentric and theocentric love instead of preaching the Superman. But he does wish to remain 'in possession of power', and this flaw in his answer explains why he put so little check on the outrageous delineation of the Superman. He always wanted to be one of the Cyclopean architects of the future, to be a Titan. And the more he indulged in this fancy the cruder did the image of the Ego become. The Ego despises the weak and the ignorant. 'The ignorant, to be sure, the people, they are like a river on which a boat floateth along; and in the boat sit the estimates of value, solemn and disguised.' The philosophers are pretentious fools. 'I like not these coquettish bugs with an insatiable ambition to smell of the Infinite, until eventually the Infinite smells of them.' Of the psychologists—those of the English brand—he writes: 'But I am told that it is simply a case of old, frigid and tedious frogs crawling and hopping around men and inside them, as if they were as thoroughly at home there as they would be in a swamp'. We have heard what he thought of the priestly class. What is worse is that as the Superman took more and more hold of him he came to think of the submissive, the masses, as fitted only to be slaves. 'The misery of those who live by labour must be made yet more rigorous, in order that a few Olympian men may create a world of art.'

Such a view meant that his mind under the stress of passion was out of all control, and the inevitable followed. The pessimism comes back with a vengeance; the dead worlds of science begin to rule the Supermen. 'Life is a plurality of forces bound by a common nutritive process, a lasting form of forces, establishing processes in which the various contending forces on their part grow unequally. . . . It is essentially appropriation, injury, conquest of the strange and weak, suppression, obtrusion of its own forms, incorporation and at last exploitation. Life is essentially amoral.' This is the old pessimism of Schopenhauer, and, as might be expected, what is the symbol and sure sign of despair and death makes its appearance in the doctrine of the 'everlasting recurrence'. In the Orphic mysteries the emancipated soul sung of having escaped from the wheel of necessity. The wheel image is always the symbol of helplessness, whether it be that man is carried round and round upon it or slain upon it. Egoism has tired of its revolt and gives up the ghost.

In Nietzsche the motifs of Eros and Agape which have shown considerable variation in the writers so far discussed, come together and manifest more clearly than ever before their characteristics and mutual relations. If we keep Agape for heavenly love, then Eros keeps flitting uneasily between an inordinate love of self and a despair of self so violent that desire exhausts itself in one last act of self-abdication and death. This, as I hope to show, is not the final analysis nor the correct one. Agape in man, when God so wills, is far above such weakness, but if she is the free woman, there is also Agar the Egyptian, by whom Abraham has a son, and this bondwoman, as her name signifies, is a slave and a daughter of sorrow. It is she who welcomes death, and not Eros. But for the moment, let us keep to the borrowed language which seems to assign to Eros the pride as well as the abjection of human beings. Yet, in order to bring out the significance of the writers still to be studied, it will be well to anticipate and hint that the egocentric tendency is associated with what is virile and masculine, whereas the yielding movement of the soul is thought of as feminine. That the two should coexist in every man and in every woman is consistent with such a division of roles. In Nietzsche the masculine and egoistic note is so pronounced and exaggerated as to give us an admirably clear idea of its nature. It may begin with magnanimity and high pride, but as it develops it turns more and more to solitude and to violence; it begins to show itself as the rapacious and usurping tyrant to whom all must be subject. On the other hand, in the divorce of reason and passion in the nineteenth century it is not too difficult to see the very opposite of this monstrous egoism developing and bringing with it melancholy and despair. The will to live weakens and the soul of man begins to devour itself and be half in love with its own degradation and slavery. Man is no longer the glory of creation; he sneers at high thoughts of himself, and as Baudelaire said, is 'at home in dishonour as a fish in water'. Death, the dark monster, is caressed and wooed.

Nietzsche told the Germans so much about themselves and their dreams, that he could not fail to influence their literature and outlook. Some time passed, however, before he was fully recognized in France and England. But the name of the early friend of Nietzsche, Wagner, appears constantly in the writings of the French romantics and pessimists. At the height of his egoism Nietzsche dismissed Wagner, as we have seen, as *un névrosé*. Posterity must judge which of the two is the greater subject for pathos, Nietzsche shouting on the hilltops the glories of the Superman and ending his life in collapse, and drumming with his fingers in everlasting repetition, or Wagner, who begins with that most symbolical of stories, the *Flying Dutchman*, so like to the legend of the Wandering Jew, the recreator of the fatal stories of Siegfried and Tristram and at the close chanting the twilight music of *Parsifal*. To de Rougemont, Wagner represents in the nineteenth century the old Eros of the Gnostics.

> *Now fades the world with all its glamours,*
> *Life in holiest loving, never more to waken,*
> *Truest, deepest soul's desire.*
> *Away in the night to draw thee hence,*
> *Where delusion's dreaded dream should vanish,*
> *With thee to drink eternal love:*
> *With me ever made one,*
> *Thee unto death I doomed.*

This *motif* of death recurs again and again in the French romantics and pessimists, who found in Wagner an inspiration second only to Edgar Poe. In France, however, as contrasted with Germany, the note of pessimism is challenged by that of the Catholic faith, and in this respect nineteenth century France is like to early medieval Europe. Baudelaire, Villiers de l'Isle Adam, Barbey d'Aurévilly, Verlaine and Huysmans and so many others having in their very bones the memory or the latent strength of faith, do not bend over so far in their homage to death and destruction. They are sick in soul and take a pleasure in their sickness, but they do not salute the night in mad ecstasy. Their evidence is therefore ambiguous, and in quoting some of it, I must ask the reader to remember this. Their work, however, is a phase which ends in Gide and Proust in France, and in England, where the defences were weaker, in the surrender of D. H. Lawrence and the mystical absorption of Aldous Huxley. In Baudelaire the images of death and the tomb and night occur again and again. 'Dans une ténébreuse et profonde unité, Vaste comme la nuit. . . .'

> *Mon âme est un tombeau que, mauvais cénobite,*
> *Depuis l'éternité je parcours et j'habite,*
> *Rien n'embellit les murs de ce cloître odieux.*

or again:

> *L'irrésistible Nuit établit son empire,*
> *Noire, humide, funeste et pleine de frissons;*
> *Une odeur de tombeau dans les ténèbres nage. . . .*

But, though he would not write of such things if he had not taste for them, it is more the notes of despair and ennui which predominate, 'une oasis d'horreur dans un désert d'ennui', and it is this ennui which takes on the proportions in his mind of immortality:

> *L'Ennui, fruit de la morne incuriosité,*
> *Prend les proportions de l'immortalité.*

Villiers de l'Isle Adam had such a passion for the music of Wagner that at times he uses a language which resembles that of the 'passion for death'. 'For that which thou callest the universe is nothing but the result of this pretence of which the secret is in thee. Escape then from this gaol-world, thou offspring of prisoners. Free thyself from this doom of Becoming. . . . But decide that it is hard to become a God again—and pass into nothingness: for this very thought, if thou dwellest upon it, becomes base, it contains a sterile hesitation.'[1] But no Wagnerite could have turned away from this thought of self-annihilation and fusion to pen such words as these:

> *Si nous n'aimons plus rien, pas même nos jeunesses,*
> *Si nos coeurs sont remplis d'inutiles tristesses,*
> *S'il ne nous reste rien ni des Dieux ni des Rois,*
> *Comme un dernier flambeau, gardons au moins la Croix.*

These French writers are torn in two, and their agony is well

[1] This translation and the other passages are taken from *The Influence of Baudelaire* by G. Turquet-Milnes.

expressed by the image of Louis Bertrand: 'Desert that no longer hears the voice of John the Baptist. Desert where no longer dwell the hermit and the dove. Even so is my soul a waste, where on the brink of the abyss, one hand stretched out towards life, and the other towards death, I utter a despairing sob.' Barbey d'Aurévilly compares himself to a Laocoon: 'Are we not all Laocoons in life? Have we not all of us our serpents stealing out from the blue sea to seize us—like thee, Laocoon—at the very moment of a fine sacrifice, at the joyous foot of some altar? . . . Our sons, Laocoon, are our thoughts, our hopes, our dreams, our love, fallen victims to destiny before us, prey of those dread serpents who glide into our life unnoticed till they glide into our hearts and we have no time to escape.' Alone perhaps in Verlaine can we find that complete collapse which is love à rebours, a love which wants to be slain, a love which delights in dying dans un frisson farouche:

> Le sang de mon vieux coeur n'a fait qu'un jet vermeil,
> Puis s'est évaporé sur les fleurs au soleil.
> L'ombre éteignit mes yeux, un cri vint à ma bouche
> Et mon coeur est mort dans un frisson farouche.

Through all this French writing of the nineteenth century we can see in the background the Christian faith, like a brazen serpent in the desert. In the twentieth century it becomes less and less visible, and in England, if we except the Irish writers, the cult becomes avowedly for the pagan and for the primitive. Massis, in his *Défense de l'Occident*, puts his finger on one of the chief characteristics of the twilight of romanticism: 'All the characters presented to us by the young writers are recognizable by one trait—they have no centre . . . and this produces a strange similarity amongst them which serves to differentiate them from all human types which have existed in French literature down to the present day. . . . Never do they make an effort to concentrate their sensibility on one point; their sincerity is completely material, and the spirit plays no part in it at all. Not only have their minds and wills no distinct object, but it seems as if the subject writing were in search for some undiscoverable ego; as though modern subjectivism were bent on ending finally in a complete disintegration, a total resorption into the original chaos. So might one say that these characters arose out of the dissociations of a morbid psychology and were no longer in quest of any personal identity, in which they believed. . . .' This flight to irrationalism and sensation and an earthly or ghostly mysticism has been called by Julian Benda 'la Trahison des Clercs'. Another characteristic has been duly noted by Wyndham Lewis when he says that 'very naturally, sensation left to itself tends to get monopolized by the dominant current of sex'. For the modern writer 'desires in the deepest way to see everything converted into terms of sex, to have everything and everybody on that violent, scented, cloying and unreal plane, where there is nothing that cannot be handled, the very substance of illusion sniffed at and tasted by everybody, and put to the uses of sensation. In that world most of the values of the intellect are reversed.' Wyndham Lewis, in writing this, was thinking of Proust and Sherwood Anderson and D. H. Lawrence. They like what is dark more than what is fair, the sheer sensational more than what is controlled and the primitive in preference to the cultures, the 'Aztec blood sacrifices, mystical and savage abandonments of the self, abstract sex-rage', the intoxicating embrace of mother earth when man returns to it as to the womb.

As so often happens, these strange literary outpourings have been accompanied by a philosophy which justifies them. Whether the philosophy of Freud and Jung determined the thought of a generation or is itself partly a rationalization of it, need not concern us. The fact is that they mimic and bow to each other. The poet and painter can point to the modern psychology as a piece of scientifically drawn-up evidence to prove what he portrays, and the psychologist can wave his hand to the abundant evidence in the writing around him and take his cases for analysis from the victims of modern reading and contemporary experience.

But Freud and Jung are more than scientific commentators of present manners. They put into terms of scientific hypotheses much that concerns our problem of Eros and Agape, though they know not the word, Agape. That does not matter, because the names of Eros and Agape have so far been given to what appears to be two forms of desire and love, though there is no unanimity among writers as to the role which should be apportioned to either nor how they should be separated the one from the other. All that can be asserted so far with some confidence is that our love is not simple, that it is divided and often disturbed by a civil war. This war breaks out and expresses itself in the rivalry of a quiet or mad love, Dionysiac or Apolline, irrational or rational, romantic or Christian, in pride or abasement, in taking or giving, exploiting or surrendering, in egocentrism or theocentrism, in longing to possess life and that more abundantly, or in death and fusion with something greater. As I have said, which of these loves is Eros and which Agape is still to be determined. But now we have more than a suggestion offered to us. What is put forward with all the majesty of a definitive science tells us that there is an instinct of life and an instinct of death. This conclusion comes from the Freudian analysis of the Unconscious. In his *New Introductory Lectures* Freud corrects some of the conclusions to which he had come, and gives a summary of the latest advances in Freudian analysis up to 1932.

'We suppose that there are two fundamentally different kinds of instincts, the sexual instincts in the widest sense of the word (Eros, if you prefer that name) and the aggressive instincts, whose name is destruction When it is put like that, you will hardly think of it as anything new; it looks as though it were a theoretical glorification of the commonplace opposition between love and hate, which may perhaps coincide with the polarity of attraction and repulsion which physics postulates for the inorganic world.' Whether it be obvious or not, he goes on, there is a striking reluctance to accept it. The reason is that people like to think of human nature as being entirely good, whereas science shows unfortunately that this is far from being true. Men like to inflict pain and to be aggressive and they take pleasure too in suffering. These so-called aberrations are really typical of what we incline to do, and the right interpretation of much evidence suggests a fusion of Eros and aggressiveness, that this fusion 'is typical and that all the instinctual impulses that we can study are made up of such fusions or alloys of the two kinds of instincts. Naturally they are to be found mixed in the greatest variety of proportions.' When Eros and the aggressive instinct are fused they commonly are directed outwards, but it may happen that the aggression may be thwarted and not find satisfaction without. 'It may then perhaps turn back, and increase the amount of self-destructiveness within. We shall see that this actually occurs, and that it is an event of great importance. It would seem that aggression when it is impeded entails serious injury, and that we have to destroy other things and other people, in order not to destroy ourselves, in order to protect ourselves from the tendency to self-destruction.' The poets do speak of such a way of behaviour, and the idea is not 'foreign to physiology, where we find, for instance, the mucous membrane of the stomach digesting itself'. Is this more than a very tentative hypothesis? Yes, because 'the instincts do not only dominate mental life but vegetative life as well, and these organic instincts display a characteristic', which gives us the rule for instructive action. The organic instincts are always directed 'towards a reinstatement of an earlier state of things'. This is the rule of 'repetition-compulsion'. Whenever a given state of things is upset there arises an instinct to recreate it. 'Embryology, for instance, is nothing but a repetition-compulsion; stretching far back in the animal series we find a capacity to form afresh organs which have been lost, and the instinct of recovery, to which, alongside of our therapeutic activities, we owe our power of healing, may be the remains of this capacity. . . .' Freud gives as examples of this rule, which expresses the conservative nature of instincts, the spawning migrations of fish and also the migrations of birds, and he points too to the habit in human beings of reproducing in dreams their earliest experiences, even though these experiences run counter to the pleasure principle which rules our life. 'Outside analysis, too, one can observe the same thing. There are people who, all their lives, repeat, to their own detriment, the same reactions, without any correction, or who seem to be dogged by a relentless ill fortune, though a closer investigation shows that they are unwittingly bringing this ill fortune upon themselves.'

It is this conservative tendency which explains the death-instinct. On the hypothesis that life supervened on non-living matter and organized it, we are bound to suppose that there will be a tendency in the organized matter to return to its original state, 'to re-establish the inorganic state of things. If in this instinct we recognize the impulse to self-destruction of our hypothesis, then we can regard that impulse as the manifestation of a *death-instinct*, which can never be absent in any vital process. And now the instincts in which we believe separate themselves into two groups: the erotic instincts, which are always trying to collect living substance together into ever-larger unities, and the death instincts which act against that tendency, and try to bring living matter back into an inorganic condition. The co-operation and opposition of these two forces produce the phenomena of life to which death puts an end'. If it be said that this is a mere echo of Schopenhauer, Freud replies that Schopenhauer did have an inkling of the truth and that many another genius has brushed it with his imaginative intuition. But, in fact, this doctrine corrects Schopenhauer because it reveals that there is an instinct of life which that of death only accompanies. There is not one instinct, but two, and they both mingle in the vital process. But here in his lectures Freud stops and says that it is for future investigation to work out their relations. 'How the two mingle in the vital process, how the death instinct is pressed into the service of Eros, especially when it is turned outwards in the form of aggressiveness—these are problems which remain for future investigation.'

Apposite as this distinction is, it must be confessed that Freud has here built up his theory on the vaguest of hypotheses. He takes an example from the bodily organism of what he calls the 'repetition-compulsion'. This in itself is not very sharply defined. An organism when disturbed does strive to get back into a state of equilibrium and health. Again, when a habit is imposed on an organism there is a tendency, until the habit is firmly established, to a retrograde movement. Once the habit is established it tends to repeat itself, and in turn resists new habits being imposed upon it. This is all very obvious. Something similar can be observed in psychical and mental processes. We speak of psychical mechanisms and of the mind becoming stereotyped; we watch ourselves and others growing into a routine which, the older we get, the less do we like to have disturbed. But how out of this can we infer that there is present in us a death instinct? The migratory habits of birds do not seem to be remotely connected with what we want. Moreover, in order to reach his conclusion Freud has to make the hypothesis that life is formed out of dead matter and that the living organism has a tendency to go back to the inanimate stage. If he meant merely that tissues wear out and that there is within the organism a principle—so to call it—of decay and dissolution, most might readily assent to the view. But to insert an instinct for death is to go beyond the premises and the evidence; and we may well ask how an instinct, which belongs to the living, can have any craving for an inorganic state of which it can have, of course, no memory, and feel no association. It would be intelligible for a sensitive organism which includes within its unity apparent vegetative processes to have a tendency to degrade itself to the vegetative, but there is such a gulf between the organic and the inanimate that to bridge them with an instinct seems merely fanciful. Lastly, the unitive instinct is ascribed to the erotic and the death instinct to the aggressive. This is very strange, because the only evidence which Freud uses is drawn from perversions of the erotic instincts. Truth to tell, Freud has not in the passages which I have quoted given all the reasons which have driven him to his hypothesis. The decisive argument in his mind seems to have been the evidence for carnal self-love, which goes by the name of narcissism. He thought that the evidence proved that this form of self-love was normal and a phase through which all individual human beings pass. If this be true, he knew that he would have to recast his theory. He now was bound to hold that the ego was the reservoir not only of what he called the ego-instincts but also of the erotic instincts, seeing that the latter arose within the individual independently of any external stimulation. He had, therefore, to find some way of differentiating the ego from the erotic instincts, and to do this he fell back on the new distinction of the life and death instincts. A fundamental hypothesis of all psycho-analysis is psychic conflict, and this entails there being within us at least two forces which can conflict and be to each other as attraction and repulsion are in electricity. Within each individual, therefore, is an attraction to life and also a repulsion.

Once taken over, this theory became all too convenient an instrument to explain everything. He even tries to interpret judgements of knowledge, that is to say, affirmation and negation, by means of it. 'Judging has been systematically developed out of what was in the first instance introduction into the ego or expulsion from the ego carried out according to the pleasure-principle. Its polarity appears to correspond to the opposition between the two groups of instincts which we have assumed to exist. Affirmation, as being a substitute for union, belongs to Eros:

while negation, the derivative of expulsion, belongs to the instinct of destruction.' Such an explanation is bound to be nonsense since it reduces all knowledge, including the statements in the quotation, to derivatives of instincts, and therefore to something below the level of knowing. But apart from this the attempt to exploit these instincts to explain a new number of problems makes them so vague as to be useless for scientific purposes. As Dalbiez writes in his *Psychoanalytical Method and the Doctrine of Freud*: 'So far as the life-instinct is concerned, this concept has obviously become so general that it has lost all essential association with sexuality. . . . The death instinct also seems to be a thoroughly confused concept. The tendency of a whole to its own destruction is conceivable in either of two ways. A first instance is that of a tendency of the parts, regarded simply as parts, to regain their independence in relation to the whole. The whole would be regarded as a unity of superimposition, which never becomes successfully imposed, as an extrinsic super-order which sooner or later must fail. If the death instinct meant nothing more, we should have no objection to raise against Freud. It is quite obvious that the being's chemical constituents exist just as well apart from as within him. But this would be a minimist interpretation of Freud's thought. The second instance is that of a tendency of the whole, regarded simply as a whole, to self-destruction. Here we are dealing with something inconceivable. If the concept of a death instinct has any semblance of intelligibility, it owes it entirely to the idea of the emancipation of the parts in relation to the whole. When this explanation is excluded, and the death instinct is conceived as a tendency of the whole, regarded simply as a whole, to its own destruction, we are confronted with the unintelligible pure and simple.'

This is a severe criticism by one who is well disposed to Freud, and we shall later see how far it is justified. An inorganic whole can clearly have no instinct to its own destruction, but it is not so clear that there may not be a latent tendency to non-being in organisms. But be that as it may, what is certain is that Freud has given no proper explanation of his two instincts. Indeed, he is precluded from giving an intelligible account by his exaggeration of the pleasure principle. To him it is a dogma which he never sufficiently questions: 'it is simply the pleasure principle which draws up the programme of life's purpose. This principle dominates the operation of the mental apparatus from the very beginning; there can be no doubt about its efficiency, and yet its programme is in conflict with the whole world, with the macrocosm as much as with the microcosm. It simply cannot be put into execution, the whole constitution of things runs counter to it; one might say the intention that man should be "happy" is not included in the scheme of "Creation". What is called happiness in its narrower sense comes from the satisfaction—most often instantaneous—of pent-up needs which have reached great intensity, and can by its very nature only be a transitory experience.' With this unduly pessimistic admonition we can leave Freud, recording only his recognition of a dual form of desire, one positive and the other negative, one towards life and the other towards death.

Jung has so much to say about myth and religious symbols that his views seem to have almost a direct bearing on Eros and Agape. And indeed, despite the obsession which makes him force the most obvious story or symbol to suit his theory, he does, when the chaff has been winnowed from the wheat, leave much which it is useful to gather. In his *The Integration of the Personality* he tells us that the ancient alchemists were nearer to the central truth of the Psyche than Faust and Nietzsche with his Superman. In the age of the Enlightenment and 'in the age of scientific rationalism what was the psyche? The psyche was "what I know". There was no psyche outside the ego. Inevitably, then, the ego identified itself with contents restored to the psyche by the withdrawal of the projection.' (By 'projection' Jung means the habit of externalizing in myth and symbol the figures or archetypes of the unconscious.) 'Gone were the times when the pysche was still for the most part "outside the body"—and still "imagined those greater things" that the body could not grasp. The contents of the former projection must now appear as personal possessions, as delusive fantasy pictures belonging to the ego consciousness. The fire was chilled into air, and the air became the wind of Zarathustra and caused an inflation of consciousness that can apparently be checked only by the most terrible catastrophes to civilization—nothing less than the deluge with which the gods visited inhospitable humanity.' By an 'inflated consciousness' Jung means exaggerated egoism, which as he goes on to say, inevitably destroys itself. The war of 1914–18 was such a catastrophe, due, according to this theory, to the inability of man to make terms with his unconscious and so integrate his personality. There are two grave mistakes which can be committed, the one is to give up all control by the conscious ego and surrender to the unconscious, the other is to ignore the unconscious and assume that the total personality is comprised by the conscious ego. (These, as we have seen, are the two ways of Eros, the pride and conscious assertiveness of Nygren's egocentric man and the romantic barbarism of de Rougemont's Tristram.) Now in past ages the unconscious was able to influence the ego by externalizing itself in myth and fairy tale and in various sorties of the imagination. But in modern times the ego has come to be identified with conscious thought or mind. When asked in what personality consisted many philosophers answered self-consciousness. Jung, who takes the word 'ego' as equivalent to self-consciousness, distinguishes between the ego and the personality or the whole self, and his point is that disaster follows the claim of the ego to be the whole personality. I need not point out that the traditional view of personality never made the mistake of identifying the person with the self-conscious, and Christian thought is therefore so far in agreement with Jung. But when Jung goes on to assert that religion and the doctrines and symbols of religion are projections of the unconscious and that the archetypes of the unconscious reappear in constantly similar images in religious history and in mythology, he generalizes in an unscientific way and far too carelessly misinterprets evidence to prove his argument. He is of opinion that for some time the myths and symbols, as he calls them, of Christianity, have ceased to be more than dead memories: 'the more we are accustomed to them, the more has constant usage polished them smooth, so that what remains of them is banal superficiality, clothed in almost senseless paradoxes'. But he hopes that as once people were gripped by Christian ideas, so now they may be attracted to the East, to the 'grandiose conceptions of divinity in India and the abysms of Taoistic philosophy in China.' In the last twenty years poets and artists have obeyed Jung's request, and they have stood under modern tauroboliums and tasted of blood and initiated themselves in Aztec or Hindu mysteries. They do not show any signs of having integrated their personalities by such habits and ways of thought, nor do the events of the last few years suggest that the healing of society lies in the direction suggested by Jung.

Jung, then, distinguishes between the conscious ego and the unconscious. Of this latter he is not prepared to say that it has any centre. It is too disordered in its behaviour to allow us to have any certainty about it. Hartmann thinks that it has a cosmic centre. Janet, in attributing to it only what has passed through consciousness and been discarded by it, is, in Jung's opinion, surely wrong, for the unconscious is capable of springing such surprises on us, and at time it shows contents which can never have been in the mind; and what is more, it can never be integrated into the ego. In dealing with neurotic cases we may succeed in integrating the contents of the unconscious and the ego, and when this is done the patient is healed. But this is not so in many cases of insanity. Here we have contents revealed which belong to a world apart. Instead of this kind of unconscious being drawn up into the conscious, the danger is that the conscious may be dragged down into the unconscious. From evidence of this kind Jung concludes that besides the ego there is a strange world existing below it and that it is timeless, and that even with normal persons it projects itself into his dreams and imaginings by means of images which belong to the childhood of the world. There the long experience of the human race is installed, there the age-old consciousness is 'in potentia', to use the exact expression of Jung. It is more life than thought, a life of many colours and violent and amoral. The conscious ego emerges from this unconscious, and we see in the history of primitive tribes how fearful they were lest they should be sucked back into the dread life from which they had sprung. Their magic, their sorceries, their taboos and their rituals were protective devices against the dark mystery which they projected outside themselves into nature. But if the ego arose from the unconscious, must there not have been some kind of a centre in the unconscious? To this question Jung answers that he does not know; that there may have been a centre which has been lost; that the West would wish to restore all in a super ego, but the East in seeking for an unconscious state of perfection may be nearer to that which has been lost. But though psychological analysis cannot give us any certainty here, it does seem to point to traces of personality. The reason for saying this is that the unconscious does personify. Just as biologically in each human being there is both a masculine and feminine element, so too the unconscious forces on us a distinction of what Jung calls the anima and the animus. These two are undoubtedly primordial figures or archetypes, which are so surely projected that they cannot be dismissed as arbitrary or accidental.[1] Theyhave to be accepted as natural archetypes of the uncon-scious, and amongst the principal. In fact, Jung enumerates only three, the shadow, the anima and the old man. As the shadow fades off into the anima, and the old man bears a certain likeness to the wiser part of our conscious life, we can do Jung little injustice if we concentrate on these two, the anima and the animus.

Having in this way sharply separated the conscious and the uncon-scious, Jung asks how it is possible to put these two 'halves' together, halves which are so incongruous and stubbornly separatist. We know how the rationalist dislikes the irrational element creeping in, and the ordinary traditional advice is to control the passions by the reason. This is so firmly taught by Plato and Aristotle that it has become part and parcel of our education, and many of us think that the spiritual heritage of the West, the clerisy as Middleton Murry or the 'fonction des clercs' as Julien Benda would say, is at this moment threatened by the barbarism

[1] To those not well acquainted with psycho-analytic terms the word 'projection' and its meaning may be puzzling. Jung says that an unconscious happening that is not grasped by consciousness nevertheless portrays itself somehow and somewhere—for instance in dreams, visions and fantasies. In *The Psychology of the Unconscious* he says again that 'the projection consists in the repressing of the conflict into the unconscious and the setting forth of the repressed contents into seeming objectivity, which is also the formula of paranoia'. The element of truth in this is, I think, that in phantasy a wish may easily be described in story and symbol, and the more childlike our imagination is the more effortless is the process. But obviously any number of dubious and even false suggestions and hypotheses are covered by the general term of 'projection'.

of the libido in man. Jung admits rather drily that the past masters of the art of domination in the East—the yogis—'wind up with samadhi, an ecstatic condition that seems equivalent to an unconscious state. The fact that they call our unconscious the universal consciousness, does not change things in the least: in their case the unconscious has devoured the ego-consciousness'. On the other hand he confesses that in the West 'while our intellect has been achieving colossal things, our spiritual dwelling has fallen to pieces. We are thoroughly convinced that even with the latest and largest reflecting telescope, now being built in America, men will discover behind the farthest nebulae no empyrean where fire and water intermingle; and we know that our sight will wander despairingly through the emptiness of immeasurable extension. . . . The spirit, indeed, may claim the patria potestas over the soul, but not so the earth-born intellect, which is man's sword and hammer, and not a creator of spiritual worlds, a father of the soul.'

Having, like Solomon, ordered the cutting in half of human nature, Jung has set himself a false problem of how to bring the halves together again. But there is no need to accept his general view nor his wild surmises in order to profit from what he has to say. His magnifying glass does distort but it does reveal. Most of us realize that in the fairy tales and in the myths and fantasies there is much that is suggestive though partially hidden. It is to these that the psycho-analysts have turned, and though they have been fanatic and wild in their interpretations, they have thrown light upon their meaning. The method of analysis, has, as Jung insists in *The Psychology of the Unconscious*, 'showed us that there are typical cycles. The stutterer imagines that he is a great orator. The truth of this, Demosthenes, thanks to his energy, has proven. The poor man imagines himself to be a millionaire, the child an adult. The conquered fight out victorious battles with the conqueror; the unfit torments or delights himself with ambitious plans. We imagine that which we lack.' So, too, crude and now forbidden symbols and fantasies, which once upon a time flourished, slumber still within the soul and are by no means dead. 'That which was once so strong as to give rise to a worship among a highly developed people has probably not wholly disappeared from the human soul during the course of a few generations.' Therefore, as Jung maintains, there is a tendency for us, in childhood, 'to go through a period in which the impulses toward these archaic inclinations appear again and again, and . . . through all our life we possess, side by side with the newly recruited, directed and adapted thought, a fantastic thought which corresponds to the thought of the centuries of antiquity and barbarism. Just as our bodies still keep the reminders of old functions and conditions in many old-fashioned organs, so our minds, too, which apparently have outgrown these archaic tendencies, nevertheless bear the marks of the evolution passed through, and the very ancient re-echoes, at least dreamily, in fantasies.'

This view, in should be noted, is expressed in a way which is quite independent of any particular theory of the unconscious. Indeed, the words used, such as thought and tendencies, belong to the common tradition of belief about the self rather than to any special doctrine of the unconscious. So, too, when Jung proceeds to explore the underworld we can follow him and agree or disagree without committing ourselves to his special theory, which in fact shows its artificiality time and time again. He tells us that the majority of people, and especially his patients, show a great unwillingness to look at their underworld. One of the favourite symbols of it is water, a kind of lake in a valley, lying below consciousness. 'The water is the valleyghost, the water dragon of the Yao, whose nature resembles water—a yang embraced in the yin'; and almost invariably it is thought of as below not so much materially as morally and spiritually. 'Spirit always comes from above. From below comes everything that is sordid and worthless. Spirit means highest freedom, a soaring over the depths, a deliverance from the prison of the chthonian element.' But as according to the new teaching man has relied far too exclusively on his ego, that is to say, his consciousness, he has grown sick. The overblown egoism of Nietzsche is a warning, and as we have seen, among the writers of the French and English decadence a *nostalgie de la boue* has manifested itself, a kind of earthy mystique. Jung rightly criticizes the view that our personality consists in mind and in self-consciousness. As we have already seen, the Neo-Platonic tendency to despise matter and live in the mind alone is dangerous. But when Jung goes on to say that the ego must come to terms with the unconscious and go down into its limbo, he becomes, as we shall see, a far less safe guide. 'No lofty, well-grown tree', he tells us, 'ever disowned its dark roots. In fact, it grows not only upward, but downward as well.' He would not have us return to the dark places to live there, but he does give Lilith as proud a place in the family life as the true spouse. He would deny this, I have no doubt, and claim that he distinguishes between what is evil for the self and what is healthy. Lilith, who, according to a Talmudic tradition, was the demon wife of Adam before Eve, is an enemy. She always destroys. She corresponds with the Greek fantasy of Lamia, the spectre of the night who terrifies children; she is even the sea monster which devours the sun hero, the mouth of death. But on what grounds does Jung distinguish between what is good and what is bad in the unconscious? He has already told us that it is a world in which such distinctions have no meaning. He can only do so, therefore, by appealing to the spirit or the ego, and in doing so he restores to the spirit and the conscious all that supremacy and that right to control which he has criticized. How well at times Jung realizes the dangers to which he is exposing us in opening the box of the unconscious is shown in the following passage on the symbolism of the Greek god, Dionysus. 'Dionysus signifies the depths of the passionate dissolution of all human particularity in the animal divinity of the aboriginal soul—a blessed and terrible experience that a humanity strongly hedged in within its culture believes it has escaped, till it succeeds once again in giving rein to a new orgy of blood about which all well-minded persons wonder, and for which they blame high finance, the armament industry, the Jews and the Freemasons.' A Christian culture keeps the passions in restraint and in the service of an ideal. When that restraint is withdrawn and men peer into forbidden places and salute new masters, they prepare the feast of blood. That is what Jung's warning comes to, and it is strange that he does not on the strength of it review again some of his assumptions about religion and morals. How inadequate they are, we shall see. But I did not quote this passage merely to illustrate the weakness of Jung's view. The language used, 'dissolution of human particularity', is the death *motif*; 'the animal divinity' and 'the orgy of blood'; all these expressions recall the excesses and perversions of Eros, which have already been noticed. There, as Brunhilde sings: 'Laughing let us be lost—Laughing go down to death!' —or in the still more expressive words of Nietzsche: 'Solitude surrounds and embraces him ever more threatening, ever more constricting, ever more heart-strangling, the terrible Goddess and Mater saeva cupidinum.'

The common conviction that the world below consciousness must be shunned needs, in Jung's view, to be modified if the human personality is to be restored to health. The ego must be persuaded to look at it; otherwise it will be like the tree which ignores its roots. 'The unconscious is the psyche that reaches down from the daylight of a mentally and morally lucid consciousness down into the nerve system that for ages has been known as sympathetic.' It preserves the equilibrium and by mysterious ways helps the mind to get into touch with the feelings and natures of other beings. It is a kind of sixth sense; it anticipates the slow moving reason; it intimates and throws out antennae; it reaches to the heart; and 'in this sense it is an exceedingly collective system, the actual basis of all "participation mystique", while the cerebro-spinal function culminates in separating out the specificity of the ego, and always, through the medium of space, grasps surfaces and superficialities alone.'

What then does the ego discover if it braces itself to the task of meeting the unconscious? Jung mentions three primordial functions or archetypes. The first is the 'shadow', the image. In the water man sees his face.

The mask he has shown to the world is gone and he sees himself without flattery. This is the narrow way to the unconscious, but once it has been passed we are beside ourselves and plunged into something vast which overwhelms the artificial ego we have constructed in our consciousness. In the prescientific days when symbolism came naturally to man the unconscious projected itself into beliefs, and so men lived under the tutelage of the gods or kind fates and they were protected by these friendly powers against the other hostile projections surrounding them, be they monsters or demons or dark deities. By such beliefs and fancies primitive and even cultured societies were able to live in a happy equilibrium, because the conscious and the unconscious worked together. But since the rationalistic age we have grown to rely on our ego alone and on the dry light of the reason. The result is that we have become so impoverished that we are in danger of perishing, and since beliefs now no longer carry any conviction, and heaven and hell are empty, we have to take the more arduous path and seek within the unconscious what used to be projected outside into nature. So it comes about that whereas in former days men used rituals and religious practice to protect their newly found egos from the waters of the unconscious, now we have to do the opposite and escape from the narrow cell of the ego to the source of all symbols and beliefs. The ego contrived to think of itself as a master of its fate and captain of its soul. The savage and the primitive know better, and so hand themselves over in part to the care of the gods. For salvation, therefore, we have to do likewise, without totally losing ourselves and letting the unconscious triumph over our prostrate spirit. 'Since the stars have fallen from heaven, and our highest symbols have palled, a secret life holds sway in the unconscious. It is for this reason that we have a psychology to-day, and for this reason that we speak of the unconscious.'

The first danger when we have crossed the threshold is that the shadow or image of ourselves will lose all reality or become infantile. The reason is that in passing from the ego to the shadow we become part of the unconscious, and it is the childish figure of ourselves newly arisen from the waters or, to change the picture, the tumultuous life of the instincts, which alone is left. If we cling on to this we become childlike, and possess that single eye of the poetic genius. But it is equally possible that we may become childish. Patients under analysis too often retrogress into an infantile state, which if it be not transitory but permanent can lead to catastrophe. In the experience of the unconscious, however, the anima is more important than the shadow, and the shadow imperceptibly fades into it. The self is in the unconscious so associated with the feminine principle as to be almost identified with it, and in turn the dark world of the unconscious figures itself in the archetype of the anima. The witch, the noxie, the psyche, the anima mundi, such symbols tell of its complexion and gender. It is the Lilith, the Delilah, the Helen, and the Venus, who like a siren, entices us to her abode. 'For the child, the anima lurks in the supremacy of the mother. . . . To the primitive and to the man of the classic age, the anima appears as a goddess or demonic woman', while, as Jung gravely informs us, the medieval man turned to Mother Church, paid homage to the Queen of Heaven and feared the witch!

In this farrago of meanings which Jung attaches to the anima it is difficult to pick out one central trustworthy idea. He seems to have hit on what is important, but in his effort to find illustrations from all quarters the idea is dissipated. If we were to say that the psyche has not been given a feminine gender without some reason, that as contrasted with the animus or reason she is not so much interested in herself as in being dependent on others and living for them, that she spends herself on the species more than on the individual and so, like nature, is prodigal and can be dissolute, we may have a clue which is worth following. Nature herself is thought of as feminine; she has her savage side, but she is there to provide, to be exploited and loved, and she has her secrets and her dark mystery. The soul feels that it belongs to her by its lower nature and that it will return to her, and that by listening in to 'nature's secrecies' it can learn a strange wisdom. Jung tells us that one of the attributes or functions of the anima is sophia. 'Behind all the anima's cruel sporting with human fate, there lies something like a secret intention which seems to spring from a superior knowledge of the laws of life.'

This sophia, however, is an underground organization, a secret society and only for the initiate. It has always historically had an esoteric flavour; it is to be found in the stars or by consulting witches of Endor or holding hands at séances or putting one's ear to the earth or gazing at tarot cards or forming cabalas and joining some group of gnostics. The Catharists had their veiled wisdom and the troubadours sang of it in a language with a double meaning. It is not so surprising then when Jung introduces another archetype, which emanates, so to speak, out of the anima. For, as he tells us, when science and philosophy are of no avail, 'and still less the traditional teachings of religion', when human interpretation fails and 'we sink to a final depth, to a spiritual death—as Apuleius rightly says: ad instar voluntariae mortis—a new archetype emerges which is the archetype of meaning as the anima was the archetype of life. He is the magician, the mysterious old man, the master and the teacher, the father of the soul, the medicine man, the enlightener, the Logos, the Thoth of Hermetic literature, the Hermes Trismegistus.

These and many other forms of religion are the projections of the unconscious, working, as Jung thinks, at its most salutary, but as some others may suggest, with the help of the great tempter, the Prince of this world and the Father of lies. That Jung should find his best evidence from the pagan myths and the literature of the mystery cults, the Neo-Pythagoreans and the alchemists, and that almost always when he draws an illustration from Christianity he has to force its meaning, that he should make his heaven out of the abyss, argues strongly that his explanation is upside down and that he is mistaking the counterfeit for the genuine. He may be right in his supposition, for which he argues with fascinating interest, that the alchemists were rather pseudo-mystics than chemists and physicists. It may be true that the dragon of these alchemists was a 'symbol combining the earth-principle of the serpent and the air-principle of the bird', that Mercury is the divine, winged Hermes, the divine and all-creating spirit concealed in matter, that the tail-eating serpent is the symbol of the One-and-the-All. This but reminds us of the Gnostic and Catharist heresy which did battle with the Christian faith. So, too, does the suggestion that the Pneuma or Nous of Neo-Pythagorean literature is 'identical with the God Anthropos: he appears beside the Demiurge, but is an opponent of the planetary spheres. He rends the circle of the spheres and stoops to earth and water. . . . His shadow falls upon the earth, but his image is reflected in the water. This image inflames the love of the elements, and he himself is so charmed with the mirrored reflection of divine beauty that he would gladly take up his abode within it. But he has scarcely descended when Physis or physical nature, embraces him with passionate love. . . .' This and much more like it can be found in varying form in the esoteric cults which have sung in the wake of Christianity and held out their hands to the unwary Hylas. But their enchantments have always been resisted by the Christian Church, their falsehood exposed and their sophia repudiated as a demonic aping of the everlasting truth.

Jung definitely refuses to recognize this distinction between that which comes from above and that which comes from below—and for the simple reason that what is above is for him always a projection from what is below. In his *Psychology of the Unconscious* he makes this quite clear: 'Mankind wishes to love in God only their ideas, that is to say, the ideas which they project into God. By that they wish to love their unconscious, that is, that remnant of ancient humanity and the centuries-old past in all people, namely, the common property left behind from all development which is given to all men, like the sunshine and the air. But in loving this inheritance they love that which is common to all. Thus they turn back to the mother of humanity, that is to say, to the spirit of the race, and regain in this way something of that connection and of that mysterious and irresistible power which is imparted by the feeling of belonging to the herd. It is the problem of Antaeus, who preserves his gigantic strength only through contact with mother earth.' In this and other passages the psyche is the mother of all invention, and it is she who gives to man all those visions which take him out of himself and offers him the possibility of falling in love with what is nothing more than a cloud shape or figures seen in a fire. The love which he gives to them is, however, only a reflection of the love he has for the lost property of the species, the age-old things which have been left behind. This, when all is said and done, is a cold douche for lovers and should mean the jettisoning of many a love story and love poem. Love, in fact, is just a ramp of the unconscious. It is comforting to repeat that immortal sentence: 'I say, assez, Rimbaud; like John Randolph's dead mackerel in the moonlight, he shines and stinks.'

But having turned from contemplating the heavens what method does the psycho-analyst adopt to bring back the spiritual health, which he has declared to be lacking? Well, 'it is rewarding to observe what happens quietly in the psyche' and to have 'reverence for what happens in the human psyche'. At the same time it is very hard to know what is happening in the psyche or to know what is the psyche. 'It is not describable'; 'it is a mere postulate, and nothing whatever can be predicated as to its possible contents (except those of the conscious sort).' It is rather like Kant's 'thing in itself', quite outside experience, and serving as a 'purely delimiting concept'. For this reason it is impossible to set any limits to the self, and therefore it is not surprising if it shows the marks of bound-lessness and indeterminability in space and time. 'In all times and places this is the quality of the numen and is, therefore, alarming to a careful consciousness that knows the value of precisely delimited concepts. We are glad that we are neither philosophers nor theologians and do not have to confront such numina within our own academic field. But it is all the worse when it becomes increasingly clear that numina are psychic entities that force themselves upon consciousness, in that, night after night, our dreams philosophize on their own. Even more: if we try to avoid these numina, and angrily reject the alchemized gold proffered by the unconscious, then it is an empirical fact that we fare badly and may even develop symptoms, in violation of all common sense; while as soon as we return again to the stumbling block and make of it—even in a hypothetical way—a cornerstone, then the symptoms disappear and everything goes "inexplicably" well.'

The method and answer to the troubles of humanity which Jung offers are clear. The pharisee of the conscious must link arms with the publican of the unconscious. We have to get over our fear, not only of the formidable but also of the malign and evil. We have to grasp the nettle of iniquity. In Jung's words: 'The inner voice brings forward what is evil in a temptingly convincing way, so as to make us succumb to it. If we do not succumb in part, then nothing of this apparent evil goes into us, and then also no renewal and no healing can take place.' This is Jung's recipe for the welfare of our age and for all humanity. It is by this means that the highest beauties, religious and artistic and social, can be brought back to civilization. We are neither to refrain nor to succumb completely; we have to make a covenant with 'the inner voice', whose name, Jung tells us, is Lucifer. If we abstain we shall shrivel for want of refreshment; if we succumb, then we shall invite disaster. But if we succumb only in part, keep our self-assertion and assimilate the 'voice', then we shall be both enlightened and healed.

Whatever we may think of this advice there can be no doubt of the good intentions of Jung. The evidence of this is that he has clearly in mind the heroes of myth, whose virtue consists in meeting evil. He is aware of the grave dangers in the adventure he recommends, but then he is thinking of the knights who braved evils of every kind, sorcerers, witches, Circes and dragons and monsters. The shepherds of the flock, he tells us, lead their sheep through many dangers and find the way to safety. But unfortunately he is so led astray himself by his imagination that he forgets that there are different ways of meeting evil. Lancelot, because he was stained by sin, did not find the Holy Grail; Moses because he disobeyed God was not privileged to lead his people into the Promised Land; David because he sinned brought dire affliction on the people of Israel. They succumbed in part, to use Jung's expression, and if he were right it ought to have been accounted righteous. This ambiguity in Jung's solution is no accident. The very character of his hypothesis of the unconscious demands that the conscious must surrender in part to the unconscious, and if this be so, then the only criterion for limiting the surrender must be the survival of the ego or the conscious. As long as the ego can come up from the depths and breathe again, all is well. And who can tell the power of man to accept what is dark and evil and live? And again, once the ego has yielded to the passion for the dark and been charmed into any sort of captivity to the unconscious, how can it be sure that it will be able to free itself from the drug or even want to be able to free itself? The ego, once it has admitted the embrace of the dark goddess, loses strength and inclination; it ceases more and more to be itself and may have to live an unseemly life by the troughs of Circe.

The truth is that Jung has failed to distinguish the heavenly Agape and the dark passion of Eros. He mingles together myth and truth, the dreams and thoughts of man hankering for reality and setting up false gods and the real religion which comes to man from a living God. It may well be that in his myths man has been helped to enjoy glimpses of divine truth, for God 'in sundry times and in divers manners' has spoken to man. Truth and falsehood, genuine communion and wild passionate desires may well have mingled together to produce the religious symbols and practices which Jung likes using for evidence of his hypothesis. All religions have marked the difference between the good and the evil spirits, between God and the devil. The medicine man, so it is now widely held, is the opposite of the sorcerer. One of the functions of the medicine man is 'to smell out' sorcery and drive away the ghoul. Independently, therefore, of Christianity human societies have been able to separate what is genuine from what is counterfeit, and the good numen is not just a projection of the unconscious but a happy, if confused, glimpse of truth. But in Christianity the truth is free from subjective fancyings; it comes down from above and exercises the severest control of symbol and image and fantasy; it can be as cold as ice and as inflexible as the historical fact on which it rests, and it beats down upon the soul with all the alien power of an existent truth which is not a dream. I insist upon this quality, for in contrasting existence with essence we come to the heart of the matter. Thoughts and dreams and symbols may be spun out of my own soul; they are my familiars, and all the philosophies which splash about with essences end up in substituting for the living God some idea like the One or the Whole or Truth or Mind, abstracts which betray their origin. Alone Christian philosophy tears the veil of all such temples of thought. It begins not with the One or the Absolute, but with 'I Who am', and instead of my being able to think of myself as an emanation of the One, a step in a thought process, I know myself as dependent on another, my small I whispering ' "Thou", my Creator'. There is no system of thought which can include in its philosophy God as a creator save Christianity, no system which allows persons and not processes to make history, which lays all its stress on persons and freedom and can find a way out from the supposedly closed universe to a living God whose will sustains it. 'Antike Tempel', as Goethe said, 'concentrieren den Gott im Menschen, des Mittelalters Kirchen streben nach dem Gott in der Höhe.' It is sad if men like Jung should really believe that the highest ideals to which men have aspired should be only a projection of their psyche. Can Jung really think that, once a man knows that all he believed to be beyond himself and real with a worth which wins his heart, is his own invention and an illusion, he will be comforted and content with life and glad to aim at the heroic and at perfection? It is surely more likely that he will fall back on a Schopenhauerian pessimism and ridicule his self-made gods for all the playacting.

In a dream which one of his patients narrated to him Jung records that she saw a rainbow. 'The rainbow is to be used as a bridge. Yet one must go, not over it, but through underneath. Whoever goes over it falls to his death.' Jung interprets this dream as follows: 'Only gods succeed in walking on the rainbow bridge: mortals fall to their death, for the rainbow is only a beautiful semblance that stretches across the heavens, and not a road for corporeal human beings: they must go through underneath. But under bridges flows water, which follows its own gradient.' Water is the symbol for the unconscious, and the dream is supposed to warn the dreamer that it is not by flying to a vain belief in heaven and searching for a heavenly guide that she will be relieved of her trouble. She must go down under the bridge by the way of the unconscious. That is the only way for mortals. The ego, that is, must descend to the lower world. I have already explained what Jung means by the ego and what by the self or psyche. But we are by no means bound to follow him in his explanation. Indeed, his error begins here. Neither self-consciousness, conceived as an ego living a life of its own, nor an unconscious which is a world without centre or circumference, answers to the facts as we know them from experience. In self-consciousness we do have an indirect knowledge of our psyche, and that is why it must strike all readers as very odd to confine the ego to that which is given directly in conscious experience. We know, too, that this so-called unconscious is ours. As I shall return later to the question of the nature of the self, I need only point out here that common-sense supports the view that all that can come into our conscious mind must be due in part to the activity of the self which is ours. A purely passive state is inconceivable; fantasies and night-mares come in part from our own activity, and if this is so then the unconscious is always part of our nature, and it is false to call it boundless and to suggest that there may be a racial unconscious or that the psyche is more than what we are. As we call our body our own and know that in a mysterious way it is what we are, so too the impulses, the instincts, all that reveals itself in dreams and symbols, all this is one with the self. But—and here is the essential point—the conscious and the unconscious are not two kingdoms, each with its own rights and privileges. The underworld is the matter for the spirit, and the word of command and direction lies with the spirit. It is by conscious reflection and striving that we come to know what is the truth about ourselves and where our destiny lies, and therefore what Jung calls the potential, the multifarious powers and urges have to be disciplined and directed in accordance with the far-off divine event to which the spirit moves. In a sense what is below the threshold is neutral in that it can help the aims of the true self and so be an ally in the building of character and personality, or it can be lawless and anarchical and so thwart the true end of the self. In the latter case the unconscious is an enemy and its progeny is evil. The libido, for instance, if it be taken in its narrow sense, is concerned with sex.

Now Jung says that the ego must make friends with it or die, but he does not and cannot define the proper relations between the two. All he can say is that the ego must surrender in part and let the apparent evil into its sanctuary. Such advice might well be an invitation to immorality, though Jung does not intend it to be so. At any rate the advice is ambiguous and disquieting. But once we know that the ego is the eye and steward of the character and the true self, and that the end of human life can be marked out, then the treaty between the ego and the libido can be correctly formulated. The libido has to be directed to one of the ends of the spirit. When so used the whole act is good, whereas its unlicensed acts are evil. This is well seen in the recent history of legislation on marriage in Soviet Russia. Experience there taught the Government that lawless love endangered the good of society, that there were fundamental laws which could not be infringed without peril; and so new legislation corrected the excessive liberties permitted at first. And that such bridling and direction are necessary is obvious. In our relations with others we come into contact with a 'Thou', and we recognize that we must respect and honour the rights and ideals of the other. We cannot use him or her to indulge in our libido and make them a means for a supposedly fuller life for ourselves. The higher our conception of the beauty of another's personality, the more does it become incumbent on us to lift our desires to a spiritual level. By such acts and by such mutual consideration our ideal for ourself, for our friend and for society, take on a new aspect far removed from that of lust and the other dark suggestions of the unconscious. Indeed, we come by this means to see quite clearly that there are heavenly desires as well as earthly ones, that love has two mansions, one in the spirit and the other in the viscera, that the two mingle in most human acts and that the one leads to God and the other to furious egotism or death in dark places where the *gens lucifuga* dwells.

This distinction between the loves is decisive in any true account of love and human desires. There is first the spiritual and heavenly love, and secondly a human love composed of light and darkness. Human beings are made up of spirit and body; they are half-angel and half-animal. In the unconscious the animal lives, espoused to spirit but not yet married to it. When brought to the altar of the spirit in conscious mind, it has to promise union and eternal fidelity. But before it is joined in marriage it tries to exercise the stronger part, and the stories in myth and the long history of orgy and fanaticism in religious cults show how often it gets its way. I call that, for the moment, the dark passion of Eros, and it is strange and significant that Jung should pick his best evidence from alchemy and magic and voodoo and the secretive sects and cults, like Gnosticism. Certainly their teachings bid us go under the rainbow, to plunge into the waters of the deep pools, to go down into Hades. But even here, without even the help of heavenly love, there is a better way, and Dante pointed it out when he chose Virgil to be his guide. Virgil had in imagination travelled down into the dark places, where *patet atri janua Ditis*, 'the gate of dark Dis stands open', where live the 'silent ghosts and Chaos and Phlegethon, the wide dumb realm of night'; he has passed through 'the empty dwellings and bodiless realms' and seen at the very threshold 'Death and Travail, and thereby Sleep, Death's kinsman, and the Soul's guilty joys, and death-dealing War. . . .' To Dante he was a safe guide, not because he sought to conciliate the spirits of the dark or to learn some secret sophia from them, but because he could lead him in an ascent, not unsubstantial like the rainbow, but through fire and over rocks to where beyond the flames a voice could be heard singing: 'Beati mundo corde'. To that singing Virgil had taught him not to be deaf—ed al cantar di là non siate sorde—and he had led him to his Beatrice. Dante's way is not Jung's; they stand in direct contrast, but who can doubt that Dante's is the better? In Dante's view the spirit of man is represented by Virgil, man as he is at his best before the divine Beatrice brings him to that light supreme which uplifts man above all mortal thoughts—O somma luce, che tanto ti levi dai concetti mortali. As Mr. Charles Williams says so rightly: 'The Aeneid has pietas and not caritas, the divine Agape is lacking to Virgil. But he is perfect in his humanity; he is 'the author and guide'; he is the 'anima cortese Mantovana'. He is far from the overblown egoism of a Nietzsche or the decadence of a Huysmans; his spirit is that of the early paintings of Tuscany, a humanism which makes no compromise with barbarism and never parleys with the devil. Those who surrender the reason even in part to the unconscious are 'le genti dolorosa c'hanno perduto il ben dell'intelletto', the miserable race who have lost the blessing of reason. Dante does not here side with Nygren in his disparagement of reason; he would not even sympathise with the answer of Heim. The intellect is not Eros in violent contrast with Agape; it has too noble a task disciplining and humanizing the savage part in us, the underworld which is for ever dashing itself against the bar of reason. It is with 'wit and with art' ('con ingegno e con arte'), that Virgil has led Dante through Hell and Purgatory to where that 'sweet fruit whereof the care of mortals goeth in search on so many boughs' is to give to the hungry their peace. But if it is so noble, if personified in Virgil the human spirit can show the path, it also comes to 'a place where I, of myself, can discern no

further'. The highest motion of the human mind, Eros, as some understand it, at its best, has to give way to Agape. The way to heaven is
reserved to the divine Beatrice. It is she, the symbol of grace and heavenly
wisdom, who leads man beyond the rainbow over the water, 'out of the
swing of the sea'.

CHAPTER SIX

LOVE AND THE SELF

He gave man his desire but sent therewith a lean heart.

Nothing but men of all unvenomed things
Doth work upon itself with inborn stings.

—J. DONNE.

That is to say, genius is the power of leaving one's own interests, wishes and aims entirely out of sight; thus of entirely renouncing one's own personality for a time, so as to remain pure knowing subject, clear vision of the world. . . .—SCHOPENHAUER.

All originality is an eaglet which breaks through its shell only in the sublime and fulminating atmosphere of Sinai.—LOUIS BERTRAND.

It is now time to examine more closely the meaning of some of the principal ideas, which have so far been used, ideas such as those of the self, of love and the relation between love and thought, anima and animus. All men have some understanding of what love and the self mean by themselves, though it is not easy to analyse their meaning and free it from ragged edges. The advantage of keeping to literature and common speech in using such ideas is that we are always in touch with the best of all crucibles, experience. Experience does not allow a gross lie to have a long life; it challenges it with constant contradiction. The philosopher, on the other hand, may invent meanings and receive an imprimatur from fellow thinkers; even the scientist, in so far as he separates his branch of study from contact with other branches or general experience, is not so well off as the man who has to live what he knows and test it in everyday experience. Now the notions of love and of the self are universal, and most must have a fair idea of what they mean because they have their own experience to guide them and a long heritage of common sense and wisdom. All that philosophy can do is to remove ambiguities and so clarify the ideas that arguments drawn from them work together to form a wider and higher conception of the meaning of life.

In distinguishing living things from non-living we are aware of what may be called an embryonic selfhood in them. That is to say, we realize that they are growing of themselves and by their own effort. There is the beginning of a new unity and inner life, for which the word growth is often used. Most on reflection would say that there is no need to postulate anything beyond the life of the bodily organism to explain what happens. The bodily metabolism, the reflex actions, the instincts and impulses, the formation of habits, the life of the senses, all proceed within a determined end, which is specific and limited and transitory. We can speak of an organic unity and even of individual characteristics, but only by metaphor, of a person. That is to say, the self of an animal has not come into its own kingdom; it cannot take charge of its own being and appoint its own objectives, weigh them, reckon its own powers by reference to its past and its future hopes, retire behind its desires and activities to a deeper self, which has its scouts and patrols in thought and conscience, and suffers loss or gain in all experience. Selfhood, at least, means this, and in the world we know it is the prerogative of human beings alone. Man has been called a tool-bearing animal, but he is far more than this; he has a power to mirror himself and to mirror within himself the length and breadth of reality, and he can stand off from his impulses and thoughts and guide them in a direction which he himself chooses. Moreover, one part of himself, and that the most intimate, does not belong to any thing, being or power in the world. There he knows himself morally, and not physically, subject to an absolute, a subjection which is first discerned in the duty of keeping his word, saying what is true and choosing what is right. It is on these grounds he claims to be regarded as a moral person with rights and duties, a self in the full and proper sense of the word.

As sharing a body with the animals and possessing mind and a rational will man begins a new order. What is animal will not be destroyed but taken up into the life of the unified self. Freud tends to ignore the new setting in which the instincts and desires are grouped, and even Jung argues as if the spiritual self were only a voyager out of the racial self, who must return to seek health there when he grows impoverished. Taking facts at their surface value they argue that there are several selves, egos and super-egos and ids, but in fact in their very explanation they presuppose a fundamental unity, only they ignore it or misunderstand it. It is true that neither consciousness nor self-consciousness sums up what is meant by being a self and a person; the mind which thinks, the will which is desire in action, are activities of the same self which animates the body. One does not work without the other in this life, and the thoughts which I think, the hopes I have, the memories I cherish, the habits I have grown into, the aches and disappointments, the physical and spiritual scars, are mine in a sense which they can never be to any other. I am their owner, the only being who has suffered them or enjoyed them in the past, who is conscious of that past as being present to me now and to no one else as both past and present; and who now can make them work together to the fulfilment of my personal destiny.

If then the self has an inseparable unity which takes in all the phases of it which we see in the mirror of consciousness, all our desires and what has been called the unconscious, it embraces the animus and the anima and must be sharply distinguished from the ego or empirical self or the other limited meanings assigned to it by many modern psychologists. Much, however, of what they say can be admitted provided that we do not swear by their assumptions and hypotheses. Much, too, can be left open for free speculation so long as that speculation does not impair the integrity of the self. There are some, for instance, who believe in what has been called, 'the fine point of the soul'. Mystics sometimes refer to this; they seem to feel that in their experience it is as if spiritual fingers had felt their way right down into the depths of the soul and touched a last nerve, which was more tender and alive than any other part of themselves. Here is the lair of their individuality, what has made them to be distinct from all others and most responsive to the touch of their God and Lover. If this be so, the Anima, as for instance as she appears in Claudel's parable, could very rightly be said to stand for this Cinderella, who dwells in the most inner recess of the self, the work-a-day maid who is also the sleeping princess of the fairy tale and most inaccessible to vulgar reporting. Some, dropping the imagery, have recourse to a theory of the self as an hypostatized longing, a love-dynamism with multitudinous desires all flowing out from one ultimate blindfold longing, which is only enlightened when the other desires have been purified or negated and God graces it by his presence and love. Or, again, we may use a favourite distinction of the philosophers, to which we shall have to return later, between essence and existence. All the contents of my being, as human, are common to other human beings. A scientist cataloguing human nature can refer to Tom, Dick or Harry indifferently; they all serve his purpose, because as examples of human nature they are all alike. But Tom as a living, existing being can never be the same as Dick or Harry, and it is this positive and singular perfection of Tom, this having a life and existence of his own, which makes him address other persons as 'Thou' and not as 'It', and give loving homage to God. Still another view has been expressed by the poet, Gerard Hopkins, among others. The version of it, however, by Hopkins is little known and is of such a rare quality that it deserves a special notice.

He starts with the customary, scholastic definition of a person, which is taken from Boethius. A person is 'the individual substance of a rational nature'. In this definition Hopkins distinguishes the self, which is the individual substance, from the nature with which it is clothed or 'overlaid'. A 'self is the intrinsic oneness of a thing', and to bring out, as I think, the importance he attaches to the word 'intrinsic', he sharply separates off the self from those broken fragments of things, like a branch or log of wood, or artificial unities, such as a billiard ball. Both the billiard ball and the branch have an independent existence; they are separate from other things and exist by themselves. But they are not true selves, for their unity is accidental and there is no positive individual character in a billiard ball which makes one different from another. (The very fact that superstitious people do sometimes attribute to a favourite golf ball or a lucky penny a peculiar, intrinsic quality brings out Hopkins' point.) A true self like a baby has a determinate character from the beginning. It is not an artificial unity; it does not result from anything else; it is not completely indifferent, a neutral, which gets all its positive character from the nature of which it is the individual component. Hopkins insists that this self must be prior to all determination, and even before it exists the bare self must be positive and intrinsically different from every other self. 'A bare self, to which no nature has yet been added, which is not yet clothed in or overlaid with a nature, is indeed nothing, a Zero, in the score or account of existence, but as possible it is positive, like a positive infinitesimal, and intrinsically different from every other self.'

In asserting that the self is positive even before it exists Hopkins, as must be observed, separates himself off from those above mentioned who connect up personality with a human being's existence as contrasted with his nature or essence. He argues that the facts cannot be explained satisfactorily in any other way. Suppose, he says, that there are various natures A and B and Y and Z and various selves a and b and y and z. Now if a and b and y are all capable of receiving any of the natures mentioned, and, in fact, we get the combination aA, bA and yZ, these combinations must be quite arbitrary 'or absolute facts not depending on any essential relation between a and A, b and A . . . but on the will of the Creator'. Further, a and b are in the same nature A. But a uses it well and is saved, b ill and is damned: these are two facts, two fates, not depending on the relation between a and b on the one hand and A on the other. Now as the difference of the facts or fates does not depend on A, which is the same for both, it must depend on a and b. So that selves are from the first intrinsically different.'

This argument is clear enough, if we keep in mind that he is writing of human nature. An example from a nature below the human will not do. Let us take the example of bird nature to stand for A and two eggs or chicks to stand for a and b. The chicks have both the same nature; that nature, therefore, cannot be responsible for the different lives or fates of the two chicks. The difference must come from the individual and positive differences in the two chicks. But Hopkins does not believe that they have real selfhood. 'Two eggs precisely alike, two birds precisely alike, will behave precisely alike; if they had been exchanged no difference would have been made.' (To prevent a possible objection it should be noticed that Hopkins is not saying that all eggs or all chicks are exactly alike. In wartime we know only too well that eggs are not all alike. His point is that if you start two human beings from scratch they will not breast the tape together, whereas two chicks, from two identical eggs would always be identical.) Only in human beings is the self unique and able to differentiate itself from all other selves. The nature which is ours as human beings 'supplies the exercise', the self supplies the determination. In other words, two eggs are not free, and therefore they are determined by their nature; but a human being is free and so he is always determining himself—and for that freedom to have any meaning the self must, so to speak, have its own say, must contribute something which is peculiarly its own. This kind of freedom Hopkins calls freedom of pitch, and he distinguishes it from freedom of play which is attributable to the nature.

But what is the relation of this freedom of pitch, which belongs to the self, to the personality? Hopkins has declared that the self, *quâ* self, is prior to nature; it is not merely a cipher, the instance of a universal or nature with which the scientist likes to deal. His objection to the scientific account, necessary as it is in its place, as a complete statement, is that then personality would be unimportant and men and women no more different from one another than two pins or peas. Each self must be positive and unique even prior to its being clothed in a nature. But is this self prior also to freedom of pitch? No, he says, that cannot be, for if there 'were something prior even to pitch, of which that pitch would itself be the pitch, then we could suppose that that, like everything else, was subject to God's will and could be pitched, could be determined, this way or that. But this is really saying that a thing is and is not itself, is and is not *A*, is and is not.' The pitch or inclination, the personal way of behaving must be identified with the self or else we should have a process going on *ad infinitum*, the pitch being the pitch of something which itself must have a pitch. Therefore, the self, even in the stage of possibility, before it has become united with the nature so as to be a full existing human person, is positive precisely as having 'pitch, moral pitch, determination of right and wrong'. This pitch is present when nature is added, and then we have freedom of exercise as well. The personal self is presented with a choice; just because it has a self and a pitch it is always inclined towards one of the alternatives, but as it has now a nature it can be so far indifferent as to choose one or the other, and this exercise of freedom is what Hopkins means by freedom of play—and also by a third kind of freedom which he now introduces, that of field. This freedom of field completes his analysis of self and person, and fortunately he gives several examples to illustrate the difference between his three freedoms. That of field, as the word denotes, refers to the field of operation, or choice; that of play is in the execution, and that of pitch in self-determination. 'Thus it is freedom of play to be free of some benevolent man's purse, to have access to it at your will; it is freedom of pitch to be allowed to take from it what you want, not to be limited by conditions of his imposing; it is freedom of field to find there *more than one coin to choose from.* Or it is freedom of pitch to be able to choose for yourself which of several doors you will go in by; it is freedom of play to go unhindered to it and through the one you choose; but suppose all were false doors or locked but the very one you happened to choose and you do not know it, there is here wanting freedom of field.' All these three freedoms should belong to us in our human and earthly condition, but for the perfection of the self only one is essentially required, and that is freedom of pitch. It is this which belongs most intimately to the self, and the more perfect the personality the less may any other freedom be needed. Choice in the sense of taking one alternative and leaving another implies some imperfection when the choice is between good and evil. There is no field of evil open to one who loves truly, and for this reason theologians teach that God could never have that kind of freedom of field, nor any field where love of Himself is concerned. God's freedom is the perfection of that which is called pitch, and it is true freedom, indeed the plenary freedom. 'It is choice as when in English we say "because I choose", which means no more than (and with precision does mean) I instress my will to so-and-so. And this freedom and no other, no freedom of field, the divine will has towards its own necessary acts. And no freedom is more perfect; for freedom of field is only an accident.' Hopkins's next words sum up his doctrine of self and this freedom of pitch and show what exactly he meant by person or self as opposed to merely artificial and independent or merely natural units. 'So also *pitch* is ultimately simple positiveness, that by which being differs from and is more than nothingness and not-being, and it is with precision expressed by the English *do* (the simple auxiliary), which when we employ or emphasize, as "he said it, he did say it", we do not mean that the fact is any more a fact but that we the more state it. . . . So that this pitch might be expressed, if it were good English, the *doing*be, the *doing*choose, the *doing* so-and-so in that sense. Where there was no question of will it would become mere fact; where there is will it is free action, moral action. And such "doing-be", and the thread or chain of such pitches or "doing-be's", prior to nature's being overlaid, is self, personality; but it is not truly self: self or personality then truly comes into being when the self, the person, comes into being with the accession of nature.'

Hopkins seems to think that this self which he has with such diligence unearthed is identical with what Duns Scotus, a thinker he much admired, meant by the 'haecceitas', the 'thisness', which constitutes the inner core of personality. The better-known theories of the self do not allow for this special, positive selfhood which is prior to nature. The upholders of them maintain that human personality can be adequately explained without recourse to this 'infinitesimal'. They, too, do however make a distinction between the individual or person and the nature sufficient to justify the distinctions employed in preceding chapters between two forms of love such as Eros and Agape and that of anima and animus. It does not matter essentially what view of the self is held so long as these distinctions are seen not to be arbitrary but to have a true ground. Nevertheless, a view which explicitly demands a sharp distinction and throws light on it is of interest, and that is why it is well worth while mastering the theory which Hopkins has so carefully thought out, or else adopting one of the views which have been given above. Common sense, joined to some knowledge of the great movements of love as shown in history or recorded in prose or poetry, can find the right answer. But there are behind the answer such great issues connected with man's destiny, his relation to others and to God, that in the following pages the solution will have to take on more and more a philosophical character.

Whatever view we take it is clear that the self is more than mere consciousness or even self-consciousness. The self has the power of thinking and willing; it is real and alive even when it is asleep or robbed by illness or immaturity of thinking; it is independent and unique and has rights and duties. All indeed that is human in us, and that is everything, is of and from and by the self. Some would hold, however, that when we have enumerated the attributes of a human being we have no need to go further to find a self beyond these. The self will be the permanent and subsistent source and unity of all the movements of the body and mind, though it will be expressed more representatively in those higher movements, such as thought and will, which are exclusively human. If that is so, the anima will be this determining form, or again the form or soul with the one exception of the reason, or again the soul at its highe t (which could serve as the 'fine point of the soul'), or, lastly, the massed and cryptic potentialities of the self, be they noble or ignoble. Our impressions of human nature do correspond with these divisions. We think of men as able thinkers but without an interesting personality, but at the same time, while we distinguish character from intelligence, intellect and will are the marks of a great personality. And often enough we are in doubt because we feel that there are latent powers in a man which may prove his making or undoing. By means of animus and anima we are able to link together these various aspects of the self.

These distinctions, however, within the self though real must not be so exaggerated as to cause us to lose sight of the radical unity of that self. The caution cannot be too often repeated. It is our misfortune that the divisions we are forced to make are too easily translated into a series of private properties, each with sharp and fast boundaries. We talk of the eye seeing, the mind thinking and the will acting and deciding, and worse still, of the unconscious influencing us; but really it is the self which has eyes and a mind and a will that is the subject of seeing and thinking and willing. Nor can we separate the various powers and activities of the self off from one another so sharply as we should like. Our very instincts and senses are impregnated with soul and thought, and will overlap in a most confusing way. The picture we form of ourselves is convenient, but misleading; it is usually oversimplified and too rigid. The self is set behind or below its different powers; it is supposed to manipulate the body and to delegate its authority to the senses or the mind; it is at one moment confounded with self-consciousness, but on other occasions it is enthroned behind or hidden in the dark cellars of the unconscious. The poet shows that the self is living vividly in the imagination, the artist has his soul in his finger tips, the conscious and the 'unconscious' are in constant correspondence, and the mind is a blank without some interest to quicken it, and the will cannot be itself a spiritual power unless in some sense it is itself or, through its intimacy with the soul, awake and aware.

The self, therefore, however retiring a part it may seem to play in many books of psychology, is necessarily the key to all the works of man. Even what is called the 'unconscious' seems to have been dangerously separated off from it. Freud and Jung and Adler and many others have done valuable service in showing us the influence of the non-rational factors of the personality in life. But their theories are defective because of the lack of proper consideration of the self. The various *fonctionnaires*, the policemen, the dissident parties which they have to create for the unconscious realm in order to make it intelligible are at best what Eddington would call in another context, pointer readings. Having been deprived of consciousness they are often reinvested with conscious authority, and their phantom existence usurps the place of real, conscious experience. That is not to say that they have no true message. Perhaps we understate the all-pervading influence of the self which is ours. For a long period psychologists confused it with the mind or the self given in self-consciousness. They seem now to have rebounded from the manifest inadequacy of this idea to a conception of the self which makes it almost totally unconscious. It becomes a materialistic poltergeist. To correct this it would be well to re-emphasize the spiritual nature of the self. Whatever else we may say about it it is at least the originator and owner of those activities of mind and will which prove it to be of the spiritual order, and therefore above any materialistic or organic explanation. We do not take this fact of the spirituality of the self sufficiently seriously and press it to its logical conclusions. We are content to admit that in mind we have a power which is immaterial in its essence and commit the rest of the self to the nether regions of matter or organic life. But the unity of the self precludes this and if spirit cannot abdicate and accept an inferior status, we ought to be able to perceive spirit in all that is not completely impervious to its operation. Now we know that much happens in the so-called unconscious which is different from the conscious operations of the reason, and we have enough evidence to conclude that the seeing and hearing, for example, of a human being, the gestalt and the general impression, the fancy and the memory are very different from those which belong to an animal. If this be so, then we can suppose that the soul is alive and operating in all the activities of man, which permit of it, that it makes sensation and feeling protoplastic of mind, turns sight into perception and imagery into imagination, and at times of stress, when its life is threatened or it is full of expectancy of meeting the longed-for Unknown, it even dispenses with normal channels of communication, it makes contact by secret signs, and tokens and telepathy and ecstasy and the beating of the heart. Its relation with the various powers works according to the Communist formula: from each according to his capacity and to each according to his needs. The sensitive and pyscho-physical faculties and impulses determine the kind of way the self can work in and through them, and it has to keep step with their capacities and answer to their needs. This holds true even of the mind and will. The mind of man is a function with a definite end, and the interests of the self are to that extent forwarded by it. But as we all know the mind can be an embarrassment; its aim is pretentious, but its bag is disappointing; it has to paralyse the living reality before it can make it its own; philosophy is not the warmest of professions, though its object be truth. The self is deeply implicated in its thinking, but it is more than its thought, and its deepest desires reach beyond it. The will, too, which seems so intimately personal, is so often rebellious and confuses the self by bursting, like a rocket, into a number of divergent desires. Owing no doubt to Original Sin, the self has to spend its time bringing order into its desires, instead of being able to discover and concentrate upon what is the true desire of its heart.

The self, then, works in and through its various powers, but just because each of them has its own special virtue and perspicacity, it must not be identified with them, and moreover it is troubled because of their very variety and their conflicting appeal and possible domination. The anima is always having to listen to what the reason tells it with intransigeant authority, and if it becomes rebellious it is in grave danger of yielding to the importunate desires, giving up its reason and imperilling its immortal self. The animus, as we have seen, is imperious; it cannot help wanting to grasp reality, to make it its own and so form a body of knowledge. As I have suggested, it is the spiritual and sublimated form of the acquisitive and domineering appetite of the animal; it is the spiritual self acting necessarily to its own best interests, growing to its own perfection, that Eros which Nygren denounced as ego-centrism. The anima, on the other hand, is used to express both this self, and the self with animus left out. As the latter, in its spiritualized and sublimated form, it is the analogue of the yielding, self-sacrificing impulse. As human it is a longing, like to a maid with arms outstretched, expectant and in search for what it may adore. Its only safety, as it would seem, lies in keeping close to animus. No sooner does it part from reason than it begins to sing the song of death and annihilation. At first it is thrilled with the apparent freedom and passes through a period of romance. Such romance, however, feeds on illusion, and as time goes on the anima begins to bend before strange gods and to play with the dark passions until, in the end, it passes into the dark night and succumbs to a wholly irrational craving for oblivion.

I have said that the only seeming way of safety for the anima is to live in close companionship with the animus. But there is another alternative which has been sometimes followed, another turning, to a *terra incerta et invia*. Instead of the descent to the dark regions of the unconscious those who are the priests of this other way call it an ascent through purification and unworldliness to the absolute. In our day Gerald Heard and Aldous Huxley have been active in advocating it, and it has been the immemorial practice of the East. The Dionysiac cult and the mystery religions taught also this mystical way. What judgement should be passed on this mystical flight which takes the anima beyond the understanding of the animus? I do not think that experience or philosophy can give a safe general answer. The reason for this is that we have no means of knowing God's will or man's individual correspondence with grace. Because God is so silent, we are inclined to leave His part out of our explanations, and yet in the final issue all depends upon Him. So far as we can guess, God does work upon souls which have given themselves to this way of self-negation. Whatever the intrinsic value of the choice and of the method,

God can make what is deficient good whenever there is a right intention. It may well be, therefore, that many find the true God by becoming initiates of this uncovenanted mysticism. But when this has been said there is need also of caution. No way of life is more open to delusion, and many seem to confuse the means with the end, or, what is worse, to find in the emptiness to which the exercises in self-denial lead a substitute for that supernaturalization of the self and communion with a living and bountiful God. They mistake, that is, a relation which may suit beings other than persons with one between persons. The latter cannot end in any diminishment on either side. A person cannot throw away his unique status and lower himself to a means. He can at most pervert his being, sound its depths and get lost there, and then in the great emptiness enjoy a feeling which may be called atavistic, but is in no sense the glory of a spirit and a person. Nor can the other with whom a person is in love drain out that personality and leave him so crushed as to have no resemblance to himself. Love between persons means that each wants the other to be more himself. Each is unique, and that uniqueness can become so precious that other people may be forgotten or treated merely as servants of that love. In this sense we are jealous for the beloved and long to see the whole world offered up in sacrifice for him or her. And if this be true as between human persons far more is it true in the relation of God to the soul. But so invisible is God and so infinitely removed in point of excellence, that the self is overcome at the comparison and blames its limitations. The only way to find God is by the path of unknowing—and it is here that the danger begins. The spiritual anima has awakened to a life which reason cannot fully understand or supply; it does not want to possess but to give, and in this state of inquietude it is impatient of the golden cage which is what a full human personal life now seems to be. The desire may turn to a frenzy or to a deliberate ascesis; the search is out beyond all that is associated with selfish ambition; and so it may happen that the anima may find methods, a technique for adventuring into immensities and down into abysses without madness; it learns to model itself so as to be receptive of the highest experience a human being can reach, to be in a state of tension and receptivity such that the mystical language used in describing it resembles closely the most authentic divine union. But it does not follow that the divine union has taken place. The language which a genuine mystic uses must always be inadequate; it must give the interior impression, the effect upon the soul rather than a description of the being who has made the impression. He is by nature one whom language cannot describe. It is from indirect evidence and from the context that the acquaintance or reader of the mystic can be fairly sure of the objectivity of the experience. But when the experience is described in terms which seem to exclude a personal God it is possible that the soul has stretched itself out to its highest receptivity and it is this very condition which is being related, as the sound of words can have a magical effect upon the emotions and bring them into accord with their meaning, though the meaning be missed; or as pursed lips can automatically give the response to a note struck. But as the spirit cannot be entirely inactive it sublimates the desire inherent in the anima and conceives itself as lost to itself and fused with some all-comprehensive perfection or Absolute. The grave danger here is that the spirit has borrowed from the lower levels of the anima and, if it be not watchful, it slips down to that level. That this may happen is borne out by the evidence of so much religious experience and the oscillation in many mystery cults and mystical movements between the holy and the obscene, the pure and the savage sacrifice. From the *Varieties of Religious Experience* we have all learnt how easy it is to ape the highest movements and inspiration of the spirit, whether by drugs or suggestion or rhythmical exercises. As sleep gives rest to the body, so can a mood of absorption give repose to the spirit and be mistaken for eternal peace. And there is, moreover, always the danger of a decline to that animal craving for perpetuity outside its own individual existence, the joy in subjection and belonging to another.

Civilized man tends to build a rampart round his humanity to protect himself from the enemies to his happiness, whether within or without. He likes to be in control, to manage his fate as far as possible, to be a lord within a definite kingdom, however small. In accordance with this desire Coventry Patmore sings of the body as 'creation's crowning good, wall of infinitude'. 'The great immensity of space makes me shudder', said Pascal, and though without the Incarnation the city of man is tiny and closed and may bore and certainly never endures, it is yet a consolation and a protection. This is why the classical ideal never dies, and sets up its tents in the desert and rejects the romantic mirage. Animus and anima come together and form one being. In their unity they are human nature, and they are meant to complement each other. In segregating them and keeping them apart one has to some extent committed oneself to abstractions. They are both movements of the one soul or self; they overlap, and like the intellect and the will belong to each other. There is no mind without interest and no will which is completely blind. Even the mind in its essential activity can be considered as partly passive, though it ends in possessing itself of the object to be known; and the will is active in its desires and the seat of mastery, though it never seeks to possess in the same way as the mind. It is just because they are so blended that we have difficulty in separating out their basic aim, and fail, perhaps, to realize

that the possessive mind dictates to the desire what it wants and the desire
checks the mind from being totally egocentric. They are, therefore, like
the positive and negative, the rise and fall in the rhythm of the body and
in the arts; they make up the natural life of the soul; and so long as they
are able to play their parts together without frustration or discord they
define the humanistic ideal, what Aristotle and many another philosopher
would have defined as the happiness of mortal men.

I say 'happiness of mortal men', and there is the rub. Human beings
live in time and create civilizations, in which the foolish hope to find an
abiding joy. But the joy is mortal and not abiding. Immortality lies elsewhere. Claudel spoke in a parable of the anima having an immortal lover.
This it is that enlists our sympathy with the multiform attempts of the
anima to play truant to the animus. Firmly as we believe that animus and
anima must be reconciled and work harmoniously, it seems that this can
only be done if their respective roles are at times changed. The anima
must take the lead and the reason be led into a friendly and wise captivity;
the egocentric part of man, while surviving, as it must do in all persons,
must play second fiddle to the agape of the soul. But is this not to give
up all the glory of reason, to relax its control and surrender to the
Dionysiac stampede perhaps to the heights, but more likely to the
depths? That would indeed be the danger—and has proved in history to
be a supreme danger—were there not one chartered way which the anima
can take in order to find the true God and the trysting place of divine
love. According to the Christian philosophy that way does exist, and it
is the way of faith, which, as the definition goes, is an act of the intellect
commanded by the will. By this faith the soul commits itself to believe
the word of another, the word of God Himself, who has divine news to
give. It is the beginning of the new love story, which has its source in
the agape of God and the corresponding agape of the soul lifted above
itself. Reason remains and is dowered with a new power to help out the
anima in its peregrination. There is a darkness to be entered, the darkness
of faith and the dark night of the soul, but this darkness is totally unlike
the dark passion of romance or the unconscious world of Avernus, to
which in the old days it was bidden to descend. It is a darkness which is
due to excess of light and neither the human is lost nor the personal. The
living God is there, the Shepherd who leads his flock, whose rod and
whose staff are there to guide and hold; and the Word made Flesh is 'the
truth and the way and the life'.

LOVE AND THE SELF

INDIVIDUAL AND PERSON

In recent years certain French writers have made great play with a
distinction between individual and person. The first to bring it into
currency was M. Maritain. So great was his success in showing that the
terms of this distinction, which belong properly to the philosophy of
St. Thomas Aquinas, are alive and relevant to modern problems, that a
group of younger thinkers, led by M. Mounier, the former editor of
L'Esprit, has made of the distinction the chief plank in their sociological
programme. The name, Personalism, which they have given to their
views marks the importance they attach to the word, person, and they
claim that it and the word, individual, are the clue to the solution of one
of the most vexing problems of our time. Their argument is attractive.
They diagnose the trends of the age as, on the one hand, towards security,
uniformity and collectivism, and, on the other hand, towards freedom
and responsibility. Science and economics have brought nations closer
together and produced vast systems and uniform groupings. The individual tends to be squeezed out by co-operative societies, *laissez-faire* to
be succeeded by State control. At the same time it is seen that society
must have as its end the development of free and responsible persons.
Every human individual must be treated as a person and educated to be
such. Otherwise a State becomes subhuman. The problem, therefore, of
how to harmonize these two tendencies exists now in an acute form. But
unfortunately so blind are political thinkers and reformers that their plans
are often completely one-sided and strangle one or other of these two
apparently divergent tendencies.

Now the Personalists claim that the principle which should guide all
reform and can serve to reconcile these two opposing tendencies is contained in this distinction of individual and person. It goes back to Aristotle
and is fully formulated by St. Thomas Aquinas, but not till now has its
importance in the practical order been realized. Man is spirit and body,
and because of his body he is an individual in the species, one amongst
a countless number of others. If we consider a man as such, prescinding
for the moment from what constitutes him a full person, he is only a
part of a whole, an individual of a species, a member of a natural unit of
society, such as the State. The State deals with him as belonging to it,
as one of the multitude who compose it, and it can demand his service
and obedience, even at times to the sacrifice of his life. But though a
human being can be considered in abstraction as a mere individual or
unit and have an identity card and a number on his passport, this is not

the full story of him. He is a person, and as a person he has rights which the State cannot touch, and an end which is above that of the State. Looked on as a person, a human being is more than a unit of human society; he is the steward of his own being, an image of God, free and holy, concerned with truth and goodness, and destined for an immortal happiness.

In a well-informed article in *The Modern Schoolman* (January 1945), the writer, Jules A. Baisnee, brings out by quotations from its authors the metaphysical and moral basis of this distinction. He quotes these words of Maritain, taken from *The Rights of Man*: 'Whenever we say that a man is a person, we mean that he is more than a mere parcel of matter, more than an individual element in nature, such as an atom, a blade of grass, a fly or an elephant. . . . Man is an animal and an individual who holds himself in hand by his intelligence and his will. He exists not merely physically; there is in him a richer and nobler existence; he has a spiritual superexistence through knowledge and through love. He is thus in some fashion a whole, not merely a part; he is a universe unto himself, a microcosm in which the whole great universe can be encompassed through knowledge; and through love he can give himself freely to beings who are, as it were, other selves to him.' In this passage it is easy to recognize the philosopher writing, and easy, too, to recognize the philosophy on which he is relying. Not all would admit that Maritain's distinction is a legitimate application of the well-known Thomist theory of individuation, but he can point to both Père Garrigou-Lagrange and Père Gillet for support.

The apparent advantage of this distinction is that with all its metaphysical strength it lends itself to important applications in the moral and social order. We are able to see the ground of the State's authority over the individual, and the limits of that authority. We can work out a programme of social legislation which is both philosophical and practical. This is the view of Mounier and his confrères, and by laying stress on the high vocation of man as a person they claim that they are able to adjust man's private claims to those made upon him by society. Mounier, in *A Personalist's Manifesto*, defines a person as a 'spiritual being constituted as such by its manner of existence and independence of being; it maintains this existence by its adhesion to a hierarchy of values that it has freely adopted, assimilated, and lived by its responsible activity and by a constant interior development; thus it unifies all its activity in freedom and by means of creative acts develops the individuality of its vocation.' The person, he tells us, grows by progressive integration; the individual falls apart and becomes a shadow of his true self. The person is open-minded and generous; the individual is increasingly avaricious and narrow, he is a dog in the manger and fastens on to a hard and exclusive notion of ownership, whereas the person is spurred on to 'a constant effort at advancement and detachment, therefore at renunciation, dispossession, and spiritualization.' The individual is content with a bourgeois noli-me-tangere conception of freedom, while the person seeks for emancipation, for a spiritual liberty from all that thwarts his highest impulses and interior freedom. Lastly 'we find human communion implanted in the very heart of the person as an integrating factor of its existence'.

It is these contrasts rather than the philosophical truth of this distinction that are relevant to the theory of two loves. Many philosophers will hesitate before receiving the distinction as it stands. There is no doubt a distinction which must be made, but it needs a very skilful philosophic practitioner to apply the Thomist one without confusion; and it does not appear that Mounier and those who think with him have altogether escaped confusion. The contrast they emphasize is too drastic, and seems to go wrong at certain points. It is too drastic because it seems to hand man as an individual over to the State as a mere part or unit, and then by reaction to remove man as a person from out the jurisdiction of the State and society. This is to underrate the purpose and authority of the State, which is concerned with more than man's material interests. Denis de Rougemont, whose views on romantic love I have already examined, is one of these Personalists who strain the distinction. For him man as an individual is part of a whole, and his activities are wholly absorbed by the State. As Mr. Baisnee says, there is in de Rougemont's account an 'irreducible antithesis between the person and the individual: while the individual is shut up within itself like an amorphous cell which is lost in the mass, the person affirms his responsibility, is conscious of his mission among men, and is willing to take whatever risks are involved in his mission even at the cost of an heroic effort.'

Here the contrast is too forced; the individual belongs, as it were, to the 'closed' universe, the person to the 'open'. As a result this strange consequence is accepted that it is the individual who is selfish and self-centred in all his activities, and the person who is altruistic and free from selfcentredness. This conclusion has an eye on only one aspect of personality. It may be true that as persons we are magnanimous, but the more we develop the thought of the person as independent of the State and society, as free and autonomous, as, what Maritain calls, 'a microcosm in which the whole great universe can be encompassed through knowledge', the more does the person appear to be self-centred, and not so very unlike the well-known magnanimous man of Aristotle. If it is as an individual that man belongs to the State, then it is as an individual that he is less self-centred. What he is flows out from him instead of curdling within into egocentrism. This criticism is well put in a passage from Père Descoqs (*Archives de Philosophie*, XIV, cahier 2, 1938), which is quoted by Mr. Baisnee: 'As a member of the human species, man is never entirely separated from his fellow-men, but is in constant vital relationship with the community of which he is a member, and "open" to the influence of the other members. Nay more, the individual man, because of the higher degree of perfection and differentiation he can attain, is the more "open" to all forms of expansion and more capable of deep and delicate love, as he is the more free with regard to his fellow men. He is all that precisely because he belongs to a species and therefore is an individual in the sense given to the word by our modern authors. Inversely, it is because of his personality that he exists "for himself" in self-defence, in resistance and in attack. His conscience is literally an inviolable asylum which can never be forced. Under duress his freedom of action may be restrained to the point of vanishing, and yet his inner freedom remains untouched. It is only in the measure in which he is a free person that he directs and controls his moral activity to the best of his own interests. Therefore we may say that it is as a person that man is "shut-in", impervious to external influences, and as an individual that he is "open".'

It does not seem, therefore, that this distinction between individual and person can serve, as it stands and as it is understood by these Personalists, to throw light upon the problem of self-centred and disinterested love. But it is not for that reason to be regarded as useless. It adds further confirmation to the truth that we cannot dispense with some distinction. Our own experience and the long record of human history and literature exhibit a see-saw of conflicting desires, a contrast so striking that Hegel was led, prematurely and unwisely, to force it into a logical pattern of thesis and anti-thesis. This experience, which Mounier and his friends have defined under the terms of individual and person, is more appropriately expressed in the language of Eros and Agape, animus and anima, though it has many names differing according to the context in which the distinction has to be made. When, for instance, the leader writer in the *Times Literary Supplement* (17 February 1945) comments on the literary movement of the 'Nineties, he is made aware that the story of that romantic twilight has 'an urgent practical interest for our own time'. For 'we are on (if not already over) the threshold of a new era when weariness, disillusionment and escapism will be kept off only by the hardest of gem-like flames of watchful energy and self-control'. And when Santayana looks back upon the *Persons and Places* of his past life he tells us that he was struck by a distinction which, as belonging to the fabric of human nature, is older far than the terms which Nietzsche invented or rediscovered for it. 'The *Bacchae*, however, was a revelation. Here before Nietzsche had pointed it out, the Dionysiac inspiration was explicitly opposed to the Apollonian, and although my tradition and manners are rather Apollonian, I unhesitatingly accept the Dionysian inspiration as also divine. It comes from the elemental god, from the chaotic but fertile bosom of nature. Apollo is the god of measure, of perfection, of humanism. He is more civilized, but more superficial, more highly conditioned. His worship seems classic and established for ever, and it does last longer and is more often revived than any one form of Dionysiac frenzy; yet the frenzy represents the primitive world soul, not at home in the world, not settled in itself, and merging again with the elements, half in helplessness and half in self-transcendence and mystic triumph.'

That is to say, in the inadequate language of individual and person, that man as a person tends to be Apollonian, to rule himself by his reason and to look to his own interests in freedom and with well-poised judgement. This is the world of 'measure and perfection'. But, as an individual, man can be less than this or more than it. He can descend to the 'chaotic, but fertile bosom of nature', be carried away by what is elemental in him or lose himself in some community or in the State; and he can also seek for 'self-transcendence and mystic triumph' with grave risks to his own integrity; or finally pray that by the power and wisdom of Another he may be taken away from self-interest and helped to love even as he is loved.

CHAPTER SEVEN

ANIMUS AND ANIMA

Wait without thought, for you are not ready for thought:
So the darkness shall be the light, and his stillness the dancing.
Whisper of running streams, and winter lightning
The wild thyme unseen and the wild strawberry
The laughter in the garden, echoed ecstasy
Not lost, but requiring, pointing to the agony
Of death and birth.

T. S. ELIOT.

A bourgeois who has not lost his illusions is like a winged hippopotamus.
—L. BLOY.

For I was flax and he was flames of fire.

F. QUARLES.

In medio duorum animalium innotesceris.—OFFICE OF GOOD FRIDAY.

'All is not going well in the home of Animus and Anima. It is a long time since their short honeymoon, during which Anima had the right of speaking at her ease, while Animus listened to her ravished with delight. After all, did not the household live on the fortune brought by Anima? But not for long did Animus allow himself to be reduced to this inferior position; very soon did he show his true nature—vain, pedantic and tyrannical. Anima is an ignoramus and a fool, she has never been to school; whereas Animus knows a heap of things, he has read a heap of things in books . . . all his friends say that it is impossible to be a better talker. . . . Anima has no longer the right to say a word . . . he knows better than she what she wants to say. Animus is not faithful, but that does not prevent him being jealous, for *au fond* he knows well (no, he has finished by forgetting it) that all the fortune belongs to Anima, and that he is a beggar, and lives on what she gives him. So he is endlessly exploiting and tormenting her to get money out of her. . . . She stays silently at home to do the cooking and clean the house as best she can. . . . *Au fond* Animus is a bourgeois; he has regular habits, and likes to eat the same dinner every day. But something strange had happened. . . . One day Animus came in unexpectedly . . . he heard Anima singing to herself behind closed doors a curious song, something he did not know; there was no way of discovering the notes, or the words, or the key—a s range and wonderful song. Since then he

has slyly tried to make her repeat it, but Anima pretends not to understand. She is silent as soon as he looks at her. The soul is silent when the
mind looks at it. Then Animus thinks he will play a trick on her; he
takes steps to make her think he is not present . . . little by little Anima
reassures herself, she looks here and there, she listens, she sighs, she
thinks herself alone, and noiselessly she goes and opens the door to her
divine lover.' (Claudel.)

In this parable Claudel gives us his version of Eros and Agape; but
Agape is here heavenly Agape, the Beatrice of the Divine Comedy. I
must try to show in this chapter how the notions of active and passive,
egoism and self-sacrifice, classical and romantic, life and death, masculine
and feminine, animus and anima are the two constituents or factors which
give the clue to the workings of nature, the self and the love of the self
for God. The anima is the feminine principle, which is described by the
modern psychologists in terms of the unconscious or the libido. What
they say of it might be correct if human beings were animals; but they
can only reach at most a half-truth in their interpretation, because the
instinctive and vital urges have been taken over and uplifted into a new
life in the human personality. The instincts as they describe them belong
rather to human personalities as they are in process of retrogression to a
level unworthy of them—to which in fact they can never finally descend.
The anima, therefore, stands both for the lower levels of the human soul,
the unquiet soul of Saul who visits Endor, and also for the soul with
boundless desires, the anima when moved to its proper delight by
heavenly Agape. What is said of the anima is also true in its own fashion
of animus. At its lowest level it is the magician of the unconscious, the
savage, the warrior, the titan and the tyrant; and finally it is the Prometheus, the strong and formative reason, which has for its duty to rule
the self and acquire knowledge. But it, too, must cease to play the
bourgeois and the complacent lover when anima is drawn by heavenly
love.

From time immemorial man has sought to answer what has been called
the Riddle of the Universe. His mind will never be satisfied until some
unity or system be discerned in the manifold variety of nature. He looks
for order in what is at first sight almost chaotic. To the answer to this
problem of what has been called the One and the Many philosophers
are dedicated; but interest in the Universe is not confined to them.
Primitive people felt that nature was both very near to them—they were
in rhythm with it—and at the same time far off and strange. They were
impelled by a desire to seize its secret, as they felt that, if they could
possess it, they would have a closer communion with it and at the same
time be able to control it magically. This desire has always persisted,

and is to be found, for instance, in the well-known lines of Tennyson:

> And came on that which is and caught
> The deep pulsations of the world,
> Aeolian music, measuring out the steps of time. . . .

Many felt that the secret lay in numbers, in harmonies and proportions. Pythagoras and his school are famous for their efforts in this direction, and the effect of their teaching is to be found in the writings of St. Augustine and many another distinguished thinker down to our own times. How impressive this line of thought can be is well shown in the remarkable book, *Le Nombre d'Or*, by Matila C. Ghyka, in which the amazing uniformity of what is called the Golden Number in architecture, painting, sculpture, music, and human beauty is demonstrated by drawings and photographs. He offers extremely interesting arguments to prove that in those rhythms of language which have a magical effect and produce by incantation an effect of hypnosis or ecstasy on the listeners, there is always present this golden number. He would even show that there is the closest connection between this number and the law of Eros.

Equaly interesting is the attempt to explain all by what is called the law of opposites. Heraclitus and Empedocles are remembered by many who are not technically philosophers because their theories arouse in all of them something of the old expectation. From the fragments of Heraclitus we can reconstruct some of his main teachings. It is customary to think of him as a physicist who opted for fire as the universal principle of nature. But he is more than that. He seems to have seen all things as existing in a kind of tension, like a bowstring drawn back or like fire which lives by consuming. Nature is, in Gerard Hopkins' words, 'million fuelled' and ever burning. But there is a rhythm which gives harmony to the strife of the opposites. In this description a glimpse is given to us by a genius into the everlasting rhythm of nature, the balance of opposites, the process of becoming, of birth and decay, of life with its dominant and recessive notes. Even more picturesque is the picture of nature and life by Empedocles, as he introduces into the mixture of the fundamental elements the moving forces of hate and love, Eros.

Here in embryonic form is the partly scientific and partly imaginative apprehension of the secret of the processes of nature. In one from or another this belief in the harmony or unity of opposites has persisted down the centuries. Fair and foul, strong and weak, the light and the dark, right and left, the opposites are always together confronting one another and doing battle in mythologies and legends. The seasons of the year, the movement of the sun, the rhythms of music and poetry are taken as pointers to the truth, and more than one majestic philosophy has made this alternation the central principle of its system. It is worth noting that the most famous of all these systems came into being at a time when romanticism had taken hold of men's minds. The Hegelian dialectic, which has left an indelible mark on the German mind, which inspired the Marxist philosophy and the later Idealism of Croce and Gentile in Italy, moves away from the egoism inherent in Fichte, and has its most resounding successes in the heyday of romanticism; it then spills over into its opposite as the nineteenth century drew to its close. In its structure and pessimism Spengler's *Decline of the West* is the strange but legitimate offspring of Hegel.

Long before Hegel, however, this hint of a struggle of opposites for existence was firmly dealt with. In his *Metaphysics* Aristotle dresses a table of these opposites. They consist of the limit and the unlimited, the odd and even, the one and the many, right and left, male and female, resting and moving, the straight and the curved, light and darkness, the good and the bad, the square and the oblong. In the *Physics* also, amongst other places, he gives his solution to the problem of becoming, of generation and death. His predecessors had been puzzled by the apparent contradiction that if a thing changes it must both be and not be at the same time. What is not turns into what is, and what is ceases to be and is not. The earlier thinkers, like Heraclitus, had tried their hand at an answer, an answer which is both scientific and poetical; they had used striking images, such as hate and love, which have more than an archaic value, and they played with a theory of numbers. But Aristotle tackled the problem seriously, and he used for its solution two principles which, whatever we may think of them in the precise formulation Aristotle gives to them, have proved indispensable in any philosophic explanation of nature. I will call them the determinant and the determinable. It was Aristotle's conviction that both of these must be present in any object which can suffer change. To take the simplest, if most baffling, example: I can divide up a line into a number of parts, let us say ten. Now before the line was divided it was one, and even now if I choose to go on dividing it, I can do so. For this to be possible there must be the capacity in an extended object to have parts, to have a hundred or more parts when it actually has only ten parts. Again, a piece of marble is in the rough; it is taken hold of by a sculptor and given a form of a man. Unless the marble in some mysterious way was of a material which could be so shaped, the change would be impossible, and that means that there was more in the marble than we imagined, though before the work of the sculptor upon it, it was actually nothing more than a lump of marble. This seems to force us to admit that there is something really there, which is not nothing and not actual. This is what Aristotle called the determinable, something which is not actual, but which can be actualized. As everything that we know is, in fact, actually something, the conclusion which follows is that it is made up of two coefficients: first, a form, which could not exist unless it were forming something; and secondly, a matter which, though here and now determined by the form to be this actual something, this lump of marble, is determinable in the future to be something else, for instance, this statue. That is to say, at the very time it is a lump it is also capable of being a statue. If we wish for other examples of these two mysterious coefficients which are present in every actual thing we know, the growth of the body and mind or the transformation of food into our bodily tissues will serve. Since the writing of this paragraph I have changed in mind and body. But in order to explain this change I must have recourse to these two principles: I must have had in me, though not actualized, the real capacity to be what I am now. The change here, however, is more subtle than in the examples I have already quoted. Better to take the example of eating and digestion. The bread which has been consumed undergoes a transformation through the activities of my body and in time becomes part of me. It is the bread which has changed, and so there must be some connection between the tissues into which it has changed and the original bread. There cannot be a gap of nothingness, for then it would not be the bread which has strengthened me, and yet it is no longer bread.

The writ of these two principles runs throughout nature and human life. The names we give to them have come to be part and parcel of our lives; they occur again and again in the distinctions we make in everyday speech, though we know not the ancestry of these destinctions nor our own metaphysical lore. They are essential for any discussion of the arts or industries; they carry with them the undertones of the positive and negative in physical science and good and bad in morality.

To detect order within apparent disorder and to group under one or more headings the infinite variety of nature and life is a delight to the mind, but at the same time dangerous. The danger is that we may think that the heading will serve as an immediate principle of explanation and prove to be a magic formula dissolving all problems and mysteries. Since such groupings and headings are often quite superficial, I do not ask the eader to accept my emphasis on the two principles save as a pointer. A metaphysical inquiry into their value would be irrelevant, and I give the Aristotelian statement of them chiefly as a preamble to what he says about generation and death. For simplicity's sake I will quote Sir David Ross's summary, in his *Aristotle*, of how, according to that thinker, the change in generation can be explained. 'The answer to both our questions lies in this—that the destruction of one substance is the generation of another, and vice versa. I.e. the material cause of generation-destruction and of its perpetuity is matter which can assume first one and then another substantial form. Generation seemed puzzling because it seemed to be coming to be out of what sheerly is not, but now we see that it is not this. The perpetuity of generation seemed puzzling because the sum of existence seemed to be constantly wasting away by the passing of things into nothing; but we now see that passing away is not that—what is imperceptible to sense is not necessarily nothing. Generation and destruction are the two sides of a single transformation of substance into substance. Yet of such transformations some are more properly called cases of coming to be, viz., those in which the substance produced has a higher reality, a more positive character, than the other; thus the production of fire from earth is unqualified coming to be and can only with a qualification be called passing away, since heat is the form of which cold is the mere privation.'

The point where Aristotle improves on his predecessors is this, that they tried to explain the change of one thing into another, while under the impression that each of those two things was fully itself and in no sense anything else. Holding this, they were at an impasse and all their attempts were bound to break down. If a thing, for instance, is nothing more nor less than a cabbage, it can never be anything else than a cabbage; the only change in it could be in its ceasing to be a cabbage. Between it and human tissue there would be an unbridgeable gulf. Nevertheless it is the cabbage which changes into human tissue. Aristotle said that no explanation could be forthcoming unless there were present in every real thing two principles, the one which gave it the positive actual reality it had and another which was the determinable. This latter in so far as it is never actually anything itself outside the conjunction with the other principle is a kind of non-being, though obviously it is not nothing. It is this strange determinable which allows for the decay of actual things and allows too for the actual thing passing into something else. And what is most remarkable is that these two principles account for destruction and generation without recourse to any new principle. One thing perishes and is changed into another, which then is actual or alive; but there is no gap between the two; there is no need to invoke a new creative power when the first dies. The loss of the one reality is the coming to be of the other; the very death of one is the generation of its successor.

Now this short account of a subtle and metaphysical change is necessarily crude and possibly obscure. All that needs noting is that in whatever we find in nature there are two principles, the one positive and the other negative—negative, that is to say, in so far as it is no more than a determinable, which allows for the possibility of change and death. One principle gives light, the other shadow; one makes for unity and form, the other for multiplicity and dissolution and not-being. The tension between what, on the one hand, asserts itself and gives definition and order, and the principle which is passive and receptive and without positive rights and proprietorial claims, gives the short or long-lived life to the various objects, inanimate and animate which we know, including ourselves. Aristotle puts this idea forward in a passage well worth noting. He says that he admits with the philosophers who preceded him that 'there is something divine, good and desirable'; but 'we hold that there are two other principles, the one contrary to it, the other such as of its own nature to desire and yearn for it'. Now, he goes on, if we take our opponents' views that there are two *positive* principles in change, the result will not work out. One of them will have to desire its own extinction, and this is absurd; for the positive principle which gives any positive object its reality cannot desire to have what it already has; the other positive principle which is the contrary of the first, just because it is admittedly contrary, cannot at the same time desire the positive perfection of the other. 'The truth is that what desires the form is matter, as the female desires the male and the ugly the beautiful—only the ugly or the female not *per se* but *per accidens*.'

This distinction of the determinable and the determinant is in Aristotle a metaphysical one, and it would be very rash to apply it to any actual and physical distinction within a living being. Aristotle's aim is wholly other from that which Freud, for example, had in mind when writing of the life and the death instinct. Nevertheless, the image of matter as a female desiring the male and the great discovery that there is an element of non-being in every finite reality, are suggestive and helpful. Though Aristotle might well repudiate the translation of his metaphysical ideas into terms of Eros and Agape, the lead given by Empedocles and the Platonists is too inviting to be rejected. Eros keeps insinuating itself into the driest Greek philosophy, and so it is not fantastic to think of Aristotle's thought as running on lines not too dissimilar to those already sketched in the last chapter.

The determinable and the determinant, the matter and the form make up every living being. The one gives notice of death to come, the other sticks to itself and keeps chaos at bay, and neither can be without the other. Life therefore is an affair of two principles and by their marriage it persists. Let us go further and say that in the receptivity and going out of itself of one, and the embrace and possession by the other, the mingling of these two together has its analogies with breeding in nature and marriage among human kind. The duality which is fundamental to nature expresses itself, when nature has separated itself off into two distinct beings within a species, into a determinant and a determinable, a masculine and a feminine. These latter are the separate types of what is in a lower and more fundamental level of nature a rhythm and duality present together as positive and negative, form and matter. It does not matter at all whether, in fact, in certain species the feminine is the dominant and the masculine the patient, so long as the two are there. The point is that, however assigned, these roles are necessary and universal; they are always present and it is by their marriage that life proceeds, dies and comes to be.

Now if this be so we should expect in the animal world the obvious presence of these characteristics, and we ought to be able to see the workings of desire and love—whether we call it Eros or not is of no concern at the moment—according to these two principles. On the one hand, we ought to find love as dominant, as aggressive and brutal, and on the other hand as also expressing itself in passivity, in victimization, in surrender and even death. There is no need to do more than mention these characteristics. Immediately we realize that the evidence is overwhelming, and, what is very relevant, the evidence is confirmed by the study of human behaviour under one of its aspects. The long and close study of pathological states under analysis reveals the fact that in stages of regression men and women begin to display more and more one or other, if not both, of these two characteristics. They are states of regression and they are looked upon with abhorrence as perversions. I shall go on later to show that man as a spiritual being must regard such behaviour with disgust, where it is culpable, but it should be observed that what is degrading for man is natural for an animal. This no doubt is one of the reasons why so many are shy of facing the obvious and admitting that everywhere and at all times animals' love exhibits itself in the lust of violence and surrender. It has the rhythm of an apache dance, and if we rid ourselves of the 'pathetic fallacy' and cease to regard animals as semi-human, their habit of love-making will seem quite normal. It may be even that much that we take to be pain and evil is to the animal a form of ecstatic pleasure. If it be true that even amongst human beings suffering can be a kind of inverted joy, a malady they cherish, the suffering and passage to extinction on a level below ours may be a death-motif and the supreme moment of a short life. The *motifs* of the dark passion and death which ring through the poetry and music of Tristram are a purified memory of the joys of the underworld or the unconscious. Still more akin to the emotions felt by animals would be the sufferings which fanatics impose upon themselves, often in the name of religion. The gruesome rites of savage tribes, the gashings and tearings in orgiastic dances and ceremonials, the shrieks of corybants, the whirlings of dervishes, the inhuman ascesis of fakirs, these and similar phenomena are far too widespread and constant in history to be dismissed as inexplicable aberrations. Mankind turns to pain as to dirt. There is a vice which is a close attendant on submissiveness as there is on mightiness and lordship. In winning mastery over others there is a special joy which can coarsen into bullying and cruelty, and it may even happen that the very overcoming of obstacles, with all the hardship involved, brings with it a pleasure which is heightened by the pain. The one consolation in reflecting on this is that nature, red in tooth and claw, may be a source of happiness to both pursuer and victim.

This savage and subhuman side of man's passions is the open and normal life of living things below him. I have said that the evidence for the two movements of desire in the brute world is overwhelming, whether it be taken from the farmyard, the jungle, the air or the sea. So obvious is this that, though we do not like to advert to the fact, we nevertheless use the images of bull and cock and buck and ram to cover one set of desires and their counterparts to express the other mode of loving. 'A man that's made a great peacock for the pride of his eye.' But it may be said that these obvious distinctions do not justify any extreme view of love, and certainly not one which attempts to build itself on two principles, the one of mastery and assertiveness and egocentrism and the other on passivity, subjection and surrender. And yet is there any other satisfactory explanation of the recurrence of that kind of love which de Rougemont has described as the dark romantic passion, or of the permanent phenomenon of Apolline and Dionysiac conflicts or of the curious problem caused by the contrasting movement of centripetal and centrifugal love, egocentrism and self-sacrifice? We do find in nature and in the behaviour of living things a rhythm and tension, especially in mating, an analogy, which it would be foolish to ignore. Moreover, when our own desires and actions fall to a subhuman level they betray the characteristics of this animal rhythm and create out of the 'unconscious' the symbols of life and death, of brute strength and decadence, the primitive male and female. In every generation the wise counsellors and the saints have sent out warnings of the peril of playing with the subhuman and the esoteric and the *pseudo-mystique* lest man fall into the abyss.

The evidence, therefore, leads us to treat as fundamental this distinction of the determinable and the determinant, which as we rise in the scale of creation, will be translated into the more congenial distinction of the active and passive, the dominant and the receptive, the taker and the giver, the male and the female, the animus and the anima. Aristotle had already called attention to the fact that there is in every finite being a principle of non-being or death as well as a principle of life or form. He never said, however, that a living thing could have within it a desire for its own extinction. To a Greek, like him, who believed in reason and what we now call the classical ideal, the romantic passion could make no appeal; he would have repudiated it as barbarian and irrational. He would have considered the Freudian instinct for death as belonging to a debased coinage in philosophy. But between Aristotle and Freud there is no need to make a choice. Their conflicting interpretations and markedly differing philosophies can be left on one side, so long as we agree on the nature of the evidence.

Now there is abundant evidence that desire turns in on itself, that man has melancholy moods, that he suffers from a *nostalgie du néant*, that he can persecute himself and find a morbid or maniac joy in suffering and self-surrender or in fusion with darkness or a Whole in which he will not personally survive. Millions of men and women for centuries have embraced a creed in the East according to which they must detach themselves from all desire for self. In the Indo-European mystery religions the wildest forms of self-destruction were practised and in the decadence of romanticism the note of melancholy is most pronounced. But whereas in man there is a contrary tendency which is stronger and demands that he seek life and that more abundantly—an imperative ordering him to guard his life and never surrender or lose his soul—in the animal kingdom life seems to be of no great price; it is given and taken with spendthrift haste. Infinite waste and prodigality and running to seed; constant corruption and regeneration! This is the spectacle which meets our eyes, and if it be denied that there is a principle of death, there is such an outpouring of life, such squandering as to be almost equivalent to it. If explanations be sought one can be found in the doctrine of St. Thomas Aquinas that in the operations of nature it is not so much the individual with which it is concerned as the good of the whole. Where beings fall below man and lack the worth conferred by personality much less care is shown for individual life, and, what is more, there is not such a hold on it by the individual. The Saint teaches that in the animal species the good of the universe is constantly procured by the destruction of individuals. Furthermore, in generation animals desire perpetuity, but as they do not possess knowledge nor a personal life of their own, the desire is rather for the perpetuity of the species. 'Those creatures . . . who have in their natural constitution strength enough to preserve perpetual being, so as to remain always the same numerically, have a natural appetite for perpetuity even in respect of sameness of numbers; while those whose natural constitution has not strength for this, but only for preservation of perpetuity of being in respect of sameness of species, also have a natural appetite for perpetuity. This difference then must be noted in those creatures whose desire of being is attended with cognition, that they who do not know being except in the present time, desire it for the present time, but not for ever, because they have no apprehension of everlasting existence; still they desire the perpetual being of their species, a desire unattended with cognition, because the generative power, which serves that end, is preliminary to and does not come under cognition.' (*Contra Gent.*, Bk. 2, ch. 55. Translation by J. Rickaby, *God and His Creatures*, p. 114.)

This passage does suggest an answer which meets the facts without the awkwardness of supposing a direct desire of a being for its own extinction. To some this latter idea must appear contradictory; for how could a dynamic structure whose very being consists in living contain within itself a contrary desire not to live and be? If, however, we take account of the twofold principle in every such organism, the one positive and the other negative, a way out of a difficulty is offered. All we have to suppose is that the negative principle is directed to some aim which belongs to it but reaches beyond its own existence. Such an aim is the preservation and increase of the species to which it belongs. Hence the female of the species gives itself in love and enjoys the giving without regard to its own death. Indeed, the pleasure is of a kind in which death and propagation are felt as inseparable.

The interpretation of animal experience is bound to be at best problematical, and it is given only in order to throw light on the experience of man. Man is half an animal and he will therefore show in his experience the transvaluation of the animal appetites into something much higher. The writ of the spirit runs throughout the kingdom of the instincts and passions, for a man is a single self and being, not composed, as a remark above might suggest, of two halves joined together. There is nothing in him which is purely animal; his whole being is infused and informed by what is called the rational soul. The life of the plant has been compared to an angle, that of the animal to a triangle and that of the rational animal to a quadrilateral. The animal has functions which belong to the plant level of life, but these latter are now like the angle within the triangle; man has functions which belong both to the plant level and to the animal level, but they are taken up into the higher life as the angle and the triangle are included in the quadrilateral. This we know without recourse to any particular theory of the relation of the mind to the body. Our moral experience is such that we know that the passions must be regulated, that the beast must be made obedient to and a friend of the spirit. It is the mind which takes cognizance of what we are and where we are going and what we ought to do about it. It is the mind which in its conscious life can indirectly be made aware of its own proper self and the essential unity of that strange self which is ours. By these and other reflections man has come to realize his dignity, his rights and his duties and the sacrosanct uniqueness of every individual, which the State has to respect and protect and forward in its legislation. What is meant by civilization and the advance of man is just the growing acknowledgement and appreciation of the rights, duties and worth of every single human being.

The proper understanding of Eros and Agape hangs on the appreciation of this peculiar nature which man has, its likeness to that of the animal and its striking difference. In animals we have argued that there is a twofold principle of love, a rhythm which exhibits itself in taking and giving, in what for short may be called a tension of the masculine and the feminine. The sexes in all higher degrees of life are separate and individual. Nevertheless in each individual the characteristics of each remain to this extent that there is a positive and a negative principle or movement, and one is called masculine or feminine according to the dominance of one or other of these two in the individual. Each person has an animus and an anima, each is in different proportions masterful or clinging and submissive, fierce or gentle, hard or soft, Apolline or Dionysiac, intellectual or emotional, selfish or devoted. I give this list of opposites because by their very diversity they serve to show the character or meaning which the two forces or appetites possess. Each has a character which produces a state of tension with the other, but neither is of the kind which can be defined precisely; and we have always to allow for a more or a less in their mutual relations. Nevertheless, it is possible to make clearer, as we proceed, what these relations are and what the animus and the anima do. They are the human equivalent of what the dominant and passive, the masculine and the feminine are in the animal. We have to look, therefore, for what in the spiritual part of the self corresponds with the dominant and possessive and what with the recessive and sacrificial. The search need not be a long one, for by the reason, the animus, the self dominates the passions and regulates them into order; it is a judge, and also it grows by acquiring and possessing. We are what we are essentially by storing knowledge after pillaging the universe of its secrets and formulating an ideal which all our other activities must subserve. This ideal is bound to be our own perfection and the happiness which attends on self-realization. In all these respects, then, the animus is analogously what the dominating instinct is in the animal. It is essentially an imperialist. The reason is not, however, an absolute king who can rule unchallenged. The animal side of man still survives, and when the reason is forced to abdicate or is tempted to lower its dignity, it descends to the level of brutal mastery or cold selfishness or becomes a mere prejudice, a rationalization, a judgement which is swayed by passion. The feminine or sacrificial principle in human beings is equally easy to find, though we are handicapped by having no such simple a name for it. Anima is not nearly so precise as animus. The reason for this is that outside the mind we can only think of the self as a creature of longings and urges and instincts. The proper word for the spiritual anima would be 'will', but unfortunately the connotation of this word is confusing. We speak of men of will power, of strength of will. What we really mean by this is that the mind's steadying influence on the passions continues, that our judgement remains unswayed, that our gaze continues in focus. To get the correct idea of anima we should think of it rather as a longing, a breaking away of desire from the self towards an object or a person; and that is why the selfish impulses of man have to be balanced by consideration for others, sacrifice for the community or the family, and, as we shall try to show later, by a movement of the anima towards its Lord and lover, God. Again, because the anima is thought to be more intimately the self than the animus, and to contain all that we are; because, besides, the anima is always affected by what is personal and individual, whereas the animus moves in a world of abstract science and philosophy, dwelling among essences and never among existences, it is used as a synonym for the personal self as well as for that part of the self which is not animus.

For the sake of clarity, then, let us distinguish the various uses of anima. There is, first, the highest level, which is intended in the parable of Claudel's and canonized by Bremond in his *Prayer and Poetry*. Secondly, there is the level, which is symbolized in Dante by Virgil, who is the guide through the dark places and the purgatory of life up to the portals of the heavenly regions. On this level anima is perfectly human, the partner of the animus, and its activity is seen in the altruistic desires of every human being, the balancing of egoism by service and affection for family and society. Thirdly, it expresses all that is in the self when reason is excluded. This covers much that is called romanticism; the soul is free to take wings in imagination, to race ahead of reason by force of love, to leave the highroad of reason for the thickets of mysticism. But as, confessedly, on this level anima is playing truant from reason, a feminine and also a sinister note is struck. Helen of Troy is changing into Aphrodite and Aphrodite into Astarte. Romanticism beginning in hope declines to melancholy and to the worship of the dark goddess. The level below this, the fourth, is one in which the spiritual disappears. The anima is the irrational, the vital centre whence come the dark passions and impulses and instincts. It is the abode of the unconscious, and both the aggressive and the seductive forces dwell there, the eagle and the serpent, Vishnu and the consort of Siva. This level has become well known to us through

the studies of the psycho-analysts, especially Jung. Here dwell the archetypes, the shadow and anima and the old magician. But granted these
levels we can now make a cross-section. In contrast with the reason,
animus, *all* the workings of the unconscious and the irrational can be
called anima, irrespective of the various manifestations which arise from
the abyss of the unconscious. There is a logic in so naming it which
connects together all the uses from the highest to the lowest and makes
it possible to use the name anima without inconsistency for all the levels.
It would be too wearisome to stop each time that the name is used and
explain the particular reference, and as there is this unity of meaning, and
the context generally makes the sense clear, the general word of anima
will suffice without further qualification.

In his chapter on the anima in *Prayer and Poetry* Bremond quotes a
number of passages to bring out its meaning, and, unwittingly, he confirms the divisions just made and shows how closely and strangely the
variations in emphasis and meaning are threaded together. His own view
is that animus is the surface self and anima the deep self: 'Animus, rational
knowledge; and Anima, mystical or poetic knowledge. Ah! when a poet
is doubled by a philosopher, he has strange ways of humbling us. All
that I could find (and with what difficulty) to make this distinction clear
was to oppose the I to the Me: the I, who dances round the circumference
of the soul who affirms himself, and is always afraid that he does not do
so sufficiently, absorbed in the contemplation and renewal of the shadows
of his Chinese lantern, so busy in the narrow wings of the little theatre
that he ends by no longer hearing the concerts which are given behind
the scenes, the symphonies of silence; and on the other hand, the central
Me, who also acts, but with such peaceful intensity that the I thinks she
is asleep, inert and passive; the I who feeds on notions and words, and
enchants himself by doing so; the Me, who is united to realities; the Me,
who receives the visits of God; the I, who often delays them, obstructs
them, volatilizes them in words, and thus loses the benefit of them.' There
is no doubt which of the two lovers Bremond prefers, and his exaggerated
liking for anima and impatience with animus makes him both unaware
of the virtue of the latter and the dangerous fits of lunacy of the former.
But his independent witness is useful in confirming the analysis of anima
as feminine, as being in prayer like to Beatrice and in poetry like to Virgil,
and of animus as being assertive and dominating and feeding on essences
and abstractions. The highest level of anima is described in one of the
quotations which Bremond gives from Ruysbroeck: 'Our most hidden
and intimate home, the extreme point and summit of the heart, the marrow
of the soul'. Louis de Blois leaves the anima open to visitants from the
lower regions as well as from heaven when he calls the anima 'a bare and

shapeless abyss, beyond space and time, its *raison d'être* being a certain perpetual adhesion to God, and yet it is essentially within us, it is us, the very essence of our soul.' This is the reason why the mystic way is the most dangerous of all; the soul must somehow be supported by God throughout the journey; He must keep it from losing itself in nothingness in that abyss, where, as another writer, Père Cyprien de la Nativité, says, 'There is no foothold' (This is one of the reasons why the Christian mystic never completely loses sight or contact with the Incarnate Christ, who is the way and the life). In these descriptions we can see how easily one can pass to different levels of the anima, and how even the language for these different levels contains identical words and images. Bremond himself in assembling together passages from the great mystics and saints and poets and philosophers like Bergson and Marcel Proust, does not seem to have altogether avoided the confusion. Dante was a surer guide.

From this description of animus and anima we can see that they conform to the universal pattern of nature and life in that they too work together as positive and negative, dominant and recessive, masculine and feminine. They are differentiated, however, from all lower types by being the characteristics of a human being, that is, of a person. It might well be true that in physical nature the tension of opposites could be at the expense of one of them or even of both. The Heraclitean image of fire represents very well the constant destruction of one in order to insure continuity. Nature is careless of life because its interests are for the species or some far-off end. The give and take involve real loss, and the giver seems to have no self-respect, no centripetal urge; its surrender is total and its desire, if desire be present, is to lose itself in what is more important than itself. The desire might almost be called a pseudo-mystic one, a form of delirium or ecstasy in which the supreme joy consists in the very passion of self-abandonment or what Scheler has called 'sympathetic fusion'. The victim of animal lust is, as it were, hypnotized into passivity or self-destruction. The relics of these twin passions of brutality and abasement or prostration abide in the anima of man, in his animal instincts, but they are taken up into human nature and undergo a transformation.

Here is the critical change and central point. What were before but instincts become the expression of a personality; they have a moral ideal and they should work together, according to that admirable phrase of Milton, 'in lowly hope and high humility'. Every being below man may be used, if needs be, as a means; it has no personal worth; it expresses itself in violence or beauty for a season and it flows out, passing on its treasures to a world whose motto is the struggle for existence and whose aim is a continuity by species. But with the advent of mind and spirit all is changed. A greater one than the world is in it now, and not the gaining of the whole world is worth the loss of one single soul. Man has been described as a denizen of two worlds, the infinite, everlasting world, and the restricted and temporal one of this earth: as living on the horizon of time and eternity. As a member of the human species, he is, to use a valuable, if imperfect, distinction, an individual; as a soul endowed with will and reason, he is a person.[1] In so far as he is an individual he can be used as a means by the State or society, when the good of society requires it; he may have to relinquish some of his freedom, give of his time and strength and gifts and be prepared, when the safety of the family or the State demand it, even to risk his life. But such sacrifice presupposes a willingness on his part as a reasonable man to share common needs and dangers with others, and there are sacrifices which cannot be asked of him, which on no account is he allowed to make. No one can punish him if he be innocent; no one can take away his entire freedom; no one can rob him of his essential rights; and he on his part is bound to look to the interests of his higher self, to serve truth and to obey the eternal moral order, which is the will of God expressed in an enlightened conscience. He cannot treat himself as a means, sacrifice his honour for gain, lie to do good, yield to his uncontrolled passions.

It is because these prerogatives of man are ignored that Jung's advice to modern man to compromise with his unconscious might mark the unmaking of man, and is, in any case, so dangerous. Jung does not realize that by the unconscious we are bound to mean the barbaric and animal elements in us and that the glory of man consists in this, that the whole of his activities belong directly or indirectly to the spiritual order and should be the thoughts and gestures of a person. What then was licit to an animal becomes a perversion for a man; it means his sinking to the level of a brute or degraded victim. The desire to dominate, to be an oppressor and Bluebeard, as well as the desire to belong to the herd, to crawl and be a parasite and perform suttee, belong to human nature in the same sense that Satan is kith and kin of Michael and his angels. In rude and degenerate civilizations these desires emerge from the dark, and their continuing presence and the toleration of them are the sure signs of coming collapse. Barbarous tribes which are not strong enough to control them do at least fear their power and by taboos and magic strive to immunize them. But when they are flaunted in a sophisticated society and the herd is worshipped and youth falls on its knees before a superman, the desire has turned into a song of death and extinction.

The ideal human life should consist in Animus and Anima composing their quarrels and coming together in amity. They are both human in their excellence and ought to be on the best of terms. The self to which

---

[1] v. Appendix at end of chapter.

both belong needs their combined help. They fill up each other's wants, and in the rise and fall and positive and negative rhythm of their interplay, they keep the self from lapsing into one opposite or extreme. The imagination supplements the reason and renders it flexible, the desires prevent the mind from losing itself in abstractions and so impersonalizing itself, and the unselfish love checks the egocentric and gives it dignity with condescension. Such a happy marriage should constitute perfect human and temporal happiness, and it is, in fact, an ideal which the best of our pagan philosophers are preaching to-day. They think that the quarrels can be patched up; they believe that the pathetic story of the human race so far is due to maladjustments which can be rectified, and so they are for ever looking into some golden future when all external obstacles to peace having been removed, animus and anima will enjoy an authentic paradise. The conflict, however, is far too deep-seated to be removed by the improvement of external conditions alone. A cursory glance at history will show that in conditions good and bad a brief and hazardous courting of animus and anima has occurred, as in fifth-century Greece and thirteenth-century France. But even then the appearance is deceptive. Let us grant, nevertheless, that the ideal of natural goodness has helped mankind and that it is not a mirage. Dante thought of it under the image of Virgil, and as an ideal it can be seriously considered from some vantage ground by a Christian poet or theologian. The theologian is sure that without the grace of God the ideal can never be lived consistently, but, as the grace, which alone will permit of it, is invisible and works in usually with nature, we can write about the result without explicitly bringing in grace. Even he, however, has to confess that human perfection is rare and that the happy give-and-take of animus and anima is as fragile and light as gossamer. Countries and civilizations are more conspicuous by the conflict between animus and the lower levels of anima or by the undue exaltation of one of them at the expense of the other. The East is supposed to be more passive than the West, that is to say, its way of life is the anima with all the attendant dangers of surrendering to the lower manifestations of it. The West is thought to admire action and to have been influenced by the Greek love of balance and reason. Saved from sterility by the Christian faith, it is in danger in its turn of losing its soul when it abandons that faith. By interesting contrast it is in the East that the seraglio and the veiled woman are to be met, whereas in the West the token of the woman is worn by the warrior, and in romance she is like the light of the moon across dark and troubled waters.

The truth is that man cannot keep the animus and the anima abidingly together, and he is ever in conflict either by having to try to heal their discord or in experiencing the very discord which undoes him. The

Christian theologian explains why this is so. Independently of experience he has been told of the doctrine of the Fall of man, and the doctrine fits in exactly with the mystery of the conflict of the two love-forces. The point of the story of the Fall is that God had given to the first human beings an integrity such that the animus and anima were in perfect accord. I say 'given an integrity' because it is held that whatever the harmony which existed by right of nature God had added to it by a special gift. By this gift all temptation to rebellion was removed. If we wish for an example of this accord in a great and sinless nature, we can take the biblical account of the fall of Lucifer and the sin of Adam so majestically portrayed in Milton. The two stories fit in neatly with the supposition of the separate functions of animus and anima, and without such a supposition it is by no means easy to think out what could have happened. In both the stories we have to believe that beings whose desires were in perfect agreement with their reason could be tempted to do such a foolish and irrational act as to reject God's will and infinitely wise providence on their behalf. That they could have been moved so to act must indeed appear difficult unless we can point to two different phases of love, the one egocentric and the other theocentric. If in both these cases there were working a desire which of its very nature tended to promote the self and another which moved away from the self to cast itself before Almighty Goodness and love, these two, no matter how closely linked they were together so as to form perfect human loving, would nevertheless leave the possibility of animus separating itself from anima. The pulsation of self which can never cease so long as there is a living being which is itself, is, as we all know now, so insistent that it focuses all desire upon itself. Even in a paradise or in heaven where sin had not entered in to sow a lasting discord in the self, self-love would exist and might make itself appear so glorious that the voice of the anima could be silenced. Indeed, the more glorious the nature of the self the easier would it be to rest on that grandeur. If we add to this what is also hinted at in the story that God was not always immediately present, the answer to the problem is rounded off. The egocentric impulse is strong just for this reason that we are so immediately present to ourselves; love of another, even God, varies with the felt closeness of the other, and it is of the nature of this love, until the consummation comes, for the loved one to be or to seem now near now far away. And if he or she be far away the love can become drowsy or be beguiled; and it is at such moments that the love of the self, because it is so intertwined with the other love as to be almost one and the same as it, can intrude and produce a false choice.

This theological digression throws, I hope, light on the nature of the human self and confirms the importance of the distinction of animus and anima. It shows how they tend to separate off from one another and how infirm the love of anima can become because of the absence of the beloved. The well-known tale of Eros and Psyche is built on the mingled misery and happiness of this experience of loving in the dark. But in the conditions of human life as we know it further misery has befallen both sides of the self. The two are almost constantly quarrelling, and the one wants to stay at home to nurse its own pride and resentments, while the other goes afield to meet God knows whom. Of the animus, with its selfishness, we have said enough at the moment; the anima has still more secrets to reveal. One is that we have been doing it wrong in ever describing it as affianced to animus. That, as Claudel suggested, is the conceit of animus, his way of regarding anima. She is so lowly in some of her manifestations, she looks so much as if she had come from a lower level of society that the reason is apt to think that it will need all his efforts to make this beggar maid into a queen. That is what most sensible persons think, and what the humanistic ideal demands. The rationalist Greek looked upon all within him which was not lit by reason and controlled by it as barbaric. The Dionysiac and mystery religions swept away the parterres of reason and carried the anima to infinite heights—and depths. They revealed to her that her destiny and her love were beyond all that animus could propose; but the trouble was that they took her out into the night and abandoned her there.

Now it is true that the soul is afflicted with a passion which nothing finite can satisfy; this has been certified once and for all by St. Augustine in the famous sentence about the restlessness of the soul and the inward famine by which it is driven. Philosophy intent on the intellect usually pays no attention to this, but so unmistakable is it that within recent years Heidegger and other existential thinkers, following out a clue given by Søren Kierkegaard, have resuscitated it under the name of 'Angst', inquietude, and made it the central point of their philosophy. But neither they nor any other naturalistic thinkers have been able to do more than be Job's comforters. They can certify the symptom and charge the soul to remember its condition, but they cannot provide a Beatrice. To what shifts Jung had to have recourse we have already seen. The mystery religions invented a technique for inducing self-forgetfulness and fusion with an unknown, and in the East multitudes have followed a similar path. Please God many have made contact with the true God who has come down to meet them, but in itself the system seems to be little more than a device to turn loss into gain and nothingness into a semblance of the All. Consciously or unconsciously those who perfected this device played upon the weakness of the anima, its temptation, that is to say, to descend to the lower levels where the individual does not count and the animal trembles with passionate joy in self-abasement and fusion with another.

In the West, it may be said, the extremes of the Grand Turk and the harem have been avoided, and the relations between animus and anima have been at least legalized. For this comparative success the Church by its powerful influence on western thought and its unbending resistance to the erotic religions and gnostic revivals has been chiefly responsible. Love was ruled by the Logos as well as by reason, and as a result the status of woman was raised. Custom might still make her a chattel, a maid of all work, but she, who had called herself 'the handmaid of the Lord', transfigured all women and gave to their function—and to that of the anima—a new honour and glory. Nevertheless, human nature has been out of harmony with itself since the Fall, and the egocentric and ecstatic impulses have refused to bear with one another, and each has gone a whoring. European history is full of strange episodes, of mad fits, of great and petty tyrannies, of superstitions and crepuscular loves and orgies of passion. Even when the civilization is progressive we can detect an undue preference for one love and the denigration of the other. The romantic gains by his dislike of the classical and the classical has no good word for the romantic. The aristocrat despises the vulgar herd and the herd envies the aristocrat, and the revolutionary is crowned in Notre Dame in the name of Reason and in the person of a woman. In a previous chapter I have tried to sketch the decline of romanticism, the rise and fall of philosophic egoism and the final wandering of anima in a waste land.

'Two loves made two cities,' said St. Augustine in a well-known passage: 'The earthly which is built up by the love of self to the contempt of God, and the heavenly, which is built by the love of God to the contempt of self'. The Saint had principally in mind no doubt the conflict of grace and nature, and before his eyes the city of the Roman Empire, now smitten with creeping paralysis and awaiting destruction from the barbarians, a destruction which the Church would survive. Yet he bears witness to the struggle between two kinds of love, and without prejudice it is possible to see in what he says the sterility of animus left to itself and the impotence of anima when it knows not its true God and lover. For too long a time now the intellect of man has been divorced from the soul and the soul has lost its faith and with it its bearings.

CHAPTER EIGHT

RECAPITULATION

Said the Sun to the Moon—'When you are but a lonely white crone,
And I, a dead King in my golden armour somewhere in a dark wood,
Remember only this of our hopeless love
That never till Time is done
Will the fire of the heart and the fire of the mind be one.'
—EDITH SITWELL.

There is no woman's side
Can hide the beating of so strong a passion
As love doth give my heart.
—SHAKESPEARE.

Three senses of love which it is important to distinguish are symbolized in the three Greek terms, Eros, Philia, Agape. The first of these, Eros, may here be ignored, because although Eros has frequently been opposed to Agape, the nature of Agape is perhaps not best brought out by contrasting it with Eros which retains its connexion with sexual desire, and in which the elements of taking and self-assertion, rather than giving and self-effacement, stand out. Agape is best contrasted with Philia, for in both there is emphasis on giving rather than on taking.—*Creative Morality* by L. A. REID.

The theories of Jung, however unacceptable, provide an admirable map to see the windings and crossings of Eros and Agape, as well as their many derivative streams. But lest the reader be confused by the variety of suggestions contained in the two writers so far examined, I will pause in order to gather up what has been said into a unity and show its bearing on the problem of love. If I am right, the very variations on the theme will of themselves be of a nature to display the true ending to the questions with which we started. That such different views of Eros, for instance, should have been expressed is no evidence that Eros can mean nothing definite. Far from it—though on kindred subjects the varying senses given to words does lead critics at times to give up in despair. I have used, for example, the word 'romantic' and have quoted passages in which it is closely associated with Eros as the dark passion. Many assume that the word 'romantic' has no definite meaning, and that the contrast of classical and romantic has been so overplayed that it corresponds with nothing real. But such a verdict would be mistaken. Classical and romantic is part of the furniture of our mind and we cannot do without some distinction of this sort. It keeps on reappearing in order to separate what thinkers in varying generations are sure must be separated. In the same way Eros and Agape do correspond with something real in the nature of love; the distinction keeps recurring, and the very variations are a mark of its constancy.

But when we put to ourselves the question, what is the exact nature of the distinction, the answer is slow in coming. We can endeavour by a new analysis to arrive at what we want or we can move among the varying answers given by others sifting them and trying to find something which is common; or we can attempt both methods. The last course seems to be the best. In a recent book, *The Personal Principle*, Mr. D. S. Savage gives a number of theories of the meaning of 'classical and romantic'. None of them fits altogether with the connotation given to 'romantic' by de Rougemont. As will be remembered, de Rougemont identifies romance with Eros, and he traces the influence of this wild love on the literature and on the social and moral habits of Europeans since the rise of the troubadours. The romantic is the troubled spirit who does not fit in with a society which is in any way content with a temporal, physical and regulated world. He feels like a ghost at the feast of society; he is in love with love, he is melancholic, constantly frustrated, and the poison in him which he has drunk leads him on inevitably to death, to the wooing of the goddess of night. Now none of the descriptions given of romance by other writers quite fits in with this notion. There are some who say, like Grierson, that romanticism is of the family tree of Plato; there are others who think of it as intensely personal and private as contrasted with the classical, which is cold and proper; others again think of it as the expression of the imaginative and the irrational as opposed to the rational in man. Wyndham Lewis says: 'I always think of something very *solid*, and I believe it is a sensation I share with many people, when the term 'classical' is employed, and of something very dishevelled, ethereal and misty, when the term "romantic" is made use of.' Herbert Read, on the other hand, tells us that 'there is a principle of life, of creation, of liberation, and that is the romantic spirit; there is a principle of order, of control and of repression, and that is the classical spirit.' He dislikes the classical and bids it be gone as the force of oppression. 'Wherever the blood of martyrs stains the ground, there you will find a doric column or perhaps a statue of Minerva'; and he finds salvation in that form of romanticism which is surrealist.

Now it is not, I think, fantastic to see in these statements ideas which border very closely on what de Rougemont described as the love of Eros and to detect analogies with Nygren's view and the glorification of the unconscious by Jung. Both de Rougemont and Nygren admitted that

Neo-Platonism had played a part in the development of Eros. What, therefore, Grierson and Wyndham Lewis say about the relation of romance to Platonism conforms with them. Again, most descriptions of the classical emphasize the reasonableness of it, and this suggests the ego-centric love which Nygren criticizes. The classical does not take one out of oneself; on the contrary, it is very self-possessed. But it can pass into something which is decidedly unpleasant, and this is what Herbert Read has in mind. The Eros, which exalts reason, turns into a tyrant. It wants to hold and to have, to dominate, and it is utterly selfish. On the other hand, this egoism can be corrected by romance, but romance with a curious twist. We must trespass on forbidden ground; we must cross the threshold of the unconscious and let its dark wisdom have sway and teach us. In all this there is surely much that is common, and it suggests that Eros and Agape are not just words, but movements of love, each with a particular idiom and genius.

I must try, therefore, as in a jigsaw puzzle, to fit the various pieces into a pattern. The Greek attitude gives us, perhaps, the best opportuntiy for a good start. The Greeks, like all other races and peoples of any civilization, distinguished between love and lust. This distinction is put in its most perfect form in Plato's *Laws*. 'The man whose love is a physical passion, a hunger for another's charms, like that for ripe fruit, tells himself to take his fill and gives not a thought to his minion's state of soul. But he that treats carnal appetite as out of the question, that puts contemplation before passion, he whose desire is veritably that of soul for soul, looks on enjoyment of flesh by flesh as wanton shame; as one that reverences, aye, and worships, chastity and manhood, greatness and wisdom, he will aspire to live with his love in constant purity on both parts.' Here is the sharp distinction, which later led to the complete repudiation of earthly love in Gnosticism. Marriage, however, is not denied by Plato; on the contrary it is praised as the only proper form of sexual love, and Plato suggests a law which leads 'to the suppression of the mad frenzy of sex, as well as marriage breach of all kinds, and all manner of excesses in meats and drinks, and wins men to the affection of their wedded wives.' (Translation by A. E. Taylor.)

The problem of Eros and Agape is, however, only very indirectly concerned with this distinction of love and lust. There are some who like to think of Eros as always lust or choose to use the name exclusively for it, but the truth seems to be that both Eros and Agape can be good or bad. The point is that they are different aspects of human love; but what characterizes each aspect it is hard to determine. In the *Symposium* Plato gives us many hints, though I do not think that he reached a full answer. He first distinguishes love and lust, the two Aphrodites, the one the daughter of Uranus and the other the daughter of Zeus and Dione. The next speaker tries to put this dual aspect of Aphrodite on a more philosophic basis. He says that this twofold love is present throughout the universe, in every art, in gymnastics and in medicine, in the relations of moist and dry, hot and cold, in astronomy and in the intercourse of the gods with man. This idea is carried on by Aristophanes, though he pretends to be ridiculing his predecessor. His belief is that there were originally three sexes, man, woman and the union of the two. But the gods found these creatures too dangerous; they actually tried to storm the heavens. So Zeus cut them in two, and so disabled them. From that time onwards each half has been in love with the other. 'The reason is that human nature was originally one and we were a whole, and the desire and pursuit of the whole is called love. . . . Wherefore, if we would praise him who has given to us the benefit, we must praise the god Love, who is our greatest benefactor, both leading us in this life back to our own nature, and giving us high hopes for the future, for he promises that if we are pious, he will restore us to our original state, and heal us and make us happy and blessed.' Agathon is the next speaker, but as he says little to honour the god of noble love, I will pass on to the contribution of Socrates. Now Socrates does not admit that love is so perfect in all its ways as Agathon wished to make out. Love is always of something which we have not; we love the beautiful when we lack it and wish to enjoy it. Therefore love is not a god at all, but a mean between fair and foul. Love is the son of Plenty and Want. Want plotted to have a child by Plenty, and succeeded. Therefore Love is like his mother, poor and always in distress, and like his father, too, in that he is bold and strong, 'a philosopher at all times, terrible as an enchanter, sorcerer, sophist'. He goes about searching and longing to satisfy his needs, and that is why we say that love is a desire for what is beautiful and good. By possession of the good he is made happy, or rather as Socrates hastens to correct himself, by possession of the everlasting good. But that is not the whole story; for love is not content with the mere possession of the good and beautiful; it always wants to give birth to beauty. 'For love, Socrates, is not, as you imagine, the love of the beautiful only. "What then?" The love of generation and of birth in beauty. . . . Because to the mortal creature, generation is a sort of eternity and immortality . . . and if, as has already been admitted, love is of the everlasting possession of the good, all men will necessarily desire immortality together with good. Wherefore love is of immortality.' Socrates, quoting the wise Diotima, develops this thought, and argues that mortal nature constantly seeks to continue itself beyond death; and this it does by generation, whereby a new existence is left behind in place of the old. Everything is coming to be and passing away, but nature survives and hands on its life and heritage. This holds true of the creatures of the earth; they live not for themselves but really so as to beget offspring and so live on vicariously. How much more true is it then of the spirit? The soul begets its own offspring, and at the last when it has risen so high as to be able to contemplate true beauty, 'divine beauty, I mean, pure and unalloyed, not clogged with the pollutions of mortality and all the colours and vanities of human life,' it seeks 'to bring forth, not images of beauty, but realities . . . and bringing forth and nourishing true virtue to become the friend of God and be immortal, if mortal man may.'

Here in germ are most of the ideas of which we are in search; the two-fold character of love, in which respect it is compared to the struggle of opposites in nature; the masculine and feminine elements which have been divided and therefore seek to be at one; the poverty and want of one element, the demoniac energy and power of the other; and then the special and favourite idea of Plato that love is a movement to possess and to beget. We shall see that none of these ideas can be neglected. But there is one point which does not receive emphasis in the *Symposium*, which is supposed to be ever-present in Plato's thought because of his knowledge of the Pythagorean teaching and the Orphic mysteries. It is a point which belongs more to religion than to philosophy and has been fully recognized, if not overstressed, in modern accounts of Greek religion. I refer to what Nietzsche called the Apolline and Dionysiac cults, and these names do serve to mark two movements which have had very different histories in Western civilization, have mingled at times and then been in grim conflict. The Apolline creed is one of light; it is fully human, the very noontide of human perfection. Many think of it as the Greek contribution to humanity *par excellence*: the idea of man as an animal endowed with reason and ruled by reason. Man by the light of his reason looking before and after, conceiving a noble end to his endeavours, training his barbaric instincts and passions to serve the purposes conceived by reason, conducting himself by the light of the four cardinal virtues, prudence, justice, fortitude and temperance, observing the golden mean, poised and controlled, and producing those classical works of art which have by so many been cherished as the embodiment of human perfection. And on the opposite side a revolt against all this moderation, this too human ideal, which so easily becomes self-centred and complacent and is so well illustrated by Aristotle's magnanimous man. At its worst it is bourgeois and at its most exalted it is an enlightened selfishness. The wild passions revolted, but they came sweeping in to the marble temples behind a god, Dionysus. At his coming we have orgy and ecstasy; he can tear the contemptuous stranger to pieces and devour his limbs, and he can be worshipped in a deep silence and become one with his worshippers. The civilized Greek liked to have fixed boundaries, to impose form upon the indefinite and the void; he made for himself a closed universe. But the Dionysiac religion broke down the boundary walls and showed a way out, leading either to the infinite sky or to the dark regions. The message of the new cult was ambiguous and of its nature undefined. It had all the obscurity of the irrational, the anima, which may be above reason or below it. It belonged to the orgiastic Indo-European group of religions, which had such an influence in the Mediterranean area at this time, the worship of Cybele and Isis and Mithra. To all of them belongs the Mother Goddess, that mysterious one, who could incite her followers to the most unearthly mysticism or to a madness which often showed itself in self-torturing, blood-violence and repulsive rites.

We have, then, on the one side a Greek ideal, which is often called classical or humanist, and on the other a superhuman or irrational impulse which may be mystic or barbaric and is thought by some to be the parent of the romantic movement. The issue, however, was complicated by an intermarriage of the two in Neo-Pythagorean and Neo-Platonic thought. A further complication arose owing to the influence of Platonism on the formulation of doctrines of Christian revelation. The early Christian Fathers repudiated the syncretistic religions around them and viewed with a deep suspicion much of the Platonic system; but in order to state for themselves their original and divine message they had to borrow terms from the philosophies in vogue. This alliance led to the problem investigated by Nygren and Rousselot. The marriage, however, of the mystery religions with Neo-Platonism led to an esoteric cult which could be made to look so like Christianity as to endanger it and rouse fierce opposition. This rival was of its very nature semi-mystic and cryptic, and owing to the opposition to it was forced to infiltrate into the rapidly growing Christian civilization by ambiguities and symbols and apocryphal writings. It had many names and many variations, and I have used generally that of Gnosticism. But the point to be noticed is that it could look so Platonic as to be almost indistinguishable from the Greek rationalism which the Church had adopted, and at other times it took on all the habiliments of an Oriental goddess.

This may explain why de Rougemont calls Eros the romantic love which was born from the Gnostic and Catharist heresies, whereas Nygren takes Eros to be the Greek ideal of love as contrasted with the specifically Christian Agape. But the distinction of anima and animus will serve still better to show how what de Rougemont and Nygren and some of the other writers say can be made consistent. The soul or self is the anima, and if we apply it to natures below the human it is irrational. But in human beings owing to the advent of mind the reason is the determining factor and dominant, and this is called the animus. As contrasted with the anima in man the animus is controlled and lordly; it brings the passions into order and directs them as a team. As such it is opposed to the barbaric and dark passions, whether we think of them as conscious or unconscious. De Rougemont has in mind these dark passions which are either in open revolt against reason or, like a *gens lucifuga*, form an underground movement; and to these he gives the name of Eros. But if we think of his reason as part of the self or anima, instead of contrasting the two, the reason itself, or animus, can easily be identified with Eros. Nygren is looking at it from this angle, as the self-assertive impulse of the anima, that which is egocentric and possessive. His nomenclature fits, too, more readily a distinction I have already made between the masculine and the feminine. As will be remembered, Aristophanes suggested that originally human nature was dual and composed of both the sexes. This idea, fanciful in itself, has this basis that in every human being an active and dominant instinct works with a passive and self-squandering one. There must be fuel as well as fire in nature. But the force which shows itself in the animal nature as aggressive and brutal turns in a human person into the rule of reason, the mastering faculty which directs its anima to its own end and perfection. This is what Plato spoke of in the *Symposium* as the Love which is 'a philosopher at all times, terrible as an enchanter, sorcerer, sophist'. It searches for the good, and by possession of the good is made happy. To Nygren this is the work of anima in its rational capacity, and it is essentially self-centred and the work of Eros. Agape is, on the other hand, more like to the receptive and self-giving part of the anima, though Nygren does not advert to this. He, for his part, thinks that only by divine Agape can the soul be unselfish. It would seem more likely that below the divine Agape there is to be found a movement in the anima which bal nces the egocentric and centripetal urge by a centrifugal love which carries it beyond what reason can clearly delineate. But it may well be that such a movement is exceedingly dangerous, because if it be in discord with the reason it may all too likely be a stirring of the depths, an opening not to the sky but to the lower world.

This, in fact, is the solution which I hope to establish; but before doing so it will be well to try to substantiate it from the evidence already gleaned. The suggestion so far is that the mystery religions clothed themselves with mystic, Neo-Platonic philosophy and lived on in various forms side by side with Christianity. So like could they make themselves to the Christian faith that even the 'faithful' could at times be deceived. On this hypothesis the thesis of de Rougemont is erected. As we have seen, he holds that the troubadours were infected by the Catharist heresy and that the Catharist heresy was only a version of the Indo-European Gnosticism. He therefore explains 'romanticism' as the religion of Eros, the consecration of the dark passion, which is a rebel against reason and the searcher after the forbidden fruit of Sophia. The entry of this Eros into Western civilization had dire results. Despite all opposition it succeeded in gaining a permanent place in literature and in the thought of the centuries to come. He traces its influence in the change of manners and modes of thought, the gradual dissolution of the Christian synthesis and its final effects in our present *nostalgie du néant* and surrender to war and fatalism.

It would be more correct, I think, to say that romanticism has always been haunted rather than possessed by the Gnostic Eros; for, as Christopher Dawson has pointed out in his *Medieval Religion*, 'there is little evidence that the troubadours showed any active sympathy with the doctrines of the Albigenses. The anti-clericalism of poets like Peire Cardenal and Guilhem Figueira has no theological foundation, and the remarkable Sirvente of Guilhem Montanhagel against the Inquisition expresses the views not of a Manichaean but of a humanist in revolt against the puritan spirit which condemned the extravagance and display of the courtly society.' Dawson assigns the origin of Provençal poetry to Arabic culture. Like the Norman kingdom of Sicily the land of Languedoc was in the twelfth century a cosmopolitan centre. It is true that the Catharists flourished there, but it is difficult to think that their influence was paramount. Their views, as heretical, were not deliberately adopted, but what they taught fitted in with the soil and atmosphere. In Moslem theology and poetry there is a strain not unlike Gnostic thought. Such verse, for instance, as the following, which is quoted by Dawson, recalls the dark goddess:

> Declare the absoluteness of beauty and be not moved to deem it finite
>   by thy longing for a tinselled jewel,
> For the charm of every fair youth or lovely woman is lent to them from
>   Her beauty.
> 'Twas She that crazed Qays the lover of Lubna, ay and every enamoured
>   man like Bayla's Majnun or Azzar's Kutbayyir.
> Every one of them passionately derived Her attribute which She clothed
>   in the form of a beauty which shone forth in the beauty of form.

How near, indeed, thought of this kind came to what de Rougemont calls Catharist and romantic and Nygren Eros is well illustrated by Dawson's comment on this poem: 'This Platonic idealism received a still more elaborate treatment at the hands of the writers of the Spanish school, such as Ibnu'l Arabi. They combined it with the metaphysical theory of a series of emanations through which being and Intelligence descend from God through the celestial spheres and intelligences to the sunblunary world, a doctrine which is common to all the Arabic philosophers from Avicenna to Averroes. In accordance with this theory, the Beloved is conceived as the symbol or embodiment of a metaphysical idea.'

There is no reason, therefore, to reject de Rougemont's main thesis, even though it be an over-simplification and pressed too far as an explanation of the history of European civilization. It is enough if we accept his view that romance did contain a special doctrine of love. When the Provençal romance united with the Celtic myths and dreams, the characteristic traits of that doctrine become unmistakable. Love is a rapture, a divine transport; it desires union with the infinite, and from that union there is no return. This means that it is a form of death, a night into which we must pass. Night, therefore, and darkness always figure in this love when it is described. And thirdly, the desire personifies itself in the symbol of a woman or dark goddess. Eros, then, is a madness which takes one out of oneself and ends in a complete surrender of all that one is, the night of death in which one is united to the All.[1]

The romantic ideal lived on long after the troubadours and the courtly ideals of the early Middle Ages had passed away, but it came back in full strength in the nineteenth century. The story of Tristram shows the identity in outlook of the nineteenth with the twelfth and thirteenth centuries. Schopenhauer is the philosopher of that spirit and Wagner is its dramatist. Love becomes a frenzy, the *motifs* of night and death recur, and romance ends in a decadence of melancholy and a preoccupation with corruption and death. And if a critic be inclined to argue that this tendency in romanticism is only an unfortunate accident, he must face the fact that both Freud and Jung accept it as a universal experience. Freud, as we have seen, reached in the end the hypothesis of two instincts, one for life and the other for death; the Liebestod is the song of the death instinct. In Jung we have a panorama of mythology and legend, the projection of the unconscious. The unconscious is the lair of the racial experiences, and the ego must listen to its voice if it intends to live serenely. And in that unconscious are the great archetypes, the shadow, the anima and the magician, Lucifer. The woman appears in dreams; she is often veiled, she is the goddess of the mystery religions, she is, also, death to those who do not woo her as she would be wooed. In general, moreover, we

---

[1] I have given many illustrations of this tendency, but one of the most striking of all is to be found in Tardieu's *The Truth about the Treaty*, p. 96. Clemenceau is speaking of the Germans. 'Cher ami, the nature of man is to love life. Germany has not this cult. . . . These people love death. The divinity which they contemplate with fear, but with a fear mixed with ecstasy and intoxication, is death. Where do they get their divinity? I have no idea. . . . Re-read their poets: death everywhere. . . . War is a pact with death. There the Boche encounters his best friend.'

can say that the ego must surrender in part to this unconscious, this anima, if it is to escape celibacy and that swollen egoism, which leads to madness.

To return now to the wanderings of the animus, the mastering power, which Nygren terms the egoistic or self-centred expression of Eros. It is the opposite of the romantic, melancholic impulse, which is centrifugal and ends in an act of *felo de se*. Reason is the characteristic of man, his distinguishing principle, and it is the spiritualized version of the aggressive instinct, Adler's desire to power, Jung's archetype of the magician—Lucifer, who cried out, 'I will not serve'. This kind of love, as Plato said, is 'a philosopher at all times, terrible as an enchanter, sorcerer, sophist'. Naturally, therefore, he describes its happiness as a possession of the good, and Aristotle in this matter does not differ from his former master. To him, too, the highest perfection for man consists in possessing the good, and because man's good must be found in his highest activity, perfect happiness lies in the knowledge and enjoyment and possession of the supreme good. This is what Nygren calls the egocentrism of Eros, and he would have us believe that Christian love, Agape, lies in denying all place to this kind of love. He is certainly mistaken in this, and he is unable to hold the view consistently. But he sprang a problem on us, which after all allowances have been made for the exaggerated form in which he stated it, remains to be solved.

In the Middle Ages the problem took another form, though it was the same in substance. The Christian thinkers had adopted, by the time Scholasticism took its rise, much of the Greek philosophy. They took for granted, therefore, the principles of Plato and Aristotle and agreed that every nature developed from potency to act, from imperfection to its perfection. It followed that the end of all the activity of each living being was its own perfect life and happiness. Man as a living being who develops seeks his own perfection by his very nature. How then can he at the same time love God more than himself, as the Christian religion taught that he was bound to do? We have seen some of the attempts to answer this question, the way in which Rousselot argues that St. Thomas answered it, and the contrary opinion of Gilson and others. Put in terms of the Eros problem the question to be answered is, how is egoism reconciled with altruism or how is possessiveness compatible with self-sacrifice? Can I really love God and my neighbour for themselves and not as merely means to my own happiness. The doctrine of enlightened selfishness has always attracted certain minds, but it will not do as an answer for a Christian.

In his Hulsean lectures Burnaby suggested that the answer lay in the neglected notion of Philia, Christian friendship. Aristotle had declared that in all friendship the lover loves the other as himself and that ultimately the love was self-centred. Burnaby denies that this is a true analysis of friendship. He is supported in this by the interesting distinction which has been made by certain German theologians between the love of persons to persons and to things. The relations, they say, are quite different and ought never to be classed together. In the 'I'—'It' relation the soul is in relation with things; the mind is feeding on them and absorbing them; it extracts the essence and turns it into an idea, and that idea belongs to the ego, even though the thing itself, existing outside the mind, is not the property of the ego. But when it comes to another Self or 'Thou', there is a resistance to this possession which can never be overcome. I may think that I have seen through another, that I have exhausted all the meaning there is in his nature; I can study man or my fellow men and write a book about them. In so doing I treat them as things, as matter for thought, but I have ceased to regard them as persons, to address them as 'Thou'. Every person, whom I meet, has his own secret and his own initiative; his consciousness is his own and cannot be taken over. He is another world from mine, and each one has a unique world, which is sacred and inviolable. That is why Buber and Heim maintain that the relation between the I and the Thou is so different from that between the I and the It. They do not, however, attempt any alliance between the two, and they do not develop the implications of this analysis of theirs. They were deterred by their belief in a philosophy which limited the valid use of reason to sensible experience. This prevented them from any use of reason in the development of their discovery, and they failed to see that reason can still function though it has been shorn of some of its exclusive powers and has had to call in aid from outside. It is true that persons escape the clutch of human reason, but a person is not a person without this reason, and it is to be expected, therefore, that in the meeting of persons reason should still operate as well as, shall we say, will or whatever activity it be that brings persons together in love. The presence of reason and thought need not necessarily make lovers egocentric; the thought may serve to keep our high desires at the level due to contact with other persons and prevent a false love creeping in,—a love that could look very like the romantic in the death swoon,—to which a completely unselfish love might succumb. In other words, if the presence of another person stirs up in us a love which is not self-centred, as our reason is wont to be when dealing with things, a smack of reasonableness in turn will prevent us from going to the opposite extreme to that of egoism, and of losing ourselves in the other.

The two extremes of egoism and abandonment are closer bedfellows than one might expect. The reason is that what Freud tries to describe by calling them the instincts of life and death, work in a less obvious way in human experience even when the higher faculties seem to be solely engaged. We have seen to what degradation the high melancholy of the romantics can descend, to the *nostalgie de la boue et du néant*. The animus or reason, too, is bound to the fierce animal aggressiveness by an umbilical cord. The note of will and power was sounded by Fichte in Germany at the beginning of the last century. Many a noble passage can be culled from the pages of Fichte and his philosophic friends and philosophers. But not so long after the high note had grown sharp and fierce and become a call to arms and violence. A superman stepped on to the stage and then a race of supermen. Even the idealist movement in philosophy exalted the human mind to the place of God and held that all nature and all persons fell within the processes of mind, as it gave out only to suck back again what had come from it; and strangely enough this happened at the very time when the romantics were gazing with fascinated eyes at the spectacle of death. Egoism and abandonment showed themselves as bedfellows. They were both the outcome of Eros, the present manifestation of a love which had in its earlier years displayed the aggressive pride of the ancient tyrants and the orgies of passion and the mystic raptures of love for the dark goddess. All the difference is that the modern is more jaded when he thinks of the *crépuscule embaumé*, child though he is.

> *Si je désire une eau d' Europe, c'est la flache*
> *Noire et froide où vers le crépuscule embaumé*
> *Un enfant accroupi, plein de tristesse, lâche*
> *Un bateau frêle comme un papillon de mai.*

CHAPTER NINE

LOVE AND SYMPATHY

Dedit ei Deus latitudinem cordis quasi area quae est in litore maris.

How can we know the dancer from the dance?—W. B. YEATS.

> *O thou undaunted daughter of desires!*
> *By all thy dow'r of Lights and Fires;*
> *By all the eagle in thee, all the dove;*
> *By all thy lives and deaths of love;*
> *By thy large draughts of intellectual day,*
> *And by thy thirsts of love more large than they;*
>
> . . . . . .
>
> *By all of Him we have in Thee;*
> *Leave nothing of my Self in me.*
> *Let me so read thy life, that I*
> *Unto all life of mine may die.*
>
> —R. CRASHAW.

The distinction which I have described under various headings, according to the nature of the context, as Eros and Agape, animus and anima, intellect and will, masculine and feminine, egocentric and altruistic, operates throughout the ascending levels of living things. In man, however, it takes on a quite new complexion. The principle of power and aggression becomes with regard to others a constitutional and reasonable authority, and with regard to the human being himself the assertion of rights and duties and human dignity. Naked power and brutal aggression, therefore, which are natural to an animal and to be seen in the murderous play of a cat with a mouse, or the selfish greed of a dog with a bone, are forbidden to a human being. In like manner the submissiveness to the herd or the pack, and all that we mean by words and phrases like 'henpecked' and 'downtrodden' and 'treated like cattle', what Freud, whether rightly or wrongly, calls the death instinct, would be vicious in a man or woman and unworthy of them. But the fact that human beings do so often act as brutes or as slaves to a master or to a herd shows the complexity of their nature, the presence in them of instincts and urges which are partly expressed in the most human and spiritual of their activities, the mind and the will, and partly have to be tamed and humanized. When they fail, when an individual, as J. T. MacCurdy says in his *Problems in Dynamic Psychology*, cannot adjust himself to society, he either becomes intensely egoistic or 'if reality is difficult to endure . . . then a most natural regression would appear with a dissolution of consciousness associated with some expression of return to the earlier type of existence. One would expect the latter to be formulated as ideas of death, and in fact, this is a universal phenomenon'.

The necessity of the integration of these two principles in human life and of the evil results of any degeneration could be illustrated from many fields, and it is tempting to examine both the plans for the improvement of our modern society as well as the evils from which it is suffering in the light of these same principles. But the importance of them and their working is all that must now be emphasized. The cardinal mistake of Freud, for instance, is to ignore the difference between the human and the animal level after having hit upon the distinction in his medical analysis between two kinds of 'instincts', as he calls them. This flaw in the Freudian theory is very clearly pointed out by Rudolf Allers in *The Successful Error*. Freud 'conceives of love only as a particular way of attaining instinctual satisfaction'. His view is hedonistic, and he naïvely assumes that this pleasure principle covers all human activities. Moreover, Freud adopts a hedonism 'of a primitive and simple kind. It lacks the refinement of Epicureanism, which at least recognized essential differences of value and of the pleasures they procure'. Allers has no difficulty in showing the disastrous effects of this naïve and narrow view of love, and he touches the heart of the matter when he writes that 'it is, in fact, not true that the other person appears in Freud's theory as another person to be loved and to love. His name is not person, his name is—object. He is a "sexual object". There was never a name given to the human person which more clearly disregards the essential dignity and the particular position of the human person. The beloved or desired individual becomes an object among objects. His value depends on cathexis, on the amount of libido attached to him, just as every object receives its meaning, its importance, its value for the subject by the very same process. What is there to distinguish, basically, essentially, a human person from any other environmental element? There is nothing. The human person as such has been denuded of all distinguishing characteristics. "All things have a price; man alone has dignity". This famous saying of Kant has lost its meaning in psycho-analysis. Man has a price as things have a price. Man's price is measured and expressed in units of libido.'

The human level is properly and fully expressed in the appellation of person and the realization of human dignity. How slowly this realization grows is witnessed in history in the story of slavery and in the position of women in many early civilizations, and we can not be sure that this realization would have come without the aid of Christianity, which promised a still higher dignity to man and gave a new meaning to love. And despite the influence of Christianity every society and every individual in every age has to struggle to keep at arm's length the savage and sub-human. The two primary loves make themselves felt, and each pulls at times against the other and can all too easily decline to a lower level. Hugo Münsterberg in a chapter on 'Society and the Dance', in his book on *Psychology and Social Sanity*, points out how effective an instrument certain forms of dances are in loosening self-control and exciting both the violent and the passive emotions of sexual love. 'The uniformity of the movements, and especially of the revolving movement, produces a state of half dizziness and half numbness with ecstatic elements. We know the almost hypnotic state of the whirling dervishes and the raptures in the savage war dances; all this in milder form is involved in every passionate dance.' But nothing, as he suggests, is more marked than the loss of self-control. The rhythm produces a kind of hypnotic state, not unlike that of the drunken man, and the victim of it becomes the slave of his excitement and open to every kind of suggestion. In certain dances the rhythm and the accompanying music excite to violence and brutality; in others to a loss of reason and control; in both the anima is listening to the sirens. Münsterberg is not, as the context proves, maintaining that dance and music unman us and let loose the irrational in us. In all the arts, just because they are so distinctively a human creation, mind and emotion partake. The mind, instead of walking, is carried, but it likes to exercise some discipline and have its say, and the happier the partnership the better the art. This is true; but there are arts which are closer to the earth and to the animal in us than others. Wyndham Lewis, for instance, in *Time and Western Man*, makes a very suggestive if disputable contrast of music and painting. The former of these two arts is all movement; it belongs to sensation, to the infantile and to the irrational, while the latter has fixity; its effect can be seen by the mind as well as by the sight; it is cool and permanent. The one takes us out of ourselves; we are carried out to sea on the waves by a sympathy we did not know that we possessed. The other does not attempt to allure us; it challenges our critical admiration; it gives a new vision and appeals through the senses to our liking for what is dimensional and composed. We know, however, that in making such contrasts we have been unfair to both the arts. It is dance which is farther removed from the sway of mind. As games are in part the harmless expression of the more primitive desire to fight and dominate, so dance is the ritual of surrender, disciplined in civilized communities to more innocent aims. Without too much exaggeration it can be called a rhythm of sympathy, and the outgoing movement of the love of anima.

LOVE AND SYMPATHY

The dance is not the solitary or an isolated piece of evidence proving the presence of the two loves and the different levels of their manifestation in human life. Mr. Iovetz-Tereschenko in his book, *Friendship-Love in Adolescence*, quotes and analyses the diaries of some young adolescents, and claims their evidence as proof that there is a love of friendship quite separate from the lust which Freud, for instance, assumes to be the basis of all affection. He does not tell us, however, whether these two loves can mingle, and we are left to guess if they ever meet, or whether the higher has any analogy with the lower love. Max Scheler, in his *Nature et Formes de la Sympathie*, is more informative. He distinguishes carefully between sympathy and love. In its proper sense sympathy is indifferent to values and to moral worth. An actor or poet can enter into the feelings of the character depicted, an onlooker can relive the sentiments of hate and the desires for vengeance of another, without any regard for the moral value of these feelings and sentiments. Love, on the other hand, rejoices in the perfection of the beloved and is pained at any short-comings. It looks to an ideal and cannot bear that the beloved should fall short of that ideal. The distinction here made is probably too rigid, but it serves to bring out the variety of desires and loves which the self can exhibit on different levels. Scheler himself wishes to separate off the vital from the spiritual tendencies and he would have us believe that there is one universal life, which is super-sensible and super-individual, below that of the personal and spiritual life of each human being. He is in agreement with Bergson and Driesch and others in postulating this, and he points to the many monistic systems, philosophical and religious, in East and West, as evidence for this supposition. But his evidence suits far better the doctrine of the two loves and their coexistence on different levels in the soul. If the active and passive principles show themselves in human nature in the animus and the anima, in the control of reason and in infinite desire, and these can all too easily be swamped by the irrational elements in the soul, we should expect to find traces of this in all experience and even in the philosophies and religions which man has striven to create. The animus will manifest its exaggerated claims in a scientific cosmos of its own devising, in a philosophy of egoism and of the 'thing', and it will be haunted by the shadow of supermen and savage aggression. Scheler observes that this is constantly happening, and he calls this movement of the soul 'egocentrism'. 'When it presides over the conception of objects in the real world, egocentrism is called solipsism; when it expresses itself in desire and in conduct, it is called egoism; and finally the egocentric attitude in matters of love goes by the name of 'auto-eroticism'. But the common root of solipsism, of egoism and auto-eroticism consists in the tendency to identify personal values with the values of one's own narrow world and that narrow world with the world in general; and it is this which I call timetic egocentrism (from the Greek word Timé = value, price), or, for the sake of brevity, egocentrism, *tout court.*'

A still more decisive comment, however, follows on this analysis. The egocentric, just because he refers all values to himself, tends to make objects in the world, and persons too, instruments to his own purposes. They are not considered as possessing values of their own, or, if they are, they never rise above the status of 'things'. It is in this criticism that Scheler brings us back to the doctrine of love, the views of Buber and Karl Heim and the sin of animus or reason, when it is divorced from anima. The mind is acquisitive and insists on making its own all that it meets in experience. But as the common man and the poet and the saint have all agreed, there is something very incomplete in the life of science and philosophy. The scientist and the philosopher preside over a dead world; they leave aside the world we all love, of colour and movement and intimate, personal intercourse. Their world is the world of things, and even persons are marked, like the poor Jews in concentration camps, with this stigma. They live to give a Roman holiday to the mind; at the very best they make up its beatitude. Animus is a selfish lord; he takes more than he gives.

But here again Scheler supplies what is needed to correct this bias of the soul. He thinks that 'sympathy' sets the balance right. Its function, he tells us, does not so much consist in giving us a positive knowledge of things as in 'suppressing the illusion' of egocentrism. In one of its expressions sympathy consists of a 'participation affective', an affective sharing. The primitive savage loses his identity for a moment in some object or group: the more developed man enters into another's feelings, and senses him as alive and like himself. As might be expected, the more primitive form approaches to the lower level of anima, and it is best seen in childhood and amongst savage tribes. The child before the use of reason and adolescence has moods of aggressiveness and cruelty; it bullies other children, hurts the animals with which it plays and can tear the wings off an insect. But it is not the dominant and egoistic phase but its opposite which gives the clue to the later activity of the anima. The child loves to identify itself with objects and persons, and at times can hardly distinguish the imagined from the real. If taken to a Punch and Judy show or to a theatre it lacks the power of its elders of living their own life while watching the portrayal of the struggles on the stage. The child suffers so much with the hero or heroine that when they are unhappy it too is unhappy; it has identified itself with the characters on the stage and at their sadness it loses all its enjoyment. Amongst savages the individual seems at times to be absorbed in the tribe; he is like to a member of a pack, and though no human being can be less than human and personal, that personality is in abeyance. Instead, his senses are highly developed, and he feels telepathically with the crowd. How near even the civilized man is to this state is clear from the behaviour of crowds and the contagion of excitement which can spread and overwhelm the ordinary, rational reactions of the individual. The primitive is nearer to nature and depends upon its assistance; he can lose himself in it or be terrified of its influence, malign more often than good, upon him; he confuses the great god with the natural objects around him, and though we now know from research into primitive religions that he preserves an idea of a god above all, he is prone to worship natural forces and to identify his existence with the totem of the tribe. Scheler refers us for evidence of these habits to Lévy-Bruhl and Westermann and von den Steinen. 'According to von den Steinen, the Boroso pretend that they are really identical with the red paroquets (Araras) and that each member of the totem is identical with a red paroquet. It is not just a question of a causal relation between the destinies of the totemist (birth, sickness, death) and his totem animal: the causal relation is itself a result of a true identification. There is even an identification with inanimate objects, for example, with stones (Foy calls them "human stones"). The identification of man with his ancestors belongs to the same type', and also, as Scheler argues, his identification with a god. The mystery religions were capable of raising the worshippers to a high ideal, but we have only to read a summary of some of their practices as described by Rohde in his *Psyche*, to be convinced of the truth of Scheler's argument. Rohde is describing the Dionysiac rite: 'The Bull-God, in the most ancient and primitive form of the belief, appeared in person among the dancers, or else the imitated roaring of a bull, produced by hidden "Mimes of Terror", served to suggest the invisible Presence. The worshippers, too, in furious exaltation and divine inspiration, strive after the god; they seek communion with him. They burst the physical barriers of their soul. A magic power takes hold of them; they feel themselves raised above the level of their everyday existence; they seem to *become* those spiritual beings who wildly dance in the train of the god. The worshipper who in his exaltation has become one with the god, is himself now called Sabos, Sabazios. The superhuman and the infra-human are mingled in his person; like the frenzied god he throws himself upon the sacrificial animal to devour it raw. To make this transformation of their nature outwardly manifest, the participants in the dance festival wear strange dress; they resemble in their appearance the members of the wild thiasos of the god; the horns they set on their heads recall the horned, bull-shaped god himself, etc. . . . At the same time it is something more than mere drama, for it can hardly be doubted that the players themselves were possessed by the illusion of living the life of a strange person. The awe-inspiring darkness of night, the music, especially that of the Phrygian flute, to which the Greeks attributed the power of making its hearers "full of the god", the vertiginous whirl of the dance—all these may very well, in suitably disposed natures—have really led to a state of visionary exaltation in which the inspired person saw all external objects in accordance with his fancy and imagination.'

In these scenes it looks as if man were attempting to lose himself in a greater reality and to imagine himself as one with a god, and as Rohde remarks, it is a universal phenomenon. 'The shamans of Asia, the "medicine men" of North America, the Angekoks of Greenland, the Butios of the Antilles, the Piajes of the Caribbees are merely special cases of a universal type, essentially the same in all its different manifestations. Africa, Australia, and the island worlds of the Pacific are equally familiar with them. Both their performances and the range of ideas that lie behind them belong to a type of religious experience that occurs with the regularity of a natural phenomenon, and must therefore not be regarded as abnormal. . . . The impulse to union with God, the extinction of the individual in the divine—these are what form the fundamental points of contact between the mysticism of the most highly cultivated and talented peoples and the emotional religion of primitive "savages".'

Scheler gives other cases of this 'affective participation', such as the condition of a patient under hypnotism, the instinctive love of a mother for her offspring, what may be called a communal consciousness and the hysterical state into which a crowd may pass. He considers the excitement aroused in mating to be a notorious example, because both participants 'believe that they are plunged into the same vital current, in which there is no longer any separation between the two egos, though there is no awareness of any "we" or plurality. It is certain that this phenomenon lies at the basis of the primitive, vital metaphysic, whence are derived the orgies and bacchic mysteries, in which the initiates make an ecstatic renunciation of their entire individuality and believe that they have sunk into the same primitive source of the "natura naturans".' Scheler thinks that these and other phenomena justify him in his special theory of a vital unity running throughout the cosmos, the natura naturans. He distinguishes between this vital unity and the higher spiritual self. This latter can never surrender its personality and does not want to do so, but in the sphere of vital union individuality is a hindrance. 'Whether we are concerned with the effective fusion which takes place between the vital centre of the hypnotizer and that of the hypnotized, or the reciprocal fusion in the acts of mating which transforms two lives into one vital

and impetuous stream, or the affective fusion of the mother and her child
(in the case of maternal instinct and not of maternal love), or the kind
of coincidence which exists between vital processes and modes of operation of the animal of prey and its chosen victims; whether, again, we are
concerned with the affective fusion as manifested in the crowd or the
herd, or the ecstatic fusion with the life of the gods, or that which lies
at the base of those phenomena which manifest themselves in the doubling
of the ego, or the pathological fusions, the experiences of primitive man,
the dream states—it is always the same layer which is engaged in the
process of affective fusion, namely, the vital sphere be it of man or of
other living things.'

There are many difficulties in accepting this theory of Scheler. He
wants to separate off the vital from the spiritual in a way which fails to
explain their close connexion. Again, it is not easy to see what this vital
cosmic unity can mean, and lastly the processes which he would be bound,
by his theory, to confine to the vital urges manifest themselves clearly
in the intellectual order. In the mystery religions, for instance, there is
no sharp dividing line between the crude ecstasies and the highly spiritual
union sought by many of the initiates. In philosophy, again, as Scheler
himself admits, there is an obvious connexion between the monistic
systems of the Absolute idealists and the affective fusion of the instincts,
or, as I should say, the selfless movement of the anima. Just as the egoistic
philosophies proceed on a higher plane from the same source as the
acquisitive and domineering urges of the soul in other spheres, so too
the absolute philosophies which resolve all individual units of consciousness in the whole are of the same order as the desire of the mystic to be
fused with some divinity or dark goddess; and this phenomenon belongs
to the same type as those to be found in, for example, the merging of the
individual in the pack or community. To confirm this general similarity
of type we can trace the process from below upwards. At the lowest end
of the scale the anima can hardly call her soul her own. Without the aid
of the Argus-eyed egocentric love she would lose all individuality. As
it is she is drawn out of herself to mingle with the vital life around. She
is drawn into the rhythm as a cobra is fascinated by the snake charmer's
piping.[1] Higher on the scale this translates itself into a sensitivity, an

---

[1] 'He [Espinas] begins by considering the lower polycellular forms of animal life. Among
them, especially among the hydrozoa or polypes we find compound or colonial animals;
such an animal is a single living mass of which the parts are in substantial and vital connexion
with one another, but is yet made up of a number of parts, each of which is morphologically
a complete or almost complete creature; and these parts, though specialized for the performance of certain functions subserving the economy of the whole animal or coherent group
of animals, are yet capable, if separated from the mass (as they sometimes are by a natural
process), of continuing to live, of growing, and of multiplying. There are found among
such creatures very various degrees of specialization of parts and of independence of parts;

overdeveloped awareness, a finely wrought sympathy with nature and, above all, with the species to which the being belongs. Instead of eyes within and without, as in the Apocalypse, it is all ears, or like a radio station picking up messages from all quarters. This telepathic communication with nature and with other members of the tribe is very noticeable among primitive savages and those who live close to the soil or in the company of animals. By this time, however, we have reached the high end of the scale. Long before the reason takes full cognizance of what is around it, the 'apis argumentosa', the busy anima, has been feeling a presentiment of what must be rationally explored. The spirit of man has drawn the shutters and is in love with what is not itself; it is preparing loyalties and devotion; it is whispering the other's name. It is from these sorties, these expeditions and secret trysts that man learns to live for others and subordinate his selfishness. The animus left to itself would be, as we have seen, an isolationist, a solipsist, a tyrant without friends. In collaboration with the love which comes from the anima the animus becomes a constitutional monarch; the human person grows ever more personal and at the same time a devoted member of a family and of his nation and a lover of humanity. I say 'humanity' because there is still another stage. Usually the harmony between the animus and the anima is precarious. They tend to draw apart in civilized societies, and especially in our modern society when science can build a screen between us and nature. The mind assumes more and more sway to the neglect of the other activities; men see nature through spectacles and through books and pictures, and those of the city forget the seasons' rhythms and the constant coming to be and passing away of life.

Scheler does not notice how the one stage passes imperceptibly into the other and that all are found in some degree in human life, though the lower instincts are now subordinated to a higher ideal. He does, however, bear out fully the theory of two loves and their at times conflicting but normally complementary aims. He is wide awake, for instance, to the salutary presence of a dose of egoism to prevent the extreme to which the self-sacrificing love tends when left to itself. Were it to disappear entirely, he says, the answer of the Buddhist or the Idealist would be right. It is the excess of egoism, what, in fact, we generally mean by the word egoism, which is wrong. In agreement too with the distinctions

and in those cases in which the specialization and interdependence of parts is great, the whole compound animal exhibits in its reactions so high a degree of integration that we seem justified in supposing that a common or "collective consciousness" is the psychical correlate of these integrated actions of the separate parts.' (*The Group Mind* by W. McDougall, p. 33.) Another interesting example of the influence of the group on the individual is quoted from Streseman by Koffka in his *Principles of Gestalt Psychology*, p. 655: 'The little birds which come into proximity to an impressive and usually noisy swarm are attracted to it; they hurl themselves into the living maelstrom and are not easily able to extricate themselves from it.'

in this book, but inconsistently with his theory, he sees this egoism working itself out especially in the activity of mind. Nothing could be more apposite than the following passage: 'We ought then once and for all to rid ourselves of the idea . . . that man's attitude to nature should be solely to master it, control it and direct it. This is a Jewish idea, one which, despite all the efforts of reaction and resistance to it, as for instance in early Christianity or by the Franciscans, or in the philosophies of Goethe, Fechner, Bergson, or romanticism, has become a kind of axiom in our Western world and has ended by raising the mechanical view of nature into an absolute truth.' We are, in part, the children of nature. The true tiller and husbandman has an inborn reverence for the land as well as the flocks of the fields, and long experience has taught him to serve it and to treat it as alive. But the age of reason, of science and mechanical invention moves in haste and would exploit the earth without love. The old instinct of domination and destruction reasserts itself in the disregard of the mind for the life with which it has to deal. Economic and physical science, when they become objects of worship, are like the ancient gods who spread death in their train. The West presents a notable example of the neglect of the anima to the undue exaltation of the ego and the rule of science. 'It is thus that the history of the West, from the time when it began to be dominated by the idea of human progress . . . has developed by an implacable law and with a stony logic. It is the woman, in that she represents the eternal feminine, it is the child, in that it is the primitive and childish element of human nature . . . which have particularly suffered in this hardening of civilization.'

The masculine and the feminine, these are the old potent distinctions, and just as the latter has been crowded out in the business-like, hardheaded West, in the East she has had no master in the house to keep control. There the ego is of little account. Buddha, as Scheler says, 'recommends the point of departure of love but not the end to which it leads; in other words, it is only the self-detachment, the self-denial, which love implies, that he approves, the self-renunciation which can reach to the extreme of complete abandonment of the self. . . . It is for this reason that there is for him neither a "love of God" nor a "love of self", as distinct from egoism. The love of God is absent because, at least in Buddhism, God himself is absent; there is no love of self, because there is no spiritual and individual "I", who, in regard to his salvation, is as worthy of love as the spiritual "I" of another.'

This is an extreme as obvious as the one which Scheler accused the West of holding, and he is surely right in arguing that perfection should consist in a balance between the two. We have seen, however, that Scheler is not so sure in his cure as in his diagnosis. His spiritual self is cut off from the tendencies he has observed in the 'vital' sphere. The anima mundi he seems to postulate is not needed, for the conception of Eros or the animus and the anima, or whatever one pleases to call the two principles of living things, suffices to span the streams of energy from the lowest form of life to that of man. Every living being has some kind of individuality, however shadowy it may be, and as we rise in the scale that individuality is accentuated, and shows itself naturally in more and more assertiveness. But while this individuality everywhere persists it is accompanied by and sometimes almost overwhelmed by the greater reality to which it belongs. It is always part of nature and part of a whole within nature. This is most noticeable in the relation of the individual to the species or a group within the species. The bees and ants live for one another and have hardly any separate life; each plays its part and dies for the community. In mating, often enough the life of the individual is sacrificed that the species may continue, and we must regard this tendency to sacrifice itself as as much part of its function as the preservation of its life. This being so, we can look upon the member of the species or the group as having two tendencies or fundamental urges, the one to be itself and live, the other to live for the species or group, and it is these two tendencies which can be called the two fundamental desires or loves. These loves can be described in terms of animus and anima or masculine and feminine, life and death instincts, self-assertiveness and self-sacrifice, taking and giving. They lead up to the distinction of Eros and Agape, but they do not quite fit it, for a reason which I hope is by now apparent to the reader. On more metaphysical grounds the same conclusions can be reached. From the Greek philosophers onwards life has been thought of as an imminent process, a process, that is to say, which consists in a certain degree of self-development. In a living thing, as contrasted with a piece of inanimate matter, there is a principle of internal activity, and this activity proceeds by reacting to external stimuli, absorbing what is congenial into its own life and promoting the particular kind of life which it has as distinct from other things. Translated into simpler language this is no more than saying that a living being is able to look after its own interests and does so primarily and, so many have thought, almost exclusively. In other words, unless we reserve the word 'love' for what is conscious, self-love is synonymous with life, or the desire to live.

But this is not the whole story. The more definite and organized an individual member of a species is the more self-love must it have, and so we tend to forget that in the species below human nature the individual never has a complete individuality or self. It is always a member of a whole, and this is just as much part of its being as its individuality.

Indeed, its being an individual and a member spell what it is; they are the two phases of one life. As a result we must think of it as living for what is beyond its own particular needs, as having a tendency to live and to die for others. In the lower species it happens again and again that the male or female's function consists in dying to pass on life, and in the maternal instinct while it lasts there is frequently entire self-forgetfulness. Such life is a service, a giving, and the individual is only a means to the prolongation of the species. To give, therefore, as well as to take, is inherent in living organisms, and in the more developed animals we may well suppose that this mounts up into a desire equally strong as that of self-love and equally enjoyed. Two loves co-exist in every living thing.

Man, too, is partly an animal, and we should, therefore, expect to find in him the marks of these two loves. But the issue becomes now no longer so simple, for with the advent of the spiritual soul, a new order begins. In so far, however, as he is an individual, man must have this self-love, and by reason of his new grandeur a self-love intensified. In so far as he is an animal this will show itself in the old tendencies to assertiveness and brutality, but above all it will show itself in his spiritual activity in the wish to possess and to become humanly wise. The sacrificial or feminine desire will also persist, and in its animal guise will exhibit itself in the tendency to be a chattel or the slave of another's passion, to be rapt into a dark passion, to be swept away in orgiastic dance, to be lost in the herd and sink into nothingness. On the fully human level, however, the role of the anima is more subtle, and this is one of the reasons why the name Eros is given to such various forms of love. Nygren assigns it to that self-love which is so masculine and so conspicuous in Greek philosophy. De Rougemont, on the other hand, calls Eros the love which is peculiarly the anima's when it strays away from divine grace and reason. Both have grounds for their choice, for the truth is complicated. As contrasted with divine grace and the love which springs from its influence in the anima, the acquisitive self-centred love of the Greeks can rightly be called Eros. But if we leave out the grace of God, then the anima, instead of loving with Agape, tires easily of its *ménage* with animus, becomes forlorn and seeks after false gods. It forsakes reason and displays a darker side of Eros, the Eros which walks in the night and loses its identity in the dark. It is difficult to describe all the wanderings of the anima, for no sooner does it sever itself from reason than its shape becomes almost indistinguishable. There is a good and a bad romance, there is a wise and foolish mysticism, just as affairs of the heart may be tender and generous or wild and foolish. At its most human the anima acts as the handmaid of the mind, serving it and coaxing it, running ahead to make contacts with the world which the reason has to meet, warming the home of the soul so that the visitor may enter not as a stranger but a friend. But beyond all other services it creates a world of persons. The mind, it cannot be repeated too often, reproduces on a higher level the characteristics of the acquisitive, masterful, self-centred love. It tends therefore to exploit the world and all whom it meets; it leaves out the homely and personal and lives in the abstractions, the concepts with which the scientist and philosopher like to deal. So it is that the animus lives amongst things, and though it cannot but be aware that it is surrounded by a mass of living beings, it pays no conscious attention to this fact. But then one day St. Martin meets a beggar, as he thinks, naked or in rags. He makes to pass him by as he has passed by hundreds as if they were all the same and were of no use to him. But the beggar importunes him and on a sudden impulse Martin takes his immense military cloak, and dividing it, gives one half to the beggar; and as he does this, in the very gesture, anima makes herself heard, and instead of looking upon a thing, he recognizes a person, like to himself, but oh so different from himself, another unique universe of love. He says no longer 'It', but 'Thou', and he is ready for Agape.

This recognition of another as a person, as another 'I' and lover is the decisive moment in our human experience of love. The word 'love' now takes on its proper meaning, and the event happens when animus and anima rejoice together in an undivided act. Much of our dissatisfaction with theories of love is due to the neglect or over-emphasis of one of these two factors, which should be together. We can extend and refine as much as we like the meaning of thought and marshal our findings under the heading of 'unitive love', but a vital factor will always be wanting. Love, like the pelican of fable, must wound its own breast to feed the beloved. It was this want which drove the ecstatic school, as Rousselot calls it, of Christian thinkers to look for love in self-sacrifice and respond joyously to the cross. There was danger latent in this revolt, no doubt, because the desire for self-sacrifice can all too easily become sub-human and dangerous. But it was inevitable as against the overlordship of the mind and its exaggerated claims. Nygren, in his polemic against the infiltration of Greek philosophy into the Christian faith, has this just complaint against reason at the back of his mind, but in his attempt to cure the disease his knife made a mortal wound. In his system there is no man left; only a ghost blown upon by Agape. There must be a place for mind in human love whether it be for God or for our fellow men. But it cannot do all the work itself. The presence which is only a 'thing' for the mind must become warm and intimate as a person, who gives us back all and more than we, forgetting ourselves, give to him or her. Buber feels this and expresses his experience in the relation of 'I' and 'Thou'.

Burnaby, also, realizes the need of a personal relation to explain the workings of love, and he finds his answer in the notion of Philia. De Régnon and Descoqs fill in the answer of Burnaby by their emphasis on the distinction between nature and person. Man is a rational animal by nature. We can take the rational in him as that which marks him off as a man, his essential trait which gives him his pride and his dignity and his self-satisfaction. The animal in him abets his self-centredness in its aggressiveness, its masculinity; but this animal part of him has sympathies with all that is vital and particularly with the race and nature to which it belongs. So far, therefore, love, as a spiritual expression will be rational and egocentric, and if the word pleases, unitive. But man is not just a rational animal, if by that we mean one of many who share our human nature; he is not just an individual, one member of the human race; he is also a person, and this is where we come upon the secret of the spiritual self, which has been described variously as the anima, the fine point of the soul, the positive infinitesimal of Hopkins, and it is this spiritual self which gives itself to others and enjoys a reciprocated love, and looks beyond all temporal loves to where the divine Giver of all good things abides.

That the spiritual self should have a human and a more than human love at the same time raises many problems. A word more, however, is necessary to make clear what human love is. There are some who would maintain that human love is only an extension or evolution of the 'love' which is bodily and animal. Truth to tell, we have no direct experience of the feelings and desires of creatures other than ourselves, and there are some who argue that they have no intelligence, that all their behaviour belongs to the type of reflex action, that they are automatons. It is hard to believe this, and, thank God, few put such a belief into practice. But I mention it to show how dangerous it is to argue from the relatively unknown to the known, from the non-human to the human, as some extreme evolutionists do. The psychologists are not so prone to make this error. They start with our human experience and by comparing it in its most primitive and vital manifestations with the behaviour of animals, they arrive at certain conclusions about the sensations and instincts and feelings of all living things. The temptation on their side is to deny that our human experience is specifically distinct from that of our animal cousins, to omit from their account the spiritual self. In so doing they commit a grave error, and it is this mistake which revolts so many of Freud's readers. The libido to which he resorts for an explanation of all his psychological problems would make lust and love the same, or at best variants on the same theme. Now it is precisely here in the case of love that the spiritual separates itself off so clearly from the instinctive and animal. I have already quoted from Iovetz-Tereschenko's and Allers' evidence to show that not all love is lust. They are only two from innumerable witnesses who could be cited. Blake's well-known lines are as definite as can be:

> *Love seeketh not itself to please,*
> *Nor for itself hath any care,*
> *But for another gives its ease,*
> *And builds a Heaven in Hell's despair.*
>
> *Lust seeketh only self to please,*
> *To bind another to its delight,*
> *Joys in another's loss of ease,*
> *And builds a Hell in Heaven's despite.*

'Lust seeketh only self to please'; this is certainly not true of the highest human love. These words of Blake suffice; they contain a truth to which we must bow. But I do not think that they are entirely accurate. It is rather because they suggest the dark pleasure and consuming passion of lust that we feel he is so right. Pleasure may be the sole end of lust, but if so, it can be a strange pleasure. We can slay what we love and be slain of a cruel passion. Mastery and possession, sacrifice and death, are the ingredients of lust. May it not be that nature works its ends by this strange mixture of desires, and because its offspring are fulfilling its purposes, they do more than they realize? It may be that they are not important enough to be consulted; theirs but to meet in due season, to have their pleasure, to exult and to die; nature passes on. If this be so, then lust would be a moment of pleasure without any regard or outlook beyond the moment. But however we analyse the workings of lust, it is clearly utterly different from that human love which is tender and true, which disengages itself from mere passion to fix upon the service of the beloved. This is seen in all its beauty in a mother's love. In almost all living things the maternal instinct is to be found. While it lasts the mother forgets herself in care for her young; she will defend them and die for them. But the instinct is for a purpose, and when that purpose is achieved the instinct dies away, and within a short while mother and offspring are prepared to fight and kill one another or mate together. A human mother behaves far differently; there is no end to the love. Instead of dying it can grow, and there are few sights more beautiful than to see a mother in her old age with her grown-up children around her. Her constant thought is of them, and they watch over her as she watched over them in the days when they could not live without her. Such love is separated by an abyss from the instinctive.

The same holds true of all genuine human love; such love does not dispense with the vital and the instinctive, but it changes them to a new dimension. It is enlightened and not dark; it is like one born blind who has come to see, and he sees another 'I' before him; it is lasting and not momentary. So strongly is this latter felt that lovers naturally swear eternal vows and forswear union with any other. This is why marriage and the marriage bond are unalterable. Lust would but have laughed at Diomed's cry:

> *If beauty have a soul, this is not she;*
> *If souls guide vows, if vows be sanctimony,*
> *If sanctimony be the gods' delight,*
> *If there be rule in unity itself,*
> *This is not she.*

Diomed had believed in a 'winnowed purity in love' and had defied time or anything mortal to change his constancy. Again and again Shakespeare returns to this finely human ideal of love, which Christianity did so much to uncover:

> *Since all alike my songs and praises be*
> *To one, of one, still such, and ever so.*
> *Kind is my love to-day, to-morrow kind,*
> *Still constant in a wondrous excellence.*

> *Presume not on thy heart when mine is slain:*
> *Thou gavest me thine, not to give back again.*

The reason why so many empirical philosophers and Evolutionists, like Herbert Spencer and Huxley, confuse the instinctive and the spiritual, lust and love, and assume that one proceeds from the other, is, as Scheler thinks, due to the control, the stamps and passes, which the instincts impose on love. Human love and human sympathy are regulated by passports; they are held up and sent off to determinate places by the authority of the instincts The phrase, which Scheler coins for this is 'perspective of interests', and under this phrase he groups the well-known facts of experience that nearness and distance in time and space make a difference to our affections. A handshake means more to us than a greeting through a third person; a child's headache worries its mother more than the news of a famine at the other end of the world. Love for one's village or town can hold up projects for the general welfare; party prejudice make us blind to national interests and national selfishness destroys all schemes for international co-operation. It is the bodily and instinctive life of ours which creates these oppositions, which restricts or enlarges the field of our loves; and this is why 'the perspective of interests' leads the unwary astray and causes them to confuse the instinctive and the spiritual. In reality, part of the struggle of our life consists in liberating ourselves from the excessive control of the instincts, in enlarging our vision and freeing the will like a sword from the scabbard, in making ourselves free to love wherever the lovable is to be found.

No doubt Scheler is right in his explanation of the mistake of the naturalist philosophers, and what he has to say about 'the perspective of interests' is valuable in correcting it. Nevertheless this 'perspective of interests' is not wholly satisfactory. It bears more closely on the influence of the body on the soul than on the relation of instinctive love to human love. It is because we are not disembodied spirits that we are helped by the physical presence of others, by being able to see and hear and touch. But if we ask how the maternal instinct and a mother's love are related, the relation must be said to be closer than that of perspectives. The truth is better expressed by saying that the former has been given a new dimension or that it has been transformed; and if we ask what kind of a transformation, then the answer must be that the mother is not moved by a blind affection; she understands the glory of being a mother and she delights in the personal being of the fruit of her womb. In other words, there is in this new dimension a mutual understanding, where that is possible, and a regard for the other as other.

How near the body is to the spirit is well expressed by Miguel de Unamuno: 'It (love) is something carnal in spirit itself. Thanks to love, we feel all that spirit has of flesh in it.' He does not believe that we can ever succeed 'in reducing love either to a purely intellectual or to a purely volitional element, putting aside that part in it which belongs to the feeling, or, if you like, to the senses'. Nevertheless he does not hesitate to describe what spiritual love is as contrasted with carnal love. His division is not on all fours with that of Scheler or Allers; it is rather in two degrees of human love. The first is like to that of all living things, whose aim always is to perpetuate themselves. (Unamuno is obsessed with the thought of immortality in one form or another.) He agrees that love is selfish and destructive and that it is inspired by the *motif* of death. 'To live is to give oneself, to perpetuate oneself, and to perpetuate oneself and to give oneself is to die.' 'Love is a contention, and there are animal species in which the male maltreats the female in his union with her, and others in which the female devours the male after being fertilized by him. Each one of the lovers is an immediate instrument of enjoyment and a mediate instrument of perpetuation, for the other. And thus they are tyrants and slaves, each one at once the tyrant and slave of the other'. Selfishness, tyranny, slavery, and above all death. 'Love is at once the

brother, son and father of death, which is its sister, mother, and daughter.'
But after this Wagnerian threnody he strikes the note of spiritual love.
'This other form of love, this spiritual love, is born of the death of carnal
love.' The souls of those who are joined in carnal love are by the very
act separated from each other. They are forced back into their solitariness
and they may even come to hate each other because of their physical
union. But this estrangement is overcome by sorrow, in the presence of
the sickness or death of their child, or after long years of suffering
together. Common anguish unites; 'for to love is to pity; and if bodies
are united by pleasure, souls are united by pain'.

Spiritual love, therefore, Unamuno identifies with pity. He is certainly
wrong in reducing love to pity, but it is easy to see what he means, and
he is working on a universal experience when he brings together common
endurance, common suffering and love. The psychologists have made a
close survey of the differing emotions, sentiments, and dispositions, and
they tell us that love is not self-love[1] nor pity, but either a tender emotion
or a sentiment under which are grouped a number of emotions which
will be evoked by the situation in which a lover finds himself. The lover
will fear for the beloved when she is in danger, be angry when she is
ill treated, rejoice when she is saved and be grateful to her rescuer. All
this is useful and prevents us from agreeing entirely with the view of
Unamuno, but so little positive information does it give us of the nature
of love that more is to be learnt from Unamuno's mistakes. Psychologists
are strangely silent on the subject of love. Perhaps it is because they feel
precluded as empirical investigators from dwelling on a matter which
seems to extend beyond their field of study. Psychology now, despite
its name, seldom mentions the soul or anything germane to the soul's
life; and so it is left to the moralists to wrestle with the problems of love.
Very naturally they deal with them strictly from the standpoint of morals,
and thus the most important theme in life is squeezed out.

To his credit Scheler does not burk the issue, and what he has to say
on spiritual love, or love proper, as he would define it, is enlightening.
He says that 'what essentially characterizes love is that we love an object
as it is, with the values which it possesses, and we deny that love implies
a value which the object "ought" to possess.' Nevertheless, love is not
so much an attitude or regard or judgement nor anything static; it is
essentially dynamic, a movement to bring out the best from the beloved
object. We may regard some object highly, esteem and admire it, but

---

[1] McDougall says that the older moralists by using the expression, self-love, confused
two different sentiments, self-love—self-respect. Self-love, he says, is fortunately rare;
the self-regarding sentiment of the thoroughly selfish man. He seems to miss entirely the
fundamental nature of self-love, without which a human being would have no care for
himself and no desire to be healthy and wise.

true love 'commences only when a movement towards the highest value of the beloved object starts, and this without any regard for the question whether that highest value is already present or "ought" to be present.' This is not to say that we consciously desire to improve the person or object or search round to find where we can help. We do not compare the ideal with the actual. It is the love itself, which, without awareness or reflection, is moved by the beloved, as he or she is now, and at the same time by the ideal image of the person. Scheler finds it hard to state exactly what he means, or at any rate, so exactly as to prevent misunderstanding. I quote again, therefore, his own words: 'What characterizes love is not the tendency to a soul, the desire to realize an end represented by some higher value. On the contrary, it is love itself which, in the course of its movement, causes without a break a higher value to rise in the object, and in such a way that this value "emanates" entirely from the loved object without the slightest interference on the part of the lover.' By these descriptions Scheler hopes to avoid being understood to say that we are only looking for the ideal, that we are not in love with the object as it is, that we wish to improve it or that the lover 'puts in' to the loved object virtues and values which are not really there. None of these ideas occurs to the lover; all he says is, 'Be what you are', and necessarily love in saying this moves towards the best in the person here and now loved. The lover never says: 'You ought to become something different; you ought to be better', and it is a sign of fatigue in love, a decline in its purity when it starts looking for something new or trying to teach and improve on the present.

I think it fair to Scheler to say that what he means is that, when one truly loves, the ideal and the actual meet mysteriously in the loved object, and that love unconsciously always seeks to reduce the gap between the actual and the ideal. It makes the best always of what is really there, and, thank heaven, a lover does seem to see in his beloved treasures of beauty, which are hidden from the gossip and the critic—and he often succeeds in bringing them out. This is what we hope God always does, and it is the story of the Magdalen and the Good Thief. But if I am correct in this interpretation of a theory left somewhat obscure, then surely Scheler is right in so far as he is describing a notable characteristic of love, of pure love. But all the same, there are loves which are quite genuine, but scarcely reach to the purity demanded of all love by him. Again, he does not give enough attention to the place of self-love, nor to the peculiar character of love of persons as contrasted with love for things or abstractions. I do not see, moreover, how this theory can be applied to man's love for God, for we are far from having any desire to think the best of God. He is already known to have supreme perfection, and that is why, I suspect, many theologians put aside theories, like that of Scheler's, of movement and turn back to the rejected idea of love as contemplation. Lastly, Scheler analyses what happens when we truly love, but he does not explain why we should love in this manner; he gives us the fact but not the reason, and it is this final explanation which is so elusive and yet craved for by all. He is prevented from doing so probably by his divorcing the spiritual self from the vital and instinctive energies. Man's nature comprises both, and that is the reason why the principles of self-assertion and self-effacement which rule the animal life must be sought also, but in a different and higher fashion, as an explanation of human love. The climax of human life is in the mutual love of persons, and here the two loves form a concert, the two *motifs* blending and supporting one another. The one gives and the other brings back, the self growing more and more personal the more it sacrifices itself, thus exemplifying the truth that unless the grain of wheat fall into the ground it shall not bear fruit, and that he who would gain his life must lose it.

Aristotle in his discovery of the mean in morals hit upon a truth which however imperfect in its first sketch, has become a lasting heritage of the West. He admired, like so many Greeks, the man of judgement who avoided the extremes of the barbarian and could so temper his feelings and passions as to make the right response to every situation. By yielding too much to a certain passion he would be foolhardy; in fighting shy of it he would be a coward. The brave man moves between two extremes, and knows when to stand and fight and when to retreat. Similarly with all the other appetites; a man is pulled two ways; he can let himself go and yield to passion, or he can make use of the turbulent elements in his nature and adjust them so as to make the exactly right response to what is needed. Now this doctrine of the mean which Aristotle applied in ethics can be extended so as to embrace the whole of man's response to life. There are two loves in man, two principles which arise from his being an individual and a member of a race and a society; they are both connatural with him. In lesser orders of being one of them is usually subordinate to the other, and an animal can find exquisite joy in being robbed of its own individual life. But not so in man; as an individual he has become sacred, and the urge in him is much more pronounced to live for himself and be as a god whom all others, indeed, the whole universe, must worship. He has always this tempter within him. 'I will give thee all the kingdoms of the world, if bowing down thou wilt adore me.' But on the other hand there is also a strong impetus to lose himself, to drown his soul-torment in the waters of nothingness, to become one with the earth and the sea and mother nature, to identify himself with the herd or some impersonal ideal or mystery or absolute. He is thus drawn both ways, between individual rights and duties, ambition and disinterestedness, liberty and authority, art and society, self-regard and regard for others, the present life and responsibility for future generations, and he has to make a reconciliation, to find out the true mean, if he is to achieve a full human life. The Aristotelian mean is, in fact, the way that most civilized peoples have chosen, if we extend that mean to include the fundamental movements or desires of man as man.

On each side of the mean stand the extremes. We have seen in previous chapters how one of them leads man to egotism and tyranny and the love of brute force, and how the other proceeds through romance to irrationalism, death and self-destruction. But as happens in the practice of the moral virtues the mean may be observed imperfectly without catastrophe, and when this occurs it is easy to recognize the predominance of one or other of the two loves. At its best this mean is exhibited in the mutual love of persons. The first regression comes in the substitution of the person-as-thing for the person loved. This substitution is made all the more easily in that it is the congenital habit of the reason. The thing can be made our own and become part of us or at least our property. Now if the thing is material there is no difficulty in seeing when our hold upon it is becoming selfish and egotistical. The present fashion is for denouncing all ownership as robbery and all capitalism as vicious. (Those who are so quick to denounce ownership do not realize that their motive may too easily proceed from the opposite extreme and be a love which is equally vicious; the truth being that ownership and the bearing of a common burden must go together in the harmony of the two loves.) But what is not realized is that the ownership of immaterial things may also betray the selfish and egotistical tendency. The scientific and the philosophic lives are of high degree, but they are not the highest. They tend to translate all objects, even persons, into inanimate things. The pursuit of knowledge for its own sake, whether in respect of ultimate principles or in a special field, is a high vocation, but it is at the cost of the living person. Only a part of man is engaged, and once the reason goes to work by itself, it wishes to have mastery over its subject and material, to reduce it to its own categories, to abstract it and extract the essence. This is a very one-sided relation, and the mind so acting betrays its origin in egocentric love. Many philosophers, and amongst them the greatest, like Spinoza, have mistaken the thing, the dehydrated essence, for personal life, and erected a soulless system to be the last word on heaven and earth, God and man. How near, for instance, to understanding the nature of this love, and yet how disappointing in his conclusion, is Santayana, in that he confuses aesthetic enjoyment and philosophic contemplation with personal relationship: 'The reward of the lover, which also chastens him, is to discover that in thinking he loved anything of this world he was profoundly mistaken. Everybody strives for possession; that is the animal instinct on which everything hangs; but possession leaves the true lover unsatisfied; his joy is in the character of the thing loved, in the essence it reveals, whether it be here or there, now or then, his or another's. This essence, which for action was only a signal letting loose a generic animal impulse, to contemplation is the whole object of love, and the sole gain in loving. Naturally essences seem thin abstractions to those absorbed in action, whose heart is set on the eventual, and to whom the actual is never anything. . . . It is not . . . as a quality attributed to external things that essence is best distinguished; for the colour or the shape of an apple may be supposed to exist in it, and when drawn out and imagined existing alone they may seem ghostly; neither the roundness nor the redness of the apple would be edible. To a greedy child they would be miserable cheats; but not so to the painter or geometer. . . . Interest, in marking the differences and precise characters of things, which are all that the mind can take from them, is the great revealer of essence. Herein appears the thoroughly intellectual or poetical virtue of spirit. The more intense and dominating it is, the less it dwells on the machinery which may control its existence, and the more exclusively it addresses itself to the true and the beautiful, that is, to the essences which experience would manifest if it were pure and perfect.'

A strange nemesis awaits these idealistic philosophers who have staked all on the findings of the mind; the more the mind explores the universe and stuffs itself with its contents, the less personal it becomes. As a result the idealist philosophies end in denying the permanent status of the self and declare that the personality is only a stage, or 'moment', as they call it, in the developing process of Absolute Mind. And granted their premises, this disappearance of the self seems inevitable. If we start with the self as felt in ordinary experience, our ordinary experience seems differentiated from that of our neighbours by such accidental and at times almost frivolous factors as environment and heredity, shocks in childhood, early habits and juvenile reading and first friendships. But these become first insignificant and then pass away into silence as truth is discovered and shared. Science and philosophy are impersonal; only when the view is eccentric or wrongheaded or because of the incident of time, or a first discovery, is it associated with a person's name. Truth is universal and one, and so the more it enters into my mind, the less room is there for any individual gloss or comment. The mind, therefore, which was sent out to hunt by the egoistic impulse, turns into a Franckenstein monster and destroys the ego.

So clear is this difficulty that those who do not agree with the idealist position are hard put to it to find means to save the self from extinction. Some plump for what I have called the 'accidental'; they claim that the body with its individual traits and heritage is a bulwark against destruction. Perhaps they are right, but it seems strange to locate what we feel to be most intimately real and personal in the lower part of our nature, the body and its characteristics. Others point out that your mind and my mind, if we perceive the same truth, may not differ in content, but they do vary because they are different focuses, and they are bound to have different perspectives. But another answer can be given in terms of the two loves. What it is vital to remember is that they should never be separated in thought, and that they overlap. It is not the mind which ultimately is the author of our thinking, but the self, that self which expresses an egocentric impulse most naturally, but not exhaustively, in reason, and an altruistic impulse in belonging to another and living in his love. The two together keep the proper poise of the self. Paradoxically, the self, by giving its life will find it and, what is not so often noticed, the self, when it seeks itself first, after a time grows pale and loses its soul. This is the law and rule of life. Disobedience to it brings decline and ruin, for, as we have seen, egotism changes into a melancholy romanticism, feels the sorrows of Werther and ends in the death-motif. Then is heard, faintly at first, the liebestod, and it sounds ever more poignantly, as the dark, selfish passion develops in intensity. The proper life, then, of the self is to be seen neither in the direction of the mind alone nor in the somewhat romantic and irrational craving of the anima. The two loves coexist and overlap, and if it be said that such a conception requires a further determination of the self, that can be found, if needed, in what I have already suggested about the 'fine point of the soul' or Gerard Hopkins' positive infinitesimal with its freedom of pitch.

Before passing on one other sign of the presence of these two loves in uneasy equilibrium must be mentioned. The perfect equilibrium is found in the love of persons and what surrounds them like an aura, such as home. The exile and the soldier in far-off places thinks of home and scene or incident which serves as a *vade mecum* of his love. Were all love of this kind, the world would be a paradise to live in. But unfortunately it is confined generally to special relationships, to a few persons or a small group, to families and to one spot. Only the saints have the secret of giving love to all they meet and to unknown friends; St. Peter Claver loved all the negroes as himself, St. Francis of Assisi felt 'the freshness deep down things', and St. Paul was so individual and all-embracing in his love that if anyone were hurt he was hurt, and if anyone were scandalized he was scandalized. Such a love can do without scaffolding and human conventions. But just because it is so rare the experience of mankind has translated itself into a hierarchy of values and distinctions, in order to preserve at least some of the respect which is due to human personality and its achievement. The hierarchy of function within a State, if it be fair, is based on the next best to personal relationships, that is, an order of respect which banks the fire of love and does not put it out. The eighteenth century (not the Christian) ideal of fraternity and equality denies this experience and assumes that all at a word can live the highest form of love. It is based on illusion, and almost at once adopts an ersatz love, which is known as the love of humanity.

This 'humanity', like so many other abstractions, does service for the real, personal love, and should never be mistaken for it. It is true that confusion is caused by the limitations of language, and a true lover may for want of a better expression speak of humanity. But the fruits of both show the difference. Humanity, like other abstractions, such as nationality and racism and Fascism and Communism, comes to the lips of men when true affection begins to diminish, and one of the two loves, like a swollen gland, begins to discharge too much. A noble cause rightly evokes a generous response, and as a cause always ultimately concerns God or men, its simple disciples are always aware to some extent of their rights or their unjust suffering. They are not misled by an abstraction, by a symbol which may mean nothing; but the transition from such an honest loyalty to a mob enthusiasm, to a collective fusion of wills in an irrational ideal, happens constantly, especially in these days when suggestion and conditioning of minds have developed into a scientific technique. And so it comes about that personal love fades away into the desire to save the world in general, to improve society, to be lady-bountifuls and, at the worst, to be Mrs. Jellabies, whose families are in squalour while they are busy writing letters and finding funds to help the foreign missions.[1] On the other hand, the individual may disclaim all love for others and duties towards them. He may do this by breaking rules or by epicurean disdain for what is going on round about him, by fiddling while Rome is burning, by delighting in sophistries in school and university and entangling young minds in the snare of universal relativity, moral as well as intellectual, and in ranting about the antinomian freedom of the artist. And the ideal or nadir of the egotist? 'It is mildly, pleasantly bewildering, like the first lessons in Chinese or the first round with a hypnotist. Events transpire in all declensions at once; they are never conjugated. What is

---

[1] In a broadcast on William Morris and Robert Bridges Mr. Stephen Spender said: 'Nevertheless, I think that the desire to merge one's talent into the mind of a political movement, however good a cause in itself, is more destructive to an artist than what may seem the selfish development of a writer's own craft quite independently of his audience, and the pursuit of beauty quite independently of current values.' This remark illustrates the argument in the text and shows the effect of a separatist tendency in the two loves.

not Gog is Magog—and at nine punkt Gabriel always blows his horn. *But is it music?* Who cares? The duck is plucked, the air is moist, the tide is out and the goat's securely tethered. The wind is from the bay, the oysters are from the muck. Nothing is too exciting to drown the pluck-pluck of the mandolines. The slugs move from slat to slat; their little hearts beat fast, their brains fill with swill. By evening it's all moon light on the bay. The lions are still affably baffled, and whatever sports, spits, fumes and hisses is properly snaffled. C'est la mort du carrousel, la mort douce des choux-bruxelles.'

From the examples quoted, which so easily could be multiplied, our life upon earth seems to be made up of a more or less successful attempt to harmonize two loves, to find the mean between their claims upon us. Our egotism is restrained by reason, and reason, which tends to an enlightened selfishness, is married to a large-hearted, sympathetic anima, which, in turn, curbs the libertine effusiveness of our lower nature. In this *ménage*, as Claudel calls it, the human person combines dignity and good fellowship, and he treats and loves others as persons. All, therefore, should be well. But, in fact, as we all know, this ideal is all too rarely achieved, and when it is presented as an ideal something seems to be lacking. The ideal in it excites a generation which has been afflicted with barbarism, but as soon as it becomes familiar the finer spirits are bored with it and those who test it find it deeply dissatisfying. The poised and cultured gentleman looks anaemic; he has made himself a eunuch, but for no kingdom of heaven. That is why Dionysus was so welcome to the civilized Greeks. The classical ideal in its various forms is too neat, too definite; its universe is closed; and so invariably it provokes a reaction to what is romantic and mystical. The uneasiness in the heart of man, what the modern 'existential' school of philosophy have named 'Angst', is not appeased by the reasonable estimate of the good life. This is plain even in the standard treatise of the good life, the Nicomachaean Ethics of Aristotle. How quietly the thought moves in its pages as the theory of the appropriate happiness for man is developed, and then when all might be thought to be finished the writer breaks new ground and without looking back on what he has written starts to tell us that we must 'play the immortal so far as we can', and that our immortal longings can be satisfied only in a life like that of the gods, in which we contemplate the highest and the best. He had told us in the first books that a man must seek happiness in this life, that he must be well equipped with temporal goods, that he must have friends, that he must control his passions and live a life of poise and be of good judgement and live in community. This is making the best of the opportunities of human and mortal life. But at the end it is left behind and another ideal takes its place, which at first sight does not seem compatible with it. The opposition is not peculiar to Aristotle; it runs through the ages; it is there in Epictetus and Marcus Aurelius and in Thomas More and Pascal and most of the sages. The Greek sculptors give us man without blemish, godlike in his human flawlessness; they have used *le nombre d'or* and given us a mean, which is a perfect proportion. Their gods and goddesses have not been dead many times and 'learnt the secrets of the grave'; nor 'been divers in deep seas', nor 'trafficked for strange webs with Eastern merchants'; they have none of the asceticism of St. Bruno, nothing of the tapering spirituality of El Greco and the figures in the portals of Chartres. The mind of the West has been nurtured on Greece, but its spirit is drawn to another standard of beauty.

When Scheler wishes to strike the balance between the egocentrism of the West and the monism of the East he does not go to a Greek model; he chooses St Francis of Assisi. Here, in his view, is the ideal man, the one who best knows how to love; and as his view of the saint crosses the bridge from human to divine love and brings us back to Eros and Agape, I will quote a passage at some length. Using his own terminology of 'loving fusion' and loving 'identification', he says that St. Francis was certainly at first inspired and influenced by the Provençal movement. 'He who gave himself the name of the "troubadour of God" and loved even up to the time of his death to sing the songs of the French troubadours, which he found delightful, he who in his exquisitely tender relations with Saint Clare, seemed to model himself on this ideal of the past even after he had become a rigorous and heroic ascetic, St. Francis, in short, understood, with an unexampled skill, however unstudied and unconscious, how to strip the great historical emotion in the Provençal movement . . . of its heaviness and its attachment to the earth and to the ideal woman, to strip it, indeed, so entirely that he kept only the rhythm of it, the spiritual rhythm, freed from all sensation. And this emotion, thus spiritualized, he understood how to attach as well to a personal and unworldly love of God and of Jesus. . . . This emotion then as it grew ever more spiritual and Christian took on more and more a functional role and withdrawing itself from the "ideal woman", which was its first object, it extended itself to the whole of nature and became a spiritual key giving entry to its mysteries and a spiritual eye to penetrate to the depth of those mysteries. We have said that the rhythm of the Provençal emotion was kept. Indeed, all that provided the subject matter for these sentiments and sensations, which were specifically erotic, the high gallantry, the worship of the "woman", the virile and knightly homage to her gentle weakness and beauty—all this lived on in the soul of Saint Francis and furnished the elements of that living art whereby the saint of Assisi learnt how to penetrate with his vital and spiritual centre to the core of creatures and bow down in an ever-burning devotion in the presence of the divine life with which they were animated. There is no question here of a sublimation . . . of a sentiment originally erotic to a degree of exalted love, christian in its nature, for his neighbour. Nor again is it a question of the simple flowering of love, as Hildebrand thinks, in a childlike nature, a love unworldly and original, or love for God and persons, which sprang directly from a supernatural source. How could, in truth, such an expansion be psychologically conceivable? What really happened was a meeting, altogether singular and unique in its kind, between "Eros" and "Agape" . . . in a soul which was originally holy and extraordinary, a meeting which culminated in such an interpenetration of the two loves that it produced the most extraordinary and sublime example of "spiritualization of life" and "vivifying of spirit", which has ever been known.'

A long range view, therefore, of history, its attempts to obtain and promote happiness, and the picture gallery of its heroes, shows conclusively that the reasonably perfect human life is not sufficient as an ideal, that it does not work for a long spell, and that love cannot end in human relationships. No matter what the humanist or the secularist may boast, he is but beating the air; the facts are too strong for him. While he is talking the people will have wandered off to look at a saint like St. Francis of Assisi and to feel their hearts moved by a strange new hope. The same conclusion imposes itself when we come to examine the recorded experience of human love at its best, the love story of animus and anima. The mind may be so carried away by its sense of power and the constant discoveries it makes, that it may fail to realize for a while the deadening influence it exercises on all it touches. Thought is always a post-mortem, and it misses the intimacy of individual experience. For that it has to seek the aid of sensation and feeling. But once it does fully realize the limitations to which it is subject, the self has an undying desire to get beyond them, to see not through a mirror, but face to face, to have a synoptic vision of all reality, to gather up in one rich experience all that has been scattered in space and broken off by time. And if this frustration be apparent even in the mind's masculine activity, much more is it so in the desire of the 'heart', in that longing for union, to be one with the other 'I'.

Yet in the moment of communion
The very heart of passion's fire,
His spirit spurns the mortal union,
Not this, not this, the soul's desire.

Some infinitely inner fusion,
As wave with water; flame with fire,
Let me dream once the dear delusion
That I am You, oh, heart's desire.

The union which the animal desires may well be death. Death comes in as a refrain in the language of human lovers, but if it be not stark passion death means that the dividing line between 'I' and 'Thou' has been crossed, or shall I say, apparently crossed. For the suffering of lovers consists in this that time snatches away love and that the isolation of the spiritual self can never be overcome. Against time the most magnificent of Shakespeare's sonnets are written, and yet he can only promise that the memory of love shall linger in his verse. But this is only a shadow in winter.

Yet seem'd it Winter still, and, you away,
As with your shadow I with these did play.

Or if it be not by such a substitute the poet, as, for instance, Thomas C. Carew, dazzles himself and flies from the grim reality by fancy and hyperbole.

My very ashes in their urn,
Shall, like a hallowed Lamp, for ever burn.

It is all very well for Milton to call Adam and Eve a blest pair and to add:

And O yet happiest if ye seek
No happier state, and know to know no more.

Even in Paradise, and before sin came, love could not end there. It seeks, to quote again the language of poetry, to live in and by the love of the other.

So when from hence we shall be gone,
And be no more, nor you, nor I,
As one another's mystery,
Each shall be both, yet both but one.

Each has to say:

I cannot stirre, but as thou please to move me,
Nor can my heart returne thee love, untill thou love me.

This is the ideal, but alas! it is only heralded in human love, and can never be reached. In our highest moments, our poor solitary self continues to beat alone, ticking over in an unbearable silence. Not only time defeats our dreams, but the boundary mark of the self. When Scheler wrote of sympathy and 'affective union' he could point only to a subhuman swoon of the self as examples. The secret of the joint movement of animus and anima is that our selves must recur in all our ecstasies and at the same time that self must be enlivened by the gift of the other. There is a compenetration of love; there are no reserves, nothing hidden. We have given all away and it comes back to us in the other's return of love. 'I cannot stirre, but as thou please to move me.'

> Onely another head
> I have, another heart and breast,
> Another musick, making live not dead,
> Without whom I could have no rest:
> In him I am well drest.

But when George Herbert wrote these lines he had found the answer; he had discovered that the union of mortal love was only the prelude and symbol of that immortal and divine love which brings to a close the story and the search of the human soul. Tous les amants qu'il a eus n'ont jamais été que les matelas d'un autre amant rêvé. We are back at the beginning, at the problem of divine love, of Eros and Agape.

Translated into the language of egocentric and self-effacing love, this means that the former of these two loves has as its ideal the knowledge of the other person, to see him as he is, to enjoy this supreme good; what, in fact, St. Augustine says when thinking of God. 'The happy life consists of joy in Truth: for this is a joying in Thee, who art the Truth, O God, health of my countenance, my God.' The animus cannot be ultimately satisfied with less, though it know it not and is helpless to realize it. So satisfied, indeed, is it with its temporary successes, with the satisfaction of using its own power in discoveries and practical knowledge that it sometimes disowns any higher aim. But the shadow on all our knowing brings us back to the ideal of knowing without hindrance, of draining all there is to be known in the object or person before us, of seizing the secret of the universe and of all existence. On the other hand, the anima, with its desire for self-effacement, its comparative disregard for its own interests, has no such palliative as the animus, and therefore, it is easier for us to discern the true end of the soul and its plight by turning our attention to it. It betrays by its unrest and by the infinitude of its desire how bourgeois even the classical and humanistic ideal of life is compared with its passion and its readiness for crucifixion. Unaware of the nature of its lover it is like an abyss calling to an abyss; it learns more from its emptiness and its failures than from any scent or sight. To give and to belong is its life; not to possess, but to be possessed. And this is how it lives in harmony with animus who stores the soul with treasures which it is its delight, like the Magdalen, to pour at the feet of another. Knowledge is the soul's delight, its positive and personal bliss, but without the balancing desire to live in and by the life of another, this desire would be nothing but an enlightened selfishness. The two serve each other's ends, and bring it about that perfect love is mutual giving and taking, possessing and being possessed.

CHAPTER TEN

SACRIFICE

The life here, though it is hard, is God's will for me, as I most intimately know, which is more than violets knee-deep.—GERARD MANLEY HOPKINS.

> *Whatever we inherit from the fortunate*
> *We have taken from the defeated.*
> *What they had to leave us—a symbol:*
> *A symbol perfected in death.*
>
> —T. S. ELIOT.

I begin by saying that a work of art is the work of a lover. It is a lover' worship.—ERIC GILL.

In his introduction to a work on *Chinese Jades*, which had been collected by Mr. A. W. Bahr, Dr. Berthold Laufer describes the 'philosophy of the ancient Chinese' as 'dualistic'. It 'classified all phenomena as male and female, as light and darkness, as heat and cold, as positive and negative. These two primeval forces were seen active in Heaven and Earth, and the union of the two and their constant interaction was believed to have resulted in the creation of nature and man'. Hence, as a passage in the ancient *Book of Rites* informs us: 'Sacrifices to the deity Earth were made to honour the beneficial actions of the Earth, for Earth harbours all beings, and Heaven holds the stars and constellations suspended. We derive our food and wealth from Earth, we derive the regulation of our labours from Heaven. For this reason we honour Heaven and love Earth, and we therefore teach our people to return thanks to them.'

This passage summarizes the general theory so far set forth, if we allow that man tends to make gods in his own likeness and offer sacrifice to the Unknown God in that likeness. Everywhere we find traces of this duality. Laufer gives us some of the opposites, and they could be multiplied. To set up one principle and to explain all the many things in heaven and on earth by means of it would be, of course, an absurd oversimplification. But to neglect the hint would be equally foolish, and, as we have already seen, many philosophies have been formulated on some theory of opposites and their reconciliation, whether we think of the Heracleitean fire or the Hegelian synthesis or the Marxian Dialectic. So far as the physical Universe is concerned I have been content to point to its tensions, its to-and-fro movements, its negatives and positives, without pressing the evidence. I cannot, however, refrain from quoting from the unpublished manuscript of a friend of mine, Dr. H. P. Newsholme, a passage which gives his interpretation of the processes of nature: 'That escape from inertia, in part expressed in a rhythm in Nature and a rhythm in life, frustrated finally in death, has its significance in the inward meaning of inertia itself. For inertia's outward resistance to a change in state, the insensitiveness to the external world to which it gives rise, is the outward mark of the inward preoccupation which inertia implies, between electron and electron, atom and atom, molecule and molecule, particle and particle. Thus evolution, as it progresses, is a process of emergence from a state of inward absorption into one of growing outward interest: one might perhaps say, from self-concern into disinterestedness, from selfishness into love.' In these words, in this view of Nature, we can read, if we like, an extension to nature of the views expressed in this book; and, curiously enough, though his theory as a whole moves in a different direction from that expressed in these pages, Dr. Newsholme has a parallel line of thought about death. 'Finally, this living frame, leaping rhythmically back into it, ends in surrender to death, the acme of expression of the inertia of inaction when contrasted with the life to which it has succeeded. In the once living organism inertia has found expression in *death*.'

When we come to the world of living species there is more ground for serious conjecture, especially as we ascend the scale and examine the behaviour of animals with highly developed organisms. The safest way of procedure, however, is to start from human experience and human history, to use it with discretion in order to interpret the conduct of animals, and then with the help of knowledge gained from this study to supplement our knowledge of ourselves and our fellow human beings. By this means we are saved from fantastic hypotheses about the general nature of all living things, from reading into the experience of animals what is specifically human and forgetting that the analogy of human experience must necessarily be of uncertain value. To the credit of our humanity we treat animals on the principle that the physical expression of their feelings, whether of pain or joy, corresponds with our manner of expression. But if, as we have reason to believe, our spiritual nature affects the whole tone of our sensitivity, no matter how similar the nervous system may be, and if there be no reflective consciousness in animals, no similar awareness of the past and expectancy of the future, and above all no personal sense of humiliation, no personal memory to reinforce the present with imaginative fears, no counting of the hammer strokes of pain, their degree of happiness cannot be estimated accurately by any human calculus. (How often has one not envied the repose and insouciance of the dog or cat resting by the fender when the hour for another raid draws near!) I say this because a reader may feel at first entirely out of sympathy with a theory of twin impulses, one of which surges into brutality and can be exhibited in the stalking of a prey, while the other can take its pleasure in what is self-effacing and degrading and submit to being victimized. (The word 'degrading' shows very well the pathetic fallacy of identifying what is animal with what is human.) The spiritual is so unquestionably the umpire in all man's conduct that the civilized man, and, above all, the Christian, is content with the decisive distinction between what is morally right and wrong, and he either dismisses the behaviour of the animal as beneath his notice or he refuses to see anything in his own nature which is comparable with it. Quite rightly he does not stop to stare hard at naked passion or to weigh his instincts, except in an age when civilized habits are in decay. Modern studies in psychology and anthropology and the hypotheses of the psycho-analysts have, however, confirmed the old belief in the composite nature of man. If he is spiritual he is also kin to the beasts of the field, and it is more than probable, therefore, that he should share in their impulses and emotions. The animal will be present in man, but in a new dimension, so that in a certain sense nothing is the same. But in so far as the spiritual loses control and the animal emerges, the lower nature will show features more common to those of the beasts. In a man they will be recognized as immoral and as perversions, but in the animal they will be amoral and natural.

If our argument be right, what is common, though analogous, throughout nature and the world of living things and man is a twofold movement, one to the preservation and development of the individual being, the other to the advantage of the order of the universe, the continuation and evolution of the species or race or society. The élan or impetus or desire which by metaphor, because of its highest manifestation, can be called by the name of love, depends for its success on the interaction of these two forms of it. Both must always be present in every individual, as a taking and giving, a coming to be and passing away, a determinant and a determinable, but according as one or other is more predominant it is called masculine or feminine. In human beings this distinction, simple in itself, is complicated and so enriched that we fail to see its workings and its universal import. But when we look closely at the behaviour of man when he is in a transitional stage of development from savagery to civilization, at the divagations from the normal in civilized society and at the symptoms of degeneracy, we are able to detect the common factors in animal and human nature and to watch the differing levels of these two loves. The psycho-analyst corroborates this discovery by ransacking the depths of our nature and dragging out the irrational desires which we have concealed even from ourselves; and whatever we may think in detail of the mythology he invents to explain the happenings behind full consciousness, there seems no reason to doubt the existence of some of the desires to which he gives a name. If further evidence for this be needed, one has only to consider the types of gods and goddesses which have been invented by man. Religion has two sides to it. On the one is the hunger for the true God, the awareness of His presence and a more or less pure worship, assisted by God's grace; on the other is the projection by man into the unknown of his fears and unformulated desires; man makes God after His own likeness, and in so doing distorts the image of the true God. Now when we look at these too human gods and goddesses there is a surprising recurrence of types, which seem to be but variants on two main objects of worship, no matter to what country we turn—and these objects of worship correspond with the two loves which make up human life.

Religion, therefore, in its unchastened stage, before philosophy and ethics united fully with it to purify it, and before Christianity came to do away with all man-made cults, is of great value as an expression and assessor of man's spontaneous desires. It not only defines the kinds of desires, but it shows their various stages, from the crudest to the most refined and spiritual. In other words, it exposes the animal and the brutal, the degraded and self-effacing impulses, which are so often checked and forbidden by custom and moral regulation in a community, in the delirious and orgiastic moments of sacrifice. It allows the bodily instincts full play—but it also gives expression to the very highest aspirations of man. It allows, therefore, for the whole gamut of human emotions. We are permitted to see nakedly how near we come to the animals, and yet how different we are from them as human beings, and lastly how by his universal impulse to worship man cannot be content with even the very best that human relationships can provide. In his sacrifices man breaks away from human loves to ask for communion with the divine.

For this reason pagan sacrifice serves as the best epitome and imaging forth of man's desires. The worst and the best are, as it were, projected on to a screen, and at the same time the universality of sacrifice, whether in time or place, is the clearest proof of man's dissatisfaction with mortal love and happiness and his blind search for a means of placating the unknown God and being lifted up into union with Him. It will be good, therefore, to see whether sacrificial cults set a seal on what has been already said about the nature of human love. Of the lowest forms of sacrifice a good example is the legend of the Minotaur in Crete. We have no means of knowing what truth is mixed up in the legend. 'The Minotaur story was doubtless helped out by the fantastic creations that the Greek invader found around him embodied in gems, and also, in all probability, upon the Palace frescoes. The choice of a bull, however, for the monstrous shape, was not dictated by any worship of a Bull-Man in Minoan times, nor by that of a bull either, save in so far as the bull was the chief sacrificial animal, and associated with other sacred objects in cult scenes. The principal, if not the sole reason, that the story gathered round the Bull, was the actual historic fact of the Minoan bull-ring, and the frequency of its representation on frescoes and gems.' (*The Discoveries in Crete*, by Ronald Burrows, pp. 128–9.) Be that as it may, the legend struck the imagination of the Greeks and appealed to them. As all will remember, Pasiphae conceived an unnatural passion for this Minotaur, this creature which was half-bull and half-man; it roamed about in the labyrinth, and every year the Athenians had to send seven sons and seven daughters to be devoured by the monster until Theseus slew it. The story is especially important because, if Dr. Farnell be right, it is a potpourri of the ideas of the East and the West, of the Semitic and the Phrygo-Carian ideas of worship and sacrifice. The sacred animal of the Semitic goddess was the goat, and the bull was her lover, and this myth is mingled with that of Zeus-Dionysus and Europa. What startles one is the brutality of the story and the way in which it states the passions for naked power, the lust to devour, and on the other hand the complete surrender of Pasiphae and the sacrifice of the maidens and boys. It is only when one realizes that here, as indeed in so many other pagan sacrifices and cults, is the dramatization of the two 'loves' in the most barefaced symbols, that the appeal of the legend becomes intelligible. To the Greeks Eros was not at first, nor perhaps at any time, the fair Cupid who plays with Campaspe. Before Eros takes shape in human form he is depicted on ancient vases as a winged shape, a kind of fate, and he is at one moment the impulse to life, of whom Theognis sings:

> *Love comes at his hour, comes with the flowers in spring,*
> *Leaving the land of his birth,*
> *Kypros, beautiful isle. Love comes, scattering*
> *Seed for man on earth.*
>
> (*Theog.* 1275);

and, at the next moment, the spirit of death, whose wand or voice entices poor mortals to their destruction. Miss J. E. Harrison quotes a remarkable passage from the anonymous author of the Philosophoumena: 'There is in the gateway the picture of an old man, white-haired, winged; he is pursuing a blue-coloured woman, who escapes. Above the man is written φάος ῥυέντης (Phaos Hruentes), above the woman Περεηφικόλα. According to the doctrine of the Sethians it seems that φάος ῥυέντης is light and that φικόλα is dark water.' The exact meaning, Miss Harrison thinks, of these mysterious paintings is probably lost for ever; but it is scarcely rash to conjecture that the male figure is Eros. He pursues a woman; he is winged; in that respect he is like the Eros of common mythology. But in other respects he is the Eros of the mysteries; not young, but very ancient and white-haired, the ἀρχαῖος ἔρως of Orphic tradition, eldest of all the Gods. And the name written above him as he pursues his bride inscribed 'Darkness' or 'Dark Water' is 'Phaos Ruentes', the 'Rushing or Streaming Light'. 'This is an ideal which is very different from the conventional one, and most closely connected with the passions which may break forth in two diverging streams. Even after Eros has taken human form and has been civilized under Athenian influence he can change suddenly into the shape of the beast-mystery-god: "Heads had he many, Head of a ram, a bull, a snake and a bright-eyed lion".'

The barbarity and animalism of some of these rites shocked pious-minded Greeks like Plutarch, and were used by some of the Christian Fathers to point the contrast with the Christian mysteries. 'I will not', says St. Clement of Alexandria, 'dance out your mysteries, as they say Alcibiades did, but I will strip them naked, and bring them out on to the open stage of life, in view of those who are the spectators at the drama of life. The Bacchoi hold orgies in honour of a mad Dionysus, they celebrate a divine madness by the Eating of Raw Flesh, the final accomplishment of their rite is the distribution of the flesh of their butchered victims, they are crowned with snakes, and shriek out the name of Eva, that Eve through whom sin came into the world, and the symbol of their Bacchic orgies is a consecrated serpent.' (Quoted from Miss J. A. Harrison's *Prolegomena to the Study of Greek Religion*, p. 484.)

But as we have already seen, the mystery religions can pass from what is bestial to what is intensely spiritual. The 'red and bleeding feasts' are abandoned and a purer sacrifice, as 'dear to these gods', is initiated:

> *Wool of the sheep was there, fruit of the vine,*
> *Libations and the treasured store of grapes,*
> *And manifold fruits were there, mingled with grain*
> *And oil of olive, and fair curious combs*
> *Of wax compacted by the yellow bee.*
>
> (Sophocles, fragm. 464.)

A sense of communion with the god or gods, which before had been half-hidden in the rites of human sacrifice and the tasting of blood, now turns into a mystic marriage. As Epiphanius tells us: 'Some prepare a bridal chamber and perform a mystic rite accompanied by certain words used to the initiated, and they allege that it is a spiritual marriage.' In the mysteries of Isis, as already related, the rite could symbolize at its best something pure and spiritual. The same holds true of the Eleusinian mysteries, if we are to believe the author of the Philosophoumena, as quoted by Miss Harrison:

'And following the Phrygians the Athenians, when they initiate at the Eleusinian rites, exhibit to the epoptae the mighty and marvellous and most complete epoptic mystery, an ear of grain reaped in silence. And this ear of grain the Athenians themselves hold to be the great and perfect light that is from that which has no form, as the Hierophant himself, who is not like Attis, but who is made a eunuch by means of hemlock, and has renounced all carnal generation, he, by night at Eleusis, accomplishing by the light of a great flame the great and unutterable mysteries, says and cries in a loud voice "Holy Brimo has borne a sacred Child, Brimos", that is, the mighty has borne the mighty; and holy, he (i.e. the Naassene) says, is the generation that is spiritual, that is heavenly, that is from above, and mighty is he so engendered.'

Sacrifice, then, exhibits all the levels of human desire and activity. It can seem to offer only an opportunity for expressing the lowest passions; it can turn into a festive occasion on which a city or nation celebrates its corporate happiness in living and loving, and it can rise to a mystic ardour to be one with the unknown god. But in truth in all the manifestations of sacrifice the centrifugal force of the human heart is active, and that is why it offers such clear evidence that man cannot be satisfied with a closed universe or with a purely human love and destiny. Dionysus disturbs the moderation, the poise which the humanists of every generation would set up as the ideal to be cultivated. The animus after setting everything in order to his own satisfaction has to take second place. He has to stand by and watch while the anima dances out of doors to another's piping. But this is not quite correct, as it anticipates what happens at only a developed stage, after the anima has been tamed by reason and told to behave in a civilized society. Before that stage at the lower levels of animus and anima the more savage impulses darken the real desire of the soul. The real longing is there, and alive, and even in the most primitive religion, it can at moments assert itself; but the two passions have twisted and defaced the image of the true God and substituted the image of their own crude desires. The god is a Minotaur or Juggernaut or Moloch or at best a Homeric Zeus and nordic Wotan; or if the other passion be predominant it is the goddess of night, the dark and horned goddess who calls her votaries to self-immolation and extinction. As civilization grows, the wilder passions are tamed and a period of pride in reason and self-control succeeds. The gods become tutelary deities at the service of the city or the State, and the worship of the unknown and great god is damped down and finds its exit in strange and devious ways. For the essential of religion and sacrifice cannot be laid to sleep nor can it be imprisoned for long. A new religion will spring up and gather innumerable disciples. It is then that the animus finds itself impotent to restrain the truancy of the anima. At this point we reach the summit of natural religion, the summit which I have described in the dilemma of the great philosophers, like Aristotle, who advocate a high-minded humanism with one breath and at the next are darting out into untrodden ways to greet the beckoning hand of the unknown God.

The varieties of sacrifice are so multiple and strange that, when they were first investigated, many conflicting theories were invented to explain their purpose. But now it is possible to see the unity of intention which underlies all the vagaries, and in the light of the perfect and Christian sacrifice they fall into place. They serve also to illustrate the workings of the two loves, and in turn these two loves throw light upon the nature of sacrifice. In the Christian sacrifice the essential is freed from all primitive distortions and unhappy accretions and shines out as the appropriate reaction of man in the presence of his Maker and Last End. (The sacrifice is, of course, much more than that by reason of its Victim and Priest, but the new perfection added embellishes and does not dim the essentials of all sacrifice.) If we suppose that mankind has always been aware of its creatureliness and the overlordship of an invisible God it will always practise some religion and express what it feels about God in terms of sacrifice. Inner feelings tend to complete themselves in some outward act, and if those feelings are profound the outward act will try to symbolize those feelings. Just as goodwill to friends is expressed and symbolized by the offering of gifts and repentance in the beating of the breast and in some form of repayment, so the spontaneous response of man to God shows itself in the acts of homage and adoration and in the symbolism of gifts. Moreover, the kind of homage and the kind of symbolism shows what man instinctively realizes to be his due attitude. The homage is not of the servant to the master or the liege man to his king; it is of a creature to the God who made it. Worship and adoration are unlike any other human act or response; they denote a peculiar and special relation, and this is made clear by the symbolism which confesses that the offering is the token of man himself. Sacrifice is a symbol of complete dependence and dedication, and also a prayer for assistance from the Almighty that he should be propitious. The response of natural religion has been, perhaps, nowhere better stated than in the play of Sophocles in the closing words of Philoctetes. 'Farewell, thou sea-girt Lemnos; and speed me with fair course, for my contentment, to that haven whither I am borne by mighty Fate, and by the counsel of friends, and by the all-subduing god who hath brought these things to fulfilment.'

But it is inconceivable that man should separate off from his religious thinking all that is to his own benefit. Without any interruption in his thought he thinks of God as one to whom he owes all and on whose will he depends and at the same time as the Rewarder, and on a higher level as the Supreme Good himself. And just because all this is in his mind when he worships and sacrifices, the sacrifice tends to end in a new covenant between God and the tribe or people and in the bestowal on them of something of God's own power and holiness. This is symbolized in the acceptance of what is made over to God by God so that it becomes God's property and sacrosanct, and the return of it to the people that they may partake of it and so enter into communion with the Godhead and share in his virtue and power. That this is the meaning of an ever-repeated symbolism is clear from the prayers and utterances which have been handed down to us in so many religious cults. Human beings are frightened of God, both because of His immensity compared with their frail tenure of life and because of His unerring judgements on their wrong-doing; but despite the fright there creeps in a note of hope that the 'all-subduing god' will bring their life to fulfilment and that He may deign to become their beatitude. It is in accordance with such universal fears and hopes that St. Augustine gave the dignified and confident definition of true sacrifice as 'every action which is performed with the aim of inhering in God in one holy society; whose purpose, that is, is to bring us to the end by which we can truly be made blessed'.

Unfortunately the true aim of sacrifice is often obscured by the primitive passions which deflect man's ideals and also by the intrusion of other motives. At one moment magic and superstition have usurped the place of religion; at another, the desire to make religion profitable and to exploit the invisible power of the gods. But these are the parasitical growths; they do not help to show us the main stem. In its purest and therefore most exemplary forms sacrifice is always homage and adoration, petition and quest for pardon, and in the end the longing to be possessed by God and to possess Him. And that this is the truth behind all sacrifice is borne out by the role of the two loves in the act of sacrifice. They are responsible for the outbursts of crude passion in the savage rites; they are seen in the fierce, despotic god and the blind and abandoned response of the worshipping multitudes. There are there in the cool, rational religious cults of sophisticated humanity, and they take their proper place when God is worshipped in 'truth and spirit'. Human reason now has to take second place and to allow love to move by faith into a darkness which is of life and not of death. If romance and irrationalism and the dark mysticisms belong to Eros, the love which moves to God because of God's initiative is the prelude to Agape.

SACRIFICE

It might seem from this description as if with the coming of Agape
reason had to relinquish its office and that love had turned into complete
self-surrender. There is, in truth, a momentous change. Beatrice, to recur
to an image already used, does take the place of Virgil, and at first sight
the roles of animus and anima appear to have been reversed. Of old by
natural right the self came first; it showed a proper regard for itself, was
conscious of its dignity and sought for self-realization. Aristotle and the
philosophers mentioned by Rousselot took this for granted as a metaphysical principle which could not be gainsaid, and as in man the directing
and differentiating mark is reason, reason takes charge and, like Aeneas,
leaves the night to accomplish his Roman destiny, although

> *in such a night*
> *Stood Dido with a willow in her hand*
> *Upon the wild sea banks, and waft her love*
> *To come again to Carthage.*

In all human loves the Roman yields to Dido at his peril, and even when
the soul is drawn by longings more than human and seeks for mystic
union with the One or the Absolute, experience shows how near to
drowning is the self and how near to being eclipsed the reason. Has this
risk, then, to be incurred in Agape? No, the perfect correspondence
between taking and giving, self-regard and self-surrender, animus and
anima is reached in Agape, and the manner in which this perfect correspondence is brought about is unfolded in the Christian sacrifice.

In the Christian religion God, to use the magnificent words of Pascal,
is the God of Abraham, the God of Isaac, the God of Jacob, and not of
the philosophers and savants. He is a living God, not an object but a
Being most personal, not slumbering like Endymion, but alive and loving.
So active is He that we cannot begin to think of Him or address Him;
we can only reply, and even that has been initiated by Him. We love
because He first loved us. The Christian revelation goes much further
than this and tells us that God has shown to us, so far as is compatible
with the unchanging plenitude of His nature, a love like to that of self-
donating and giving. The New Testament goes out of its way to underline
this characteristic as if the writers were determined to make clear that
God can do all in selfless love which man is required to do if he would
love perfectly. (In man, just because a Thou more perfect than himself
exists, the love rests ultimately on the Other, but in God because He is
Himself, the plenitude, the love returns to its source after gathering up
the loves it went out to meet.) Man is to be the beneficiary of God's
action, and God acts as if he were sacrificing His all. 'He dispossessed

245

Himself, and took the nature of a slave, fashioned in the likeness of men, and presenting Himself to us in human form.' In these words St. Paul gives us the first act of the outgoing love of God, and he adds to it the still more wondrous proof of generosity: 'And then He lowered His own dignity, accepted an obedience which brought Him to death, death on a cross.' In another place he goes so far as to say in a figure of speech which his converts would understand that 'the Christ, that knew not sin, he made sin for us'. To realize the full meaning of this we have to go to the full length of the doctrine that God did become man and so fulfilled in striking manner the desire which lies behind the movement of one of the forms of love. But whereas that love, as we have seen, when uncontrolled seeks for fusion with the other and to identify itself with the beloved, God remains God and yet wholly man. As a result of this, man is able to offer the perfect sacrifice and attain to the apogee of love. He is drawn by his very nature to worship God and to offer himself to God. If his love were only of one kind, and that which the Greek philosophy tended to emphasize, he would at the highest be only able to see that such a love and sacrifice tended to his own perfection, that it would give him all his desires and make him blessed. But, in fact, this most legitimate love is but the warp to the woof of another love which draws him out of himself to lose himself in the beloved. This too has its dangers, as we have seen, and if isolated from the other love would lead to self-extinction —an extreme which has been condemned by the Church. But how combine the two loves and satisfy God? The answer is in the gift of God, which surpasses all human expectation. The God-man can as man give his life and offer the perfect gift of love, Himself, to the Infinite Lord and Lover of mankind. 'He gave Himself up for us, an oblation and victim to God in the odour of sweetness'. Such love is infinitely pleasing and so proceeds to its culmination in the return of the gift to the offerers. The God-man is given back to give new life, to be the mode of union between God and mankind. That is to say, that instead of losing his self, man has that self exalted into a new unity, whereby he can live the life of God Himself. 'And the glory which Thou hast given me, I have given to them; that they may be one, as We also are one: I in them, and Thou in me; that they may be made perfect in one.' It is in this reciprocal love that losing one's life is saving it, that to give is to receive, that death is swallowed up in victory. And the language, as is only fitting, is the language of persons, of 'I' and 'Thou'; we have passed away from the philosophy of objects, from pantheisms and monisms. Persons do not die when the love is mutual; they live more fully each in the other's love. But when it comes to the infinite love of God for man, man, so far from

SACRIFICE

having anything subtracted from his being, has the personal joy of giving back to God something of that infinite love which has taken possession of him. It is this mystery of love which the Christian sacrifice figures forth.

CHAPTER ELEVEN

PHILOSOPHICAL BACKGROUND

The fact that God could create free beings *vis-à-vis* of Himself is the cross which philosophy could not carry, but remained hanging therefrom.
—S. KIERKEGAARD.

The true man, the 'man in man' as Plato beautifully expresses the new idea, is the intellectual part of the soul.—*Paideia*, vol. II, by W. JAEGER.

Other natures follow reason and their poetry is the lean music of argument and of rhetoric; ideals and noble theories and all the rest. . . (They) are the enemy, plucking the unit man, the individual, out of his sublime solitude to place him in this or that fraternity, and be in the bonds of sympathy or antipathy with his fellows.
—From letter of J. B. YEATS.

Something must now be said to fill in the background of Eros and Agape, and fortunately there is a book at hand which is admirably suited to do this. In his *Introduction au Problème de l'Histoire de la Philosophie* the Rev. Hunter Guthrie has written a remarkable sketch of the anatomy of human life, its primordial exigencies and responses. He follows the method of Heidegger and the Phenomenological or existential school of philosophy which claims that it is able to concentrate on the pure and primordial elements in thinking and desiring, and so peer into the very workshop of the self and relate the findings. As this method is not well known and may be considered to be of very dubious value I had better begin with a word of explanation of its history and nature.[1]

A dramatic moment occurred in the history of religious philosophy when the Dane, Kierkegaard, shook the dust of the Hegelian rationalism

---

[1] It must be clearly noted that the purpose of this chapter is not to enter into a philosophical analysis of any system of thought for its own sake. It may well be that several varying systems of philosophy could serve as a background for Eros and Agape. St. Augustine found the Platonic very suitable for some of his favourite ideas on love; others have found Duns Scotus to their taste. For purely philosophical reasons there may be grounds for deciding in favour of another system. If I were engaged on a critical analysis of Guthrie's theory, it might be that I should have to express constant disagreement with his detailed development of it. But such criticism would be irrelevant to my purpose. It is enough that the system is suggestive and valuable, that it works in and through some of the capital ideas of our age and that, at least, it serves admirably to bring out the original distinction of the two loves and how they co-operate in human nature. Just in so far as Guthrie fails to do justice to this theme I think criticism is needed.

off his feet. He had been brought up to believe in the dictum that 'the rational is the real' and to walk with Truth in the majestic deployment of the Hegelian dialectic. But increasingly Kierkegaard came to see that the human personal life of beings like himself could not be laid out all neatly in a human rational system, however neat or majestic. Still less could any such system do justice to the God, as known, for instance, in Christianity. The God of Abraham broke to pieces the Hegelian idol of Him. The latter could not be lived or experienced; it belonged to the world of abstraction and essence and not of existence. Abstractions and concepts are like statistics; they do not bleed. Kierkegaard, therefore, fell back on what may be called an existential view of life as contrasted with one of essence. So far his choice is not a very exceptional nor original one. On a superficial view one might say that it was nothing but the full acceptance of a Protestant outlook. It, also, could be said to fall in with a tendency in philosophy, ever prevalent since Descartes, to lean on the subjective. But what marks out Kierkegaard is both the intensely vivid religious conflict he experienced and his attempt to think out the implications of this existential philosophy in terms of this conflict. He touches on the most sensitive nerve of human nature, its radical contingency, its subsistent agony, the constant contrast between himself as part of a world of reason and order, which even lays hands on divine reality and solidifies it into human concepts,[1] a world in fact in which his nature and essence are at home, and another part of himself which has to play the rebel and defy the rules and in that very irrationalism touch with longing hands a living God. He made this rent or schism in himself the very definition of life, to such a degree that he would call true life a crucifixion. It is no wonder that he became hypnotized by the cry of dereliction from Christ upon the Cross, and that he introduced death into the very heart of religious desire.

The thought here expressed by Kierkegaard and disregarded by his contemporaries was soon picked up again. It echoed so truly the troubled spirit of his age, and it pointed to where the radical defect in the rationalist systems of the philosophers lay. Man as man is not the measure of life; thought which proceeds from the essential nature of man can only appropriate the formal and universal element from what exists and lives. There must be another way of living and making contact. Various alternatives, therefore, came to be proposed, and of these I shall mention two. The first is that of the phenomenological school with its existential philosophy. This has culminated in Heidegger, who repeats the password

---

[1] In the rationalist philosophy and theology which Kierkegaard studies there was no real attempt, as in the Scholastic philosophy, to reconcile God's transcendent existence with the limited human concept of Him.

of Kierkegaard, by summing up man in the word, 'Angst'. The second is bound up with the name of Bergson, and its stress is on movement and will. Hunter Guthrie, while by no means neglecting this latter solution, uses the method followed by Heidegger. Another Christian thinker, Rousselot, by criticism of Bergson is able to renovate a more ancient outlook on the relations of will and intellect, essence and existence.

The Phenomenologists are difficult to understand and almost impossible to explain. In common sense thinking we take for granted that we are thinking about real objects and persons, chairs, sisters and cities. But common sense gets into such difficulties that at times philosophers have parted company with it. For a long period empiricists and idealists took each an extreme view and would not hear of any mediation. Brentano pointed out that whether we really know objects or not, whether all objects are really in the mind or outside, what is certain is that we cannot think without thinking of something nor desire without something which we desire. In other words, there are objects of consciousness, and we can suspend our judgement for the time being on the problem of the status of these objects, the while we analyse them. He called them 'intentional objects', and said that we should treat them as phenomena without bothering our heads for the moment about realism or idealism. If we examine them as they belong to our consciousness and in their pure state without any presuppositions, we shall have a true and irrefutable science on which we can build a true philosophy. This belief of Brentano's has been worked to death by his followers. It might seem from what I have said to be simple and obvious; but this is far from being so. The hard task they have set themselves is to strip off from an experience all that makes it, all that is topical or historical or idiosyncratic, to get down to the essence of the intentional object. I may, for instance, desire a chicken for lunch or to go for a holiday; I may be thinking about my lunch or a friend or a problem in mathematics, or I may be anxious because of a headache or a lack of knowledge or the folly of a friend. Now what is peculiar to each of these cases has to be removed. I do not even use the cases mentioned to make an inductive generalization, but so concentrate my gaze that I am able to see the pure and undefiled essence of 'thinking about something', 'desiring something' and 'fearing something'. This can be discerned intuitively, so that at the end of my inquiry I can form a number of self-evident judgements about the species of 'knowing of' and being 'anxious about'. Husserl has occupied himself with this investigation of knowing. Heidegger, on his part, has applied himself to what he thinks the most fundamental problem of all, namely, that of 'being'. We normally think of 'being' as that indefinite universe of reality about which we gradually come to know something. We ask the question whether I, shut up in my own self and consciousness, can ever get outside my own mind so as to know the world as it really is. Heidegger says that we inherit this naive assumption. Being is in truth the correlate of consciousness, the intentional object of consciousness, and just as much or as little subjective as consciousness itself. It is the prime intentional experience, and without it none of the others can fairly be examined. That is why he gives his whole attention to it in *Sein und Zeit*, or, rather, he returns to the 'I think, therefore I am' of Descartes and treats this statement by the new method. He takes this because it is the exemplary essence; that is to say, in starting with the ego and with one's own self he has the best jumping off point for reaching the nature of 'being'.

It cannot be too often repeated that Heidegger is not engaged in analysing what we mean when we say that we are aware that we are thinking, and thinking, say, of ourselves, or that we are wishing to learn more about our character and our chances in life. All such acts of thinking and desiring are impure, that is to say, they contain a number of pre-suppositions and irrelevant details. We have been affected all our lives by influences, by our reading, by our nationality and our professional interests. What we have to try to do is to see our naked being before it is overlaid with non-essentials, and so discover what 'being an I' really is. The 'I' is the best subject for such a scrutiny because it is an essence which is existing. Earlier philosophers assumed that the ultimate subject for study was 'being', and the study of it they called metaphysics. Here they made a double mistake. They took for granted that there was a world of being to which the self, as itself a being, belonged, and that the self could look at and study this external reality. But Heidegger thinks that there is an unjustified assumption here. In our primordial experience there is indeed always a subject-object, a thinking-of something, but the two are so inseparably united that we cannot speak of one as outside and the other as inside, or of one being independent of the other. Such conclusions are secondary and must be decided later. The second mistake lies in accepting any real distinction between essence and existence. It is quite true that the objects of the old metaphysics could be thus distinguished. When I think of something I know that it is an essence, but I cannot go on to say that it must therefore exist. In the famous Ontological argument, St. Anselm held that in one case and one case only, namely, that of God, existence must be predicated if I can form any idea of such a being. But as everybody knows, this argument has been hotly disputed; and this brings out the point that reality consists of things which do exist, which may exist, and amongst those things which do exist only perhaps one which exists necessarily. Now, Heidegger says that such distinctions which arise in metaphysics are not present when we turn in on our own being. What we are confronted with is an existent being, this concrete, individual existent being that I am.

What then reveals itself when I look at this existent self? The answer is that the self is a 'being-in-the-world'. Neither can the world be thought of except in abstraction as apart from the self, nor can the self be thought of except as concerned with objects, whether it be thinking about them or anxious about them or using them. The object is correlative with the subject in a more intimate and fundamental manner than the perfume is with smell, or,—shall we say?—self-consciousness is with consciousness. Much later in thought, of course, I may well come to think of objects as outside this primitive correlation, and I may be able to distinguish between objects as thought of and as desired, as loved, and as used, but all such thoughts and distinctions belong to a more sophisticated stage and may prove to be artificial. What is indubitable is that the concrete, existential self is a 'being-in-a-world', a being whose nature can be summed up in the expression 'being concerned-about-things'. Dasein ist Sorge; the self is Concern or a Business or a Fret, according to the emphasis one wishes to place upon the word. The ego has a world at hand, a Sparta to adorn, an ambient sea to use, almost as the soul has a body, and the two together spell the name of the self.

Strange as this result may sound, it can be translated into very human terms. The Sorge is not so different from the Angst of Kierkegaard and the Misère of Pascal, nor from the 'unquiet heart' of St. Augustine. Indeed, Heidegger seems to have been influenced, despite his protestations against prejudices and prepossessions, by the great religious thinkers. He tells us that the self is essentially a thing of time, a series of 'news' in time, and that mortality rides it, like death upon a horse. A man is not merely what he has been nor what he is at the moment, for he is aware of his potentialities and has to concern himself with his future. And yet he came from nothingness and he must return to nothingness; he comes from the dark through a lighted room out into the dark again. Death ends his life without completing it; he is never completed, never fulfilled, and at each moment he is aware that he is not all that he should have been. As has been well said: 'To become a man in the pregnant sense requires a courageous resolution avowing human existence to be nothing other than an advance in time towards death. Past and future are concentrated presentially by recollection and anticipation in the temporal determination of human existence as a betweenness having birth and death as its limits. Since it is incommunicably his very own, death is essential to the human individual as the source of his genuinity. To come to oneself is a process involving temporality as the condition of concern and hence as the constitutive principle of man's being. Thus in their profoundest depths, existence and historicity are one, man being the ground of historical continuity. To be is to exist in time, and existence is a forward advance to the nothing of death before which we are suspended and can halt only momentarily.'[1]

The faults in this view are many, and they have been pointed out by friend and foe,[2] but the one error which concerns us is the mishandling of a true situation. Let us grant that Heidegger has by fair means or false hit upon a truth, which as he says the dulling influence of everyday life and our herd instincts prevent us from realizing. Life is Sorge and can be Angst not because of incidental trials or the accidents of birth or fortune, but by reasons of the very constitution of the human self. That Heidegger should put his finger on this sore spot, and unlike most modern medicine men refuse to ignore it or impute it to slums or phobias or poor hygiene or political backwardness, is all to the good. His phenomenological method would make it endemic to man. But there is surely something wrong in thinking that life is a cancerous growth or at best a long sitting in a dentist's chair. The old writers said of man 'that is born of a woman' that he 'hath but a short time to live and is full of misery. He cometh up and is cut down like a flower; he fleeth as it were a shadow and never continueth in one stay'. They admitted that the 'brother of death daily haunts us with dying mementoes, and time that grows old itself bids us hope no long duration', and that it is folly 'to cling pertinaciously to what we feel crumbling under us and to protract an inevitable fall'. But all these writers clung just as firmly to a belief in immortality and so thrust aside frustration and despair; for the soul 'would not taste of death by reason of its adoption into immortal palaces'. These mortal men, to adapt de Quincey's words, 'like God whose servants they are, . . . utter their pleasures not by sounds that perish or by words that go astray; but by signs in heaven, by changes on earth, by pulses in secret rivers, heraldries painted on darkness and hieroglyphics written on the tablets of the brain'. Heidegger errs by confining man to time and missing his immortality which is not so much a negative survival of death as a new and abundant life of love. He has made what the metaphysicians would call the fatal mistake of equating man's existence with his essence and making of his essence a creature of time. In his view there is nothing beyond the self which exists, or, if perchance it does, it must be bracketed and guaranteed later from the evidence of the self's existence—a kind of footnote not worthy of a place in the text. Man's existence is the only primary and plenary datum, and all other reality is

---

[1] James Collins, *The Modern Schoolman*, March 1944.
[2] Phénomenologie pure, ou Philosophie de l'Action, par Joseph Maréchal in *Philosophia Perennis* and various articles in *Stimmen der Zeit* by E. Przywara.

relative to it and subject to it. Such a view puts man in the first place and God and all else in the secondary place; in other words, necessary existence or the identity of essence and existence, which belongs to God alone, is displaced and given to the ego. The result is only to intensify the misery of man, for he becomes a *roi fainéant*, a being who has to be all and can make nothing of himself, the centre of existence who starts from nothingness and ends in the nothingness of the grave. To transpose the metaphysical language into that of animus and anima, animus has lost anima; she has disappeared. He has become the lord of nothing, the king of shadows. As, however, he cannot really get rid of anima, she becomes to him the symbol of change and death, a kind of writing on the wall, warning him that all his boasting is in vain, that he has no lasting habitation. She is the memento of his mortality and gives him the 'angst' of bad dreams.

And yet how easy it is to restore the balance in the light of what has already been said about the two loves and their expression in animus and anima, or, let us say in accordance with this existential philosophy, in terms of essence and existence. And it is here that Hunter Guthrie's thesis serves so well. He does not commit himself to a wholehearted and exclusive use of the phenomenological method, but he avails himself of it to establish the existence of the Homo Irrequietus, the restless heart, which St. Augustine so vividly described. 'Our method', as he says, 'makes use of a primordial sentiment which we will show to be commensurate with the existential and essential activities of human life. A direct analysis of this sentiment—which will be no more, and no less, than a description of what we see with "the interior eye" of pure reflection —will provide us simultaneously with an anlysis of our existential and essential structure'. That is to say, Guthrie is not relying, as so many do, on generalizations from a number of human experiences; he is not saying: 'Look at the restlessness of nomadic tribes or gipsies or a Rhodes or Lenin or Byron or Napoleon or Francis Xavier.' All such examples might be explained away by special features in the men or by the times and conditions in which they lived, and, therefore, it would be unsafe to do, as so many do, and generalize about the nature of man. Guthrie maintains that we can go behind these scenes and see the actor, which man is, in his shift; that by a mitigated use of the method which Husserl and Heidegger and others have followed we can see 'with the interior eye of pure reflection' the secret places of the self, the to-and-fro movement of the self, which makes a man a man and protrudes itself in all his activities, whether the level be that of the body, the senses or the spirit.

There is no need to give a summary of the arguments with which Guthrie established his point that restlessness is the mark of human life.

He is at one with many of the greatest thinkers and religious geniuses in saying it, and he can enlist on his side the work of many artists and the hypothesis of evolution. This latter presupposes a struggle of some sort, and for existence, unless the hypothesis be stated in the extreme form of purely physical permutations and combinations. Where he leaves the company of the majority and links himself with Kierkegaard and Heidegger is in emphasizing the fact that this restlessness is more than a sentiment; it is life itself. This sentiment of agitation is, then, more fundamental than and anterior to the 'cogito' (of Descartes). It is in fact the primary activity which makes the 'cogito' possible, and is at the same time the revealer of the 'Ego'. From this still more fundamental point of departure we say: 'Inquietus, ergo sum'; I am in unrest, therefore I am. By this he means that all the ordinary alarums and excursions of the soul have behind them a permanent ground of restlessness, the unquiet soul, which provides the principle of sufficient reason for what happens on the different layers or tiers of the self. It will follow, therefore, that behind the conscious thoughts and desires we must presuppose a preconscious stir and movement, the tossing from one side to another of the soul itself.

Before going on to develop Guthrie's argument it may be well to adjust what has so far been said by him to the main argument of this book. According to that argument there is a love which is self-regarding and a love which is self-sacrificing, and these two loves can be gathered up in the general expression of 'giving and taking'. These two loves, which we easily perceive in action, in human experience, have their counterparts all down the levels of the self and are imitated in sometimes gruesome, sometimes pathetic fashion in the brute creation. They seem, then, to belong to the primordial structure of all finite living beings. The one which is self-regarding and possessive exhibits itself peculiarly in the world of reason, the animus; whereas the self-denying love belongs to the anima, to that side of the self which cares little for its dignity and rights and tends to romanticism and even irrationalism. The first is set on self-realization and proceeds with Aristotelian backing to argue that man must by his very nature love himself even when loving others. The second shies away from such an idea and prefers fusion with the beloved and death to itself. The two have, however, to live together. (It is only by an abstraction that we think of them as separate.) The partnership fails very often because the anima being blind to its vocation and espousing irrationality reduces man to a savage condition. At other times a species of humanism is courted and praised, and it is supposed that the anima can find its satisfaction in obeying the reason and being thus highly civilized. Lastly, there is the moment when the anima tires of the bourgeois ideals and self-satisfaction of the so-called humanist culture and goes roaming after a hidden and perfect lover. This can take two forms. It may result in a vogue of mysticism, with all the danger of the self losing itself in an absolute, in some dark night lost in the embrace of a god without a name; or it may wait with hope on the coming of the God, who spurns neither the anima nor the animus and sets up a relation of personal friendship. What we have, therefore, is the uneasy habitation together of two loves, and it is in their interaction that the soul is unquiet. The animus tends to make itself the measure of reality and to put its own happiness in the first place. It resolves all that exists into its own essence, as if human thought and thing were correlative and, at the end, identical. Kant knew better and went to the opposite extreme, but Hegel would not admit of extras outside the scope of the human mind and devised his giant dialectic to take in everything in heaven and on earth. But all existence cannot be spirited away into human thinking like this, and a sensitive soul like Kierkegaard's felt stifled by such human logic and systematizing. He felt the crack within his own being, the cleavage between the pretensions of the human mind and the frailty of his own existence and life, the dead categories of thought and the immeasurable longings of the heart.

These tensions and contradictions fall into place in the distinction which Guthrie makes between essence and existence. The inquietude or restlessness which he has unearthed has, as he says, a double movement. One of these is more obvious than the other, for the reason that it is centred in the ego. It is entirely occupied with the interests of the ego. 'This current of agitation draws me ever forward to the most complete possible evolution of the species of being which I am. It demands the complete development of all the powers on the psychical and corporeal levels (of the self), the expansion of all the forces of the soul. It presses man to the full realization of himself, in so far as he is a man.' There are two features of this movement and development which are outstanding. The first is that it has a limit, however uncertain our marking of it may have to be, and that limit is defined by the possibilities of our human nature. The warning not to seek to be more than human, for that way lies madness, appears again and again in the proverbs and counsels of the wise. We have then to suppose that one kind of restlessness would be appeased if we exhausted the possibilities of our nature and reached saturation point. The second feature is the absence of spontaneity. We do not ourselves initiate the movement, as a person is stirred to imitate a beautiful dancer or learn medicine to help the sick. The ideal of self-realization is too vague, no more than a pure possibility, and so it is that we may direct our movement once it has started, but we cannot create it ourselves. For the origination we must look elsewhere.

It is to the second great movement expressed in our restlessness that we must attribute the origination of the movement just described. This latter, as we have seen, is concerned with the preservation and development of our ego. Philosophically this means that we have been looking at the self living and evolving towards its own perfection, becoming what it should be. Every being is some sort of a thing which is definable. We may not know how to define it, but we do know that we cannot feed a cat and a cow on the same food, and we should be startled if cats and cows and red herrings began to crave for a common life and common destiny. We think of them, roughly, as having different natures or essences, and the best specimen in each nature is full-sized and healthy and exhibits very definite characteristics. Let us grant that our knowledge is so infinitesimal that we do not know the limits of various species nor their order and connection with one another, and, this being so, we are prepared to find that many of our divisions are provisional and that unities hitherto undiscovered may pervade whole sets of species of genera. A moderate evolutionist theory allows for definiteness of species and perfection of type within these species as well as development from one to another. The difficulties caused by our uncertainty about natures below man disappear when we deal with man himself. Man stands by himself; we know something of his possibilities and can draw a line round his capacities somewhat in the same way as we know that there are limits to a man's power to jump or run a mile, even though the reference books have to keep changing the records.[1] We are justified, therefore, in speaking of the nature of man and postulating a movement in each single man towards his own perfect being.

The word which covers this aspect of a man is 'essence'. Guthrie sharply distinguishes this from 'existence'. The two movements which he describes belong the one to existence, the other to essence, and he maintains that the more fundamental of the two is that of existence. The essential movement is not self-originating because it is directed to a pure possibility, the perfection of itself. But the movement of existence is towards something real, and so it is able to originate its own movement and that of essence as well. But what does Guthrie mean by this mysterious 'existence'? We have a clue already in what Kierkegaard and Heidegger have said about the flimsiness of life, the feeling that a sword of Damocles is always hanging over our head. We are what we are and there is no

---

[1] I am here more or less interpreting Hunter Guthrie's argument and his use of the word, essence. I must add that we should distinguish what a man can do of himself and what he may be enabled to do by the help of God. A human mind is essentially limited, and even after death, when its powers may be greatly increased, it would still be limited, if a man is to remain a man. But we also know that the divine power might make such a gift to man that his passive capacity could become what for want of a better word we must call 'divinized'.

ground for pride or assurance in our being. Though we are bound by our nature to cherish and support our ego, to make it the focus of all we think and will, we are also only too well aware how unnecessary that ego of ours is. It seems hardly to count in this vast universe; it is ignored by countless millions of our fellow men, and they like ourselves hang only by a thread to life, they make very little impact on it, they are ruled by absolutes which they did not themselves invent, they are not themselves what they should be, and they leave the world maimed and thwarted and uncertain whether their part in it has been of any lasting import. Now in saying this of man I am referring to living man, past or present or to come; men who exist. And it is in their existing that they are made conscious of their mingled strength and weakness. The stress here is on existence, and the meaning of existence can be understood still better if we reflect on the fact that our nature or essence can be thought of independently of its existence.

In scientific inquiries the investigator is interested in the perfect specimen; he does not want to be distracted by peculiarities and odd behaviour; he prefers to see a description of an insect or formulation of it on paper to watching its slimy wriggling behaviour. Or take a person with a prophetic mind or the gift of second sight. He might be able to see a human being before he or she had been born. At the moment that human being is not existent, but he is clothed in his full individual nature or essence, just as the idea in the artist's mind is complete in all details before he translates the idea into reality. A being is complete therefore in essence before he exists, and for this reason we have to distinguish between them. Existence gives no new attribute to an essence, and yet a live cat is better than a dead king; existence is all important. Without some being existing there could be no coming to be, no ideas, no possibilities, no essences at all. Again, if a being were necessarily existent, if his essence were such that it existed necessarily, then there would be no fear of decay, no dread of the future, no other kind of essence which would by comparison be worth having. The sin against the Holy Ghost is for a finite essence to think of itself as necessarily alive, for that would be to make itself God. The truth, however, is that human beings are dependent through and through on what is not themselves. The body has to be fed and supported, the senses informed, the mind to learn, and the individual is part of a community. Nowhere, not even in the deepest layer of self and personality can complete independence or self-sufficiency be found. Falling in love with his own essence, like Narcissus with his image, man might almost be unconscious of his lot if he were, so to speak, kept preserved and in a bottle. But as he is, out of the world of pure essences and by himself in a world of impersonal and personal friends and foes, he is made aware of his weakness as well as of his strength, of his relation to others, his needs and longings and his dependence upon an Absolute Will. As an existent being he has to move beyond the bonhomie of the essential self and cry out:

> '*Thee, God, I come from, to Thee go,*
> *All day long I like the fountain flow*
> *From Thy hand out, swayed about*
> *Mote-like in Thy mighty glow.*'

The self, then, senses itself in two ways; it feels lovingly towards its own ego, and it feels its derivativeness, that it bears the name of Another imprinted on it. If a melody could be conscious of its own beauty we might suppose that it could both admire itself and think of itself as being nothing more than the expression of a master musician.

Guthrie describes one of the movements of the soul as limited and without spontaneity; that is the self-regarding love. The other moves towards an ultimate and absolute end. 'This movement . . . is for me the first revelation of the possibility of an *exterior* (world), by the fact that I am not the sole and unique end of the vital activity in me. Furthermore, this restlessness drives me to an end much more vast than that of the completion of myself. It drives me ever onward towards an ultimate, an absolute. I discover in it the revelation of my own insufficiency, the weakness of my own instability, the poverty of my self-perfection. Like the other movement this also has two features. The first is the absence of limits and the second is its spontaneity. These two features are the opposite of those which were said to belong to the movement of essence. In thinking of a nature or essence we are, except in one case, forced to think of it as definite and finite; but this is not so if we think of existence. To exist does not imply any limitation; it is only when we think of some being, say a cat or a laplander, that limitation enters in. It would seem to follow that existence is reduced and limited not of itself by its union with some essence. For this reason Guthrie argues that the restlessness in the love which issues from our existential self is due negatively to the unease at the restriction of our nature. We are in love with more than ourselves and groan at our own small compass. But the restlessness is not only negative, an impatience at our bonds, at our slowness in growth of knowledge, at the indecisiveness of our will; it is due also to our straining at the leash, to the longing to reach to infinite beauty, to share in a life where the ego is taken up into a love greater than itself.

The characteristics, therefore, of the two movements or loves are so different that they must proceed from different grounds within the one self, and these grounds are those of the essential self and the existential self. Because my existence is not my own and yet most intimately mine, I am restless both because of my instability and because of the restrictions imposed on it by the limitations of my own poor nature. As the mystics say, what feels itself as by comparison nothingness, calls to what is the plentitude of being; what is hungry looks for 'green pastures', what is thirsty pants for the fountain of living water. But I am restless, too, for another reason. Life has been called with some reason an élan vital. Certainly men are in constant change, and that change means for them a growth or a decline. They are in a continuous process of becoming. The child is the hope of its parents, and lives in expectancy of greatness, of becoming a superlative athlete or discoverer or scientist or statesman. The years pass and it is seen that the varying ideals are only shadows of the one ideal, to live at the top of one's being and exercise all one's powers at their highest—and the self sees that it has to use every moment of its *existence* to do this. All this is comprised in the general formula of realizing oneself and one's nature. Humani nihil a me alienum puto. H. G. Wells describes this kind of restlessness admirably: (Life) 'is a spreadout of lovely intimations. . . . We jump out of bed, and right away we tumble over our stale selves of the day before. . . . I couldn't believe that life was just the slow procession of dusty events it seemed to be. Dusty greyish events with a lot of rather forced laughter and streaks of downright painful and disagreeable experience. Uncalled-for afflictions, and a perpetual menace. . . . Presently somebody or something, I imagine, was going to draw the curtain. "Prince, your time has come." . . . Stop to think, life hustles us. Flowers and sunsets, art and music, just mock us, as we get pushed and beaten past them. Every sort of loveliness mocks us—and gets snatched away. Love? . . . We're hustled. Mind your head. Mind your step. Get on with you. Consequences! Take the consequences. We were born conditioned. The past sold us.'

How different this is from the cry of Christopher Smart: 'For in my nature I quested for beauty, but God, God hath sent me to sea for pearls'; or, again, the confession in Claudel's Satin Slipper of Don Rodrigo to Dona Prouheze:

'All the same, whence could have come to Caesar and Mark Antony and those great men whose names I have just given you to recall . . . whence cou'd have come to them the sudden power of those eyes, that smile, those lips, as if never before they had kissed a woman's face . . .? Let me make it clear, let me untrammel myself of these tangled threads of thought! . . .

'Is not a being's joy in its perfection? And if our perfection is to be ourselves, just that very person whom fate has given us to fulfil, whence this profound exultation like that of the prisoner who hears in his wall the sap at work to set him free, when the dart of death is buried quivering in our side?

'So to me was the sight of this angel like the dart of death! Ah, it takes time to die, and the longest life is not too much to learn to answer that long-suffering call!

'A wound in my side like the flame that little by little sucks all the oil from the lamp!

'And if the perfection of the eye is not in its own geometry but in the light it sees and in every object it discerns,

'And the perfection of the hand not in its fingers but in the work which it engenders,

'Why nevertheless should the perfection of our being and the kernel of our substance be evermore bound up with opacity and resistance,

'And not with worship and desire and the preference for something other than self and with giving one's dross for gold and one's time for eternity and with giving oneself up to translucency and splitting at last and opening up into a state of ecstatic dissolution?

'Of this self-undoing, of this mystic deliverance we know that of ourselves we are incapable, hence this power over us of women like to that of Grace.'

The differing aims of the two loves are here shown to us without disguise, both of them fair and both of them necessary. Without the essential and self-regarding love that of existence is without backbone. It ends, as Don Rodrigo hinted, in dissolution. The essential love guarantees the permanence of the self and personality; but again if it is left to predominate it develops into egoism and substitutes a false absolute for the true one. The two loves must implement each other, and the essential one must be subordinated to the love which reaches up to the God whose name is, 'I am Who am'. Guthrie firmly indicates this answer when he writes: 'The existential disquiet directs me towards the Infinite. This essential disquiet leads me to an ideal, but this ideal is not anything outside me, that is to say, "outside" my essential Ego. The ideal is the realization of the human essence that I am potentially. Here is a difference between the two egos which deserves to be pointed out. I am, in act, fully, my existential ego. Athwart the disquiet of this ego I tend towards the Absolute, but there is no question of my becoming this Absolute. I have not the power to do so. I seek only for rest, security, permanence in the Absolute. My existence clasped by His Existence. Per Ipsum et cum Ipso et in Ipso. On the other hand, I am my essential ego, not in act but only potentially; or, rather, I am in process of *becoming* my essential ego. I unfold myself and develop myself, not through time and space (although there is an external relation between these material realities and my essential growth), but through the closer union of my essential ego and my existential ego. Their union proceeds step by step with the realization of the essential ego. I become what I was already potentially. I am, so to speak, more and more present to myself exactly in proportion as, on the one hand, I draw near to an ideal, and, on the other hand, penetrate into the Absolute.'

In this last sentence Guthrie indicates how the two loves come together in a full personal life. Our essential disquiet is felt at first in a more or less negative way, as a repugnance to a life of somnolence and bovine stupidity. No-one wants to be a nonentity, and though many complain of their bad memory, few admit to a third-rate intelligence. A man feels that he has to put away the things of a child and think as a man, and thus he comes to the parting of the ways. He can pursue a sybaritic or stoic cult of himself and become a spiritual isolationist, or he can learn from the promptings of the inward counsellor within himself that he who will find his life must lose it, and that it is only by giving himself to some cause much greater than his own private devotion, by surrendering himself to the living Absolute, which is God, that the two sources of disquiet in him may be resolved and give way to a lasting peace.

The next stage in Guthrie's argument is an inquiry into the final cause of man's disquiet. This need not detain us long, for he has already indicated what it is. He has called it an Absolute. The question, however, arises whether this Absolute is one or multiple, and this question Guthrie holds to be of supreme importance. Certainly as bearing on the nature of love it is crucial, and, as Guthrie says, a wrong or incomplete answer can give rise to a whole set of false problems about love and lead to serious error. Most writers, if they allow an Absolute at all, take for granted that it is one and not multiple, that all our varying loves fall into one regiment and move to one end. This assumption contains a truth, but as it stands it is false. There are two Absolutes towards which man tends; the one is the Absolute *par excellence*, the other is what he calls a pseudo-Absolute. This does not mean that it is merely a cloud formation which resembles the reality, or a kind of will-of-the-wisp. It is real enough to compel supporters and disciples, and it serves as a precursor, a John the Baptist to the Messiah. Even this comparison, while useful, is insufficient; the pseudo-Absolute does not totally disappear; its position is like to that of a man who is introduced as the husband of a queen and later found to be the prince-consort. The pseudo-Absolute is not therefore a mirage or phantom; it is the ideal of the essential Ego which must be different from that of the Existential Ego. The latter, the self as existing, is always actual and complete, and at the same time contingent and unstable. It seeks therefore for stability and union with something else than itself, which really exists, and can buttress the Ego's being and give it an immortal strength. Only an Absolute, who is different from itself, can do this, an Absolute who is without flaw or shadow of instability. The former, the essential Ego, on the other hand, is not at the moment itself; it is only in process of becoming all that it wants to be, and, therefore, what it in turn seeks is that its own possibilities should be realized. Such an ideal is clearly not the same as that of the Existential Ego. The one looks within itself for its perfection, the flowering of its nature; the the other looks beyond itself: to some other being, who is Absolute.

The two, then, are so distinct that they must have distinguishable ends or ideals. That love which is founded on the self's reality and goes outside itself to seek for a support which cannot fail, tends to the real and genuine Absolute. The other love, which proceeds from the self's incompleteness and strives to fulfil itself, tends also to an Absolute; but the Absolute in this case is only relative as the childish ideal of being an air-pilot or engine-driver is relative to the child. Human nature is like a sponge which can be soaked. It has its Admirable Crichtons. We assume that there is something final and supreme which can be reached, that to speak of human perfection has meaning, and in this sense the ideal can be called absolute. But from its very description, despite the unwillingness of philosophers and humanists to acknowledge the fact, it can be only subsidiary to the love which seeks the genuine and truly infinite Absolute. When the self is living its full and proper life (that is to say, when we drop the abstractions of the two loves and think of them as inseparably conjoined in every human being's life) the lesser love plays an important part, but in some mysterious fashion finds its fulfilment as a minor partner to the love which seeks not its own.

Guthrie develops still further the meanings he attaches to the existential and the essential movements of 'disquiet'. He proceeds by means of the phenomenological method and elicits by this method a number of characteristics, some of which belong to the existential, others to the essential, side of that self. The unity of the self he attributes to its existence. We are alone with our own existence, which no one can share; it separates us from all our fellows and from all that is manifold; it makes us solitaries and at the same time nostalgic, for we are drawn by our very being towards that creative and living God, Who is our source and our home. This primal characteristic leads Guthrie on to emphasize two more characteristics, which are directly relevant to the theme of love. He says that in living and existing we are profoundly aware that our existence is not ours in the sense that our essence is; it is a gift. (That is why suicide is the supreme act of blasphemy.) In other words, we have to think of the word 'mine' differently, when we use it for our talents or our character and for our existence. Secondly, 'goodness is the alpha and omega of existence'. By this he means that it is the good, the lovable over and beyond us, which is the direct concern of the existential self. The essential self is satisfied with truth, the replica, that is to say, of the Absolute, made in our own likeness. 'The essence, the potential "I", in a certain sense, has no counterpart in the Absolute. There is nothing potential or limited in Him who is Complete, Final, Absolute. Hence it is in existence that we must see what is "inter creatorem et creaturam . . . tanta similitudo" (that great similarity between the Creator and the creature); and in the essence "inter eos major . . . dissimilitudo" (the still greater dissimilarity between them), of which the Council of the Lateran speaks.'

Here we touch upon a cardinal point in this theory of essence and existence. In the majority of philosophical theories the problem of the nature of truth has figured most largely. The mind is concerned with truth and the will with good, and it is assumed that truth has the primacy. There is an obvious reason for this assumption in that we cannot begin to philosophize without thinking, and unless we are sure that our thinking is true, all results will be worthless. Knowledge dominates every investigation, even that of morals and art, and at the end of the investigation we want to know the truth about the matter in hand. In other words, the possibility of truth is a *sine qua non* of every conscious act, and the primary importance of knowledge is proved by the fact that in order even to criticize knowledge we have to presuppose it. It is this simple fact which makes nonsense of extreme forms of pragmatism, or any views of life which try to test knowledge and truth by criteria outside itself. Nevertheless, if Guthrie be right, we can overrate the claims of knowledge, and we shall be bound to do so if we give undue attention to essence to the exclusion of existence; if we spoil essence and spare it the rod. This favouritism has been a mark of philosophers since Descartes—to such an extent, indeed, that it produced rebels at the end of the nineteenth century in the persons of the Pragmatists and Bergson. Their rebellion was justified, but they failed because they went to the opposite extreme and subordinated reason to man's practical aims. To right the balance we have to keep our minds on existence. Already we have seen that it has precedence over essence in that existence is relative to a genuine and existing Absolute, whereas essence is relative to a pseudo-Absolute. But the surprise comes when as a consequence of this Guthrie argues that the good is connected with existence and truth with the essence, and that, therefore, the good takes precedence of the object of the mind, namely, truth.[1] 'The good', as Guthrie writes, 'is the foundation of all reality because it is the *ratio sufficiens* of existence. . . . The True belongs to the essential pole of things. It is a possibility. Though it can be the sufficient reason for existing, it does not contain that reason in itself. The Good, on the other hand, belongs to the existential pole. It is actual. It *is* because it is good; and it is good because it is real.' In other words, we would have no movement at all towards knowing unless we were attracted to the object to be known by its goodness, by some preceding and preconscious desire of it which initiates the process of knowing. We are but repeating and underlining the priority of final causes, that it is 'love which moves the sun and other stars'.

This conclusion is reinforced by what we know of the disquiet in our essence. The rationalist philosophers have taken essence and knowledge of it as the be-all and end-all of their inquiries, and as a result they have ended up in queer street. Human knowledge cannot escape two defects; it abstracts all it touches and it reduces all that exists to the level of its concepts. The consequence is that life turns into logic, for 'all that is real is rational'; and secondly there are no things left over which are not dreamed of in these philosophies. The pit into which all reality is poured is the self. Knowledge started from self and ends up in self, be it self-realization or human wisdom, which goes by the name of truth. We see all reality mirrored in the self, in the ideas we have of the universe. But as a well-known writer remarked: 'A mirror is a mystical thing, but it is not half so wonderful as a window', or what points the same moral: 'It is better for a man to get his head into heaven than heaven into his head.'

If, as the preceding argument demands, intellect be deposed and give place to its rival, the will, a number of other changes will have to be made, as when a Labour Cabinet succeeds a Tory. We have now to conceive of the self as a kind of half-tamed bird which still hears the call of its mates and the open-air. "Une grande espérance a traversé la terre." The very being of the self is stirred to take flight, and it is this initial disquiet which defines the life of man, its growth and its vagaries. Of itself it is pure of all taint of self, being utterly disregarding, and for this very reason if the essential element in the self were absent it would be promiscuous or dissolute. Grafted on to it, however, is another cutting, which saves the self from indefiniteness and limits its craving and capacity. This is the nature which it possesses, the essential self, whose first duty and desire it is to make itself fit, strong, and substantial. Thus the move-

[1] The reader must, of course, remind himself that just as essence and existence go together in the indissoluble unity of the human self, so too truth and goodness work together in proper unity without infringing the rights of each other. Final and formal causes do not clash.

ment outward is met by a movement inward, the love of what is not-self by a love of self, the desire for the good by a desire for the true. The animus may be selfish, but he knows his own mind and he keeps an eye on anima. These terms, animus and anima, when all due qualification has been made, are not inappropriate to essence and existence as understood by Guthrie. At all the levels, organic, sensitive and spiritual, there are present the two contrasting movements; but instinctively we give the supremacy in the levels below human consciousness to the anima. It is only because of the special character of reason that we come to think of mind as superior to all else in the human being. We forget that the soul is more than the mind and that in its most vital expression it is a movement towards its final end. As such it will express itself in will as contrasted with thought, and this will must be as it were the periscope above the waters which belongs to our submerged being. Our mind takes note and reflects on what it has absorbed and reproduces it in terms of its own being; but it has been awakened originally by what we are existentially, by our being radically a naked intent towards God, a living heartbeat and sigh for the reward of infinite Love. This implies that a vital process of natural selection is always going on wherever there is life, and that there is a preconscious movement of the soul towards certain objects before the mind can be moved in turn to take notice of them. Instead of the formula, nihil volitum nisi praecognitum, nothing is desired before it is known, we must set nihil cognitum nisi praevolitum, 'nothing is known except it be desired'. When, for instance, the distinguished Thomist, Sertillanges, says that 'I only know that I exist by this invasion (of some external object) which awakens me to myself in provoking me to live on what has been given to me', Guthrie retorts that the very life of which Sertillanges writes was already at work and in movement towards an Absolute other than myself, and that consequently it was already looking for external reality. I have not to be provoked to live nor do I suffer an invasion which awakens me from sleep. 'Knowledge does not begin in man with a shock, through some surprise or invasion of himself. Knowledge is the normal, necessary, fully developed result of the psychical activities of man, a result for which the subconscious, ontic nature of man has been ardently making preparation. The fundamental misconception of (Sertillanges) lies in his having identified life with intellectual activity. Knowledge is only one of the forms of the conscious manifestation of life. There is still another, a more elevated form of conscious life, in which the intellect plays only a secondary part, and this is the act of love.'

What really happens in the various stages of knowledge proper is that there is first an estimative intuition; secondly, desire; thirdly, knowledge of that external object as external.[1] By the estimative or appraisive intuition is meant the primordial perception of the will, the perception which seizes what is other than the self in a perspective which reaches from the Ego to the Absolute. Being an élan of self from itself to the Absolute it criticizes in its going all that falls between itself and its end. It discerns the value of what it meets and interprets it in function of the Absolute value. The body 'knows' what is good for it in the sense that we are often forewarned by it before we eat. In an analogous way the movement of the existential self gives the intellect an inkling. That the Absolute value is beyond description or understanding does not matter; it can make itself felt in the very movement towards it, even as an artist rubs out and corrects his work without having any clear idea of what the painting will look like when it is finished or of what it should have been like. Certainly the intellect will have to play a part and should be encouraged to take as great a part as it can legitimately do. But it cannot take over from the will nor claim pre-eminence. 'The common action, in which the two poles of the intellect and the will meet and in which their differences are harmonized . . . is found in that spiritual act which is the most complete and the most sublime, namely, the act of love. In this act the will makes haste to aid the intellect and the intellect itself makes an effort to support the will.' In this harmony the self is exalted and rejoices in a new-found unity of its being. The external object which had been preconsciously appraised by the will is seen now in its true worth by the mind, and this in turn makes it more desirable to the will. Thus it comes about in the act of loving that both the will and the intellect are at their best, and this means that the essential movement towards self and the existential movement away from self to the Absolute cease to be in any way antagonistic. The pseudo-Absolute of the ideal self is transfigured in the rays of the true Absolute. It is seen to be relative to it and to acquire its highest expression in that relation.

[1] As there is no occasion in the text to clear up some of the more obscure points in Guthrie's account of the relation of the will to intellect, I quote from a revealing note on p. 128 of his book. Certain hoary phrases, he says, 'have given rise to or confirmed the opinion that the will has no direct intentional relation with the object, that the will must listen to what the intellect wishes to say about the world of objects; it cannot see of itself. A critical examination of the "mechanism" of preconscious knowledge shows that the first contact of the psychic self with the sensible and imagined data presented by the somatic self is made by the energic (existential) pole. This function is always in act, for, let us not forget, this function is a prolongation of the unitive force (existence) which binds and unifies the potential essence. Consequently it alone is capable of reuniting the somatic-psychic duality. Furthermore, being in act, it is the function which actualises, that is to say, starts the psychic movement of knowledge. The intentional activity of the will is, as we have said, different from, but complementary to, that of the intellect. It is different because it "perceives" the existence, the goodness, the value, whereas the intellect "perceives" the quiddity, the essence, the nature. The two are complementary because they are polarised, functions of one synthetic Ego and their perceptions are complementary aspects of one single thing. Whence it comes that an image more like to the will and the intellect would represent them as positive and negative poles of a dynamo, as right and left arms of the psychic Ego.'

In this scheme the place of honour, as can be seen, is reserved for the will and for love. The self has a limited nature or essence and it exists. The motor force of the essence which is in process of becoming is directed to that self-realization; it is a movement inward. The motor-force of the self as existing is away from itself to that Self-Subsisting Being from whom its existence is derived and on whose succour it depends. From the moment it exists the self stretches out with all its antennae for safety and union with the Absolute, and it appraises all the external objects which it meets by the measure of its longing. This primordial movement of the anima expresses itself on the spiritual plane in will and culminates in love. The motor-force of the essential self, on the other hand, thrives by appropriating to itself all that it meets. It, too, as we have seen in previous chapters, is primitive and can be brutal and bestial. But it is and must be secondary, since it issues from something which is not yet itself and ends in an Absolute which is finite and relative. The self is only in process of becoming itself, and though the perfection it is seeking is definite, in so far as it is human and limited, it is also shadowy and uncertain, like the moon which draws its light from something else. On the spiritual plane the intellect does the work of the essential self; it enlarges the self and brings the world to the foot of its throne by appropriating the world intellectually. The world is grasped in ideas of it; the macrocosm is reduced to the microcosm of a finite mind. On both these counts it is inferior to the will. The will is the sense of the real and it makes immediate contact with the transcendent, whereas the intellect knows the real only conceptually and can attain the transcendent only indirectly. As Guthrie says: 'We know God indirectly. We love God directly. Our love of God aspires towards Him and reaches Him directly. Before this mystery the intellect tends to confusion, futility and abnegation. And so it happens that the greater this abnegation and decentralization of the intellect, the more does the real self throw itself into the movement of the will towards the Absolute, and the greater will be the union of the relative with its absolute end. Here is the psychological and metaphysical foundation of all true mysticism. In the presence of God all the disquiet of the seeker and every limit and every defect of the intellect must be consumed in a complete self-denial, the while the will, which is the "sense of the divine" and had even at the beginning passed beyond the limited horizon of the relative, enjoys peaceful communion with the ineffable Absolute.'

The highest act, therefore, of man is love, and love belongs to the will, and is, as has been said, the culmination of the existential movement. There is first the preconscious apprehension or appraising of what is given as good or valuable. By this act the attention of the mind is drawn to the object and it is then translated by the inward-looking movement of the self, that is, the essential movement, into thought-content. The self wants to know the truth about the object, to form an idea of it and so to enrich itself with knowledge. At this point the search for truth ends, and the essential self is satisfied. But the existential self is not satisfied; like the intellect, the will is spiritual and it 'takes on' and uses knowledge as its coefficient. Through the limited knowledge which the self has it perceives the good which first preconsciously attracted it—and it is this fresh perception and conscious desire which constitute love. The difference between this act and the act which ends in knowing is that the latter is satisfied with the object as known, while the former not only envisages the object as known, but as it is in itself. Knowledge takes place within; the object as known is within us and it is we who have gained a prize and grown more perfect. But in love we turn to the object and it is upon it, as it is in its goodness and beauty, that our whole self is directed.

Since Aristotle it has been more usual to assign the highest position in the self to the intellect, and to place man's happiness in the act of contemplation. Guthrie will have none of this, and he criticizes the philosophers for being so exclusively interested in what he calls the essential activity of man. The result has been that philosophy has fallen into disrepute and no-one thinks of the philosopher as the ideal man. It is impossible to draw a true or interesting portrait of man if he is pictured as a thinking being inhabiting a body. He becomes all brain. A man's thinking is not the most interesting side to him. Indeed, if this theory were true, and if all men thought as they should and arrived at the same conclusions, they would all be identical. The distinguishing mark of man has been placed in his essence, and in essence they are all alike. The protagonists of this school have always felt the difficulty of explaining individuality, the separateness of one man from another, of Raphael from Michelangelo, Charles James Fox from Edmund Burke, Bernard Shaw from Hilaire Belloc. They have been forced to explain this individuality by what is lowest in human nature or by the trivial, by men's spacial contours or environment or education. But if this were true, then the whole tendency of education should be to get rid of such individuality, and the more scientists and philosophers thought truly the less individual should they become, until at last they became indistinguishable. Common sense has always rejected such a view and has never thought over highly of the philosopher. To the ordinary man the philosopher has always been faintly ridiculous. Something which gives full humanity and personality is felt to be wanting. On the other hand, those who communicate their experience of the grandeur and misery of living touch something profound in their listeners; there is a chord struck which responds. In a former chapter Scheler depicted St. Francis of Assisi as the most moving and perfect example of human living, just because he combined an intense interest in all objects and persons around him and at the same time was completely self-denying. Instinctively we admire the heroic because it issues from a choice which reveals the man and a self-denying man, and at the same time the personality is flashed forth, like lightning which illumines dark places. Moreover, when we love we do not love a man for being a man; we love something in him which is unique and incommunicable to others. That is why it is so often said, 'I love him for what he is despite all his faults'.

Guthrie takes his stand against the primacy of contemplation on the ground that, no matter what degree it may reach, it is self-centred. 'The object contemplated is a simple function of the potential "I".' This means that the Absolute itself must be a function of what is relative. The opposite should be the case. 'The relative should go to the Absolute, in self-denial and lowliness, with the perfect holocaust of self-renunciation and in a pure élan of existential activity. That is the road which love follows, and it is only love, therefore, which consummates the destiny of man.' Perfect love must consist in an abandonment of self in order that it should go with all its heart to God. Paradoxically, however, this very renunciation of self guarantees its highest possible perfection, because now the individual is free and can hasten without hindrance to its union with its last End. 'It follows, then, that the individual, by this self-surrender, is set on the way to attain his supreme good, which consists in finding itself again in its ecstatic embrace of the Absolute.'

In this summary of Hunter Guthrie's theory, and commentary on it, much has been left out which is important to his argument, but not directly relevant to the problem discussed in these pages. The outline given provides an adequate philosophic setting to what I have called the loves of giving and taking, the twin movement of egocentric and altruistic, centripetal, and centrifugal love, the distinction of the masculine and the feminine, animus and anima, Eros and Agape. These distinctions fit in almost all along the line with the metaphysical distinctions which Guthrie has discovered in his qualified use of the phenomenological method. In the one, concrete and indivisible self he finds ground for making a metaphysical distinction between the self as nature or essence and the self as existing. This is a well-known metaphysical distinction, necessarily obscure to those who are not familiar with philosophical language, but clear to those who use magnifying glasses. You and I are both human; we have a similar human nature, so similar in fact that the remains of either of us, after we are dead, would serve as a specimen of human nature to a scientist—and if he were studying the essentials of man the scientist would be quite indifferent which of our two remains he found. As human beings we have to be treated alike, our bodies are subject to the same pleasures and sufferings, our minds and desires meet, and we each of us have the same pattern of human perfection. All legislation depends upon this common ideal, individual and social, economic and moral. This covers what Guthrie means by the essential self. But though in this description we have exhausted the content of human nature, we have not said everything about you or myself. We have dealt only with a *caput mortuum*, with the image of you as it might have existed in someone's mind. As a statue may exist in a sculptor's mind before he takes his chisel to work on the marble, so we are not nothing before we are born; we can pre-exist whole and complete, so completely, indeed, that there is not a particle of difference between our prenatal features and our actual ones. And yet there is all the difference in the world. At one moment we are not; at the next, we are. To use Scriptural language the breath of life is breathed into man's face and he becomes a living soul. No comparison drawn from essential or natural differences will explain what is meant by this change from non-existing to existing, and that is why it is so difficult to state its meaning and its implications. All other changes involve an addition or subtraction from the subject of change, but here all that happens is that something already complete has been actualized, has come alive. A baton descends and every instrument in the orchestra starts; Orpheus strikes a chord 'and the spotted lynxes for joy of thy song were as sheep in the fold . . . a dappled fawn left the shade of the high-tressed pine, and danced for joy to that lyre of thine' (Alcestis 579). Just as something is communicated which gives each animal more of its own life, so we have to think of a communication which gives that life its original actuality. In one aspect it is nothing more nor less than the essence living its own being, in another aspect it is something which the essence cannot claim as its own. I mean by this that we should think it arbitrary and mystifying to speak of a friend of ours in the room as if his being alive and his being himself were different; on the other hand, we could describe him accurately whether he were living or dead. A fish, let us suppose, cannot live out of water; nevertheless we can examine the difference between a trout and a tench without reference to the water. To be existent and live is all important, but the constitution of a fly or a trout or a man defines the kind of existence it or he has. Each is perishable and in different degrees. A fly is easily destroyed, and even if left to itself is not of a nature to live long. A man has a body which is destined to death within an appreciable number of years, and even his spirit is not of a kind to laugh to scorn the idea of extinction. The proof of this is that so many are inclined to doubt whether the spirit can survive the body. It is obvious in all these cases that the perishability, that is, the limit on existence.

comes from the nature which is in existence. It is quite impossible to conceive of what by its very meaning implies actuality and imperishability fading away and perishing. But as it is quite impossible to think of real nothingness there must always have been something existing and of a kind whose essence is imperishable. This is what the metaphysician means by God, One, namely, whose essence it is to subsist and from whom all finite essences derive an existence contracted to their own limited and perishable being.

This necessarily difficult account of essence and existence has its echo in all human experience, and fortunately we can turn to the literature of that experience which vividly bears out the metaphysical story. It has already been described for us by Kierkegaard, Heidegger and Guthrie in the word, Angst, or Disquiet. Man is made sharply aware of his tenuous hold upon existence. This feeling is intensified in moments of crisis and can rise to the supreme, poignant poetry of a Nashe in time of pestilence:

> *Beauty is but a flower*
> *Which wrinkles will devour;*
> *Brightness falls from the air;*
> *Queens have died young and fair;*
> *Dust hath closed Helen's eye;*
> *I am sick, I must die—*
> *Lord, have mercy on us!*

In this cry it is the anguish at the thought of man's perishable state which is foremost, and the same cry repeats itself too often to be anything else than a manifestation of a permanent and profound human experience. But there is a more positive side to this experience which is equally often expressed in love poetry. We seek to belong, and to belong utterly, to what is imperishable and to live by its love and in its love. It is here that the final secret of love is revealed, and for this reason the language used to express it must be more accurate and careful. With one half of our being we love ourselves as our all in all. Those who concern themselves exclusively with this love tend to place its culminating joy in the experience of beholding and possessing the beloved. With the other half of our being we are aware of not belonging to ourselves. The negative side of this experience is that 'I am sick, I must die, Lord have mercy on us.' But it is also positive. Alone we die, but we are not alone. We belong to another, and our life is rescued from nothingness by the love which gave us our being, sustains us in being. To live by the life and in the life of that other would be heaven. Now this love, if stated in impersonal terms, means a total self-surrender to the Absolute to which we are relative. But these words about the Absolute and all this impersonal language is detestable. To set the matter right we have to introduce the 'I' and 'Thou' relation. I live by the gift of the Supreme Lover and I return the gift, which is myself without holding anything back. But that does not mean that I pass away. Such a thought only befits an impersonal relation. The mystics describe it as a spiritual marriage, in which the soul because of its dependence is called the spouse. The union is one of mutual love. From the very fact that the mystics like to use the analogy of marriage, we have a right to suppose that in the compresence of God and the soul, the soul experiences something in its whole being akin to that which is felt in the most perfect of human unions. I say 'in its whole being'; we err if we confine the highest bliss the self can reach to only one of its powers or activities. So to be present with another that we belong to him not by his power but by his love, so enjoy that love that we feel his being, not only alongside every movement of ours but in them as their mainspring, that is indeed a new life and more than a finite beholding.

Even this, however, is not complete. The love described is that of the existential self. The essential self which is so apt to preoccupy our thoughts in this life and to claim exclusive proprietorship cannot be discarded. It retains always that hold upon our nature which keeps us independent, and it preserves the 'I' in the sublime mutual relation of love. God's love is such that he increases the dignity of the self and makes it fit, as Richard Rolle said, to sit at the table with God and make merry with Him. Even though the primary joy of the finite love of God is to be possessed by God, we are entitled by the gift of personality to possess God ourselves to some degree, and by His grace we are so enlightened as to be able to see God as He is in His essence. If it be true that it is the intellect which represents the essential self and gives the fullest expression to its desires, we may well think that the soul will reach complete satisfaction in seeing God and in making of that vision its supreme joy. There is no reason why this happiness should not be combined with self-surrender, so long as we give priority to this latter. The essential self has to learn the paradox that it gains by giving, and by joining hands with the centripetal and existential movement it will attain to that self-realization which it craves. In loving God there is no loss. The personality is heightened, and without a doubt the joy of this should be experienced and at the same time the object, namely, God, who gives such new life, may be seen and enjoyed. The full love act, therefore, if God so will, takes in both the ideal of the essential self and the existential self. There is the sheer giving and ecstatic happiness in being possessed by everlasting love, and concomitantly with this and fusing with it is the joy of possessing God as He is by means of the beatific vision.

CHAPTER TWELVE

PHILOSOPHICAL BACKGROUND (*cont.*)

Philosophy buries its own undertakers.

Love is the leech of life and nearest our Lord Himself, and also the straight road that leadeth into Heaven.—*Piers Plowman* by WILLIAM LANGLAND.

> *Amor tu sé quel ama*
> *dondo lo cor te ama.*
> *Love it was Thou thyself that didst inspire my*
> *heart to love Thee first.*
>
> —JACOPONE DA TODI.

Such is the solution of the problem of love, and of Eros and Agape, inside the philosophic setting provided by Hunter Guthrie. The great advantage of his system is that the distinctions within love, established in the course of this book, seem to dovetail very neatly into the larger framework of 'essence and existence'. Were I committed to this system of philosophy I should have to show that it is, as a system, sound and solid, and that not only does it throw light on the nature of love, independently ascertained, but that, in turn, the nature of love provides additional evidence to the general truth of the system. This, however, is not my task at the moment. It is sufficient to have found a system which offers so suitable a background and furnishes new material for reflection on the nature of love. The truths about love and the truth of this system do not necessarily hang together. There may be many who, as I hope, agree with the general analysis of love given in these pages; and it is open to them to look with grave suspicion at this 'existential' philosophy. They may feel very antipathetic to the priority which Guthrie gives to will over intellect and be critical of many other points. This is not the place to inquire into the validity of Guthrie's general standpoint. But as some might be inclined to reject the theory of the two loves because of their hostility to Guthrie's general views, it will be well to show that the two are independent of one another. This can easily be done by sketching another line of thought which may not seem so contentious.

Throughout these pages it has been assumed that the intellect is essentially self-centred. Its function is to increase the spiritual life of the self. It has an analogy with the bodily appetite. We feed on what is good for our body; the food is eaten and transformed into flesh and blood. Using a just analogy we can say that the mind feeds on the world around it. No physical change takes place in that world, but nevertheless its content is absorbed and transformed into ideas. Truth, according to a famous definition, is said to be the correspondence of thought with thing; the implication being that we know truly when what is within the mind represents or, in a certain sense, is identical with the object outside the mind. Each person's mind is a small cosmos reflecting the existing cosmos, and the ideal of human knowledge is to possess all truth about the universe and God in this manner. The kernel of Aristotle's theory of knowledge is that the mind is 'in a sense all things', and it is worth noting that those philosophies, which start and end with human knowledge as their criterion, generally finish up in some form of idealism or egoism.

Nevertheless such a view of the mind may seem to many unconvincing. When I look at something and think about it I am trying to understand the thing and not myself. My interest is in the object and not in myself. Self-consciousness is a distraction, and the best thinking, like the best art, is done when the self is forgotten. Moreover, in all accounts of the process of knowing an element of passivity has to be included; the mind has to be impressed and informed. Now it is true that the mind has to some degree to be passive. But all that that means is that the human mind cannot create. It has to learn, and owing to the infirmity of the human mind in this life, often laboriously and painfully. If we wish to be learned we must be industrious and be patient; if we want to assimilate the wealth of the whole universe we must clear our mind of all that can distract us from the matter in hand and study it. But the very formulation of the difficulty shows the answer to it. Our patience and passivity, our engrossment in the object is the means to an end; a necessary means, no doubt, but no more than a means. The end we have is quite clear; we wish to make our own what we are studying, to master it and acquire knowledge. The mechanism we have to employ may look altruistic, but it is our own interests we have been consulting all the while.

But this answer does not entirely solve the difficulty. It may well be said that the great scientist or the great philosopher has an interest in truth for its own sake and that many a man loves what he studies. It is not at all easy to analyse what is meant in saying that a thinker may love truth for its own sake. One meaning, I think, is as follows. In solving a problem or in making a new discovery in science or mathematics or philosophy there is a peculiar pleasure, which has been likened to that of the artist's. Pieces of evidence are before one, hypotheses which do not fit, and suddenly a new light comes, and one discovers at least an apparent unity. The joy in making the discovery can be very great. Probably part of the pleasure comes from reaching an end to one's efforts and anxiety. There may, too, be some self-satisfaction in that I have made the discovery. But the principal pleasure is, I think, of a kind which is illustrated in a less serious way in the jigsaw puzzle game. When different bits of knowledge, hitherto scattered, come together in a new unity, the mind is satisfied. It is the function of thought to unite and systematize; it cannot abide chaos. It is always restless if it sees a mess. Just as beauty implies organized masses and colours, so, too, the world must have meaning. In the jigsaw puzzle every bit must fit in somewhere; in the universe one thing must be related somehow to another, and we feel sure that we are well on the track of truth when fewer and fewer bits are left over. What is meant, then, in saying that we love truth for its own sake is this: we are prepared to sacrifice all our immediate prejudices and all the short cuts in order to discover what really is the objective nature of things; our pleasure is in the discovery of the unities and systems within nature, and, if possible, the ultimate nature itself, and we refuse to prostitute this kind of knowledge to any other end.

Does, then, the love of truth for its own sake take us out of the orbit of self? Yes, if we mean by self a form of selfishness which seeks immediate satisfaction or pleasures at the expense of knowledge and truth. But we can dismiss such a self, as it is a false one, and unworthy of consideration. A man dishonours himself and acts against his own best interests when he sits lightly to truth. To have a fair answer to the question we must take human nature as it is essentially and at its best. Is the love of truth more ultimate than the quest for self-perfection, for the full realization of what we should be? Is it altruistic? The answer to this will depend in part on our attitude to the world of reality outside us. If we regard it as a vague, mysterious unknown which we are impelled to understand and master, I do not see how we can avoid saying that ultimately our own interests come first. 'Knowledge is such an excellent thing'; 'Truth and liberty of thought are the two sole incontestable glories of human life'. These and similar encomiums of knowledge drive us back on ourselves. But if, on the other hand, we regard the universe as the expression in shadowy form of the wisdom of an infinite God, then our search for truth is an act of homage to God, the living Truth, and we are prepared to submit ourselves to what belongs ultimately to a higher order than ourselves.

But it is now the turn of Guthrie and those who think like him to raise difficulties. This expression 'love of truth' is often on the lips of thinkers, but they seldom try to tell us what they mean. (The point at issue is not, of course, about telling the truth. That is a moral consideration. To tell the truth is a virtue and to lie is morally wrong.) Guthrie writes rather scornfully that certain writers would have us believe that in their judgements they are interested in truth and truth alone. But despite all their protestations and rhetoric they are worshipping an abstraction. 'Truth has never been and can never be a final end. Moreover, the man who believes that he is philosophising for love of the truth, the savant who is persuaded that he is labouring solely for love of scientific knowledge, for truth, for reality, for the final triumph of man over ignorance, is playing with words. A man is a philosopher because he loves to be a philosopher. He is a savant because he loves science. He thinks it a good thing, worthy of his devotion, he regards it as a sacred vocation, he flatters his *amour propre*, or—and here is a subtle variety of *amour propre*—it provides him with a means of assisting his fellows. All the activities of life, the vocations, the occupations, the pursuits, the hobbies of man are undertaken in view of an end—whatever it may be—the pursuit of the final end, the improvement of oneself, self-satisfaction, self-denial, amusement or sensible enjoyment.' That is to say, every action of man, intellectual, moral or physical is motivated by the good. 'Truth as such is sterile; it does not attract; it is incapable of stirring devotion, and certainly incapable of producing martyrs.' Aristotle at the beginning of his *Metaphysics*, lays it down that 'every man *desires* to know'. This is true. 'Renouvier, on his deathbed, avowed to his disciple, M. Prat: "J'ai cherché sincèrement d'une façon désintéressée, la vérité". But neither Renouvier, nor anybody else, has ever searched for truth, in the sense that it has been the sole and final motive for his researches. Along with truth there has always been another motive force. This motive force, in its purest aspect, is the nature of man, developing towards his ultimate end, which is the attainment of the Absolute good.'

Such a view is uncompromising. Nevertheless it is not quite clear whether Guthrie denies the possibility of having truth as an object of love or whether he places it with other tributary ends like self-improvement and amusement which, as he seems to admit, can be loved. Let us look at the subject, therefore, from a slightly different angle. If we spell Truth with a capital T and claim that we think and work for its sake, it ought to be indifferent to us what subject matter we take up to study. We shall always be looking unconditionally for truth. But if we try in this way to consider truth independently of the subject matter, does not truth become very unimportant? It is like the grin of the cat without the cat, the smart performance of a drill for the drill's sake and without any further purpose in view, or spelling correctly in a dead language. In fact, the right word is 'correct'. Truth means little more than 'not making a mistake'. Can we be said to love this very negative aim? The use of the word 'love' which keeps creeping in to all descriptions of the use of our mind shows that we cannot separate the object studied from the truth about it (unless we mean the exhilarating sense of thinking well—an aesthetic pleasure like to that of romping and dancing). But once we introduce the object we let in the 'good'; our interest is really in the objects, and what we want to know is what they are like and how to make the closest possible contact with what they are in themselves. To say we love truth is, then, only an abbreviated expression for a desire to know the truth about objects outside ourselves. We love them and not truth primarily.

Yet such a statement runs counter to the diagnosis we have already given of knowledge as having its end in *our* possessing and making our own the universe around us. This is an apparent contradiction, but so far from being a real one, it illustrates once more the presence and working of the two loves. The first point to notice is that love comes in even through the portals of knowledge. We desire to know, to have truth, to understand the object or person we are thinking about. For the moment let us leave aside which has priority; let us leave, too, the kindred question whether Guthrie is right in assuming a preconscious act of the will before knowledge can start. What must be accepted without qualification is that desire and love must in no way interfere with the integrity of the mind and the pure passion for truth. But we are warranted in saying that even in knowledge this desire or love can and should show itself in two ways. So far, knowing has been treated as a mode of self-love, as the supreme manifestation of the masculine and dominating 'instinct', the animus as compared with the anima. But as the reader has been warned again and again, the two loves, while distinct, belong to an indivisible self, and therefore the two modes of loving are present in every act of the self, though one of them may be so faint as to escape attention. For the sake of economy it has been necessary to treat each of the movements apart and to hold up a notable example of one as if it were quite independent of the other. All of us do the same when talking of the reason and the will or of manly and feminine traits in human beings. Even the most feminine of human persons has some manly trait, but it would be waste of time to keep referring to it. So, too, the love of truth covers both operations of human love.

When we desire to know the nature of some particular object we are drawn out of ourselves by our interest in that object and at the same time want to have the truth about it and to be better informed. This twofold end can be detected in most of our acts. Are we moved, for instance, when eating food by our interest in the delicious dish the chef has put before us or by the desire to satiate our appetite and feed our body? The answer is that both motives operate. And if this is true even with regard to food, much more is it so in our attitude to objects which have a higher degree of beauty and goodness. The distinction between the liberal and servile arts is, if Eric Gill is to be believed, radically false, but it is based on the belief in a rising scale of values in what we observe and use. The husbandman must love and serve the land and not exploit it, the craftsman must know his material and reverence it, if they are to be true to themselves and their work. In the Book of Ecclesiasticus it is all set down. The whole talk of the holder of the plough is to be about 'the offspring of bulls'; the craftsman 'shall give his mind to the resemblance of the picture'; the smith sits by the anvil and 'considereth the iron work'; the potter turns the wheel and is carefully set to his work; 'their prayer shall be in the work of their craft, and searching in the law of the most High'. What is true of the craftsman holds with still greater force of the artist, the scholar and the professional man. The cultured man has a genuine love for the things of the spirit; he does not make a business of them and so seek to profit by them. Similarly a genuine friend does seem to love one for oneself. And thus the paradox of the Gospels is proved right, that one saves one's life by losing it.

The reason for this is that the self is governed by this interplay of self-regarding and self-sacrificing loves. There are exceptions, and they but prove the rule. To love the vile is to become vile, to make a god of duty without love is to sterilize one's being. It may happen also that one of the two loves gets out of control, and we have already seen how easy it is for this to happen. Animus knows what is to its own good, while anima is spendrift of self. The *ménage*, which should be a relatively happy one, may be broken up, and then the excess of the one has a bad effect upon the other, and the whole self suffers. Animus comes to believe that enlightened self-interest is the goal of life; it becomes a snob and a tyrant. Anima becomes bored with the, at best, sweet reasonableness of animus, and shows herself wilful and unbalanced. We find her asserting violently that some cause, social, national, international or religious, must be worshipped at any price and that nothing else is worth while. But in their proper interplay one of the two loves exhibits itself as a form of self-development, as a movement of growth. Just as a boy grows bodily by healthy feeding and exercise, so the character and personality develop by the attainment of the self's desires. The youthful personality develops into a full personality by feeding, as Plato said, on what is best. Such a love tends to perfect the self; it is the love of essence. The other love presupposes a self already actually and fully existent; it is also directed to what is actual and existent, and it consists in acts of self-renunciation in favour of the thing or in the mutual giving of themselves in the case of two persons.

To return now to knowledge. It is galvanized and interpenetrated through and through with love, and we can detect in it the expression of the two forms of love. In so far as its end is to acquire knowledge, to make the agent wiser and be 'all things in some sense', it is moved by the essential, self-regarding love. In so far as it respects and reverences the object, desires to get acquainted with it, and seeks to make known and to do honour to the value of the object as it is in itself, the love belongs to the sacrificial and existential self. Both these loves are requisite for a proper act of knowing. It is often said that the mind has for its proper object the essence or quiddity, what is universal, in contrast with the senses which are affected by the particular, '*this* green', '*this* sound', '*this* man', and there is truth in this statement. Our ideas are universal. When we have a concept of man, that concept is applicable to every being we meet who has the characteristics, the nature which conforms to our concept. It is a universal, and as a universal it does not exist in the world outside us, however true may be its application to objects in that world. It is ours; it is our true way of thinking of reality; our nature has determined the way we shall look at things and possess them. Knowing, from this aspect of it, by-passes the existence of things as they are in themselves and gives them a new existence in terms of my mind. The movement terminates in the self. But there is another aspect. We want to know what things are like in themselves, and at least to be sure that we are in touch with them. How do we know that we are not living in a world of our own? This is a problem which has vexed many a philosopher. If the object of his mind are his thoughts, how can he be sure that he is thinking about objects as they exist outside—if indeed there be any objects outside? This question presses on us all, for there can be no doubt that we want to be in touch with what is not ourselves, with a real and loved world; and it is the presence of this want which suggests, perhaps, the answer. There are some who think that the mind enters reality by means of the senses. The senses are in contact with the external world and supply the material for the mind to work on. The senses and the intellect thus work together, the senses insuring the individual and the real nature, the intellect extracting the essential. This may be so, and excellent philosophers follow this line, but it must be confessed that the senses do not keep a very good look-out.[1] They are easily deceived, and few modern philo-

---

[1] Étienne Gilson, in his *Réalisme Thomiste et Critique de la Connaissance*, severely takes to task those Scholastic thinkers who assume either that realism can be justified by sensation (the common-sense view) or by a critique of the concept or judgement. 'We are faced with a dilemma, the terms of which have been clearly defined by St. Thomas: Est enim sensus particularium, intellectus vero universalium. It does not help that existence should be singular: for as it is not a sensible quality, the senses cannot perceive it. It does not help that it should be intelligible.' His argument is that the senses cannot give us anything more than sensible qualities, and that the intellect cannot give us more than quiddities or universals. How then do we get into contact with the existent world around us? He thinks that most of the modern

sophers are confident about how much they tell us about the nature and reality of external objects.

Let us begin, therefore, from another quarter. I have said that the object of the intellect is the essence, the universal. What exists is always singular, and it is the singular and existent, which, in terms of something good for us or good in itself, excites and interests us. Truth is of the universal and it lies within; the good is particular and real, and it lies without. As this may sound cryptic I must try to explain it. When Samuel Johnson wished to disprove Berkeley's idealism he stamped on the ground. His argument may not have been a good one, but his intention was obvious. When St. Thomas the Apostle had doubted the reality of Christ's bodily appearance, Christ said to him: 'Bring hither thy hand and put it in my side.' This would prove that the body was real, that it was not an apparition, that there was no illusion. The point is that only something real 'does things' to us, and what we want is always ultimately something real. If we are awakened and if our interest is stirred, the cause must be, at least, partly real, that is to say, something existing. We are not satisfied with apparitions or ideas; if we want to eat bread and butter, we shall not be satisfied with the idea of butter or imaginary butter. If we are thirsty we shall be disappointed if the oasis turns out to be a mirage. Always when we take action it is because something not ourselves has knocked at our doors and excited our interest. The external contact is not sufficient; it must advertise itself as interesting. Then, and only then, does the self spring to attention and take action. What this comes to, in philosophical terms, is that we can only be moved by what appears interesting and valuable, i.e. good, and this good is something existing.

Knowledge proceeds upon this initial stirring of interest. That this is so can be shown to follow from metaphysical principles, and it answers to experience. I will take only the latter. Where we have only a minimum of interest we fail to take notice, and in pathological cases when the poor ego ceases to take interest in anything except its own self external realities turn into phantasmagoria; the ego dwells in a subjective world of dreams and illusions. It has lost its sense of a real and existent world outside itself. In normal lives there is a close correspondence between interest and understanding. How this works I will show a little later. For the moment the important point to make clear is that the initiative comes from the good which interests the self and starts the dynamism of the act of knowledge. We need not bother to ascertain whether the interest is evoked

Scholastic philosophers have started off in the wrong direction in treating this question owing to the influence of Descartes and Kant. His own solution is different from that suggested in the text, and it is too long to summarize. I quote the book because it bears witness to the fact that the answer to the problem is not so simple as it looks.

through the lower levels of the self first and then transferred to the higher level of the intellect and the will, or whether there is a kind of pre conscious act of will, a stretching out, which, because of the unity of the self, brings in the activity of the reason. The internal vibration once started the reason follows its own movement to turn the experience to the advantage of the mind and self. It seems to monopolize the energies of the self, and picks up and carries back the nature or essence to the nest of the mind. But, in fact, the self never loses contact with the external objects in which its real interest lies; it keeps desiring that object, and hence in the final act of judgement the self stamps the knowledge as true by reference to the existing, external object. When I say, for instance, that 'marriage is a contract', I do not intend merely to make a neat combination of ideas of my own, nor even to express my own individual views; I am making a statement about reality, as I believe and hope. (This is what logicians mean when they say that there is a supposition of existence in such propositions.) I am not satisfied with the egocentric movement of the intellect. I benefit by that, but I use the intellect as the best way I have of getting into contact with the real object, seeing it for what it is and entering into union with it. If this be so, then interest in the thing which exists outside me has been a motive throughout the whole act of knowing. Both will and intellect have co-operated and both the self-regarding and the self-sacrificing, the essential and the existential loves, have been active.

The ground is now prepared for an alternative setting to these two loves, an alternative, which though in many respects resembling that of Guthrie, is constructed on Thomist principles. In his *L'Intellectualisme de St. Thomas* Rousselot presented a fresh interpretation of the Thomist theory of knowledge. His premature death in battle in the war of 1914–18 deprived us of a complementary work on metaphysics. He published, however, three articles in which his views on love and knowledge can be seen taking shape.[1] He begins by showing that in experience there is a close correlation between knowing and loving. Intense love makes us blind, and at the same time intense love makes us see. A fond mother is blind to the defects in her children, and yet she is the first to notice if they are not well. Now a lover is not conscious that he is being swayed by passion; it is not as if love were outside the thought giving it directions. As modern psychologists have brought out so well, desire regulates our

---

[1] These three articles, 'Amour Spirituel et Synthèse Aperceptive', which appeared in the *Revue de Philosophie*, March 1910; 'L'Être et L'Esprit', *Revue de Philosophie*, June 1910; and 'Metaphysique Thomiste et Critique de la Connaissance', *Revue Néo-Scholastique*, November 1910, have been translated by my friend, Mr. Ralph Harper, with an excellent introduction by himself, and are, I believe, to be published. I have made use of his translations. The thought in these articles is not complete.

knowledge from within and determines not only the exercise of judging but the sort of judgement we make. No two men agree on everything; each has his own point of view, and the majority of men feel strongly on some subject or other. The more strongly they feel the more do they see to confirm their opinion. One man can see only the objections to planning; another only its advantages. We read a short account of the views of a stranger or we are told about them. We say to ourselves, how can anyone be so silly as to hold that nonsense? Then perchance we meet the stranger, and we are astonished to hear what a good case he can make for this apparent nonsense, how almost convincing he can be. 'The blinder one is, the better one sees.'

The explanation of this paradox lies in our power of abstraction. 'Just as acid draws from salt its base exclusively, "abstracts", so to speak, from salt its base, so the eye, we can say, sees the colour in things, because, as the Scholastics used to say quite rightly, it is "moved" by colour. And, again, a beast of prey knows its victim by a natural, irresistible, instinctive "sympathy"—in as much as it is good for him, the right sort, and tasty; he abstracts the aspect which interests him.' Men, as well as animals, select and fasten on what they like. 'The optimist sees everything in rose: his formal object, in as much as it is such, is the cheerful aspect of objects. The pessimist sees everything in black: like Shakespeare's Jaques, who "sucked melancholy out of a song" with the instinct of an animal, he sucks the melancholy out of things naturally and irresistibly: he extracts from it the dismal aspect, which rules it, which masters it, which imposes itself upon him.' This is a common feature of everyday life. The business man looks at a field in terms of money, the farmer in terms of its fertility, and the poet in terms of its visual form and colour. The hypochondriac sees all in the light of his health, the selfish man in terms of his comfort and advantage. Where your heart is, there is your treasure. 'But the sensual man perceiveth not these things that are of the Spirit of God: for it is foolishness to him . . . but the spiritual man judgeth all things.'

Now, as Rousselot says, it is most perilous to let the mind be swayed by personal inclinations. 'Keep the inner spirit pure', Stoicism used rightly to say. Truth is bound to suffer if we let knowledge slip into the hands of prejudice; it can be so easily twisted to serve the end desired. But such perils arise because we stop half-way and desert our first love which began when we were first impelled to know the truth about the world around us and about ourselves. Here was a pure love which identi-fied itself with truth, and, as Rousselot says, if once we admit the presence of this love in knowledge itself, in the 'domineering, lordly, uncompro-mising character' of its claims, we shall be able to understand far better both our own selves and the end towards which we move. Indeed, if we accept the truth that knowing is 'an entirely natural appetite', we shall be forced to infer the legitimacy of its speculative pretensions, and even the reality of the good which attracts it, commands it, and can alone satiate it: pure truth exists. Even as the hound abstracts from all else and follows after the fox or deer, scenting it and ignoring all else, as the eye singles out colour and the carrier pigeon moves unerringly home, so the mind moves out to attain what it alone can possess, a final Truth which exists. 'Just as a man possessed by a love which blinds him, is thoroughly dominated by it to the depths of his faculties of knowing, and sees according to this love with an evidence the stronger the more he is bewitched; just as a faculty of sensible apprehension is entirely, irrevocably, enslaved by the charm of its formal object, however narrow and relative this be; so the human intelligence is attracted by being and by truth as the only object which charms it, only because its very nature is to be an inclination towards infinite being in so far as it is the Good of intelligent beings, that is, in so far as it is the supreme truth.' And whereas a debased love debases the evidence, here the natural and pure inclination presses towards pure and genuine intellectual evidence.

If the supreme good desired by the self in knowing is perfect truth, we may expect Rousselot to argue that both God and the self are the objects of our love. This would follow from what we have learnt from Guthrie and from the arguments at the beginning of this chapter. The Good lies on the side of existent being, and it is outside us and beyond us; it is that to which we in our unstable existence fly, away from ourselves. The truth, on the other hand, lies on the side of essence, within us; it is in the beholding and possessing of the good. And this is what Rousselot proceeds to say and develop. For him, however, in accordance with Thomistic principles, all is consummated in the highest activity of the intellect. He begins with the formula, 'Intelligence is the sense of the real because it is the sense of the divine'. To prevent misunderstanding Rousselot insists, first, that this does not mean that God must be an object known prior to our knowledge of sensible objects; nor need there be any conscious desire of God. There is abundant proof now that the complete and final end of a desire or impulse may not emerge for a long while. The law or dynamism governing our desires is more often than not latent. Secondly, there is no tampering with the sovereign power of the mind, as mind, to know truth. This power is unassailable. In the very act of knowing we are aware of its competence and its truth, and it is because of this that even those who are foolish enough to impugn its power presuppose its validity in their act of criticism. But it is one thing to be aware of its function and competence and another to see its drift, or— shall we say?—its place and importance in the vast amphitheatre of reality;

and again, why we finite human beings, with body and spirit, with various fears and loves, must be so attached to it. The fact that so many wish to know more about the purpose of knowledge and feel that they have a new understanding of it when it is integrated with the famous saying of St. Augustine, 'that Thou has made us for Thyself', is clear evidence of the value of re-examining it in the light of love, and especially the love of God.[1]

Having begun with the formula that intelligence is the sense of the real because it is the sense of the divine, Rousselot qualifies this. It expresses one of the two loves, the existential one, that of the anima; but the self is also self-regarding. Hence, as he says, we have to insert between the two parts of the formula, 'the sense of the self'. This admission of the presence and activity of two loves is worth noting, as it confirms the

---

[1] In an interesting article in the *Recherches de Science Religieuse*, 1929, entitled 'Sur l'Analogie des Noms Divins', Ch. de Moré-Pontgibaud argues that the difficulty implicit in all arguments from analogy between God and creatures, between divine perfections and finite perfections, can be overcome if we hold fast to this relation between love and intelligence. The difficulty is that the analogy between the infinite God and finite creatures is unlike any other analogy in that one of the terms, God, is unknown and infinitely surpasses any finite attempt to express Him, and no matter what stratagem we use we remain in the finite. Out of bad eggs we can never get the taste of a fresh egg. But if the imperfect is a falling short of the perfect and there are degrees of imperfection and an orientation discernible in those degrees, then, no matter what the distance which separates, we can have some real inkling of the nature of the perfect. We can, though obviously the comparison fails, form a true idea of the personality of a headmaster if, though we have no acquaintance with him, we observe a definite kind of improvement in behaviour and ideas in the schoolboys who come from his school. A clever listener might from the first fumblings of a Beethoven, have formed a correct if faint idea of the form his later and great works would take. If infinite love set us on our journey and be the end of our journey, everything on the way will point to Him. In this way, though our knowledge still be finite, we shall not be limited by it, for we shall have an 'intelligence poursuivant sans cesse son bien final et saturant à travers et par le moyen des vérités particulières, ne saisissant celles-ci que *parce que*, et donc *selon que* inclinées vers Celui-là.'

De Moré-Pontgibaud is also careful to safeguard the absolute character of knowing in itself. He says: 'En parlant *d'inclination* et de *désir*, ce que nous nous proposons, ce n'est pas tant d'expliquer notre intelligence *en tant qu'intelligence*, que de manifester, entre toutes les conditions qui président à l'actuation de *cette* intelligence (et proportionellement, de toute intelligence finie), la plus profonde et la plus intime. Si, en effet, cette intelligence est foncière-ment dynamique, c'est-à-dire astreinte à passer successivement, selon toutes ses démarches, de la puissance à l'acte, il est nécessaire que cette actuation se fasse sous l'influence d'un appétit (au sens large), qui soit l'âme de ce dynamisme, et qui, antérieurement à la connaissance même, en règle le jeu. Et si ce qu'il faut avant tout résoudre, pour expliquer le pouvoir et l'ampleur virtuelle de l'intelligence finie, c'est l'apparente antinomie entre la nécessaire immanence de l'objet, participant, en tant qu'assimilé, à la condition de sujet, et son *extraposition* comme objet, saisi dans la connaissance même comme un *absolu relatif* et indépendant du sujet, il est naturel que l'on aille chercher la solution dans l'inclination radicale de la puissance intelligente vers un terme qui soit intérieur à cette puissance, en tant que son premier principe et qui, en tant qu'objet, *précontienne* déja en lui-même tout ce à quoi cette puissance est inclinée. Mais d'abord, nous ne prétendons pas par-là (c'est trop clair) *suppléer* l'évidence que l'intelligence a de la vérité de ses jugements, mais seulement expliquer, en quelque manière, comment cette évidence est possible. Et, de plus nous ne nous proposons pas tant par-là d'expliquer et de définir formellement la vue (i.e. la substance intelligente, en tant qu'elle est *elle-même à elle-même selon certains objets*), que d'expliquer comment la substance intelligente peut être *mise dans la situation de voir*. Et alors nous disons qu'elle ne peut être ainsi *elle-même à elle-même selon toute la virtuelle ampleur de son pouvoir*, qui si *d'abord* et premièrement elle est à *Dieu*'.

main argument of this book. And that it is not a chance agreement is proved by a passage in the essay on Thomist Metaphysics, where he says: 'One can, besides, regain, in the throbbing duality which characterizes the first apprehension (of the mind), the distinct trace of the two loves which draw the soul along; in so far as it translates the sensible given into a something, into essence, the soul desires itself, it wishes to realize itself as humanity; in so far as it affirms that being exists, it wishes to realize itself as being, it desires God. But these two loves are not external to one another; the love of God, as St. Thomas explains it, is internal to the love of self, it is its soul. Furthermore, it is the first source of our intellectual light; if the soul is sympathetic to being as such, it is finally because it is capable of God.' The two, he says, have the same root; a finite spirit can only find itself in the measure in which it finds God, and it is by finding itself, its true life, that it is enabled to know God. To know oneself as one is would be to discover that one is *ex Deo* and *ad Deum*; we should see ourselves as simply dependent upon God and suspended from Him; we should be aware that we were a kind of vibrating echo on an inferior instrument of the divine chord. But since we are deaf to our own being we are deaf also to God. It is our own darkness, the black-out within our own being which prevents us from knowing God. 'It is as if the love of God were solidified in our *unconscious* nature. That is what gives to our intellectual certitudes their character of impersonal coldness and of "an evidence imposed". It is our blindness which makes us see.' But 'if our spiritual nature were an object of our intuition, if, instead of searching ourselves, we possessed ourselves, then . . . we should know everything sympathetically. We should be aware of the love which guides us, we would see, so to speak, the law which defines knowledge come out of ourselves, we should feel the kinship of our object with us'.

Rousselot, therefore, lays great stress on the acquisition of self and its function in opening out to us the love of God and our dependence on it. It is because we are absent from ourselves and feel this absence that we tend to treat the love of self independently from the love of God, and to overestimate it. It becomes our primary concern, and even contrasted with the love of God, as though the one could be opposed to the other. Owing to our estrangement from ourselves our knowledge both of ourselves and of the world around us becomes strange and unfamiliar. We deal in abstractions; we have to think of *a* thing, *a* man, because we ourselves are only in process of becoming ourselves. In more philosophic language: 'To say that the human soul is a form in a subject, is to say that man is an hypostasis who does not equal his essence, a person who does not possess his nature intelligibly; and, if he is made thus, to actuate himself, to realize himself, and pass from potency to act, will be for him to tend to this conquest, to this adequation. So it is, therefore, on the one hand, that the sense of the operation characteristic of humanity, which is its intellection, ought to be taken from the innate desire which the human subject has of equalizing itself, of winning its own nature; on the other hand, that the specific note of this intellection, is the distension which we have said exists between the nature conceived and the subject (exterior) connoted. At the moment when the interior distension of man ceases, the representative distension, the distension of his concept, will also cease. Man would *envisage* his essence, his substantial self; man would live his soul, his whole soul, and at the same time, he would know exterior being by sympathetic intuition. All material *apathy* would vanish in spiritual *sympathy*; not having in itself a remainder to reduce, the soul too would no longer find an obstacle in penetrating objects. In short, the deep root of the conceptual distension, of the abstraction proper to the category of thing, is the incompleteness of our spirituality; if man cannot bring his object to light, it is because he is not himself enlightened.'

Rousselot here applies the laws of love found true in ordinary experience to the very nature of our human knowing. Experience proves that love blinds and love makes us see. What we love we become; the lover of self becomes selfish and other human beings lose their individuality and turn into 'things' which can be of use to him. A St. Paul, on the other hand, because he loves other persons, identifies himself with them; his heart beats in unison with them, so that he can cry out, that if one of them is hurt, he is hurt, if one of them is scandalized, he is scandalized. He has what Rousselot calls a feeling of connaturality, and Scheler an affective fusion, with them.[1] This law of love Rousselot daringly uses as an interpretative principle of the very nature of our knowing. He uses examples from experience, which at first sight may seem poetic or metaphorical, and then inserts them into the metaphysical framework of Thomism. His view, in short, comes to this that at the high point of self-realization, when self-love has reached its climax, the coldness and impersonality of our subject-object relation will vanish; we shall sense and savour our own being, I being always I to myself and not an object with shadow around it; and then I shall feel my being and essence vibrate in unison and sympathy with all other beings; and because my existence is derived, vibrate also to the voice of Him who called me into being and now sustains me in being.

[1] An excellent example of the same sentiment of connaturality is to be found in the *Autobiography of Miss Dorothy Day*, the apostle of outcasts: 'Solitude and hunger and weariness of spirit—these sharpened my perceptions so that I suffered not only my own sorrow but the sorrow of those about me. I was no longer myself. I was man. I was no longer a young girl. . . . I was the oppressed. I was that drug addict, screaming and tossing in her cell, beating her head against the wall. I was that shoplifter who for rebellion was sentenced to solitary. I was that woman who had killed her children, murdered her lover.'

The image which he draws from experience is this. 'When a vague anxiety weighs upon the spirit—when the half-conscious apprehension of a painful hour restrains the freedom of the soul—when we know that we have something important to do, and that we have forgotten what it is, we cannot apply ourselves wholly to the occupation of the moment. We feel something between ourselves and the objects. We cannot give ourselves to them. The soul is elsewhere, it is as separated from itself, it is distracted (Dis-tracta). It is not the object which is more obscure, it is the soul which is less supple and less vigorous.' This absence of the self from itself and the consequent haze over the object gives us an idea of the reason why the human mind in the process only of discovering itself sees the world around it in terms of the abstract idea. So, too, when a man begins to love, but is not aware of the passion which has come upon him, he feels that the world he has known formerly has changed. 'A certain alien quality has spread over all objects; why has the world changed? Why is the world new? But what is new is himself; he has acquired a new category and because of this he penetrates his object imperfectly. When he will have become aware of his attitude, that is, of his love, the *sense* of things will appear to him.' In this comparison the darkness of things corresponds with the inclination as unconscious and imperfect. The more perfect the love, the more is the object comprehended and *possessed*. Still another comparison is needed to explain the effect of love upon our present form of knowing objects. Rousselot takes the example of an aesthete who is passionately fond of his country, France. Gradually he has acquired a most delicate perception of the peculiar virtue and quality of the French spirit. 'He gets to the bottom of a song, a speech, a story, in which the national spirit is expressed. Attractive, because he vibrates in unison with the least French object, *recognizing himself in it*; a mere nothing, a gesture, an intonation, a word of a ragamuffin passing, will suffice to stir him to the depths with an emotion chock full of intelligence.' A stranger, on the other hand, just sees things in a general way, and he cannot distinguish what is individual and distinct. If I may vary the example: a stranger, say, in China makes the remark that all Chinese look alike and that their customs are either unintelligible and silly or like those of his own country. But if after a time he grows to like the Chinese, he is more and more struck by the native originality, the variation in facial look, their turns of phrase and, finally, their humour. When a man enters into the spirit of the humour of another country, he has reached a stage near to that of Rousselot's connaturality or sympathetic vibration. The law of the intelligence is that 'a spirit who would be *self-conscious*, could penetrate to the heart of the real. "The more spirit one has", says Pascal, "the more original things one sees", and for the pure spirit, there are only originals. He, who is all spirit, is all affinity with beings, all *noumenal affinity*; everything real is sympathetic to him; all his quality is "connatural" to him; he does not find there, to speak in Hegelian language, a *"suchness"* which he comes up against, but he insinuates himself and flows into the inmost place where we cannot penetrate. The pure spirit, says St. Thomas, knows the individual in its very singularity; the human soul abstracts at its own opportunity the idea of quiddity. Still absent from itself, how could it *apply* itself entirely to objects?'

These examples drawn from experience are, as I have said, supported by an interpretation of the philosophy of St. Thomas. Rousselot claims that in every affirmative judgement, both the final stage of self-realization is affirmed and prophesied, and also a final relation between that self and an existent Truth or Good. This is too complicated an argument to summarize in full. In short it comes to this: the judgement that a 'being is such and such' is a cumbersome expression of our imperfect mode of knowing. We separate and join, and we affirm absolutely that the subject and predicate are one. The imperfect manner of seeing and stating this unity is like a bud which precedes flowering; the very structure of the judgement contains a presage of a perfect state of knowing in which we would intuitively and connaturally sense and see the unity and originality of that which we have come to know laboriously and by abstract concepts. In other words, we are pricked on to self realization by love, and when our essence will be an open book to us, so too will be the book of nature. But the judgement does not only contain in it implicitly the philosophy of the self as essence; it intimates also a relation of our contingently existing self to a Being in whom essence and existence coincide. When I say that 'being exists', I am again making a distinction which is due to the imperfection of my knowledge. I can see that being always contains a reference to existence (even when I am thinking only of possibilities or imaginary things). But such a foresight supposes a state of affairs in which there is perfect unity between what is and what exists; that is to say, the existence of one who can say of Himself, 'I am who am'. Just as in the light of my perfect self, or essence, I foretell in every judgement a state of affairs in which I see intuitively things for what they are, so in the light of my infirm existence I adumbrate in every judgement another most perfect kind of knowledge, the scientia Dei which is causa rerum, the knowledge which belongs to a being in whom essence and existence are one.

Both Rousselot and Guthrie agree in emphasizing the two-pronged movement of love, and it is for this reason that I have dwelt at some length on the philosophic settings which they provide for a full understanding of the nature of these loves. They differ in that Guthrie keeps steadily to the view that the self-denying love is more important than the self-regarding love, that the intellect represents the latter and the will the former, and consequently that the highest life of man is to be sought in the will and not in the intellect. Rousselot while walking the same road at the beginning as Guthrie forks at a certain point and seeks man's perfection in the intellect. This is not the place to enter into any formal criticism of the two theories; they are both serviceable, and it is as serving to elucidate the meaning of love and its place in human life that they have been quoted. Their strength is that they give full recognition to the importance of love and are able to work it into the very fabric of their system without weakening in any way the great philosophic tradition of the West. That tradition comes to us philosophically from Greece and religiously from Palestine. The Greeks, as Gilson very pertinently pointed out, gave us a philosophy of essence, the product of reason, while the Hebrews, and above all, Christianity, taught us life, and so introduced 'existence' into Western thought. The Greeks never grasped the idea of a living God, who could create. They, like Santayana, dwelt amongst essences, they delight in human concepts and measure all by them, and one can always recognize their accent when the talk amongst philosophers settles on to 'emanations' of the 'One', divine process and becoming and dialectics of the Absolute. The best they can reach to is the idea of Truth and Goodness and Beauty. Into their highest thought the note of the impersonal and the necessary keeps coming in. No wonder the Christian sense of Kierkegaard revolted against such purely intellectual constructions. The emphasis of the Christian thinker is on existence, and as a consequence on freedom and personality. But though his emphasis should lie there, he is in the happy position of combining a doctrine of essence and existence, of holding fast to the worth of reason and human thinking while adoring a personal God, whose nature is far beyond the reaches of the human intellect. He may at times, for it is a very natural temptation, slip back a little into the Greek ways and concentrate on essence. In so far as he does this he deserves the lash of Nygren's criticism. But Nygren, and many others like him, are far too ashamed of man and his thought. They will have nothing to do with man's thought of God; God must ignore his own gift and creation, that godlike reason, which has the power of looking unabashed at truth and rising from the visible, modico cordis ictu, to the invisible and perfect.

Now one of the great virtues of Rousselot is that he gives full weight to the intellect and to the love of self, and yet is sure that in doing so he is reinforcing the doctrine of the sovereign and, to use an Old Testament adjective, the jealous love of God. But it may be said that in placing the highest act of man in the intellect he has failed to exorcise self, and failed, too, to do full justice to the existential side of man. There is no doubt that Rousselot considers the act of knowing to be possessive and directed to the well-being of the self. He expressly says that it is 'possessive' and he plays upon the Aristotelian dictum that the intellect 'is in some sense all things'. But he believes that he escapes the difficulty by his view of the relation of man to God and the connection of the love of self with the love of God. We have already recorded this answer in the first chapter, and suggested a criticism. The work in which that answer is to be found was the first of the writings of Rousselot. The essays in which he developed his theory of the relation of love to knowledge came later. He does not restate the old answer that the part in a whole loves the whole more than the part and the part only as part of the whole; he is content to show that the self as being *from* God and *to* God sees itself in that relation, and in that sight is all its joy. The soul can love itself properly only in loving God first; 'a spirit fully conscious of itself would know itself only as wholly dependent on God, caused, attracted, charmed by God'. Such expressions do not perhaps quite settle the problem of the relation of the two loves, nor do they explain why we should love God above all as Truth. There is, however, one rather cryptic and suggestive remark in a note. He says that he does not think that Maurice Blondel, the author of *L'Action*, has completely mastered 'the Thomist idea of intellection'. It would seem, indeed, from one of Blondel's articles, 'either that he does not see that in the creative and beneficent intellection of God, knowledge and love are identical, or that he does not wish that this be the intelligence which makes us penetrate to heaven, to the very interior of God. But if our perfection truly comes to us from an *Other* than ourselves, is not the act which ought finally to perfect us be that one which causes this Other to be more fully immanent? *Since it is God who is our Beatitude, and not we His, our perfection consists still more in receiving Him than in giving ourselves*'. Here is a new note struck, which may well be decisive and final.[1]

---

[1] The answer, however, in Rousselot's mind may have been that of St. Thomas. St. Thomas is often represented as saying that the bliss of man consists in an intellectual act, the contemplation of God's essence. But such a statement is far too simple to do justice to his thought. In an appendix at the end of the next chapter I give some passages from St. Thomas which help to explain his position.

CHAPTER THIRTEEN

PERSONALITY

Mere legal persons (*Personae Juris*) are persons by a figment, and for the sake of brevity in discourse. All rights reside in, and all duties are incumbent upon, physical or natural Persons.—JOHN AUSTIN.

Je suis mon maître entre les mains de Dieu.—BOSSUET.

As it is persons, and not things, who know and love, it remains to say something about persons and personality. Neither Guthrie nor Rousselot has much to say about personal relations and the reciprocity of love. This is a loss. Guthrie generally describes the movement of love as towards the 'Absolute'; Rousselot falls back upon the idea of God as Truth. The danger of such language is that it suggests that all the love comes from one side, and that the relatively unimportant side. The image left in the imagination is of a human being who alone is active and loving. For this reason all the descriptions of man in pursuit of Truth and Beauty and Goodness are imperfect. As well might a child at its mother's breast say that it was learning to enjoy reality! The self may turn from its worthlessness in longing for the Absolute or seek passionately for truth in order to possess it. But perfect love has another language. It will not do that the 'I' and 'Thou' relation should be treated as if it were the same as the 'I' and 'It' relation. Again, and perhaps as a result of this, the meaning of 'individual' and 'person' remains obscure. One has to guess what Rousselot has in mind. Guthrie in several passages makes the unity and individuality of a human being depend upon his existence. Here is the most explicit statement of this:

'It is because of my existence that I am one, that I am this supra-sensible reality, *this* very personality and not another. This becomes more obvious when we reflect for a moment and see that by my essential self I am metaphysically indistinct from any other individual considered under the same heading. The metaphysical individuality is, therefore, due to the existence, which is the principle of unity. This unity does not merely produce an interior individuality, consisting of an organized whole, but it also separates it radically from all others who possess similar essences.'

This view is arguable and has been accepted by some thinkers, but it is difficult. It treats individuality, personality and existence as if they were one, and that is a courageous act. It will be remembered that existence adds nothing to the essence save to make it actual. How could it do more?

The distinction between the two has been forced on the mind by such facts as that a pound note means essentially twenty shillings and that this is true whether a pound now exists or whether it does not. Everything which is intelligible, everything which we can say about a real object is covered by the essence, and it is only when we have completed all that can be said about the nature of a thing that the question arises, 'To be or not to be'. If we suppose that a scientist has thought out a new and most devastating explosive down to the last detail, and now asks himself whether he will allow that explosive to be produced, we have an illustration of the difference between a thing complete and not existing and a thing existing. In the moral order moralists distinguish between an intention fully formed and the execution of that intention. I may intend to take a sick friend for a drive, but it is not the mere intention which gives my friend fresh air. Hell is paved with good intentions. In the order of artistic creation, again, the work of art may be complete down to its smallest details in the mind. Robert Bridges, so I was told by a friend of his, was not satisfied until he had a poem all written out 'on the palm of his hand'; he then merely transcribed it on to paper. These and many other examples serve to bring out the difference between nature and existence, and it should be clear from them that the difference does not lie in any addition to the nature as such. It is true that for the comparison to be perfect, the examples should have been of living things, which have their own existence and independence. The cold statue of Pygmalion must come to life. But as the point of the comparison is that the statue of Pygmalion, whether in his mind's eye or dead or alive, is the same statue in nature and essence, the defect in the comparison does not matter. If there be any doubt left, let us accept a suggestion on the lines of Dunne's Experiment with Time, and imagine a dreamer seeing a person in a dream scene before he actually existed. We could then infer that the person in the dream and the existing person are identical in nature, and from that we could pass on to the safe generalization that existence is of a different order from essence and adds nothing, therefore, in the line of essence.

Those who are convinced by this type of argument are inclined, then, to distinguish between individuality, personality and existence. They first remove individuality out of the way. They keep that word for what divides one material thing from another. The spare-parts which are now so often mass-produced are thrown away if they show any peculiarity. The aim is uniformity; all the parts are alike. Nevertheless they are separate one from another, and the reason for this is that matter is divisible and that, when it is divided, however similar in pattern the pieces may be, the pieces are individual. This law of individualism holds true of anything, which is in any sense material. Twins may be so like as to be constantly confused with one another even by their parents. They are, nevertheless, separated from each other from the first moment of conception. That is the basic ground of separation and individuation. But when we rise in the scale from simple structures to complicated and living ones, there are other ways of distinguishing things. There are different sizes in boots, and when a pair of boots has been worn by their owner for some time, they are unlike any other pair. Soon peculiarities begin to multiply. One greyhound is different from another in size and weight and colouring and temperament and speed. The more complex the individual the more does he become singular and different from anything else.

To many this explanation of individuality suffices. There are grounds for disputing this, and we have already seen that neither Hopkins nor Guthrie, for example, is satisfied with it. But it is wiser, I think, to choose for a battleground not this question of individuality, but that of person. In the language of to-day the words 'person' and 'personality' often stand for peculiarity or originality of character. We speak of a 'kindly person', of an 'unpleasant personality', or of 'having personality'. The direct reference in these uses is to character, and so to avoid confusion with the old use some writers distinguish between what they call the 'psychological person' and the 'metaphysical person'. At times it may be necessary to recall this distinction. One of the many phenomena, which have been closely studied in recent years, is that of split personality. The patient suffers from alternating 'personalities', as if there were two or three characters of very different temperament and outlook inhabiting the same body. One Sally Beauchamp dislikes the other, and a third claims to be aware of the other two and to interfere with them. The fact that such personalities can be integrated again proves, if proof were needed, that they all belong to one subject. The problem of split personalities has nothing really to do with the metaphysical person, except in so far as we are bound to be interested in how our conscious and habitual way of thinking of ourselves is related to what, for the sake of a word, I shall call the true self or Ego. Everything we think about ourselves and feel about ourselves is about ourselves and nobody else. We are, to use a graphic word of de la Taille's, 'self-enclosed'. We move round in the circle of ourselves and we can never escape being the individual 'I'. As children we may have asked ourselves the question: What must it be like to be someone else? Reflection, however, shows that this is an absurd question. If I am another person I am not myself, and there is no reason for delaying with Bertrand Russell over the question: If Plato were a donkey would he be wise? The words 'I' and 'my' must be singular. Nothing else can resemble this self-being of mine, 'except in so far as this, that other men to themselves have the same feeling. But this only multiplies the phenomena to be explained so far as the cases are alike and do resemble. But to me there is no resemblance; searching nature I taste *self* but at one tankard, that of my own being. The development, refinement, condensation of nothing shows any signs of being able to match this to me or give me another taste of it, a taste even resembling it.' (Notebooks of Gerard Hopkins.)

But if I cannot get away from myself, that does not mean that I know myself or have full command of all that is in me. I knock up against myself as existing every moment and at every turn, but my nature remains a dark wood in which I can get lost. If what Rousselot said about love and knowledge makes sense, then I am a self-lover whose knowledge is measured by his love and his love by his knowledge, and until I reach to an intuition of my own being, when what is seen is the seeing, the tasted the taste itself, the expressed the expression of it, as when a man puts his whole soul into what he is composing, I shall continually get surprises. Now it is this self, the owner of the actual nature and final subject of attribution, which deserves the name of the metaphysical person. It is more than the character, more than the 'I' we are accustomed to when we start to describe ourselves to our friends. We may be so accustomed to living in one palace, let us say, Windsor or Balmoral, that we think of ourselves as the owner of Windsor, whereas, in fact, we are the owner of these palaces because we are the King of a land in which these palaces have been built. What we want to know is in what does our royalty precisely consist? There is, indeed, a connection between our character and our empirical self. When we use the word 'person' of these manifestations of ourselves, we are mentioning our personality, though we are attending to its stage production; we are referring indirectly to what is the root and basis of our being. That is why there is no separation of an impassable kind between the old and modern uses of the word 'person', no more than there is between the use of the word vanity in such varied connotations as 'the vanity of human wishes' and the 'vanity of a "movie star".' From the psychological personality of men and women we can pass easily to the deeper meaning of what it is for each of them to be this human being, individual, independent and incommunicable. And if an investigation of character is interesting, how much more so the quest of that which throws light upon the deepest and most intimate feature of our being. In our advice and exhortations to our fellow men we are always having recourse to this mysterious word 'person'. The lawyer needs it in a mitigated form for drawing up his briefs and laws; the moralist insists upon the respect for persons, and the democrat is for ever proclaiming the rights of persons, their dignity and their essential equality; so much so that it is evident that democracy is dependent upon a right estimate of what it is to be a person.

When we turn, however, to the professional thinkers for aid to know what meaning to attach to the idea of a person, we are met by a strange silence or a stranger discord. What is dearest to us, most intimate and congenial, causes a black-out when we try to dive down into it. Mr. W. M. Thornton, in an article in *Mind*, has gathered together what the chief thinkers have said about it, theologians, philosophers, lawyers, and moralists. Many of them confess their inability to give any description: 'Its meaning we know so long as no one asks us to define it, but to give an accurate account of it is the most difficult of philosophic tasks' (W. James); Herbert Spencer wrote that it is 'a thing which cannot be truly known at all, knowledge of it being forbidden by the very nature of thought'. Others skate round it. Hume says, 'person or thinking being', and Kant, 'A person is the subject whose actions are capable of imputation'. Nearly all see that mind or consciousness has something to do with the personality: 'Consciousness is inseparable from the idea of a person or intelligent being, but does not make Personality'. (Bishop Butler.) The great Christian thinkers were more than most concerned to state its exact meaning, for their thoughts were bent on the mysteries of the Trinity and the Incarnation, but even they were not unanimous. Most of the Scholastic writers took off from the definition of Boethius, already given. But with their clear distinctions between nature or essence and existence, and the difference beteen mind and thing, they were troubled how to find a proper place for this property which, as they saw, was peculiar to beings who were not only independent but self-conscious and self-directing. They employed the intelligible theory already described to explain the individuality of material things. Every material thing which exists is particular, but the particulars may share a common nature. Two pins may be so like that all we can say about their difference is they are two and not one; for the rest, they are identical. If you wish to use a pin it does not matter which of the two you use. What makes one and not the other is not then the 'nature' which it shares with the other, but the fact that it is made up of this particular amount of stuff, while the other is made up of another amount of stuff. When we turn, however, to more complex and organized natural objects, such as wild roses and acorns, we find a greater unity and independence and at the same time variation in the members of the species. Still more is this the case with animals, such as cats and foxes. The aforesaid principle of individuation may still be applicable, but they seem to have something of their own, which makes them positively distinct and private. The word for this is individual substance or subsistence—preferably the latter, because the word substance is often connected up in men's minds with the general nature of the animal—which is not here in question. I have used the phrase 'individual substance' and 'seeming to have something of their own' for an important reason. We have to distinguish between a prerogative a substance may have and the substance itself. If we grant that in human beings the body is a substance, it is clear that it has no independent existence of its own; it is our body, and when we say 'our' we mean a being who is spirit as well as body. The 'I' who makes the body and spirit one being and owns both and is responsible for the combined action of the two, is the individual who is subsistent—not the body nor the spirit by itself. If we grant also that the spirit survives the death of the body, we have the problem, which may be more than verbal, whether the spirit can then strictly be called a subsistent being or person. I put this question because it brings out a feature which is said to belong to a person.[1] The spirit after death is still a spirit which did belong to a body and is of such a kind that it is natural for it to belong to a body. If this is so, then it does not possess the prerogative of incommunicability. It is separate and substantial, but it is not so sovereign and private as to be incommunicable. As such it lacks the final flourish and signed signature to the content which makes it personal, so much mine that no other can possibly claim it as his own.

In these last sentences I have passed from the notion of subsistence to that of person. The transition is easy. That which gives a cat a life of its own, and possession of its own being, we call subsistence; when the being has a life of its own and is rational and self-conscious and self-directive, we call the subsistence personality. A rational subsistent being is a person. We are back at the definition of Boethius that a person is the individual substance (or the subsistent being) of a rational nature. Every cat is a permanent individual and all that it does must be attributed to one subject. It cannot, however, call its actions its own in the same sense in which a conscious, self-directing, and, therefore, free, human being owns itself. The interior life has reached such a pitch in human beings that it is free, utterly the subject's own, responsible and so private that it cannot be another's. This is what is meant by being a person.

But now arise conflicting voices. Is this prerogative of rational and spiritual beings a new mode of being, a something extra which escapes the attention of philosophers, or a relation, or something which comes into play as soon as a concrete being exists? The Christian thinker has naturally the revealed truth of the Incarnation in mind when he sets to work to answer this problem. Christ, he knows, was fully a man, and he was also fully God. Yet he is not two beings; the being to whom the Apostles spoke was in all appearances a human person, an individual and

[1] For a fuller treatment of this problem v. my *Death and Life*, c. 4.

existing man. But even they before the end came to realize that he was more than a man, that this person with a body and mind was truly God. The only possible explanation is to say that the 'I', the being who is addressed, is God—the person of God or a person of the godhead. We know what this means by the very fact that we are forced to say this, but at the same time it raises very acutely the problem of the relation of a person to nature and to existence. For it would seem that there can be a full human concrete nature, everything requisite in order to speak of Christ as a man; and yet Chirst is a divine person and not a human person. Our first thought may be that the answer is not so difficult; we can form an image to suit the facts in saying that the human nature is owned by God. But we are almost bound to be misled by thinking of physical or human analogies. A property or benefice is owned by one proprietor; if however it with several others passes into the hands of one man, we have a plurality of properties or benefices and only one owner. But the ownership is here external; the properties remain just what they were. A slave owner or tyrant may have life and death powers over his subjects; they may be said to belong to him 'body and soul'. The slightest reflection, however, shows us that this is still an external relation. If we take the case of physical or living compounds, the compound may have a unity, but it will be at the sacrifice of one or other or both of the ingredients. The chemical processes and the vegetative continue in the body of a man, but it would be quite false to think of them as complete beings or natures subsisting together under a new headship; they are part of the one life of the body. This is true even of the unity of the body and the spirit in any living man. A man has only one nature, his human nature, and the body and spirit compose it. Now in Christ the ownership of the human nature is not an external and accidental one; the human nature has no actuality, no subsistence of its own; it *is* Christ's, and Christ is God. To understand the point, we should have to imagine that the concrete human nature which is, for instance, St. Paul's, should cease to be Paul's and become St. Peter's, in the same sense and degree in which it had been Paul's. The very fact that it seems most absurd for us to think of this human nature which is Paul's without it being Paul's, shows us how closely the conception of personality is bound up with the concrete nature or essence. I can almost hear critics saying that the supposition is ridiculous, as ridiculous as supposing that Plato could be a donkey. Theologians, however, dispose of this difficulty by showing that the union of a finite nature to an infinite person would not bring confusion into our thought of the concrete, finite nature. Our difficulty arises from our habit of either thinking of the psychological personalities of Peter and Paul or comparing the personality to the ownership of properties. In the first case we so identify Peter's character with his personality that we do not and cannot think of them apart. In the second case we picture the personality as so apart that the property remains unchanged when the owner is an absentee landlord. This oscillation in our minds between two errors is an excellent warning to us how to look on personality. It is in neither of these extremes, and we shall be well on the right road if we keep steadily in mind that the characters of Peter and Paul, their psychological personalities, are so truly what they are, as living human persons, that everything that is done and thought and felt is Peter and Paul, respectively, acting and thinking and feeling. The writs of Peter and Paul run through every human movement in their domain. There is only one substantial human being. Peter as a person is not something outside himself.

These distinctions serve, as I hope, as range-finders and enable us to get right on to the target. Expressed in terms of essence and existence, the person must be looked for not as an extra, something outside the concrete, human and existing being, nor again in the concrete human nature or essence by itself. Once again we have to ask whether it is in the correlation of existence with the essence. When we speak of a human person, we mean not the character nor the superficial 'I' of our experience, but the 'I' who makes me to be myself and nobody else. But if I possess my own nature and existence I do not own it as a property outside myself —like a benefice. The nature, therefore, which I have seems to enter into the definition of my person, as well as the fact that I exist. Nevertheless the nature can be complete, and not be personal—it might be owned by a divine Person and have no personality of its own. If this be so, then the clue should be sought in the direction of the nature *as existing*. On the other hand, existence seems to be empty of any content. The coin that was lost and found is the same coin; whether it exist or not makes no difference to the worth we attribute to it. The nature of the supposed buried treasure in the Spanish Main is the same whether it really exists or not. Existence, therefore, adds nothing to nature or essence; all that it can do is to actualize the nature. In terms, then, of essence and existence, all that appears to give positive content to my thought of Peter is on the side of essence, and yet essence by itself is without personality; and all that existence gives is the actualization of the nature of Peter; it does not add anything to my idea of Peter's nature.

Will it then suffice to say that a person springs up, like a Jack-in-the-box, when essence and existence are correlated and come together? Many great thinkers answer in the negative. Some, like Suarez, say that existence brings with it, or after it, a new and real mode of being, a kind of flush or flowering to the being which now exists. The difficulty in this answer is to see what meaning can be attached to such a mode or flowering, and how it escapes being an extra. Others maintain that as existence does no more than actualize what is already present, personality must precede this actualization of it. To suppose otherwise would be as absurd as to say that a bird in the hand was more of a bird than a bird in the bush. A man launched into existence is like a ship. The cable is cut and the ship glides down into the water. It is exactly the same ship after launching as before. Personality must therefore reside in the essence of the concrete human individual. What then is it? Cajetan says that it is that in the nature which makes the nature fit to have a substantial existence all its own. This, however, seems to be a roundabout way of saying very little. What he says, however, becomes more intelligible if we understand him to mean that there is always, first, a fine point or tiny seed of distinctiveness, the 'I' which shows itself so individually in the behaviour of different babies and in mature life countersigns every thought and act with its individual name; secondly, there is the nature with which it is overlaid, its essence in which it has to work and be itself. Indeed, it cannot recognize itself save in this nature, and so identified with this nature is it that it takes for granted that its perfection consists in making itself a perfect instance of this nature. Within its nature it determines itself, and has scope for free action within this playground. Thirdly, there is this 'I' clothed in a nature, and now existent. As existent the self is positively incommunicable. It is in the midst of other existents, and they are all, however near, physically or spiritually, at an infinite distance because of their separate existence. The self is solitary and has, as Whitehead noted, to learn what to do with its solitariness. This aloneness is an ontological experience; the experience, that is, which comes from its being positive, a substantial élan existing for itself. The convex, however, of this experience is that of contingency or exigence; it is a person which exists for itself, but it cannot subsist by itself. By and in its nature it lives for itself, for its own perfection; but as existent it moves out to other existent beings and to God.

The last group I shall mention are opposed to this view of personality. They say that it is unnecessary to invent this positive 'I' and that it can have no *locus standi* on the side of the concrete essence, which can be nothing but a potency waiting to be actualized; it is as awkward as a nigger in the woodpile. It is impossible to conceive of a concrete nature as personal unless it is existing. An essence thought of in abstraction from existence is always dependent; it is a mere possibility, present, for instance, in somebody's mind, and therefore dependent on some other existent. But by personality we must mean a being which is itself and dependent upon itself—in fact, a being with an existence of its own. The one exception to this is, as we know from Revelation, in the Incarnation, and that exception only confirms the general answer. Normally the human nature possesses existence; it has an existence of its own. In Christ the human nature is possessed by the personal existence of one of the Persons of the Trinity. Normally a human nature has existence; in one exceptional case the human nature is held by Another. In the relation between human nature and existence, whoever holds the other is the person. The one exception only brings out the meaning of the general rule. As a rule when the concrete human nature is actualized it has an existence of its own; it then exists and is the ground of all action and thought and the ultimate subject of responsibility. As de la Taille writes:[1] 'What do we call a person, or a subsisting individual, in opposition to a mere nature? We mean one that exists as a complete whole; not as a part of a whole, like my hand; nor as an associate only, like my body; nor as a mere belonging or dependency, like Christ's humanity. We mean one existing separately as well as independently; self governed no less than self-contained. All that is verified at once when you have, in the created sphere, a complete nature fitted with *what is required* to make it exist by itself and for itself. What then is required for this? Nothing more than the ordinary connatural existence of a human nature. Have that, I would say to the nature, and at once, you are a man, you are somebody; because to exist in such a manner is to subsist as a whole, as an independent unit. On the contrary, failing such existence, the nature depends at once on the higher One, who by union with Himself can associate to His existence the humble consort of Divine Majesty.'

This answer may appear to many to be the final one because it looks to be both clear and complete. It fits the theory of the two loves, but it would fit that theory still better if it were combined with some of the advantages contained in the alternative view of the positive self. This change, moreover, might serve to remedy one or two apparent weaknesses in the answer as just given. This answer pretends to find in existence the clue to human personality. This may well be right, but it remains true even in this theory that the 'I' of Peter and Paul, though it is a person because it now has its own existence, refers primarily to the nature or subject which has the existence. In the explanation of the theory it is usually said that the complex of soul and body is endowed with an existence connatural to it, and personality is defined as 'the ownership of commensurate existence'. The words 'connatural' and 'commensurate' are illuminating, and they betray the delicate place in their armour of the 'existentialists'. The words serve to repel the thrust of the 'essentialists'. The latter urge that personality must be sought in the concrete nature of essence, because all that existence does is to actualize that nature. The answer is to the effect that it is wrong to dissociate the thought

---

[1] *Essay in Incarnation*, edited by C. Lattey.

of the essence from that of its existence. Whenever we think of a man, we can, if we wish, fix our attention on his nature and prescind from the fact that he is alive. But such abstraction is really incomplete, because we have always in mind this particular man, Paul, with this particular kind of existence. Our eyes cannot help straying from the image to the reality. In other words, a substantial being of the sort which exists by itself and not by another bespeaks this particular kind of existence. Essence and existence are correlates, and each in its own way is superior to the other. Essence in one respect is inferior to existence, because existence actualizes what would otherwise be a mere possibility. Existence has no limitation in itself; it is an act which is limited by the nature which possesses it. On the other hand, existence is for the sake of the essence, and in this respect essence is superior to existence. It is always some perfection of a limited kind, of this particular greyhound, for example, or this particular racehorse, which makes us glad that it exists. We wish, to take another example, that penicillin should be produced because we believe in the efficacy of penicillin, and that, in more abstract language, is to admit that existence is for the sake of the essence.

If this be so we are forced back from our exclusive emphasis on existence on to the essence again, and it must be some special virtue in the concrete human nature which is implemented by an existence which is its very own. If we take this special virtue to be the 'I' or person, we shall have to face all the old difficulties over again. But we can take a hint from the language about correlates and the definition already given of personality as the 'ownership of commensurate existence'. The 'I' of the essence is a positive; in this light it is an absolute; but in respect of the existence it is a pure relative. When we consider the essence in abstraction from the existence, we have to think of an ego within a nature. This is the self-regarding movement whose one ambition is to be *itself* irrespective of all else. On the other hand the nature as such in relation to the existence is no more than a potency which has to be actualized, and in this regard the existence of the self is far more important than its own toilet. The existential movement is quite free from this self-regard. The one human being who owns the commensurate existence is therefore as turned in upon his own essence a lover of self, but as the owner of the commensurate existence he is subject to a higher power. He is near the bottom of the rung of existing things; he can call his existence his own, but at a price—and the price is that he remembers constantly that his essence is only a potency which has had to be actualized, however much he tends to admire his own essence when he gazes in the mirror. Paul is a person; he possesses an existence which is all his own; he is this individual with a human nature who has his own independent existence. The human nature is his and the existence is his. What does this mean? Within the one inseparable being which he is, composed of essence and existence, we can separate out the various parts. As a subject with a human nature he is to all intents and purposes a self in the process of self-realization. Perfection here lies in self-realization, and by means of the differentiating power of human nature, the reason or mind. But this same subject, who in respect of his essence, is an intellectual and self-regarding individual, has to exist if even a beginning is to be made in self-love. Everything on the side of essence waits on existence to become actual, and therefore even the movement of self-perfection is dependent on the self being existent. In this sense self-love is always inferior to the movement of the existential self. Self love is not destroyed, but it is put in its place, and that is the second place. The self as existent is, therefore, the source of all our behaviour and our relations with real things and beings, which exist outside us. As in his essential movement a human being turns within, in his existential movement he turns without —and if we ask the ultimate reason why there should be such diverse movements within the one self, the answer is that it is limited, that the essence of the finite self is not its existence, and that only in God do the two loves unite. God is what he is, and hence the centripetal love is a movement between persons who are one in essence. Their love is one of perfect union. As Descoqs writes (*Institutiones metaphysicae generalis*, pp. 403–4): 'Love, in the true God made known to us by Revelation, is not for a single instant, egoist. The Father does not know himself in order to take pleasure in himself; he knows himself in constituting by that very act a personal term to which he communicates his nature, and the second person gains from his father a new and sufficing title of necessary existence. . . . No subordination of any kind in dignity and perfection can be admitted in the divine persons; between them there is only an order of origin. The love of one divine Person for another divine Person which should put love for his own Person first would straightway upset the whole order of the Trinity; for in doing so each of the divine Persons would make himself an end in regard to the other two, and this is impossible. The infinite perfection of the divine Persons demands, therefore, complete disinterestedness in their mutual relations. . . .' A human person, on the other hand, is bound to have a love for himself, because he has a limited nature which he has to perfect; but the disinterested love, which comes from his being an existing self, while it allows for this self-regarding love, gathers it up in its movement towards that self-subsistent Being of infinite love, from whom its existence has come and to whom it belongs.

Human personality is, therefore, rightly described as the 'ownership of commensurate existence', if we give full force to the relativity contained in the word 'commensurate', and in this definition of person the secret contained in the to and fro movement of the two loves is fully disclosed. There is the love which is self-interested and the love which is dis-interested; the one is introvert; all is grist to the mill of the essence; its business is to adorn the nature, however Spartan, to preserve it and increase its worth. The other is extrovert; it is not directly concerned with the essence (existence gives nothing to the essence; it only actualizes it); it is, if I may use a metaphor which is metaphysically correct, only too aware that its co-partnership with the finite essence has limited it to the status of the finite. It moves, therefore, away from the limited, unstable life it has towards the existent ground of all being; it hangs on the Word of another. Now the 'I' as person holds these two movements together. It builds itself up, it supports itself, it is self-conscious and ever in process of realizing itself, and bringing to their proper perfection its potentialities. But it cannot do so without an existence of its own, and once launched into existence, it is solitary, incommunicable, but also dependent. A human being is not self-sufficing; to be himself he must depend all the while on other existent beings, who are not himself. To be without existence is to be an abortion—and fortunately the 'I' as person exists. But as existing he has to submit to the rules of the divine game of love, for what exists cannot keep within the bounds of the self; it is irresistibly drawn out of itself towards the source of all bounty, towards other persons who can give and take, and by the divine initiative towards that existent Trinity of Love which is so perfect that mutual giving and taking sum up its personal life. We can compare human life to a stream which flows to the ocean and at the same time by its own motion makes a floating island which instead of perishing grows ever more beautiful as a piece of nature. The love of self is not swept away by the love of God; it forms a nucleus which develops ever more richly its own form, the greater the sweep of love beyond it. The love of self is a true love; it is necessary for the permanent selfhood and splendour of our finite beauty; it is not just a part of another love; it is a co-efficient with it; the animus and the anima give each other mutual assistance and love; the essential self and the existential self together make the 'I', the person; Eros and Agape are not enemies, but friends.

APPENDIX.—THE VIEW OF ST. THOMAS AQUINAS ON THE RELATION OF LOVE AND INTELLECT

Because St. Thomas says that the highest act of man consists in the contemplation and vision of God, it is often supposed that he gives the primacy to knowledge as against love. Such a bare statement of rivalries does not do justice to St. Thomas. He does, indeed, say that 'happiness or bliss consists substantially and principally in an act of the intellect rather than in an act of the will' (St. Thomas, *Ia-IIae*). But he equally insists that love follows on the knowledge and also precedes it. 'There is no passion of the soul (*passio animae*) which does not presuppose some love.' 'Everything has a natural consonance with or taste for what suits it, and this is natural love.' 'Hence whether in the case of animal love or intellectual desire, love is a certain consonance of the desire with what is apprehended as suitable.' Knowledge, therefore, is initiated by love and accompanied by love, and he makes much use of such words as consonance and connaturality of subject and object. Charity, as might be expected, dominates all. 'The contemplative life, though it consists essentially in knowledge, has nevertheless its origin in love, in so far, that is, as one is stirred to the knowledge of God by love. And because the end corresponds with the beginning, it comes about that the end and completion of the contemplative life has its being in the love of affection; for one takes delight in the sight of the beloved object, and the delight increases the love. . . . In this consists the ultimate perfection of the contemplative life that the divine truth should not only be seen but should also be loved.'

In this doctrine then loves presides, and inspires even knowledge. But as knowledge has its end in truth, and truth tells us all we want to know about the beloved object, the act which gives us the truth about God and enables us to see God is that of knowledge. The movement of the intellect is started by love: 'First there is the love which moves us to it (the end); second, the active desire for it, and the active steps which proceed from this desire . . .; thirdly, the goal and viewpoint gained; and fourthly, the delight which ensues, which is no other than the satisfaction of the will in the end gained.' He then goes on to compare this process with the movement towards any natural object, and says that as it is always the object which we seek primarily and not the delight which comes from having it, so 'the ultimate goal of an intelligent creature is to see God, and not to take delight in Him. The latter accompanies that attainment and, as it were, rounds it off. Still less can the longing and feeling of love for the end be the ultimate end, seeing that they exist even before the end is obtained.'

The point of this argument is that the possessing of an object is what is first sought and only secondarily the pleasure or delight in that possession. Now the love, which proceeds from the will, is always towards an object which remains outside the self; it is only the intellect which can have the object within and possess it fully. This is the old difference, so

U

often emphasized in the argument of this book, and it may seem to some to leave out the important difference between persons and things. Things may be possessed, but others are loved for what they are in themselves, for what is personal. We give and they take, and it is only in this way in their giving that we take and possess. If the matter ended here we might well suspect that St. Thomas was working too much on the Aristotelian formula of love necessarily being self-interested, and so, consistently with this formula and the Aristotelian ideal, is placing perfection in the intellect, whose function it is to possess. But St. Thomas sets the balance right by remarking that when the object loved is of a higher order than the lover the situation is changed. The lover has to be taken out of himself. The two following passages bring this out:

'The perfection and dignity of the intellect consist in this, that the likeness of the object known is present in the intellect itself; that is what the activity of the intellect brings about, and this is what gives it its dignity. The distinction of the will, however, and of its activity, consists in this, that the soul pays heed to some object that is noble, and to that object precisely as it is in itself. Now, absolutely speaking, it is more perfect to have within one the nobility of another thing than to be put into relation with a noble thing existing outside oneself. Hence will and intellect, if they are considered in the abstract and without reference to this or that object, exhibit this order to one another, viz., that intellect is nobler than will. But it sometimes happens that there is more nobility in being related to a noble object in a certain way than having its nobility in oneself; that is, when the nobility of that object is possessed in a degree much lower than what the object has in itself. If, on the other hand, the nobility of the object be possessed by the other in an equal degree or to a higher degree than it is in the object itself, then beyond all doubt that other is more ennobled by possessing the object nobility than by being related to it in any way whatsoever. Now the intellect possesses the forms of the things which are more noble than the soul in a way that is inferior to their manner of existence in themselves—for an object is received by the intellect according to the manner of being of the intellect itself. . . . Likewise, of things which are lower in the order of being than the soul, such as bodies, the forms as possessed by the soul are nobler than as they exist in the things themselves.

'Hence the intellect and the will can be compared in three ways. First of all, in general and without qualification, with no regard to this or that object; and then the intellect is more eminent than the will, as possessing the worth of an object is more perfect than being related to that worth. Secondly, in regard to the natural objects of the senses; here again the intellect is as such nobler than the will, seeing that it is nobler to grasp a stone by knowledge than to want one; and the reason is that the form of a stone exists in a nobler way in the intellect, when it knows it, than it does in the stone itself as desired by the will. Thirdly, in regard to divine things, which are higher than the soul; here will is more eminent than intellect, as it is nobler to desire and love God than to know Him; seeing that the divine goodness exists more perfectly in God Himself, who is the object of desire, than it does as partaken of by us when it is possessed by the intellect.' (*De Veritate*, Q. 22, art. XI, C.)

'Happiness or bliss lies in an activity and not in a disposition, as Aristotle proves (*Eth. Nic.*, I); and thus the bliss of man can be related to a power of the soul in two ways. Firstly, it can be the *object* of that power; in this way bliss is chiefly related to the will, for bliss signifies the last end of man and his supreme good, and these are the objects of the will. Secondly, bliss can be related to the power as act to potency; in this way bliss has its root and substance in an act of the intellect (though the will can add something complementary to this); since it is impossible that an act of the will should itself be the ultimate aim and object of the will. For the ultimate object of man is that which is first desired, and this object so desired cannot be an act of the desire itself. A power or faculty is directed first upon the object before it turns in upon itself; seeing, for instance, is concerned with colour before reflecting upon itself seeing the colour; similarly the will desires a pleasing object before it desires its own willing. Thus, therefore, an act of will cannot be the first object of desire, and cannot, in consequence, be the last end of the will. But as often as some external good is desired by us as our end, our very act of desiring becomes a kind of quasi-interior end to us, whereby we first perfectly enjoy the object; as when we say that eating is the end and happiness of one who makes food his end; so too the possessing money by one who makes money his end. Now the end of our desiring is God, and so the act by which we are first united to Him is, in root and substance, our bliss; and we are united to God first of all by an act of the intellect. Therefore the intellect in seeing God is, in root and substance, our bliss. But because this operation is most perfect, and its object most suited to it, there follows from it the greatest delight, which does indeed grace amd perfect the activity, as beauty graces youth (as is said in *Eth. Nic.* X. 4); and therefore this delight which belongs to the will gives a grace and complement to our bliss. Thus the origin of final bliss is in vision, but its complement is in fruition' (*Quodlibet* VIII, 9, Art. 19 c).

CHAPTER FOURTEEN

HUMAN AND DIVINE

Wisely hath Helen done in setting the Cross above the Kings' heads that the Cross of Christ may be adored in Kings.—ST. AMBROSE on St. Helen.

Its nostrils snuffed the air and sought repose
The while its glances, keen, uncircumscribed,
Projecting pictures into space,
Brought a blue saga-cycle to a close.
The Unicorn by R. M. RILKE.

Salva me ex ore leonis, et a cornibus unicornium.

Enough material has now been collected to see the shape which love always takes. We begin with the distinction which it is easiest to make, selfish and unselfish love. All admit this, and it is sufficiently clear and obvious for all to use in everyday judgements about others and to rely on in biographies and historical criticism. Immediately, however, we take it seriously and inquire into its ultimate truth we meet difficulties. Selfishness is only a vice if it means an undue regard for self; unselfishness is only a virtue if it is countered by self-respect. The two loves, therefore, so far from being opposites appear to require the presence of each other. We do not blame a man for seeking to develop his mind and will, for asserting his claims on occasions, so long as he is not exclusively bent on promoting his own interests. Similarly, we admire a person who is self-sacrificing, but we are shocked by those who show no trace of self-respect and are prepared to throw away their honour for some belief or cause.

But if this be so, a problem arises. The two loves seem to go hand in hand, but we do not know on what terms they are disposed to be friendly; we are ignorant of their relative rank and of their roots in human nature; we may even wonder whether they are so ultimately different as they seem to be. Nor can the problem be set on one side as academic, as if it were always happily settled in practice. I have tried to show in preceding chapters how the great movements in history and art and philosophy and religion are influenced by the preference for one or other of these loves, and that it is vastly important to know where we stand with regard to them. The two loves appear in every place of history like the Lion and the Unicorn fighting round the town. They take, however, such different names and appeal to such diverse motives in us that we usually fail to see the underlying identity, and it is because we are thus distracted that we fail also to have any coherent idea of what these loves are and how they are related. It is for this reason that I have taken apparently disparate kinds of examples and by holding them up to the light tried to show their interconnection. The very thinkers who had made them a subject for examination may help too by unwittingly disclosing more than they themselves notice.

The words Eros and Agape, which have come into favour recently and are in their very names suggestive, were used both by de Rougemont and Nygren to delineate two forms of loving. They gave a beginning, especially as de Rougemont was directly concerned with a romantic movement in history and Nygren with a religious one. The advantage of this is that as they started from different angles, their evidence can be taken as independent. On a first impression their conclusions seem to clash, but on a closer look a remarkable resemblance reveals itself. De Rougemont was engaged in a study of the troubadours and the Provençal romantic movement. He was struck by the fact that, at the very moment when the Church was establishing Christian manners and morals, the so-called courtly or chivalric songs and tales were idealizing a love which was the antithesis of Christian marriage and the Christian sacramental view of life. The most typical example of this love is to be found in the story of Tristram and Isolde. De Rougemont describes its features as follows: it stood in doctrine for mystical union, in its theoretical application for woeful human love, and in its historical fulfilment for hedonism and for a rare and despised passion. Christian love, on the other hand, as he understands it, stood for communion, for love of our neighbour and blissful marriage, and in its historical fulfilment for painful clashes and a strong passion. He calls the first Eros and the second Agape.

So far there might not seem to be anything which threw an unexpected light on the love of self and the love of others. Once, however, de Rougemont develops his theme, we listen to a strange and fascinating story. The opposition of Eros and Agape is not a light one, due to an historical accident; it goes down to the roots of human nature and is coeval with man. Eros is the dark passion, man's beguiler and destroyer. It is the Delilah or, in the language of romance, the witch Lilith. Romance is a form of escape; it breaks loose from the control of reason; it soars up in emotion and crashes to its death. Some time or other in the theme of Eros the death note will be heard; man in love with death and with the dark goddess, and singing of the night when his soul will be fused with the object of his passion. This passion makes itself felt in the medieval courtly tales, but it is not peculiar to them; it belongs to a philosophy and religion which can be traced back to the pre-Christian Indo-European religions which swept into the lands of the Mediterranean and strove to rival Christianity. Defeated, these beliefs were not extinguished. As the centuries succeed one another the followers of them betray their presence in a succession of heresies or rival theories. These theories can be summed up in the name, Gnosticism, and they all have this in common that the material world is evil, that the soul which has fallen or descended from the divine substance, the spiritually One, longs to escape back from the world and to be immersed again in the divine, and that it must as a consequence hate the body and all things associated with the body, such as marriage. This view, which has such close associations with Neo-Plato·nism and the mystical element in the worship of Eleusis and Isis, lies behind Manicheanism, Priscillianism and Catharism. Now, as de Rougemont points out, there is ample evidence that this philosophy, under the name of Catharism, was prevalent in Spain and spread across the Pyrenees through Southern France, even to Italy, just at the time that the Provençal songs and tales were written. What more likely then than that the ideas so obviously in conflict with the doctrines of Christianity came from the implacable rival of Christianity, the Gnostic religious philosophy. Thus the romantic development in Europe, with its cult of the dark passion, its antipathy to reason and its cult of death and mysticism, is traced back to Neo-Platonism and the religions of Asia. And it is this kind of love which de Rougemont calls Eros.

Far different at first sight is Nygren's account. De Rougemont thinks of Eros as unrestrained and passionate, hedonistic, and to that extent selfish, but also bent on self-destruction and fusion of its identity with the dark godhead. To Nygren it is the rational man, the natural man of the Scriptures, who relies upon himself and is fundmentally egocentric, who is moved by Eros. Eros belongs to the Greek way of life, and the Greek is the pagan of the Areopagus to whom the Christian teaching of St. Paul was folly. Greek philosophy makes man the measure of truth, and the perfection of man consists in his possessing truth. Eros is, therefore, equivalent to self-love. The Christian love, which Nygren calls Agape, does not negotiate with this self-love at all; it discards it utterly. God does everything; He is Agape, and freely, without any regard for the deserts of human beings, he initiates a corresponding Agape in them. He takes them out of themselves altogether, and inspires in them in place of self-love, a non-natural love for Himself and for their neighbours. No self-love is left. Pure Christianity, therefore, teaches Agape without any taint of Eros. But, as his book tries to prove, Christian theology proved unequal to the task of keeping the faith pure. Slowly at first, and then more rapidly as the Church came to esteem Greek thought, Eros returned. The Scholastic philosophy reeks of Plato and Aristotle and self-love is put alongside the love of God and the love of one's neighbour. Hence arose false problems about the relation of self-love to the love of God and of others.

Whereas, then, de Rougemont considers Eros to be unrestrained and passionate, and, apparently, more inclined to self-effacement than to self-regard, Nygren defines it as an Hellenic ideal, as intellectual, self-complacent and possessive, as, in short, irretrievably egocentric. Agape, on the other hand, in Nygren's view, is so theocentric as to leave nothing human in it, while de Rougemont sees in it something which irradiates reason and everything human. By God's love, as the latter says, 'every human relation has been given a new *direction* in being given a new *meaning*'. It is strange that two such penetrating observers should come to such strikingly different conclusions, and on a subject, too, about which every human being from his own experience has a tale to tell. On one point, however, they concur—Eros is somehow connected with the growth of Neo-Platonism. One thinks that the dark passion took philosophical shape when in its journey from the East it encountered. Greek thought; the other is convinced that the egocentric philosophy of Greece soared up into a mystical religion when it encountered the mystery religions of the East. The only difference here is one of stress; the result is the same, except that de Rougemont limits the enemies of Agape to Gnosticism, while Nygren includes the whole of Hellenic philosophy and religion. This is very suggestive. It looks as if both writers had by a too-exclusive attention to one feature or other of Eros and Agape drawn apart. What they have positively to say is valuable, but their conclusions sin by omission.

This conjecture is verified when we look at their omissions. De Rougemont has many happy intuitions to give us on the nature of both Agape and Eros. Nevertheless, his account of Eros becomes at important points too vague. He calls it hedonistic, and this implies that it is selfish, but he does not show how this idea of Eros is compatible with the one which he is more inclined to emphasize, namely, that of self-extinction. Again, he is concerned to show that Eros is a dark passion which makes its victim dash himself against the bars of reason and all that is human. As a result he seems to leave no place for reason in Eros. What is lawful and good and reasonable is felt to belong to Agape. But Agape, which, as is clear, from *Passion and Society*, is equivalent to the supernatural love of God, has now to carry too much. Human nature is impoverished at the expense of grace. Eros must include the best in man, which is his reason and will and all the ideal possessive love of which it is capable. To right the balance, therefore, Eros should stand for both the ecstatic, irrational and self-effacing mood of love and the rational, self-assertive and possessive form, as they are found in human experience; and Agape for God's special love and man's response to it as inspirited and energized by it.

But if de Rougemont overbalances on one side, Nygren leans too heavily to the other. Instead of Eros being little else than a dark passion, it is now identified with the highest activities of man, the pursuit of truth and the possession of the good. Eros is the Greek ideal, and Agape has no relation to human reason or ideals. Instead of doing the work of reason, as in de Rougemont, Agape dispenses with it, and this is to take everything human out of Agape. Man does nothing and God does all. Self-regard and self-perfection completely disappear. But Nygren does not seem to see that what he says takes us away from Christianity and leads directly to the ideal of mystic fusion which so repels him. If man can do nothing, then extreme quietism is his lot, a quietism which must end in man being swallowed up in union with the godhead. At times Nygren does seem to be uncomfortable at the starkness of his view. He has to eviscerate passages of the New Testament of all meaning, to deny the words, 'as many as received him, he gave them power', to reject the virtue of hope, and to brand even the first Christian writers as semi-pagan. To redress the balance, therefore, we are bound to accept some self-love as legitimate, to admit some place for Greek and any other kind of true thinking. Agape will be God's love, which takes the initiative and gives the power to men to be 'the sons of God'. On the one side, then, there will be man with a passion which seeks for deliverance from himself and simultaneously a just regard for himself and his own perfection; and on the other God who respects man's integrity while lifting him up into a new relation of love with Himself. With such a correction of both views the violent dissimilarities vanish. De Rougemont and Nygren are looking at the same scene and seeing the same problem, which they both describe in terms of Eros and Agape. What each has to say is valuable. De Rougemont brings out the truth that man has a love which does not end with himself. Outside the Christian dispensation that love has a habit of revolting against reason and rushing off now to lose the self in some trance and ecstasy, now to practise self-immolation in dark, mysterious rites. Nygren, by contrast, shows, despite his dislike of it, how potent and all-pervading is self-love. The self is irresistibly borne along by the desire to perfect its own being. The Greeks realized this and taught mankind the value of human nature, the splendour of reason. In their eyes the ideal of life consisted in a beholding of what is most lovely and true, and in the possessing the good'. 'You and I', as Mgr. Ronald Knox has written, 'have each of us an I that is very dear to us, a self which we think much more important than anything else in the world, which we are determined at all costs to keep safe and comfortable if we can. Our natural instinct is to set up a great capital I in front of our minds and worship it.' Any theory of life which neglects this natural self-love is bound to fail. Nygren notices it and then neglects it. He notices, too, that it is in our intellectual activity that our self-love reaches its full expression. The intellect is like a spider's web which draws all into its net; but unlike a spider, it has no need to slay its victims; its happiness is in thought, in the forms or replicas of the reality outside which it can contemplate independently of the hurly-burly of actual existences.

Nygren, then, presents us with self love and its most powerful instrument, the human reason; de Rougemont presents us with a romantic and ecstatic love, which is either irrational or ill at ease at the superior claims upon it of reason. One love takes and possesses; the other love likes to be beside itself and give. One is masculine, the other is feminine. The two are necessary for one another, and together they tell us what we are and whither we are going. To neglect either is to court death. If the self becomes entirely self-centred a monstrous egoism follows, but as the self is now living on its own conceit and without external nourishment, the inflation is followed by collapse, a period of melancholia and death. If, following the opposite line, the self abandons itself to ecstatic love, it moves like a moth to the candle, or passively, like the musk rose, it gives forth a stronger perfume in the dark to entice the robber visitant of the night. It has chosen to be a victim, to die of love and to find its sole joy in self-immolation. That these are not fantastic images or wild spectres is proved by the successive diseases of human thought and passion. The to-and-fro movement between egoism and anti-personal philosophies adequately sums up the history of thought, and it corresponds with alternating emphases on individualism or general welfare in politics and social ideals and personal or pantheistic ideals in religion. So long as the two loves are on speaking terms we can enjoy the small quarrels, the bickerings, the taking of sides in favour, let us say, of romance against classicism, liberal competition against security, activity against passivity in prayer, moral asceticism against mystical union.

The two must never be separated. Self-love is perhaps the quicker to move us in practice; we are all of us, in fact, sensitive about ourselves, conceited and proud, ambitious and determined to have our way. No matter how uneducated a man may be, how stupid and empty-headed, he is sure to deliver his judgement as if it were final when he is amongst his friends in pubs or at home. So close are we to ourselves that we can hardly help making ourselves the centre round which the whole of past and future, as well as present history revolves. The world and its events matter to us in the degree they touch our own fate or our likes and dislikes. The old man is perturbed because the world is moving towards a future condition, a hundred years hence, which he does not like. The world a hundred years away is the world of which he is an inhabitant now, and his 'now' takes no account of lapse of years and the short span he has to live. Everything naturally seems relative to the I. Even the 'planners' for the future think and work as if they could rest on the Sabbath Day and see that their work was good. But if the 'I' seeps into all activities it does not do to admit it, and so in theory, if not in practice, selfless love receives more notice. We like to think of ourselves and of others as disinterested and working to ideals which will bring no personal benefit. This love is less ready to hand, and in truth may steal on us unawares. At times, indeed, we would not like to confess to its presence. When we seek to hide our identity in a crowd or are swept away by some herd passion; when we slay the very self we love or bow down before some idol, we have become victims of this love. This form of Eros can make us happy slaves of Circe or Calypso and dance madly to strange rhythms. It tells us of greater themes than that by which our little life is led; it purges us of that restless individuality which we have unduly prized, and plunges us into the abyss where alone night is the illumination. Were we swayed by this sole and single love there could be no return to selfhood and personal life. But fortunately for us the two loves are both ours. Self-regarding love can easily be an evil and but another name for selfishness; but it has a necessary and noble function. It will be appeased by nothing less than self-perfection; it demands that we remain persons; and that is why at the level of human life the monistic or pantheistic solution spells degradation. Between persons there is mutual enhancement. In true loving we receive and give, and in the relation of the self with God we receive life and receive it more abundantly.

If this be so we must inquire more profoundly into the meaning and extent of these two loves and also into their mutual relation. Now the principle of give and take which is illustrated in human loving seems to belong to a wider field and indeed to be coterminous with life. Were it the place, it might be even possible to show that a twofold movement governs everything. Here such an idea can be no more than a suggestion which to some may be helpful while to others it may sound so vague and metaphorical as to be spurious. In all that exists we presuppose or else discover activity and passivity, the positive and the negative, energy and inertia, an up and a down or a rise and fall, a coming-to-be and a passing away. In living things this principle is exemplified in the struggle for existence, and in the evolution of species. A living thing has a whole apparatus for self-preservation, and nevertheless it may be so constituted that it propagates and promotes the continuation of the species by entire subjection, a subjection so complete that it entails sometimes its own death. The splitting up into different genders marks clearly the contrast between the two loves or desires. It does not matter whether in any particular species the male or the female be dominant; it is sufficient that one of them be dominant and possessive, the other passive and possessed. In the brute creation the two desires or impulses or instincts (the name does not matter in this regard) are more obvious because they approach our own experience and can therefore more easily be judged. The male is dominant, self-assertive and violent; the female is responsive to his pleasures, but looks instinctively beyond its mate to offspring and the continuation of the species. Eric Gill, in an amusing essay, pointed out how 'finery is for the male in all creatures except the human', and he argues that 'by the design of divine Providence vanity has been from the beginning the virtue of male creatures. That he should take a pride in his physical condition and appearance is a necessity for the male, and vanity is designed for his advancement.'[1] Vanity and pride are in man merely the exaggerations of a disposition natural to him; in women they are perverse. 'Man is, on the whole, a more reasonable creature than woman, and vanity, his proper accomplishment, may safely be left in his care without fear of its running away with him.' A woman's glory is not in brute strength nor in domination. She does not win her victories by 'hitting and having'. 'Behold as the eyes of servants are on the hands of their masters, as the eyes of the handmaid are on the hands of their mistress; so are our eyes unto the Lord, our God, until he have mercy on us.'

But there are vital differences between the 'taking and receiving' of men and that of beasts. The typical brute male has no limit to his taking except the repletion of his appetite, and he gathers round him a submissive herd. The female again may be quite indifferent to her own fate; she may give or forfeit all. She may be compelled to commit *felo de se*. But a human being is of another order, an order which is summed up in the name of 'person'. He can never be a means, and he can never allow either of these two loves uncontrolled supremacy. He is forbidden Sabine rapes. Every human being has within him both the love of taking and of giving. Now his new spiritual unity includes all the instincts and impulses of the animal order; we shall expect, therefore, to see a new orientation of these impulses, of the old desires and loves, at his best a perfect sublimation of them, and a partial retrogression to them at his worst. As we have seen in preceding chapters, in the evidence from the mystery religions, mythology and the cartoons of the unconscious, this expectation is verified. The self on its lower levels contains the impulses to brutality and power, together with those of servility and self-immolation. The images

---

[1] *Art Nonsense* by Eric Gill.

of the dark goddess, of death, jostle with those of Moloch and the Minotaur.

But what were blind and crude passions are chastened and reformed into loves and human *motifs*, when they are owned by persons endowed with reason and will. Moreover, the truly human and spiritual level in man will have its characteristic expression of these two loves; they will both disclose what he is, and they will in partnership formulate the ideal of man and help him to attain it. The caution contained in this last sentence is very necessary because it safeguards us from the error of Nygren, the mystical theories of an Aldous Huxley, for instance, and even the too narrow ideal of Greek philosophy. Nygren rejected the self-regarding love, and as a result mutilated the idea of a person. Aldous Huxley again, following an Eastern tradition of mystical thought, will not have anything human in the final mystical union with the Absolute which he preaches. A true and genuine self-regard which is inherent in every human person is needed to prevent such a mystical union stultifying itself in pure absorption. On the other hand, the Greeks gave such an exclusive attention to the ideal of self-perfection that they made it very difficult to understand how love for God and for another person could be disinterested. Both the loves, as we now see, must be active and co-operative. A person as an end in himself, independent and unique and self-owning, cannot surrender himself so entirely as to deny or maim his own personal perfection. Nevertheless, he too is swayed by a love which takes him outside himself to other persons whom he has no right to possess, and to God to whom he owes everything. We must look at the whole of man, and leave nothing out, if we would understand him, and set his love in the right perspective.

Man, therefore, like every other living thing, is moved both by a desire to take and possess all for himself, and at the same time to give himself and throw away his private interests and even his life. In the brute creation the life of the individual is not of such importance as to create a real problem. The individual is sacrificed. But in the case of a rational creature like man, endowed with reason and with a corresponding urge and duty to himself, the individual cannot be sacrificed or bartered away. He cannot suffer the loss of his own soul for any good whatsoever. Moreover, as we have seen, it is in the activity of mind that man rises above the animal world and asserts himself. On the spiritual level it is the mind which represents the love of self, which is dominating, regulative and possessive. It is useful at this point to change over from the language of Eros and Agape to that of animus and anima. The animus is masculine; it is man as rational, whereas the anima is the self, exclusive of reason, but with a special reference to its spiritual aspect. Now if everything moves by its nature to conserve itself and to be more itself, and if reason, the differentiating activity of man, is of its very essence self-regarding, it is very difficult to see how the other love can enter into a person's life. Its counterpart in the animal world could be so insouciant of the self's claims as to make it a mere means to some other object and even sacrifice its life. A person cannot allow this to happen; he must never be a means and 'at the mill with slaves'. As Claudel's story shows, animus is determined to be master in his own house and to make anima into an obedient housewife. Many a thinker has dreamt this dream in past ages, and at times a civilization has feasted on the hope of a noble humanism, when reason should spread throughout society and all should be happy in a neat world of enlightened self-interest. But to judge by the lessons of history, anima is sure to prove refractory and to go roaming. The romantic movement, the phases of mysticism and irrationalism, bear witness to this. The only answer, the only true harmony, as preceding chapters attempted to show, must be sought in religion—in the communion of anima with its divine lover. But even this will fail unless, as in the Christian religion, the divine lover befriends animus as well, and gives power to the unavailing soul to be led to the altar with God.

The distinction just made between animus and anima prepares us for an answer to the problem of the relative status of the two loves. From a natural and human standpoint the animus or reasonable side of man would seem to have the headship. It is the masculine and regulative principle, which we are inclined to think of as the proximate ground of our independence and self-sufficiency. It is natural for every living organism to live its own life according to its nature. It would be absurd if a man made a mechanical instrument and put into it parts which interfered with the perfection of the instrument. In a human body we assume that every part of it has some relation to the whole life and well-being of the body; a malignant growth, for instance, is not normal. What more natural, then, than to take as an axiom that man's activities have for an end his well-being and that the intellect, *par excellence*, is the instrument of self-realization. No doubt, in the light of what has been said previously, a reader will notice that the argument assumes what has to be proved and that a word like 'nature' is ambiguous. But he will at the same time agree with the Greek philosophers in making this principle of self-realization and self-determination the corner-stone of any constructive philosophy of human nature.

But if there were no other principle, and if this principle of self-love were totally true, then a grave difficulty would arise. For we should have to ask how it is possible to love others for themselves and how we can love God more than ourselves. Nygren stuck at this difficulty and resolved it by clearing away love of self. The Christian philosophers refused to act in this Procrustean way. Their evidence, like Nygren's, is important in its avowal of the presence of two loves, the one egocentric, the other ecstatic. Of their attempts at a solution several examples have already been given. They put the problem in the form of the question: How can man love God more than himself? Rousselot replied in terms of an analogy of the relation of a part to the whole; Gilson developed the Thomistic idea of man as the image of God. Both of these writers gave the primacy to the act of the intellect and tried to show how self-perfection turns into the disinterested love of God. The intellect, they admit, is essentially self-regarding, in that it feeds the self with reality as known; it translates that external reality into the limited idea of it which a human being can grasp and possess; and yet somehow at the end the self gives up the ghost and finds God in place of itself.

The weakness of this view is that the intellect is by its very nature possessive, and no matter how delicate any posture of it may be, no matter how incidentally disinterested its desire, it keeps a taint of selfishness. That this is so is shown by the way its advocates try to explain our love for others. They admit that in the experience of this love the self is entirely preoccupied with the other, but they are bound to say that at bottom the other is loved because he is a kind of 'second self'. (*Vide* Appendix at end of Chapter Two). It is for this reason that some writers look elsewhere than to the intellect for a solution or look for another kind of love. Burnaby accuses Nygren of leaving out Philia, the love, that is, which persons have for one another. De Régnon and Descoqs and others see something special in the love of *persons*. This special love which persons have for one another has been developed by a modern school of theologians. The gist of its teaching is given in the following passage: 'To man the world is twofold, in accordance with his twofold attitude. He perceives what exists round about him—simply things, and beings as things, and what happens round about him—simply events and actions as events; things consisting of qualities, events of moment; things entered in the graph of place, events in that of time; things and events bounded by other things and events, measured by them, comparable with them: he perceives an ordered and detached world. . . . It is your object, remains it as long as you wish, and remains a total stranger, within you and without. You perceive it, take it to yourself as the "truth", and it lets itself be taken; but it does not give itself to you. Only concerning it may you make yourself "understood" with others; it is ready, though attached to everyone in a different way, to be an object common to you all. But you cannot meet others in it. . . .'[1]

[1] *I and Thou* by Martin Baber.

'Or on the other hand man meets what exists and becomes as what is over against him, always simply a *single* being and each thing simply as being. What exists is opened to him in happenings, and what happens affects him as what is. . . . It cannot be surveyed, and if you wish to make it capable of survey you lose it. It comes, and comes to bring *you* out; you can make it into an object for yourself, to experience and to use; you must continually do this—and as you do it you have no more present. Between you and it there is mutual giving; you say *Thou* to it and give yourself to it, and it says *Thou* to you and gives itself to you.'

Hence it is that the relation of an I to a Thou is quite different from the relation of an I to an object or thing—and true love is always an I and Thou relation. 'Love does not cling to the I in such a way as to have the Thou only for its "content", its object; but love is *between* I and Thou. The man who does not know this, with his very being know this, does not know love. . . .'

In this account there is a mixture of truth and fiction. The truth which it contains is expressed more soberly and philosophically by Descoqs and Hunter Guthrie and others. They too lay stress on the difference between the 'things' which the mind makes it own and persons we greet. They would call the former the world of essences, and it is the domain and happy hunting ground of the intellect, the food of self-regarding love. Man being such by nature that he must live for his own preservation, development and perfection, is drawn to things in so far as they are suitable to his nature. A human being, just because the mark which differentiates him from the brute is his mind, will find the specific perfection of his being in growth of knowledge, in the vision of truth. When a person grows in knowledge he comes to know more and more and to unify his discoveries within his mind. All the creatures of the universe come trooping aboard into his ark, and there they are named and docketed and understood in their relationship to one another. It may be that some objects seem far superior to others and throw light upon the meaning of many of the others; it may be that some object dazzles the eyes and is too great to creep inside the ark. If it does accept the invitation it will have to send a substitute or viceroy who is not too tall to cross the threshold. But certainly with regard to the material world the mind is able to make its own, to bring into the unity of its being, all that it sees. It can understand their meaning, grasp their nature and essence and 'become all things'. This is to possess truth, to have a body of knowledge which conforms with things as they are, to enjoy a viewpoint which does not distort reality. But notice that however true a knowledge I possess of the things or persons outside me, that thing or person is not my possession. He or it goes on existing and dancing and suffering; I know the meaning or nature, but the existence of that thing or person escapes the mind.

This is why Buber talks of true love being a salute or address, a salutation of another I, and makes what is in fact too sharp a distinction between 'It' and 'I' and the work of the mind and the act of loving. De Régnon and Descoqs and Hunter Guthrie for their part do not exaggerate the divisions in the self, but they admit a distinction between nature and person. By nature we are bound to consult the wellbeing of ourselves first, and we are inclined to give the regency to the intellect and to subject all other powers of the soul under it. But, as we know now, anima is always restless when under too severe duress of the intellect, for it has another love. This other love is the love which a human person as a person has for God, from whom he has his existence, and for others as persons. It is not egocentric because a person always spells a relation, and in that personal relation the centrifugal love finds vent.

The two kinds of love, therefore, which we distinguished as 'taking and giving', masculine and feminine, centripetal and centrifugal, which are contained in Eros and Agape and expressed in part by animus and anima, are now seen in the new distinction of nature and person, or better still in that of essence and existence. The metaphysics of essence and existence and nature and person under the skilful treatment of Hunter Guthrie and others gives us a more profound idea of the diversities of love, and acts like a floodlight on the picture of it. But as there are many who are only irritated by the technical language of philosophy, I do not propose to repeat the argument of the last chapter. Its conclusions, in short, come to this: that desire or love directs all the activities of the soul, the intellect as much as the will; that intellectual desire represents the movement of the essential self, and will the movement of the existential self; that the movement of the essential self is self-regarding and that of the existential self towards God and other existing persons. We must not, however, think of the two loves as separate and independent within the one self, even though, in order to bring out their distinct characteristics, we have to treat them as if they were alone. In choosing examples from the animal world there is no grave consequence which follows from our taking them apart, but in human persons they come together so as to make the very warp and woof of personality. When we use the word 'person' we do think of something which makes a human being his very self in his independence and singularity; and at the same time the word 'person' seems to imply a relation. In other words, a person is one who owns himself and is very much an 'I', and at the same time, instead of being turned inward in deadly introspection, like an idiot, he takes up a position in the world of reality and is aware of positive relations of equality or dependence or love with one or more other living beings. He has both a self-regarding love and a disinterested love. As an essence he is proud, as an existence he is dependent. He is an absolute on a finite scale, a solitary who feels 'angst' and is full of grandeur and *misère*. This is the nemesis of a finite personality.

The secret of the two loves is, therefore, as so many of the writers we have quoted—Burnaby, Descoqs, Buber, Scheler and Hunter Guthrie —insist, to be found in persons and in the relation of persons. As has been appositely written: 'Nothing is more intimate to our selves than this mysterious I who is the underlying subject of our acts and the term beyond which one cannot go in the line of willing. "I" and "Me", and that is all. But what a mystery! See how this absolute and this incommunicable being cannot find peace in itself. It will seek—and it is not some *other thing* which it will seek, for things cannot interest it nor satisfy it— it will seek *another* I, which it will long to make its own in order to discover itself there and to lose itself. And this second I and this second Me is nevertheless also an absolute and incommunicable. It matters not. Irresistibly they will go the one to the other, for they live for one another. The person is absolute, yes, but it is also relative. Is there contradiction here? No, only mystery; the mystery of love which will not be satisfied with the intellectual likeness of its object, but desires it to live as it is in itself and to live with a life which is at the same time the life of one and the life of the other. To be a person is to be essentially in search of a person. Love presupposes knowledge, but it can to some degree do without it; what it needs is the living and actual being itself. For a person there must be a person.' ('La Recherche de la Personne', by P. Philippe de la Sainte Trinité, in the *Études Carmelitaines*, April 1936.)

How then can we work out a conclusion of the two loves in the light of what has been said about a person? Within a person we can roughly distinguish what he has, his nature, his humanity, and what he is. The foundation of self-love is in the nature, and therefore it tends in the higher reaches of the soul to rely upon the intellect and to regard all else except itself as things. We can advance a high theory of love by making full use of this natural love, but the keynote of it will always be possessiveness. Our neighbours will be loved like to ourselves; they will be as it were another self; they will give us the noblest of joys. But that which makes us finally to be this self-enclosed being, isolated from all others, living and growing, expectant and attendant on what is not ourselves, is our existent being. We are not now in a play at one remove from hard reality, we are in that swirl of reality, and we must swim or drown. And it is in this condition, when we have been plunged into life, that we first discover others and salute them and address them as persons; as beings and persons who are most decidedly not ourselves, who demand of us that we treat them as beings who possess their own inalienable individuality and perfection. We are drawn to them not as being in any sense our own; it is just because they cannot be exploited or used or partitioned out that we attend to them for what they are in themselves. And here something new happens. In loving things there is only a one-way street of love. We take and hold; the thing is ours or we lose ourselves in something bigger and disappear, and that is all. But in the relation of persons there is a return of love. Both are active and the mode of taking is to receive from another, and the more one gives the more one is likely to receive. I live by his life and he lives by mine.

This is the new law of love, and the old prescriptions will not suit it. I do not and cannot ask the question whether I am ultimately loving myself first for the simple reason that when loving another I cannot get any benefit unless I give my love to that other. The less I consider any gain to self and the more I give freely and without second thoughts, the better for me and my love. I live by another's bounty as he lives by mine. This is perfect love on earth between persons, but, alas! a word of caution is needed. There are two impediments at least to its perfect fruition. The first is that, however much lovers in the act of loving deny it, there is no certainty of equality of giving and taking, no surety that love will be returned; and secondly, there is a barrier which no human person can cross. The fine point in personality must always remain untouched. We share but in part, and we are left lonely. It is at the poignant moments when we realize this that we are most tempted to do a forbidden thing—to hand ourselves over utterly and to go into the dark that we may be lost to ourselves and fused with the other. Many times we have seen the menace of this temptation and the disasters which follow on total surrender. The anima has deserted the animus, the existential self has cut itself off from the essential self and is in love with death. Strangely enough, but consistently with the true notion of personality, the relation between persons disappears and is succeeded by that between a person and a thing. No mutual love keeps both lovers in their own lovely and loved station and being. The lover becomes like a moth which dashes itself against the hot lamp; the mystic loses his identity by absorption in some impersonal Absolute.

This temptation reminds us of the indissoluble unity in the self of the two loves and the need for both of them to be operative. A person, as we argued in the last chapter, has to include both the human essence and the existence of that essence if it is to be properly and adequately defined. The self-regarding love preserves the integrity of the self and prevents the other love from getting out of hand and being too prodigal.

There is a constant threat against the rights and independence of man in modern society; he is with difficulty able to call his body and his soul his own. For that reason it is just that those who love man should recall to him his proper dignity and ceaselessly proclaim that a State exists to give fuller scope for personal life and not to subordinate personal life to itself. Personal life suffers both by the constant conditioning to which it is subject, and also, though this is less obvious, by an appeal to its so-called better nature to belong to some movement or to espouse some cause. This second danger is more insidious because it comes under the disguise of an ideal, and may well be a genuine ideal. The interest of the anima is enlisted just because the cause is altruistic. Now, as we all know, causes and ideals draw men together and often bring the best out of them; without them good fellowship is impossible and life is anarchic. But as modern movements have shown, if proof be needed, youth can be easily seduced and lose its reason and interior virtue. It loses its power of judgement and worships before an idol.

In human affairs, therefore, the self-regarding love, which stands for reason and judgement and watches over and commands progress in self-perfection, must ever be active and even take precedence over the love of self-effacement. We have to say, what doth it profit to save the whole world and suffer the loss of our souls? Our true love is tested by our honour; it grows more pure the higher we set our own personal standard. The truth of this will become more apparent if we reflect that we are from birth to death, from the moment of our existence, absolutes who must be treated as persons; whereas we are from the point of view of our nature only in process of self-realization.[1] Our first duty is to belong to Him from whom comes our existent self, but what seems to be the most obvious and pressing duty is to direct the steps of our own advance aright, to struggle for existence and growth and be what our inward monitor tells us we ought to be. In the comparison of the relative roles of the two loves, the problem of living has been perforce simplified. In fact we have so kaleidoscopic a self at first that we have deliberately to attend to what we are and practise self-discipline and self-knowledge; and then lest this inner look become distorted and set up a habit of morbid introspection, we have to divert ourselves by care for what is around us. In ringing these changes for the sake of our spiritual health, we play within the two great loves and make a practical judgement how far we, in accordance with our weakness or strength, should commit ourselves to one or other

---

[1] The point of this distinction is brought out by the paradoxical fact that at any moment we are so fully ourselves that we can commit ourselves here and now by a decision which may settle the whole of our future, end our lives and decide our eternal destiny; and this, though we are still young, in many ways unformed and just growing into habits which may change our character considerably.

of them. Some men are said to be introverts and others extroverts, and there is an infinite variety of talent and character among men; hence it would be ridiculous to try to prescribe any one mixture of self-love and disinterested love for all alike. But what no one can neglect is a sense of personal dignity. We start, as I have said, as existing persons with a nature of our own which we have to cherish and develop. This self-regard must act as a brake upon the other love, on the tendency of anima to trust itself and its experience independently of reason. The anima, especially in an age when reason is in disrepute, simmers in revolt against its collaborator. It accuses the reason of dealing with abstractions and essences, whereas it touches what is real and has its own criteria. It is true that experience is needed to correct theory, especially when our external senses can verify what has been thought. But experience left to itself can be irrational, illusory and deadly. The champion and coming victor in the struggle for self-perfection is the intellect, the godlike reason, which looks before and after, which contemplates the beloved and sees itself in intuition one with that beloved. It is the eye of truth and it detects the impostor.

The intellect has in all our descriptions of it been placed on the side of self-regarding love, as indeed its proper expression in the spiritual order. The reason for saying this is that the mind is possessive; it is concerned with essences and natures and meanings and by it the soul becomes all things in its own spiritual fashion. But as the self is one in both its loves and operates as one the mind cannot allow love to betray it. Both self-love and disinterested love have to be kept straight by truth, and by truth is meant here what conforms with the essential nature of the self and the whole order of being to which it belongs. The mind serves our loves by spotting for them and reporting, by testing and judging. We have to know ourselves and to know something of the various objects and persons we meet in our life. Love runs ahead and may have its own guarantees and signs, and were our condition perfect these might suffice. But in our struggle and wanderings in search of our one Love and of ourselves we are at the mercy of a disordered imagination, heady passions and unruly impulses, and we are at the mercy of the cunning stranger, the congenial and the novel. Were our loves enlightened we could say: ama et fac quod vis. But it is not until the searchlight of truth has played upon the many shapes which hold our attention and the many loves which beckon to us, that we can give ourselves wholeheartedly to another in personal friendship. The law of personal friendship is, as has been said, that we give what we are and we receive from the other. The law holds and does distinguish this relation from all other relations, whether of gain or loss. A person is such that he would, while remaining himself and having a never-dry fount to draw from, give himself to another. The other likewise because he is a person gives and has no thought of gain. Thus each makes up to the other in abundance the sacrifice and the apparent loss. A new circuit of love begins where two complete one another and live together in one. This is the law and the ideal, but a flaming sword cuts it off from perfection and prevents the longed-for consummation. The solitariness of the self is not overcome, and there is no sure guarantee of the lastingness and worth of the love. And it is here that the mind comes in not as a pander but as a priest. It establishes the friendship on truth; on the knowledge of the genuine character of the loved person's response and his or her worth. Only on truth can friendship be founded, on the certainty that the honour and fairness of the self will not be menaced. When this is known, and only when this is known, can the lover freely and wholeheartedly give of himself without looking back. The interests of the self are then safe in other's hands.

The law of love exhibited in personal friendship is really a foretaste or prophecy of a state of love in which all is well. No love can be so sure in this life as to pledge itself without reserve. Even in marriage there are settlements to be made with the contract, and a child may be undeserving of its mother. We go beyond the evidence because of a faith whose strength and source we do not always comprehend. We make our vows because the ideal hero in our hearts whispers that they can be fulfilled, if we are true to the best in us; and we give ourselves into another's keeping because we know however, checked and thwarted human love may be, there is a Lover in whose heart we can live. Put philosophically, this means that we act and imitate a love, which suffers from none of our limitations; we aspire to be loved by one whose love breaks down the last reserve of the self, so that we can belong utterly to him. He is more to us than we are to ourselves; and he cares for us more than we care for our own being. We need have no anxiety about our good, no dread that we may be injured or suffer any loss to our identity, for we know that it is the nature of perfect love to lift and not to lower our being, to multiply and not subtract, to give life and to give it more abundantly. Hence in one case, and one only, that of divine love, the self may and must drop all its self-regard, strip itself and say, 'all that I am and have is yours'. The primary act of the creature is not to possess God but to belong to Him. The essential self is not, indeed, dead—that could not be so long as a person remains a person—but it is the existential self, the anima, which goes forth to greet the divine lover. No doubt the essential love prepares the way. The mind has for a long or short while to direct and fortify the anima. The true God may be hidden and have to be discovered, and when he is discovered there must be so much to be learnt about him, either by the mind's own effort or from God's own communications about himself. Owing to the infinite distance which separates the finite from the infinite there is a prolonged darkness, and the gift of God will have to enlighten the mind to see the right direction and to understand the divine will. The mind, then, will have constant work to do, but nevertheless so far as the primary relation to God is concerned, love dictates all, and the love is one of homage and sacrifice and self-giving.

It is in the perspective of divine love that all the strange behaviour of the self and its oscillation between its two loves are understood. One love tends to self-realization, the other is self-effacing; the one is dominant and possessive, the other is submissive and self-sacrificing. The first is the love of the essential self and perfects itself by reason; the second is the love of the existential self, and it reaches out to other existences and other persons. To be oneself and wrap oneself up in one's own virtue seems to be a reasonable, if despairing ideal; it is, as Hunter Guthrie maintained, a bogus absolute. To run away from oneself and bury oneself is some absorbing ideal has also always attracted man; but this too is a dream and a delusion. As persons we have our own life and independent existence; our own life is most precious to us; we are so much to ourselves that we can hardly think of anything else as real. But it is in the painful throb of our existence that we are brought back to reality, to the frailty of our being, to our solitariness in the face of other impenetrable existences. We hang by a thread on life, we are more like a live echo than a living voice; we have laws in our being which we have to obey, a song which we have to sing which we did not create ourselves. Hence it is that in being persons at the very moment we call ourselves 'I', we salute another person in whom we live and move and have our being. In this relation all comes from one side—all the power and all the love. It is poverty subsisting and deriving all its surprising winningness from the Giver of all good gifts. The essential love busy about its own affairs is a good clerk counting up its money; it is the existential self which feels itself to be only a feoffee and is aware of its dependence. The one self is upright and self-contained, the other is on its knees.

If this be so, the finite person is not primarily concerned to possess itself, still less to possess God, so much as to belong to God. He cannot be a person and not be in relation, and as a living relation he looks to the other term of that relation. This in terms of love means that we are not concerned with ourselves save to make ourselves a more pleasing and acceptable sacrifice. Our principal aim is not to have God, not to enjoy Him, but to live by Him and for Him. How far this desire is attained or attainable outside the Christian Agape we do not know. By our nature and our existence we are a work of God's hands, and it is love which keeps us in being. We are a product which can be called the past and perfect tense of the verb to love, when the first person of the verb is God. It is in our own being, therefore, with the help of nature around us, if need be, that we discover God. Our own being, essence and existence, is the school of divine love, and so we must not think of our own being as something of our own which is met by God and then loved. This idea would be quite inadequate and give rise to a host of misunderstandings and false expectations. It would suggest that God is like a finite lover, now loving and now indifferent, now storming his way into our hearts and now lying hidden. All such language must be understood in the context of infinite and creative love, which produced us and keeps us alive. Not new favours, nor new external happenings, nor rapturous experiences are so much a testimony of God's love as our nature and being itself. It is difficult to realize this, especially as so many of the old words to express the causality of God have lost their savour. The modern image of syntonization may help. It is as if the sounding of a note on one instrument produced the corresponding note on another instrument, or as if a child were to begin to hum and dance as it listened to a fiddler playing outside the window. The energy of love, which is God's own, is communicated, and an essentially inferior energy starts repeating the rhythm of the superior one in its own fashion, as when a log thrown into a stream takes on the motion of the stream or a rider on horseback sways up and down to the movement of the horse. Causality is a kind of *pas de deux*, the sympathetic response in a finite energizing to the simple, supreme energizing of the Creator. The conductor, who is also the composer, lifts his baton and each member plays and gives back to him his own music.

What secrets there are of love in the natural order between God and human persons we have no sure way of knowing; nor need we stay to inquire, since in the Christian Agape the complete revelation of love is given. Here the finite is not left to itself to repeat in the perfection of its nature the divine beauty and to crave to belong to God. The finite is lifted to a new degree of being, whose limit is measured only by the necessity of its remaining a human person. This new energizing has for object to change the relation of creature to creator into one of friend with friend, beloved and lover. This new life which is thus set going is a pure gift and beyond the natural capacity of the finite human person; the self has the joy of knowing that it is now so united to the life of God that even the beginning of its own acts and love is God's. It now echoes the words of St. Paul: 'I live; no, I no longer live, but Christ lives in me.'

The superabundant life which has been given to it, thereby increasing instead of decreasing its personality, only serves to bind it ever more closely to God, to be His and to belong to Him utterly. It expresses the perfection of personal relations; all is giving and there is no thought of taking; what one has is the gift of the other.

The definitive statement of this new love is given in the Fourth Gospel in the discourse at the Last Supper. The doctrine of disinterested love which comes into its own, first chivalrously in all personal friendships and then finally in divine love, is no more than a paraphrase of the love declared by Christ on the eve of His passion. 'I am the vine and you the branches; he that abideth in me and I in him the same beareth much fruit, for without me you can do nothing.' 'I will not now call you servants . . . but I have called you friends.' 'And all my things are thine, and thine are mine; and I am glorified in them.' 'And the glory which thou hast given me, I have given them; that they may be one, as we also are one; I in them, and thou in me; that they may be made perfect in one.' These words canonize true and divine love. They contain the lesson of 'the pure love, of the noble love, and of the high love of the free soul; and how the Holy Ghost has His sail in his ship', as we read in *The Mirror of Simple Souls*. The fifteenth-century author of this treatise and others who have tasted of this love know well the secret of it and its disinterestedness. 'For it is His good pleasure to reign in our understanding blissfully, and sit in our soul restfully, and to dwell in our soul endlessly, us all working into Him'. (Juliana of Norwich.) 'Perdue en vous, elle oublie elle-même et tout le reste, elle ne sait plus comment elle vit, ni comment elle aime; elle ne voit plus que Vous seul. Encore ne peut-elle *penser* qu'elle vous voit et vous adore; car ce serait se voir elle-même, et en de tels moments elle ne se voit pas, elle ne voit que Vous. . . . Elle sent que l'opération de Dieu a pris la place de la sienne et que c'est Dieu même qui opère en elle la connaissance et l'amour.'

But better perhaps than any of the others save St. John of the Cross does the same author of *The Mirror of Simple Souls* give us the first effect of love and its relation to the desire to know God. In the sixth and highest stage of union upon this earth he tells us of the soul that 'pure and clarified, she sees nor God nor herself: but God sees this of Him in her, for her, withouten her, that shows her that there is none but He. Nay, she knows but Him, nor she loves but Him, nor she praises but Him, for there is but He. And the Seventh keeps He within Him, for to give us in everlasting glory. If we wit it not now, we shall wit it when the body our soul leaves.' It will be noticed here that love consists in being so united with God that the soul feels and thinks in the divine life and love. It belongs utterly to its Lover. But something more is to come. The mind which because of its possessiveness had been in the background is to be rewarded; nothing in the person is to be lost or unrequited. But the very seeing, the possessing of God and enjoying of Him, is to come as a superlative gift from the Other, and it is no longer desired for its own sake. It is God's gift to make the friendship equal and to enable the soul to know God as He wishes to be known. No one makes this clearer than the master of Divine Love, St. John of the Cross, and as his words gather up all that has been said on the two loves and their interrelationship, the following passage from the *Spiritual Canticle* can fittingly bring the theme of Agape to a close. St. John has been commenting on the stanza:

> *There wilt Thou show me*
> *That which my soul desired:*
> *And there Thou wilt give me at once,*
> *O Thou, my life,*
> *That which Thou gavest me the other day.*

He says that the soul longs for an equality of love with God because 'he who loves cannot be satisfied if he does not feel that he loves as much as he is loved'. This is the reason why it is glad that in heaven it will be able to see God as He is, for then at that sight its love will be so increased that it will love with God's own strength; 'for as the understanding of the soul will then be the understanding of God, and its will the will of God, so its love will also be His love.' He explains this further by saying: 'For God not only teaches the soul to love Himself purely, with a disinterested love, as He hath loved us, but He also enables it to love Him with that strength with which He loves the soul, transforming it in His love, wherein He bestows upon it His own power, so that it may love Him. It is as if He put an instrument in its hand, taught it the use thereof, and played upon it together with the soul.' But then St. John asks himself a question, and it is both the nature of the question and the answer he gives which provide a final vindication, if such be needed, of pure love in companionship with knowledge. 'Why is it,' he says, 'seeing that essential glory consists in the vision of God, and not in loving Him, the soul says that its longing is for His love, and not for the essential glory? Why is it that the soul begins the stanza with referring to His love, and then introduces the subject of the essential glory afterwards, as if it were something of less importance? There are two reasons for this. The first is this: As the whole aim of the soul is love, the seat of which is in the will, the property of which is to give and not to receive; the property of the understanding, the subject of essential glory, being to receive and not to give; to the soul inebriated with love, the first consideration is not the essential glory which God will bestow upon it, but the entire surrender of itself to Him in true love, without any regard to its own advantage. The second reason is that the second object is included in the first, and has been taken for granted in the previous stanzas, it being impossible to attain to the perfect love of God without the perfect vision of Him. The difficulty in the question is solved by the first reason, for the soul through love renders to God that which is His due, and with the understanding which she receives from Him as a gift and does not herself give.'

In this Agape all that Nygren demanded is present. God is all in all, and there is no trace of that kind of self-love which interferes with perfect love. But self is there, the self and the intellect, for it is God who loves them and gives them both increase. 'Unarm Eros, the long day's task is done'; in Agape is rest and everlasting life.

FINIS

INDEX

ABELARD, 86, 138
Adler, 163, 203
Aeschylus, 75
Allers, 207, 220, 222
Ambrose, St., 308
Anderson, Sherwood, 135
Anselm, St., 251
Aquinas, St. Thomas, 11, 67 sq., 78, 80, 89
    sq., 104 sq., 169, 183, 286 sq., 304 sq.
Aristotle, 11, 12, 61 sq., 68, 90, 104 sq.,
    108, 168, 177 sq., 198, 203, 225, 230,
    245, 269, 275, 277, 310
Augustine, St., 11, 57, 64 sq., 78, 87, 95,
    99, 107, 115, 176, 192–3, 234, 244, 252
Austin, J., 292
Averroes, 202
Avicenna, 202

BAHR, 236
Baisnee, 170, 171
Barbey d'Aurévilly, 132, 134
Barth, 107
Baudelaire, 132
Baudouin, 87
Beethoven, 285
Belgion, M., 12
Bellarmine, St. Robert, 79
Benda, J., 134, 142
Bernard, St., 85 sq., 95, 99, 108
Bertrand, L., 134, 156
Bergson, 188, 209, 215, 250, 264
Blake, W., 21, 220
Blondel, M., 291
Boethius, 296
Bossuet, 85–6, 292
Brémond, 186 sq.
Brentano, 250
Bridges, R., 293
Browning, R., 127
Brunner, 107, 109
Buber, 114 sq., 204, 210, 218, 318, 321
Burnaby, 69, 107 sq., 203, 219, 318, 321
Burne-Jones, 28
Burrows, R., 240
Butler, 296

CAJETAN, 300
Carew, 233
Chesterton, G. K., 104
Cicero, 66, 108
Cingria, 31
Claudel, 158, 168, 175, 192, 260, 317
Clemenceau, 202
Clement of Alexandria, St., 241
Climacus, St. John, 68
Coleridge, S. T., 54
Comfort, A., 27, 90
Cook Wilson, 9
Coton, 89
Crashaw, R., 206
Croce, B., 177
Cyprien, Père, 188

DALBIEZ, 139
Dante, 35–6, 68, 104, 154, 186, 190
Da Todi, J., 274
Dawson, C., 201
Day, D., 287
de Bérulle, 110
de Blois, L., 187
de la Taille, 294, 301
de Quincey, 253
de Régnon, 95, 99, 114, 219, 318
de Rougemont, D., 10, 12–13, 21, ch. 1
    passim, 73, 79 sq., 109, 113 sq., 125,
    132, 171, 182, 195, 198 sq., 217, 309 sq.
Descartes, 121, 249, 251, 255, 281
Descoqs, 92, 114, 219, 303, 318, 319 sq.
Dill, 32
Donne, 14, 156
Driesch, 209
Dublanchy, 99
Dunne, 293

ECKHART, 38
Eddington, 163
Eliot, T. S., 174, 236
Empedocles, 176
Epictetus, 231
Epiphanius, 241
Euripides, 23, 41, 271

INDEX

FARNELL, 240
Fechner, 215
Fichte, 118, 124, 204
Francis of Assisi, St., 26, 228, 231 sq.
Francis of Sales, St., 112
Freud, 12, 135 sq., 157, 163, 180, 183, 202, 204, 206–7, 209, 219

GALSWORTHY, 81
Garrigon-Lagrange, 170
Gentile, 177
Ghyka, M. C., 176
Gill, E., 124, 236, 279, 315
Gillet, 150
Gilson, 11, 96 sq., 203, 280, 290, 318
Goethe, 151, 205
Gogarten, 119
Goldman, E., 81
Grierson, 195, 196
Guthrie, Hunter, 12, 13, 248 sq., 274, 276 sq., 289 sq., 292, 319 sq., 326

HARPER, R., 282
Harrison, J. E., 24, 240 sq.
Heard, G., 165
Hegel, 124, 172, 177
Heidegger, 119, 192, 249 sq., 272
Heim, 117 sq., 204, 210
Heracleitus, 176
Herbert, G., 234
Hopkins, G., 83, 158 sq., 176, 219, 236, 244-5
Hubert, 31
Hugh of St. Victor, 85–6
Hume, 296
Husserl, 250, 254
Huxley, A., 109 sq., 133, 165, 316
Huxley, J., 221
Huysmans, 132, 154

IOVETZ-TERESCHENKO, 209, 220

JAEGER, W., 124, 248
James, W., 296
Jammes, 37
John of the Cross, St., 328 sq.
Johnson, S., 281
Juliana of Norwich, 328
Jung, 135, 140 sq., 157, 163, 187, 189, 195, 202

KANT, 118, 121, 149, 207, 281, 296
Keats, 27
Kierkegaard, 12, 192, 248–9, 252, 256–7, 272, 290
King, C. W., 49, 52
Knox, R., 312
Koffka, 214

LANGLAND, 274
Lattey, 301
Lawrence, D. H., 133, 135
Leishman, J. B., 21
Lessius, 79
Lévy-Bruhl, 211

MACCURDY, J. T., 206
McDougall, W., 214, 223
Male, 37
Marcus Aurelius, 231
Maréchal, J., 253
Martindale, C. C., 107
Massis, 134
Milton, 191, 233
More, Sir Thomas, 231
Münsterberg, H., 208
Murry, Middleton 142

NASHE, 272
Newsholme, H. P., 237
Nietzsche, 24, 32, 125, 127 sq., 145, 150, 173, 198
Novalis, 38
Nygren, 10, 11, ch. 2 passim, 84, 88, 90, 92, 96 sq., 104 ,107–8, 117, 127, 195, 198 sq., 217–18, 290, 309 sq., 320

OMAN, J., 109
Otto, 38

PASCAL, 231, 245, 252, 288
Pater, W., 32, 44
Patmore, Coventry, 14, 21, 167
Philippe de la Sainte Trinité, 321
Pindar, 24
Plato, 21, 38, 60 sq., 84, 99, 121, 196 sq., 279, 310
Plotinus, 38, 61
Poe, 132
Pollen, P., 16

INDEX

Proust, 133, 135, 188
Przywara, 253
Pythagoras, 176

QUARLES, 174

RALEIGH, W., 84
Read, Herbert, 195, 196
Reid, L. A., 194
Renouvier, 277
Rickaby, Joseph, 184
Rimbaud, 54
Rohde, 211–12
Ross, D., 178
Rossetti, D. G., 28
Rousselot, P., 11, 12, ch. 3 *passim*, 104, 198, 203, 245, 250, 282 sq., 292, 295, 318
Russell, Bertrand, 294
Ruysbroeck, 110, 187

SAINT-EXUPÉRY, 104
Santayana, 126–7, 172, 226, 290
Savage, D. S., 195
Scheler, 188, 209 sq., 287, 321
Schelling, 125
Schopenhauer, 125 sq., 137, 156, 202
Scotus, Duns, 79, 108, 162
Scotus Eriugena, 68
Sertillanger, 266
Shakespeare, 84, 124, 194, 221, 233, 283
Shaw, Bernard, 13, 125
Sitwell, Edith, 194
Simmel, 61
Smart, C., 260
Smith, R. G., 114
Soderblom, 107, 109
Sophocles, 21, 74, 241, 243
Spencer, Herbert, 221, 296
Spender, S., 229

Spengler, 177
Spinoza, 226
Stolz, 111 sq.
Streseman, 214
Suarez, 88, 299

TARDIEU, 202
Taylor, A. E., 196
Tennyson, 176
Teresa, St., 36, 40
Theognis, 240
Thomson, G., 76
Thornton, W. M., 296
Turquet-Milnes, G., 133

UNAMUNO, M., 222–3
Undset, S., 81

VALTIN, J., 81
Verlaine, 132
Villiers de l'Isle Adam, 132
Virgil, 72, 154
von den Steinen, 211
von Hügel, F., 81–2, 107

WAGNER, 125, 127, 132, 202
Ward, John, 54
Wavell, Lord, 13
Wells, H. G., 260
Westermann, 211
Whitman, W., 127
Wilamowitz-Möllendorff, 58
William de St. Thierry, 95, 96
Williams, C., 154
Windelband, 60
Wordsworth, 84
Wyndham-Lewis, 134, 195–6, 208

YEATS, J., 128, 248
Yeats, W. B., 206